NOV 0 6 2007

W9-BXY-961

Also by Eric Lax

The Mold in Dr. Florey's Coat

Bogart (with A. M. Sperber)

Woody Allen, a Biography

Life and Death on 10 West

On Being Funny

Conversations with Woody Allen

Conversations with Woody Allen

His Films, the Movies, and Moviemaking

Eric Lax

New Lenox
Public Library District
120 Veterans Parkway
New Lenox, Illinois 60451

Alfred A. Knopf  New York 2007

This Is a Borzoi Book Published by Alfred A. Knopf

Copyright © 2007 by Eric Lax

All rights reserved. Published in the United States by Alfred A. Knopf, a division of Random House, Inc., New York, and in Canada by Random House of Canada Limited, Toronto.

www.aaknopf.com

Knopf, Borzoi Books, and the colophon are registered trademarks of Random House, Inc.

Library of Congress Cataloging-in-Publication Data

Lax, Eric.
Conversations with Woody Allen: his films, the movies, and moviemaking/Eric Lax. — 1st ed.
p. cm.
Includes index.
ISBN 978-0-375-41533-3
1. Allen, Woody — Interviews. 2. Motion picture producers and directors — United States — Interviews. I. Allen, Woody. II. Title.
PN1998.3.A45A3 2007
791.43092 — dc22   2007006350

Manufactured in the United States of America

First Edition

3 1984 00260 0128

For Punch Sulzberger
with admiration and love

Contents

Introduction

A book of conversations usually collects interviews done over weeks or months and so, regardless of the time span covered, the result is a snapshot that reflects the attitudes and feelings of the subject at a given point in life. This book, however, is an album assembled over half of Woody Allen's life, beginning in 1971, and like time-lapse photography, it offers a clear view of his transformation from novice to one of the world's most acclaimed filmmakers, and what he learned along the way.

For thirty-six years I've had the pleasure of watching an artist's evolution from close range, but I wouldn't have laid money on the chances of that after our first meeting. In the spring of 1971 an editor at the *New York Times Magazine* sent me to investigate three ideas for a possible story. One of them was a profile of Allen, a thirty-five-year-old comic who had written two Broadway plays (*Don't Drink the Water* and *Play It Again, Sam*), whose prose was now often in *The New Yorker,* and who had recently begun to act in and direct his own screenplays: *Take the Money and Run* (1969), the purported documentary of a petty criminal so spectacularly inept that he can't even write a legible holdup note, and the just-released *Bananas,* a comic turn on Latin American revolutions and U.S. foreign policy. With just enough plot to bind them, the pictures are strung together like a nightclub monologue, with little attention paid to character development or cinematic style. They are one often surreal gag after another, and they are uproarious.

The films announced the arrival of an idiosyncratic and original talent, and editors at the *Times* wanted to know more about him, as did I. I thought he was in a league with my comic heroes, S. J. Perelman, Bob Hope, and the Marx Bothers, and even more varied in his ability to provoke laughter. I telephoned his managers, Jack Rollins and Charles Joffe, to ask for an interview, and an appointment was made. I arrived at their duplex office on West Fifty-seventh Street in Manhattan with a couple of pages of questions and a brand-new tape recorder and was taken upstairs, where Woody was waiting in a small room furnished with a table and lamp and a couple of nicely stuffed chairs. He looked uncomfortable and seemed shy; I was new to journalism and nervous about meeting someone whose work I admired. We shook hands, said hello, settled into the seats, and I asked my questions like someone reading off a checklist. His answers were succinct. His shortest was "No," which would not have been so bad had any of his longest been more expressive than "Yes."

So I wrote a piece on one of the other two ideas I looked into, and figured I was done with Woody Allen.

Six months later, while riding a bicycle in Sausalito, California, I was nearly run down by a Ford station wagon with a card in the front window that read "Rollins and Joffe Productions." In that day's *San Francisco Chronicle* I had seen a short article about Woody being in town to film *Play It Again, Sam* and, being young and solipsistic, I figured that instead of mere coincidence, this was a sign that he was ready to talk more openly. I phoned Joffe to see about another interview and was summoned to meet Woody on a houseboat in the Sausalito harbor, which was being considered for a scene in the film. We chatted about the baseball playoffs and then he excused himself to look at something with the location manager. A few minutes later, Charlie came over and said, "Why don't you come to the set and hang around? But be sure to keep quiet and out of the way, otherwise you'll have to go."

I dutifully did as I was told and, after a few days, Woody came over between shots and we talked for a minute. He came back later and we talked longer. Soon we began more formal interviews. The *Times* commissioned a profile and I stayed through much of the filming. As Woody didn't direct *Sam* (Herbert Ross did), my editor suggested I also interview him while he acted in and directed *Everything You Always Wanted to Know About Sex* immediately after. I went to the old Goldwyn Studios in Los Angeles, talked with him for many more hours on and off the set, and finally, months after the original deadline, turned in my piece the day *Time* ran a cover story on him.

In journalism as in comedy, timing is all. After the *Times* killed my story, I thought Woody should at least see the result of all the weeks he spent with me, so I sent it with a note of thanks for his time. I didn't expect a response, but a couple of days later he called to say that he was sorry it wouldn't run.

"You quoted me accurately in context, and you honored my jokes," he said, meaning that I had not quoted one without including both the straight line and the punch line. "Feel free to stop by my editing room whenever you like."

I did, several times. Then one day we ran into each other while walking in opposite directions along Fifth Avenue. He told me he was about to go to Las Vegas to perform at Caesars Palace and to stop by if I happened to be there, though nothing seemed more unlikely. But a few days after that Richard Kluger, the former editor in chief at Atheneum who had just started his own publishing house, suggested I turn the misfortune of the *Times* piece into penury by doing a book on comedy with Woody as the focus. I went to Vegas after all and during a ten-minute discussion in the Caesars coffee shop, Woody agreed to cooperate. I stayed through his engagement, then traveled on with him for what would be his final tour as a stand-up comic to begin what became my 1975 book *On Being Funny,* and as part of my research I spent several weeks on the sets of *Sleeper* and *Love and Death*. It was evident from our earliest conversations about them that while these are very comic films, his ambition and interest had a more serious side. When you consider that two of his chief influences are Bob Hope and Ingmar Bergman, this is not a surprise. But it is a difficulty. Woody Allen is one of the world's funniest people. Why, many moviegoers wondered when presented with *Interiors* (1978) and then *Stardust Memories* (1980), wasn't he content to keep making funny films? The short answer is, as a young writer he saw comedy as the stepping-stone to drama, and he was willing to persist in his ambition to write compelling films on serious matters. Critics have grumbled about someone so funny disparaging comedy and wanting to play Hamlet, but they miss the point. Woody doesn't disparage comedy, which has been the basis of lifelong success; he simply prefers drama. And, completely aware of the limited roles he can be believable in, he has no desire to *play* Hamlet; he wants to *write Hamlet*.

Allan Stewart Konigsberg, born on December 1, 1935, and raised in the New York City borough of Brooklyn, became Woody Allen in the spring of 1952 when the gossip columnists at several New York newspapers started to use jokes and one-liners he sent in. The shy sixteen-year-old didn't want his classmates to pick up the papers and see his name—the gossip columns were a staple for millions of readers of every age—and besides, he thought everyone in show business changed their name; he wanted one that was light and seemed appropriate for a funny person. Soon he was being quoted so often that he was hired by a public relations agent to write witticisms that could be attributed to his clients. Every day after school Allan rode the subway forty minutes to midtown Manhattan and for three hours knocked out as many jokes as he could at the agent's office. He thought he was "in the heart of show business." Each day he handed in three or four typewritten pages (about fifty jokes; he estimates he wrote twenty thousand in his two-plus years there) and in return received $20 and soon $40 a week, very good money at the time.

Success accompanied every subsequent step. At nineteen he was hired by NBC as part of its new writers' development program and sent to Hollywood to work on the *Colgate Comedy Hour;* at twenty-two he was writing for Sid Caesar; by 1960, when he was twenty-four, he was making eighty times his first salary. Then he saw Mort Sahl, who came onstage in a sweater and with a newspaper under his arm and talked about politics and American life, and he realized that stand-up might be something he could do, and he did. On the basis of his act he was hired to appear in and write the screenplay for *What's New Pussycat?* (1965), which became the highest-grossing comedy to its time. But the finished picture bore little resemblance to his script, and later Woody said that had they stuck to what he wrote, "I would have made it twice as funny and half as successful." The experience taught him that if he was going to write movies, he needed total control of his material.

He has had it for all the films he has written and directed to date, never giving up on his hope of writing a wholly dramatic film that satisfied his intent and the audience's interest. With *Match Point* (2005) he succeeded, and he hopes to again. Other films, such as *Zelig* (1983), have entered the cultural lexicon. There also are romantic comedies; meditations on a godless universe; pseudo-documentaries; a musical; films about loyalty, the choice between leading a life of fantasy or one of reality, of deteriorating relationships, and the unpredictability of love. There are stories of families, of memory, of fantasy, of what it is to be an artist; there are slapstick and capers and ghosts; and there is magic. As the backdrop to most of them, there is New York City, particularly Manhattan, which he shows as a shimmering place and which he points out is based not so much on the real thing as it is on the Manhattan of duplex apartments and nightclubs and sophisticated people he saw in countless movies when he was growing up a world away in Brooklyn, even though the two boroughs are separated geographically by only the East River.

More by coincidence than planning, we have talked about many of his films while they were being made and about all of them many times. After thirty-six years, ours may be the oldest established permanent floating interview in New York. We've talked on film sets and in his screening and editing rooms, in dressing room trailers and cars, in Madison Square Garden and on Manhattan sidewalks, in Paris, New Orleans, and London, and in his successive homes. His answers to my questions have come in well-ordered paragraphs—thoughtful, candid, self-deprecating, often witty, and sometimes hilarious, though I've never heard him try to be funny.

Woody Allen is the antithesis of his screen character, who is usually frantic and in crisis. He is in control of his work and his time. His self-assessment is apt: "I'm a serious person, a disciplined worker, interested in writing, interested in literature, interested in theater and film. I'm not so inept as I depict myself for comic purposes. I know my life is not a series of catastrophic problems that are funny because they are so ludicrous. It's a much duller existence."

Decades of success and fame have made him more comfortable and less shy in general, and our meetings are genial and at ease. He also is an active participant. When I was researching my 1991 biography, *Woody Allen,* I figured the time to stop interviewing him would be when he started to retell stories. It was three years before he repeated himself; by then I was a year past my original deadline. One day while the book was being edited, he called.

"I've been thinking about something we recently talked about and I have some more ideas, if they'd be of any interest to you," he said.

"Sorry," I told him. "You had your chance."

Or not.

His contribution to this book has been the same. He sat for scores of hours of interviews between April 2005 and early 2007 to make our conversations current. He read the manuscript and offered clarifications in instances where he felt he sounded like Casey Stengel, the 1950s New York Yankees manager whose rococo locutions were amusing in their unintelligibility. He also offered additional thoughts as they came to him.

What I've tried to produce with his help is a wide-ranging self-examination of a life's work to date. It not only shows how Woody Allen has grown as a writer and director but also conveys what he wants to say about his films and about cinema in general. I've grouped these conversations to explore each of the seven major aspects of making movies, from getting the idea to scoring, and end them with a chapter in which he reflects on his career. Each section on filmmaking begins in the early 1970s and ends in 2006 or 2007, so depending on whether, say, casting or editing is of interest at that moment, they can be read in any order. But be sure to listen as well, as the voice is distinctly Woody Allen's.

Eric Lax
April 2007

1

THE IDEA

February 1973

Woody and I are being driven to Tarrytown, New York, about an hour north of Manhattan, where he will talk at a film weekend organized by New York Magazine *critic Judith Crist. He is wearing corduroy trousers, a cashmere sweater, and an olive green army jacket. He says he is "depressed. I saw [Ingmar Bergman's]* The Seventh Seal *yesterday and* Cries *and* Whispers *today. I see his films and wonder what I'm doing." He soon will head to Los Angeles to begin filming* Sleeper, *and he is not happy about leaving home.*

"Films made for two million are a pain in the ass, and I have to be away from New York. Everything in L.A. is automobiles and has to be done fast—twelve weeks. Keaton and Chaplin took a year to make their films." (Thirty years and more later, his films are done in eight to ten weeks to keep within their approximately $15 million budget.)

The event is held in a conference center that was once the country mansion of the Biddle family, descendants of a prosperous nineteenth-century American financier. It is near a town but many acres of grass and trees surround the property, and as far as Woody is concerned, he is heading into the deep outback. "The crickets make me nervous—that sums it all up for the country for me," he says, quoting Terry Malloy, Marlon Brando's character in On the Waterfront, *as we wend up the long driveway. "I'm afraid I'll have an attack of agoraphobia or come down with an attack of some disease unknown except to special Manhattan doctors." A man careful about his well-being, in the pockets of his jacket he has packed as precaution against almost everything imaginable, both physical and spiritual, vials of Compazine, Darvon, Lomotil, and Valium; a toothbrush; cough drops; and a book on four existential writers.*

Woody is engaging and funny at the event, and the crowd, casually well dressed, a few in their twenties and thirties but the majority older, is appreciative and filled with questions. At the end of the evening, a very pretty Yale Law student asks Woody if he will come to New Haven and be a karate expert in a mock trial. He smiles and politely declines and soon is taken up to his room. As it happens, his is next to one where through the walls he can hear two couples arguing about his films. He is offered another room but declines; he's curious to hear what they have to say. Soon one of the women begins reading his short play "Death Knocks" in the stereotypic New York Jewish voice of film comedies.

In 1980 when Stardust Memories *is released, it is impossible not to recall this weekend. It also is instructive to see how a benign experience is the seed for a story about a director on the verge of a nervous breakdown, who in his reveries imagines variations on his complicated love life, a space alien who tells him that "We enjoy your films. Particularly the early funny ones," and being shot by a deranged fan. (Judith Crist has a small part in the picture.)*

June 1974

Sleeper is finished and, to Woody's relief, he is back in New York. (In the film he plays Miles Monroe, a clarinet player and the co-owner of the Happy Carrot Health Food Store in Manhattan, who checks into the hospital for a routine gallbladder operation in 1972 and, after a mishap in the operating room, is cryogenically frozen for two hundred years, until he is defrosted by opponents of the then-totalitarian government.)

EL: I keep seeing in articles about you that the writers or people they've interviewed for the story call you "a comedy genius." What do you make of that? Do ideas come to you in a bright light of inspiration?

WA: I would hardly call it genius, but I do sometimes have a sudden flash. For some reason, funny ideas occur. Like in the prison visiting sequence in *Take the Money and Run,* the joke with the two ventriloquist dummies visiting was spontaneous. I was thinking of what to do next and the idea just popped spontaneously into my head.

EL: Can you give me an example of what seemed a great idea that instead fizzled?

WA: I was coming out of the optician's on Lexington and Seventy-seventh Street and the spider sequence in *Everything You Always Wanted to Know About Sex* hit

Two dummies visit at San Quentin along with Virgil (Woody) and Louise (Janet Margolin) in *Take the Money and Run.*

me. [*The sequence was shot at great expense of time and money but cut from the finished film. The question the sequence asked is, "What makes men homosexuals?" Louise Lasser, Woody's second wife, is suited up as a black widow at the center of a huge web and Woody, in a reddish-brown spider suit the color of his hair, is her suitor.*] At that moment I had no ending for it. I just thought it was the greatest idea that I would be a spider and there would be a black widow and we would have sex and she would devour me and that would symbolically show one possible reason why men become homosexuals.

[*"Did we do it yet?" she asks, tying him up.*
"You'll know," he replies. Then, petrified as she continues to truss him to eat him, "You're suffering from the worst post-coital depression I've ever seen."]

I thought it was a great sequence, and so theatrical—I was sure I could come up with an ending between then and when I shot it. But it wouldn't come. So I thought, I'll get Louise to play the widow because she's so great at improvising, I know we'll come up with a suitable ending. But it never went anyplace. The thing that was wrong with it in the first five seconds when I thought of it remained wrong right through.

Now, it didn't help that it was so physically painful to do. That was one of the most hateful experiences of my life and hers. I couldn't suit up without itching, my costume was terribly uncomfortable, she hated her costume, we fought all the time. Sitting on that steel cable web hurt. Still, you think you'd be able to get a few-

Louise Lasser as a black widow spider and Woody as her soon-to-be ex in a sequence cut from *Everything You Always Wanted to Know About Sex*. Despite many hours of filming, Woody felt the story lacked a good enough ending.

minute sequence out of that. We shot more than a hundred thousand feet of film over two weeks of filming, two or three cameras, all for six and a half minutes. I had a great subliminal joke to back up the whole sequence with music from *The Nut- cracker Suite*—but it wouldn't work. If I could have gotten any kind of an ending, I would have left it in. I opted for the Lou Jacobi sequence in which he plays a trans- vestite. I thought I was in too many sequences [*he was in four of seven*], and why put in another one if I'm not particularly sure of it?

But the decision whether to cut it or the transvestite sequence took a long time to make. The Coronet [*theater in Manhattan*] was going to open the film at one o'clock and I worked on it until the last moment. We had to run the wet print through the projector twice to deliver it dry.

Sleeper [*released in 1973*] showed me audiences enjoyed watching me, which I find hard to believe. The audience comes to see me, but still I find it inconceivable. I could have played in all the sequences in *Sex*, like the one with Gene Wilder as the doctor who fell in love with a sheep, though certainly not as well, but no one would have minded if they'd seen me do it.

It's just some sort of reticence, the same sort I had with my band when I started playing with them. I couldn't be the leader and they kept looking to me to be their leader only because I had initiated the band and I was known.

EL: Where did the idea for the movie come from?

WA: I came home one night after a Knicks game. [*The New York Knickerbockers are his favorite basketball team and he has courtside season tickets.*] There was a rerun of *The Tonight Show* and it was playing while I did my ablutions. Then I heard me making my joke about sex being dirty if you're doing it right. Right then I thought, Wouldn't it be funny to do several sex sketches based on the current best seller *Everything You Always Wanted to Know About Sex but Were Afraid to Ask*? I thought I was going to have a million comic ideas on sex—but it wasn't as fertile a notion as I imagined, and I had about six.

EL: Were there any that you wrote but didn't film?

WA: There was going to be a biblical sequence on Onan, but I couldn't get a good biblical look for what we had to spend.

EL: Are you always looking for the joke to move you ahead?

WA: I always think I can buy my way out of any situation by being funny. Politi- cal and social points of view, if they emerge, emerge accidentally.

EL: What was the idea behind *Take the Money and Run* [*1969*]?

WA: It originally started with two gangs coming to rob a bank at the same time. In writing *Play It Again, Sam,* there was no thought of Bogart at first. Then I wrote, "Bogart appears," then later on I did it again. When I finished I saw he appeared six times. He was a major character. I remember I was staying at the Astor Tower Hotel in Chicago when I got the idea to use him as a character. *Take the Money* was just as accidental.

[*In* Play It Again, Sam, *Woody is Allan Felix, a writer about films who admires Bogart's success with women because he has none himself. He is charming and funny with women friends—especially Linda (Diane Keaton), the wife of his good friend Dick (Tony Roberts)—but on dates he tries so hard to be cool that his true personality vanishes. With the help of Linda and of Bogart (Jerry Lacy), who materializes in critical situations and gives him instructions on what to say and do next, he discovers the appeal of his own charms.*]

EL: I guess because of *Casablanca,* Bogart is a more romantic figure than the other tough guys of his era, like Robinson or Cagney.

WA: It wasn't that I liked him any more than Edward G. Robinson or James Cagney; it's just that he had a no-nonsense attitude with women in movies and there were a lot of Bogart posters around then. I had already brought in imagined scenes in the script. Bogart was a happy accident.

EL: Is much of what you write accidental?

WA: Yes. To me, my messages are always unintentional. I was thinking about *Sleeper* today in terms of how I hate machines in real life. I have no patience with them. I can't work the simplest ones. They confound me. People close to me will confirm how many appliances I've broken. After I finished writing *Sleeper* I noticed one of the recurrent themes in it is that advanced technology doesn't work: a guy shoots a gun of the future and it blows up; I go into a futuristic kitchen and it malfunctions. Right through the writing, without planning it, I just thought of funny technology jokes as I went along. You would think that I was doing it on purpose, that I was trying to create a character that doesn't get along with machines. But I wasn't aware of it until afterward when someone pointed it out to me.

EL: So *Sleeper* is sort of accidentally autobiographical, or biographically once removed. Is *Sam* in any way autobiographical?

WA: Almost all my work is autobiographical and yet so exaggerated and distorted it reads to me like fiction. Like the character in *Sam,* I'm not social. I don't get an enormous input from the rest of the world. I wish I could get out more and mingle, because I could write better things. But I can't.

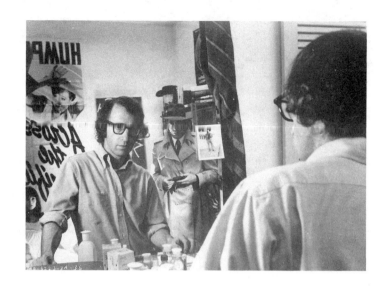

RIGHT: Bogart giving Allan Felix courage as he dresses in *Play It Again, Sam*
FACING PAGE: Bogart coaches Allan on what to say to Linda.

Sam was written at the time Louise and I split up. When we went into rehearsal with it she had just about moved out of the house. The story never actually occurred in real life. What did occur is that married friends would say, "Oh, we know a nice girl for you." Or they'd invite me to a party and introduce me to a girl and it would be an awkward evening because those things are always awkward and I'd make a fool out of myself frequently. Then I would find that the wives of my friends who I wouldn't in a million years think of romantically, I'd be natural around them and real, and they would find me much better company than the women I pressed to impress. And that's what gave me the idea. You're pressing with a stranger and you're totally at home with your friends because you don't give a damn, and it's the friend who sees you as a real person, whereas the other people see you as a nervous kind of wretch or an intense grotesque.

EL: When you get an idea for a film, do you outline it first or make notes?

WA: I outline it first, but only on one page. It's very tough. You can't believe the problems that I encounter writing for myself because of the specificity of my situation. Because I'm not an actor; I'm not going to write a story where I play, for example, a southern sheriff. I'm always going to play within my limited range. And I'm believable as me only as certain things, as an urban, studious-looking twerp my age. I would not be believable, say, as a physical trainer or a Marine hero. And people expect me to say amusing things all the time. That's what they're paying for.

So that's a problem that rules out many ideas. If I had an idea for a comedy like *Born Yesterday* [*George Cukor's 1950 film of Garson Kanin's Broadway play. Broderick Crawford plays a loutish scrap metal tycoon who comes to Washington, D.C., with his ex-showgirl mistress (Judy Holliday) to bribe enough congressmen to meet his greedy ends. He hires a newspaperman (William Holden) to polish up the*

mistress and make her more socially presentable, but his lessons also let her see Crawford for the crook he is, and she falls for Holden], I couldn't do it if I expected to be in it. I've got to get an idea that's believable, yet funny, and within my minuscule acting range. Also, there are no big crises that I can believably get into. I don't want to get into murder mysteries although I have a junk tooth for them and may indulge myself someday. [*This would be* Manhattan Murder Mystery (*1993*), *a wisecracking, old-fashioned comic mystery, as opposed to the more character-driven films about murder such as* Crimes and Misdemeanors (*1989*) *and* Match Point (*2005*) *that he will make in future years.*] I don't want to get into spies or stuff like that because they're usually silly and unbelievable to me. Therefore plot possibilities get reduced to human relationships, and because they get reduced to human relationships—and we're living in a psychoanalytic era—the conflicts become internal and not as visually active and cinematic as they were years ago. The level of conflict is much more subtle, a very modern level of conflict where little psychological things cause the problem: you strike out with women because you pick the wrong women. The seeds of your destruction are within you, which is hard to dramatize in a comedy because in a comedy it's nice to have big, physical opposing forces. So if I'm in the army, you've got more conflict right away, or if I'm being chased by the Mafia because I owe money, you've got it. But much of that kind of material is not believable for me as an actor. Or I can't make it believable. And much of it is too trivial to engage a bright audience.

Woody is at work on the script of what eventually becomes Annie Hall (*1977*). *It is the story of two lovers, told mainly in flashback. Alvy Singer (Woody) and Annie Hall (Diane Keaton) end up as great friends, but it is the second-best possibility for Alvy. (In some ways the picture resembles their real-life relationship; the two were romantically involved for several years, though not when the film was made.) He is aware of the limitations of his screen character and he is doing all he can to extend himself as a writer and an actor and move away from joke-after-joke-after-joke scripts such as* Take the Money and Run *and* Bananas.

WA: I'm trying not to anticipate what the public wants to avoid leaning toward easy, crowd-pleasing things. I'm trying to indulge my own pleasurable sense of drama as to what to come out with next, and every instinct of mine tells me to come out with a real story. Because, again, if my next film is, hypothetically, one in which I run an IBM machine for president of the United States because it's an honest candidate and would make a perfect president and I do all kinds of satire and I give it a wife and it talks to religious leaders, people will laugh at me in a distant, cerebral way, but I want to hook them into a more personal comedy.

The audience is seeing only one small facet of me as an actor and writer in *Sleeper* or my other pictures. They're seeing that part of me that can do broad, jokey comedy, but that's just one thing I can do. It's like showing them a little interesting diversion, but it isn't what I am exactly. Or more accurately put, I would like to be more than that: more dimensional to them and to open myself up more. So that's what I'm working on, trying to challenge my limitations, if only a little now and then.

I know I'm going to be working with [*Diane*] Keaton in my next movie, so at one time I was thinking about those type of things that [*Spencer*] Tracy and [*Katharine*] Hepburn did, because that would be fun. The problem is, you don't realize how old-fashioned those plots are now. You see them as old movies, so they're delightful. But they're plotty, based on mechanics the public's outgrown.

In this new script I'm trying to work from within, from the neurosis out, so it will not seem dated a hundred years from now. In *Pat and Mike,* say, they've got two characters and the writers think up a sitcom type of situation: she's an athlete who can't come through when her boyfriend is there, or it's a men-against-the-women kind of thing. They are cardboard types, not individuals, fortunately made lovely by the greatness of Tracy and Hepburn.

When you want to do a real comic story nowadays, the problems are very fine. They don't flare up in a big way. Say this girl wants to live with me but she also wants to keep her own apartment as a psychological symbol of independence. Those kinds of conflicts are interesting; they can help us learn to understand people—to try and analyze their behavior, or be aware at least that there's an element of comic psychology to exploit. But it's very tough to develop visual screen conflict from that.

When you think back even ten years, the conflicts are now different. Talk comedies were always about an external thing. It's very hard to get enough film sparks going just using character. If Diane and I were to argue in a movie realistically, it would now tend to have psychological overtones. We wouldn't argue about, "Well, darling, we said we were going to try a house in the country for a month but now the basement's flooded and we have raccoons." It would be more like she'll say, "I'd rather live on the West Coast," and I'll say, "Well you want to live on the West Coast because your family lives there, you're neurotically attached to your family." Of course, maybe the raccoons are funnier.

You can see the old example of it perfectly if you watch any TV sitcom. Sitcoms are plot-driven, it's by definition what they are: it's the situation that makes you laugh. The guy comes over to your house and you think he's the inspector general and he's just a silly clerk. It only has to be sustained for half an hour, and there's a very high level of joke writing on even the simplest, most common sitcoms. Fine jokes.

It's tougher to write it based on character, but it's so much greater for the audience. I've always said that the best comedy play in America is *Born Yesterday,* and giving birth to that was Shaw's *Pygmalion.* What's great are Henry Higgins and Liza Doolittle. The laughs come out of who they are, not jokes. *Born Yesterday* is based strictly on the juxtaposition of characters—she's the dumb blonde who's the girlfriend of a very philistine gangster and he's the intellectual.

Now, I love jokes. Nobody appreciates a Bob Hope movie more than me. But when you're laughing at character, it's great. Take Jackie Gleason in *The Honeymooners.* It's his character that's so funny, so when he and Art Carney think they're drinking liquor and it's really cider, and psychologically they become drunker and drunker and it's hilarious. Incidentally, despite the zillions of gags Bob Hope spouted, it was the Hope persona that made him last. I forget his jokes but not his character.

That's why Diane Keaton always came out funnier in the movies I played with her, because I'd write all the jokes for myself—and I can do jokes nicely and get my laughs—but she was always funny in the scene because her stuff was always character. I'm going through a movie like *Annie Hall* glib and facile as a comic, but she's going through as a character.

EL: Close to life but a bit exaggerated for comic effect, yet not a very high concept.

WA: People have trouble with conceptual comic ideas. I come up with one like a giant breast [*in a parody of mad scientist horror films in* Everything You Always Wanted to Know About Sex, *a marauding fifteen-foot-tall breast terrorizes the populace until Woody's character lures it into a two-story-high bra*] and they have trouble with it. They find it hard to say, "My God, what a funny concept that is, an enormous breast. It's so ridiculous." They laugh joke by joke within it. So I feel discouraged in terms of presenting funny *conceptual* notions.

He also is discouraged by the problems of filming the breast sequence. A man inside the inflated, air-conditioned breast had a walkie-talkie to receive instructions to maneuver it, but Woody could film for only about a half hour in the early morn-

ing before the wind picked up and blew the breast around and tore the thin fabric; plus, "I had to shoot from sixteen different angles to hide the seams."

But when I ask if he is ready to give up conceptual ideas, he details the premise for a film that instead becomes one of his most admired stories, "The Kugelmass Episode."

WA: Actually, I have a conceptual notion that I get a machine that projects me into a work of fiction because I'm in love with Anna Karenina or something, and I have an affair with her there, and I keep getting into that story and finally she comes to New York and I stash her in a hotel room in town and cheat on my wife with her. I've been toying with that idea in different forms: that my wife is involved with J. Alfred Prufrock and I go to find her, or this guy has a machine that will project me into *Anna Karenina*, for instance, or *Madame Bovary* because I'm in love with her and it goes wrong and projects me into a French grammar book by mistake and there are no humans but only verbs and other parts of speech. [*In the finished story, Kugelmass, a professor of humanities at the City College of New York, unhappily married for the second time, decides he needs "romance. I need softness, I need flirtation." A magician named Persky ("Or should I say the Great Persky?") offers to put Kugelmass in a magic box with a novel of his choosing and transport him into the story; he picks* Madame Bovary. *Kugelmass is in fact transported into the novel, and he and Emma Bovary carry on a passionate affair over several subsequent visits. He even brings her to New York, where they stay in the Plaza Hotel and she develops aspirations for a career in show business. But idealization gives way to reality, and after some difficulty (the machine malfunctions and Kugelmass is faced with the prospect of Emma forever), she is sent back to Yonville. (Though not before several readers discover Kugelmass in the story or notice Emma's absence. " 'I cannot get my mind around this,' a Stanford professor said. 'First a strange character named Kugelmass, and now she's gone from the book. Well, I guess the mark of a classic is that you can read it a thousand times and always find something new.' ") Kugelmass is relieved by his escape but after three weeks wants to try again, this time with The Monkey in* Portnoy's Complaint. *("Sex and romance," he says once back inside the box. "What we go through for a pretty face.") But yet again the machine malfunctions and instead of landing in Philip Roth's novel, Kugelmass is "projected into an old textbook,* Remedial Spanish, *and was running for his life over a barren, rocky terrain as the word* tener *('to have')—a large and hairy irregular verb—raced after him on its spindly legs."*]

The problem with doing it is you *say* the concept in one line and it's funny, but to *show* the concept you ultimately have to proceed joke by joke. You wind up still having to do a million jokes. It's not that the audience says, "Oh, my God, how funny this idea is, to be at Prufrock's party." They say, "Oh, yeah, we're there. Now what? What's the joke?"

June 1987

Woody is working on the untitled script he will shoot in the fall. In the first draft the lead character, Marion Post, is married to Ken, a cardiologist, "who ten years ago examined my heart, liked what he saw, and proposed." On the surface she seems a woman totally in control of herself, but in reality she feels so deeply that her only choice is to deny feelings or be overwhelmed by them.

EL: Now you're on to another dramatic film, about what happens to a woman who overhears a stranger baring her soul and what it conjures up in her. Is this a recent idea?

WA: I was going to do a comedy about a man who overhears an analyst and a woman speaking, is fascinated, takes a look at the woman, and sees she is quite beautiful. They continue to meet without her knowing he is overhearing. Then I thought, Gee, that's a mean thing, and dropped the idea. Five years later I thought it could make an interesting drama. There's more intensity if it evokes the deep feelings in the woman who's eavesdropping. It's still evolving.

EL: As usual, you don't yet have a title; I know that often there isn't one until long after the editing is complete. Is one beginning to form yet?

WA: I'm not as dedicated to one-word titles as before. *Another Woman* is lurking around my mind as the title. It's not very exciting, but one notion I've toyed around with. In the end it may not matter; I may not want an exciting title. It does have some resonance. Marion hears another woman, she hopefully becomes another woman, and she sees her husband with another woman. [*A middle-aged woman who shut down her emotions following an abortion when she was in her twenties is forced to confront her past when she overhears the psychoanalytical sessions of a pregnant younger woman through a heating vent in her office, which is near the analyst's.*]

EL: But your first thought when you had the idea was to make it a comedy?

WA: Yes. The idea began as a comic notion many years ago when I was interested in a Chaplinesque sort of comedy. A man lives in a tiny room somewhere and overhears a girl with problems. I'd solve them and so become her dream man. I'd make all the things happen that she wanted to happen. Then I questioned the taste of that—eavesdropping. Even in the most benign Chaplinesque way perhaps it is wrong. Then years later I thought of it dramatically—a woman hears something through a wall. I thought, What would be interesting, what could she hear that would make such a difference? My first thought was that the woman's sister and husband are having an affair. She goes home and thinks, How terrible. Then she finds that her sister and husband *are* having an affair. But that became too Hitchcockian. It was the wrong motif. So I used the sister motif in *Hannah* [and Her Sisters].

But this notion has haunted me for years and by bearing down on it, I felt I could get a story. Then the notion of someone with a closed life came, of someone who kept a wall around her but now in her fifties could no longer wall her emotions out—feelings started to seep in and reality was forcing itself on her even through closed walls. [*He laughs.*] Maybe I'll regret that I didn't do it as a comedy.

EL: Many people do hide their emotions because they're too afraid to acknowledge them.

WA: People have life-ruining difficulty dealing with their feelings and yet can be extremely proficient in their intellectual work and are active in social programs and charities. I'm probably as guilty of that as anyone.

Woody is in a relationship with Mia Farrow at this time, and her pregnancy is a new and complicating factor; she is due to deliver right after shooting is scheduled to finish and will be obviously pregnant in the film. In addition, Dianne Wiest, a regular in his recent films, is taking time off to adopt a child. This causes a number of changes, in the cast as well as the script. Farrow will now play the young woman whose voice and pregnancy release so many hidden feelings in Marion.

WA: She's pregnant to accommodate Mia, who was going to be Marion and Dianne Wiest the woman in analysis. The pregnancy is plotting through necessity. Then making Marion older seemed better, too. I want someone in the ballpark of Mia physically—Liv Ullmann, or Bibi Andersson for instance—but I don't want to use [*Ingmar*] Bergman's people; they're so associated with him. The ideal is to find an actress slightly older than Mia who doesn't look like Mia but is in her physical ballpark. [*He chose Gena Rowlands.*] I want a vivid dream of a woman seen through the eyes of Marion.

EL: It's interesting how much your idea for the film is being shaped by circumstance. Have you talked much with Mia about how best to adapt the script?

WA: It's rare that I would show the script at this stage, even to Mia. But I wanted to see if it was okay for her while she is pregnant. Her comments are important. She thinks the older woman should hear more information through the wall. She thinks that the older woman next door to the analyst should instigate everything. All good thoughts.

EL: Fatherhood is such a change for you. [*He and Farrow adopted a baby daughter two years ago and he has assumed paternity for an older adopted son of hers.*]

WA: Only recently, after being around Mia [*who came to their relationship with several children either by her ex-husband André Previn or adopted with him*] and seeing others like Dianne [*Wiest*] have I seen that children are so meaningful in helping to define parents' lives. I wouldn't have thought about it by myself. In *Manhattan* I had that list of things that are really meaningful. [*"Well, all right, why is life worth living? . . . Okay. Um, for me . . . Groucho Marx, to name one thing . . . and (sighing) Willie Mays, and, um . . . the second movement of the Jupiter Symphony, and, ummm . . . Louis Armstrong's recording of "Potato Head Blues" . . . Swedish movies, naturally . . . Sentimental Education by Flaubert . . . uh, Marlon Brando, Frank Sinatra . . . ummm, those incredible apples and pears by Cézanne . . . uh, the crabs at Sam Wo's . . .*] I got a letter from a woman who said I didn't mention my child. At the time I disregarded it. Now it seems like an unthinkable mistake. Once you have a child it is so powerful an experience it's impossible not to delight in it.

It's a bigger kick getting a laugh from the baby than it is from a whole audience. I find I'm always doing things to get that laugh because it is so gratifying. I thrust my face in rapidly toward hers, make foolish incomprehensible sounds, things that in the past I saw others do and thought they were making such asses of themselves.

EL: Have any of your films satiated your desire to do something in particular?

WA: Sometimes, yes. I noticed this completely accidentally. I noticed after I had made *Manhattan* that I didn't have the urge anymore to show New York City in a pronounced glamorous way. Now whenever I do show it, I do show it nicely. But that's strictly en route to the plot. But I had a real urge to show New York as a wonderland and I completely fulfilled that feeling in *Manhattan.*

And after I made *Stardust Memories*, I didn't want to work like that for a while. Now I do again. It satiated a yen to do a baroque picture. At least for a while.

Nine years later, in 1996, he will resurrect the notion of a man learning a woman's secrets and intimate wishes and using the information to woo her, in the musical comedy Everyone Says I Love You. *Of course he does not know that yet, but the beginning of another idea is there.*

WA: I'm thinking of my next two films now. I want to do an original musical comedy. I'm a sucker for them. I grew up with those great Broadway musicals. I can't sing, but I could act and direct one. I could play the clarinet, I suppose, but the fun of a musical is to sing the Cole Porter lyrics. I'd need to solidify the idea and give a composer and lyricist a year to work.

EL: It seems like you're always thinking of either ideas or how to solve a script problem. You once told me that even if an elevator ride is more than three floors, you turn to thought.

WA: When I go to sleep at night, put my head on the pillow, or walk down the street, I like to be thinking of story ideas. I'm always thinking about new plots. I would do anything to avoid that horrible moment of What do I do next? Paddy Chayefsky wrote about it—correctly—when he said it's the time between that a writer thinks of going into a different business.

November 1987

Woody has recently finished editing September—*for the second time. He completely reshot the picture and changed two principal cast members after he saw the first version. We are in his apartment in New York, opposite each other in the same comfortably stuffed chairs we've sat and talked in for over fifteen years. He has just returned from lunch with Ian Holm, a leading actor in* Another Woman, *which is about to be filmed, and is dressed in brown corduroy trousers, a lighter brown cashmere sweater, a brown tweed jacket, and a striped tie.*

EL: *September* is a departure for you. It is filmed in one location. What was your idea?

WA: I've always wanted to make some chamber pieces with a small cast in one location, or a limited location, and one way to do that is to work in play form deliberately. I wanted to put it in four acts, which I did. This thing, I could just publish the script, an acting version of it, and you could probably put it on in a theater with almost no changes at all. But it's not stagy because it was conceived for film. I mean, it was not a play that I put on or bought the rights to.

[*A story of the damage of past experiences, a killing, and unrequited love,* September *is a dramatic play written for film. (In his review of the film in the* New York Times *a few months later, Vincent Canby will write that "*September *is less like Mr. Allen's austere* Interiors *than like the diaphanous and lyric* Midsummer Night's Sex Comedy, *but in a hairshirt."*)

The action takes place over twenty-four hours and centers on the wishful or actual relationships of six people in a Vermont summer house: a mother, Diane (Elaine Stritch), and her daughter, Lane (Mia Farrow), with a traumatic past that has caused great bitterness; the daughter's best friend, Stephanie (Dianne Wiest), whose own life is in turmoil and who has come for a visit; an advertising copywriter, Peter (Sam Waterston), with aspirations of writing a novel who has rented the guesthouse on the property; an older neighbor, Howard (Denholm Elliott, died 1992), a widower who yearns for Lane; and Diane's present husband, an earthy physicist, Lloyd (Jack Warden). The film takes place entirely within the house. Daylight streams through louvered windows that allow no view to the outside; at night, there is only the blackness of the country punctuated by lightning.]

EL: Did it ever feel like a play to you or was it always a film as you wrote it?

WA: I always thought of it, felt it, as a film. It's hard to say, it's intuitive. The emotional points are made with a camera. It was shot as a film and it never had to face any of the practicalities of the stage. I didn't do it on the stage, like one sees a Eugene O'Neill play and you want to get that same thing on film because it was successful on the stage. When that's the case, you're very respectful of the material and very timorous about how you do it because you don't want to lose what was so wonderful on the stage. I just conceived it as a motion picture, but one done in a limited, chamber-piece way.

EL: The film opens inside a house. There are no establishing shots to show we're in the country or the city, nor do we ever see anything outside the house. It's entirely an interior piece.

WA: Having establishing shots of the outside would have spoiled it for me because, you know, usually what happens is someone buys a play and opens it up, and what you get really is neither fish nor fowl—it is no longer a play exactly, but it also never achieves the qualities of a film. I deliberately decided not to open it up, not to do all those things.

If I was going to do one or two establishing shots, I would have done what I originally wanted to do and shoot it up at Mia's place in Connecticut, because that's how the original concept came to mind. I was lounging around up at her home and thinking, My God, what a Chekhovian atmosphere this is up here; it's a house on many acres isolated on a little piece of land with water and trees and a field here and a swing out there. [*Pauses and laughs.*] No wonder people kill themselves. And I thought, Great, I'll come up and make a film here. And then I thought to myself, I could live up here for a number of months and the whole crew would have to be put up in town and there were some logistics that would have to be worked out. And then I started to get into trouble with seasonal changes, because Mia's house has some very beautiful picture windows in it and you can't avoid the outside. So if you get a sunny day and then a cloudy day you could have some real significant problems. Even so, I thought I could do wonderful scenes walking around the lake and in the weeping willow trees and things like that and that it had a real pastoral quality. But when it came down to actual scheduling time it would have brought us up there in the winter, and that's not the feel I wanted—the bare trees and the cold and, you know, then you don't walk around the lake and you don't do those things and it doesn't have the same feeling. Plus, the thought of living in the country for a few months while shooting it was enough to turn it into a studio picture.

EL: You told me that at first you thought of having people who had died appear, or fantasy sequences with other people.

WA: Yes. After I wrote it I thought, I'll have [*Elaine*] Stritch on the Ouija board summon the dead husband and have him appear. That seemed interesting, and so then I thought I'd also have Dianne Wiest's husband appear in fantasy, and Denholm Elliott's dead wife appear. But then after a while I thought, No, don't. What you've always wanted to do here is a "realistic" chamber piece, a little story that doesn't get too mysterious. Even though it was a provocative idea to me, I wanted to give myself the discipline of making adjustments to those six characters—there are the other three comic relief characters that come by briefly, but basically six characters—and not get into the other characters, which is something I tend toward all the time. I resisted the temptation because I wanted this to be like a little short story. I wanted it to be realistic. I wanted one set—one house—six people, and in the present, completely in the present, unfolding in front of you in a brief period of time. I wanted all those rigors of a play structure.

EL: Did you think about giving a sense of what was outside the house?

WA: When we first built the set we tried to simulate the outdoors out the window, so we brought trees into the studio. But that also felt artificial—not artificial in the photography, but it had an artificial quality to it. I wanted to focus everybody's attention more inwardly and not think about that. I wanted the interaction between the characters to be interesting. A beautiful sunset out the window or trees rustling never meant anything to me. What was relevant was how the characters interact. So it was a pleasure to have a set built. And the more internalized we got, the happier I was. We finally decided not to make elaborate shots out the window and simulate the outdoors but just stay, as the athletes say, within ourselves. That's how it evolved and that's how it finally gained some momentum. The idea's been germinating for years, first to do something up there, and then exactly what kind of thing to do. I'm doing this to get the ball rolling for dramatic films. If it's a disaster, at least I'll learn something. On the other hand, if it's meaningful to people and fun for me, that's great. Of course I know going in that there's not much of a market for these films.

One of Woody's most surreal and touching films is The Purple Rose of Cairo *(1985). Cecilia (Mia Farrow) is a Depression-era waitress in a small-town diner. Married to an abusive and womanizing ne'er-do-well, she spends her free time lost in the fantasy of movies, seeing the week's offering at the local theater over and over. While*

Cecilia watches a film called The Purple Rose of Cairo *for the umpteenth time, the character of a handsome Egyptologist named Tom (Jeff Daniels), who has been brought to New York by a group of wealthy Manhattan sophisticates, interrupts the scene to talk to her because he has seen her in the audience so often. He comes off the screen and they fall in love ("I just met a wonderful new man," she says. "He's fictional, but you can't have everything"), but his walkout causes havoc at the studio and with Gil (also Daniels), the real-life actor playing him, whose career is threatened. Gil comes to town, woos Cecilia as well, and offers to take her to Hollywood. Her acceptance forces Tom back onto the screen. But once Tom is safely back where he belongs, Gil leaves Cecilia behind. The film ends with her in the theater once again, lost in the fantasy of Fred Astaire and Ginger Rogers dancing their "Cheek to Cheek" number in* Top Hat *(1935).*

EL: What was the first idea for *The Purple Rose of Cairo*?

WA: When I first got the idea, it was just a character comes down from the screen, there are some high jinks, but then I thought, where would it go? Then it hit me: the actor playing the character comes to town. After that, it opened up like a great flower. Cecilia had to decide, and chose the real person, which was a step up for her. Unfortunately, we must choose reality, but in the end it crushes us and disappoints. My view of reality is that it has always been a grim place to be [*he pauses, then lets out a little laugh*], but it's the only place you can get Chinese food.

EL: You sit there rooting for something good to happen at the end to Cecilia, but it's not to be.

WA: The whole reason for *Purple Rose* was for the ending. It would have been a trivial movie with the other ending. An executive from Orion called after the screening in Boston and asked very nicely, "Is that definitely the ending?"
"Oh, yes," I said.
"Okay," he said. But I'm sure the look on his face was a grimace.

EL: How much does your original idea for the film change as you make it?

WA: *Annie Hall* started out to be something that goes on in my mind, and the love story with Annie was one big part of it, but it was only one big part. There were a million other digressions and other scenes and other ideas and I was constantly flashing into my mind, on my thoughts. Then we found the story was so strong that nobody cared about anything else. They wanted to get back to the parts about "you and Annie," so I let it grow that way.
Certain parts came from real life, but I wouldn't want to overmaximize that. Most of it was made up, greatly made up. Our affection for one another was gen-

ABOVE: Gil (Jeff Daniels), a star of *The Purple Rose of Cairo*, the black-and-white film within the film, steps off the screen and falls in love with Cecilia (Mia Farrow), who goes to the theater day after day to lose herself in the fantasy of movies.
FACING: Henry (Edward Herrmann) is amazed by Gil's ability to leave the screen and walk amid the audience.

uine, but it was a made-up story. It wasn't just the details. I didn't meet her that way. We didn't part that way. That wasn't what our relationship was like. Maybe a snippet here and there culled from an actual moment, but hardly anything. Snippets from Marshall Brickman's life and made-up stuff based on his memories put the kibosh on the notion it was my real life or my real affair with Keaton.

EL: When you get an idea, do you try it out on friends?

WA: I generally take full advantage of the people close to me. When I'm out to dinner or on a walk, I ask if it's okay to talk about an idea. With Mia [*their relationship ended in 1992 but at this time they were still a couple*], I bother her right down the line and bounce things off her. Sometimes she's helpful, or just helps me to air it. Diane [*Keaton*] and I did it, and my sister [*Letty Aronson, now the producer of his films*], too. It helps me to say things out loud. When you're in a closed room day after day you often lose focus. So asking someone and getting a response confirms your feelings or changes them. I'm operating simply on instinct, and I want to know if what I have has any relation to what other people feel or if I'm off on a toot someplace. Mia's reactions go into the cauldron of possibilities. If I'm vacillating between two or three ideas, sometimes I get a consensus from friends. I only talked with Mia about *Another Woman*. When I had the idea for *Zelig*, I knew I had a strong character. I didn't need a lot of confirmation on that.

EL: Do you write down ideas as they come to you?

WA: I do write a lot of jokes down when they occur to me. I've always done that because I always forget them if I don't. I still have a drawer full of jokes and snips. A lot of them are still scraps of paper.

Woody has agreed, along with Francis Ford Coppola and Martin Scorsese, to make one of the three short films that will constitute New York Stories. *His,* Oedipus Wrecks, *will feature a quintessential Jewish mother who appears in the sky and makes her son's life miserable in front of all New Yorkers because she wants him to find a nice Jewish girl to marry rather than the stylish WASP he is engaged to. He already has the script pretty well in hand and is thinking even further ahead.*

WA: My next movie, I'd like to try and do something different—I'm getting tired of doing realistic stories. Not that my short movie is realistic in a conventional sense, although it is: the character goes to an analyst; he goes to an office. But the mother appearing in the sky is surreal. I want to do a movie where we can shoot it differently.

There's the kind of film like *Citizen Kane*, which is shot in such an interesting way. What is *Citizen Kane* really? Pauline Kael called it "a shallow masterpiece." You could see the story of a media baron's rise to power—or any person's rise to power told realistically—and you enjoy the film or not. But *Citizen Kane* is told with such flair that the same story is transformed from just a kind of glitzy biography to a masterpiece. There are all those wonderful things Welles did in his films: the overlapping dialogue, the great camera angles, the little touches of the minor characters.

Gil's costars (John Wood; Zoe Caldwell; Van Johnson, one of Woody's childhood idols;
and Milo O'Shea), still trapped behind the screen, are first dumbfounded and then furious
that he has escaped and they cannot go on with the film. One (Deborah Rush) is stopped
by the screen as she tries to follow Gil through it.

Then there's a picture like [*Bergman's*] *Cries and Whispers* where there's very little dialogue, which is very interesting to me. And there are some things to do with cinema verité, where you just put a camera in the room. I'd like to fool around with some of these techniques and not be tied into conventional shooting.

He will make three more films—Crimes and Misdemeanors *(1989),* Alice *(1990), and* Shadows and Fog *(1992)—before he uses mostly a handheld camera for* Husbands and Wives *(also 1992), a picture with very rough transitions and cuts between shots and scenes. And he has other notions.*

WA: I'm just beginning to speculate on the type of thing I'd like to do. I've thought about doing a musical next but I don't know.

There are two types of musicals that I'd like to do. I'd like to do a little musical with already existing songs. And then I'd like to do a book musical where somebody writes a full score for a movie—like *Gigi.* If there's any way that I could be in them,

I would be. It's possible that there are one or two simple songs I could do on pre-record. You know, I could sit in a room and do them over and over and over until I got one version that was reasonably acceptable and then mouth that when the time comes. Keaton has a terrific voice. [*It's evident in* Annie Hall.]

EL: These are sort of dream projects you're talking about. Robert Altman, whose films are usually naturalistic, said he wrote *3 Women* [1977] after waking from a dream. Have any of your film ideas come from a dream?

WA: Years ago, when Altman told me that, I suggested to him that he call his agent, Sam Cohen, and have him negotiate a three-dream deal. As for me, nothing I've ever written has ever originated in a dream in any remote way. I like to use dreams occasionally in the work because you can be very graphic. I did remember my dreams when I was in psychoanalysis and I was making an effort to remember them. But when I saw how unhelpful dream interpretation was, I stopped—unless, of course, you're a pharaoh.

EL: Any other films, or rather types of films, that you want to do?

WA: I've always wanted to do a picture on one of those movie houses that I went to when I was growing up in Brooklyn, and have the whole movie revolve around that movie house, because so much of my life revolved around that in the neighborhood. You'd go there on your dates, you'd go there to meet girls, you'd go there to pick up girls, you'd go there to see films. Everything about it was fun. It was a whole other world. You had this feeling of entering a temple in a certain way, because they were big movie houses and dark and cool—or warm, depending on what you needed. It was a paradise. You'd walk in off the streets of Avenue J and when you'd think of it, Avenue J was what? Traffic and a woman with a pickle barrel selling pickles, and cold and sleety. And you'd pay your twenty cents and walk in and suddenly there was a giant screen in front of you and there would be, you know, James Cagney or Betty Grable. And there was a big candy concession. You could go and load up on that stuff and then sit down in your seat. It was just such a treat. That doesn't happen much anymore. Now kids are renting tapes. Their memories are going to be [*his voice rises in false enthusiasm*], "It was great. On a Friday night we'd get together with our friends, get all dressed up, and rent a tape."

April 2005

We begin the conversations to bring his career up to date. Match Point, *filmed in London in the summer of 2004, has been finished for several months; it will be a huge hit with audiences and critics when it is shown out of competition in Cannes in May and become his most financially successful to this time. The picture is one of the darkest Woody has made. As in* Crimes and Misdemeanors, *someone literally gets away with murder.*

EL: Where did you get the idea for *Match Point*?

WA: Originally I was just toying around with a murder story about someone who kills someone and kills the next-door neighbor to throw off the police. And starting with that, it evolved. I thought, Who would the guy be? And then I thought, He'd be involved with some woman that he wanted to kill. And she'd be wealthy and so a good job for him would be a tennis pro who is brought into contact with wealthy people, and it just gradually grew by itself.

EL: This was a recent idea or one that you'd had for a while?

WA: I had had the idea to do that murder mystery for a while. A number of those kind of stories occur to me now and again, sort of mystery stories, and I table them. There are two kinds of mystery-murder stories. There's the kind that's the airplane-read-type mystery story, and there's the type—I'm not making any comparison here—where the murder is used in a more significant way, like in *Macbeth* or *Crime and Punishment* or *The Brothers Karamazov;* there's murder but it's used philosophically and not as a whodunit. I was trying to give a little substance to the story so it wasn't just a genre piece.

[*Chris, a tennis professional (Jonathan Rhys-Meyers), ingratiates himself with a wealthy family and finds himself the object of their daughter Chloe's (Emily Mortimer) affections. Though Chris hardly loves her, he marries Chloe and is thus assured a life of success, but he is obsessed by Nola (Scarlett Johansson), Chloe's brother's fiancée at the time they meet. They have a passionate affair that is rekindled after the engagement is broken; she becomes pregnant and demands that Chris leave Chloe. Unwilling to give up the comfort marriage has brought him, he murders Nola as well as one of her neighbors, an elderly widow, and to confuse the police takes jewelry from the neighbor to make the murder seem a robbery gone wrong. He then throws the jewelry into the Thames from a walkway by the river but fails to notice that her wedding ring bounces off the railing and falls back to the walkway. When the police find Nola's diary, Chris becomes a suspect. But just as one of the detectives on the case becomes convinced that Chris is guilty, the ring shows up in the possession of a violent drug addict who found and pocketed the ring and then was killed, apparently, in a deal gone bad. Chris goes unpunished.*]

EL: Was *Match Point* always the title?

WA: Yes. It was an obvious title. I recently was doing an interview with someone from Spain and he was saying that since the movie "match point" has become part of the popular idiom. I remember watching a tennis match on television years ago and, after one of those things where the ball bounced over or back after hitting the top of the net, the commentator saying, "A favorable bounce on two or three of those in a match and you have the match. It can make all the difference." And I always remembered that. It seems like nothing, just a casual point. The ball hits the top of the net and falls back in. Yet that can be very, very significant.

EL: Did filming in London change the idea you had for the script?

WA: There were a couple of scripts before that I filmed in New York which I didn't hate but I was severely hampered by the small amount of money I had to make the films for. In London, I had enough money to open up the film, to make it more relaxed. I didn't have to shoot so confined. The European budgets are between $12 and $15 million.

EL: Wasn't this an American story originally?

WA: Yes, I wrote it as an American story and my plan was to do it in the Hamptons, and then we raised the money in England. It was very easy to transfer the story to London. It would not have transferred to every place, but London was an easy place to transfer it to.

EL: Did you have any trouble writing about the class aspect of British life?

WA: I wrote it the best I could, using my common sense, but if I made a mistake, either Lucy Darwin [*one of the producers*] or our production manager would point it out. They might say, "Oh, he would never use this phrase," or "The name Jerry is just not used, it's an odd name in England." But it was easy.

EL: This is a film with some pretty horrifying violence, not shown but implied. Two people are shotgunned in cold blood and the killer gets away with it. Under the old Production Code, this would never have been allowed.

WA: Yeah, you couldn't have done it with the backward Production Code that once ruled our kind-of-prudish country, but it has no relationship to the reality of the world. Obviously in life an enormous amount of evil goes unpunished. When I was younger, you would always hear crime does not pay. There was a very good comic book called *Crime Does Not Pay.* But when I was thirteen, I used to say it paid better than General Motors. You know, crime was to me one of the biggest, most successful industries in the country. Organized crime paid great, just great. Those guys had nothing but money and the huge majority of them were getting away with murder—and of course you can't beat the hours. But now you don't have the problems of the Production Code.

EL: Now you're on to your second successive film to be made in England. Do you have a working title?

WA: I might call this new movie *Scoop.* It's the third film that I wrote in the last twelve weeks. I wrote a film to be done in London and then after I wrote it I found that the phenomenon I was satirizing did not exist in London, so I had to scrap that film. Then I wrote another idea quickly, a dark comedy about a guy who jumped out of a window and tried to commit suicide and walked with a limp. But when I gave it to [*casting director*] Juliet Taylor and my sister to read they both felt that while it was very funny it would be perceived as very personal, autobiographical in a way that they would rather I didn't do. They thought the film would never get a fair shake, that no matter how good it came out, all the focus would be on this sense of autobiography that in fact did not exist but still would distract from the audience's enjoyment of the movie.

So I found myself with four weeks to go and no script. I had to do what I did when I was a television writer; I had to go into a room and sit down and come up with a script. There was no fooling around, no self-indulgence; I couldn't walk the streets and wait for inspiration and ponder. I had to get to the typewriter, soon. And I did. I finished it a couple of days ago and [*co-producer*] Helen Robin is typing it as we speak. She'll proofread it and tomorrow I'll proofread her proofreading and hand it out.

EL: Do you still write in longhand?

WA: I still write as I always have, writing in longhand and then going to the same typewriter. I type it out because no one can read my handwriting. Then I go over it again, usually mangle it, and have to type it again. I complain about typing it, but I don't really mind so much. I put discs on and catch up on my Jelly Roll Morton records.

My two kids love to play on the typewriter. They're always asking, "Can we type? Can we type?" I was thinking to myself the other day, when I bought the typewriter

In *Annie Hall*, Woody used a variety of cinematic techniques, among them split screen, characters watching themselves, and subtitles of characters' inner thoughts, which are quite different from what they are saying aloud. Annie (Diane Keaton), disconnected while making love with Alvy, leaves the bed to watch and he talks with her disembodied self. In the film, Diane Keaton relied on her personal sense of fashion and set a new style that was widely copied.

I DON'T KNOW WHAT I'M SAYING.
SHE SENSES I'M SHALLOW.

I'M NOT SMART ENOUGH FOR HIM.
HANG IN THERE.

for forty bucks—I was sixteen, and now I'm seventy practically, and my kids are right up there on the typewriter—a portable manual Olympia. There's not a scratch on it. It looks glistening new. [*During Woody's first years as a writer, he did not know how to change the typewriter ribbon and so would invite to dinner someone he knew who could. Then during the evening he would say casually, "Oh, by the way, could you give me a hand with this?"*]

EL: Years ago you showed me a paper bag full of ideas and half-written scripts in your desk drawer. Do you still have it?

WA: Yes. I took my bunch of ideas out of the brown paper bag it was in. It's a loose batch of papers, but I have a little clip around it. I went to it continually when I was pressed for an idea for this movie. Actually, this film is an amalgam of two ideas that came from my brown paper bag of ideas.

EL: *Annie Hall* is the film where you began to leave an empty frame, with actors talking offscreen. You did the interior monologue in subtitles of what Alvy and Annie are thinking as they talk. You had her removed and watching as she and Alvy made love.

WA: Right. It was a story where I could utilize the tools of filmmaking. There's no other medium where you can use that kind of comedy and it's all written into the script. Originally, as you know, it was written to show what was going on in the guy's mind. It's exploiting tools of the medium no different than a Western exploits the freedom of films.

EL: Were all these in the original story, the stream-of-consciousness story about Alvy's inability to find pleasure, before it turned into the story of Alvy and Annie's relationship?

WA: Yes. It was all stuff [*co-writer*] Marshall Brickman and I conceived.

EL: The ending is so bittersweet. It's a great relationship, but being friends rather than lovers is the second-best relationship for Alvy. [*The film ends with an actor and actress who resemble Alvy and Annie rehearsing the end scene of a play, which in this case is the traditionally happy ending of the couple reuniting. As the actors embrace, the camera cuts to Alvy, who looks straight into it and says, "Whatta you want? It was my first play. You know how you're always trying to get things to come out perfect in art because it's real difficult in life." Later Alvy and Annie accidentally meet and there is a montage of funny or romantic scenes between them. But they part as friends and Alvy once again addresses the audience: "I realized what a terrific person she was and how much fun it was just knowing her and I thought of that old joke, you know, this guy comes to a psychiatrist and says, 'Doc, my brother's crazy. He thinks he's a chicken.' And the doctor says, 'Well, why don't you turn him in?' And the guy says, 'I would, but I need the eggs.' Well, I guess that's pretty much how I feel about relationships. You know, they're totally irrational and crazy and absurd but I guess we keep going through it because most of us need the eggs."]*

WA: We stumbled with that. I struggled a lot at the end of that picture. There were many scenes and many ideas and finally I came up with this one by trial and error. From a Freudian point of view one might conclude men suffer through the difficulties of love relationships precisely because they need the eggs—and I *mean* the eggs.

EL: From a dramatic point of view, this is a better ending than a conventionally happy one.

WA: I never think of happy endings. I mean, unless it organically comes out of the story.

EL: But this seems like a film that would ordinarily demand a happy ending.

WA: It never occurred to me that there would be a happy ending on it. When it was first conceived in my mind as a murder mystery, I had an ending with the two people meeting and reviewing their time together in a montage and moving on with their lives. It started as a murder story, that [*nearly twenty years later*] became *Manhattan Murder Mystery* [1993].

EL: And for a time after that, it was so much about Alvy's inability to find pleasure. Your working title was *Anhedonia*.

The first scene shot in *Annie Hall*, with spontaneous laughter from Annie and Alvy as they try to wrangle dinner. "Talk to him," Alvy tells Annie after a lobster scuttles behind the refrigerator. "You speak shellfish."

WA: Originally the concept was to drive the film with Alvy's stream of consciousness. And when Marshall saw my first cut with [*editor*] Ralph Rosenblum, he just didn't think it was coherent—and he co-authored the story! It was good criticism. We worked to make it coherent.

EL: The lobster scene with Alvy and Annie laughing as they fumble with the live lobsters they're cooking for dinner worked so well as a montage. It required no sound. Was it scripted?

WA: It was scripted only in that the scene existed but not the dialogue. Then we did about seven or eight takes—it was the first scene of the picture that we shot, the first scene I ever shot with [*cinematographer*] Gordon Willis—and in one of the takes we broke up because Keaton *always* makes me laugh.

Then when I looked at the dailies I realized I had never worked with such a great photographer before, and I was impressed with the take where we broke up, and I knew that was the one we'd be using. It's the biggest laugh I've ever had and it's one of the best scenes in the picture because the spontaneity is genuine. It was a fortuitous beginning to that film.

EL: It's natural and spontaneous and shows a real relationship. There are so many things you did in the film that were a leap for you—

WA: Yes, it was a leap—

EL: —where you decided, "I don't mind putting in subtitles, I don't mind leaving the screen blank or even black."

WA: —because it was a real story about real people. It wasn't like *Love and Death* [*a farce set in Napoleonic-era Russia*] or *Everything You Always Wanted to Know About Sex.* It was real and I was working with a photographer who was teaching me things. It was just a very good experience. But it didn't come easily. We did a lot of reshooting and a lot of screwing around at the end—not just the end but editing with Ralph Rosenblum.

EL: Can you give me some examples?

WA: I don't remember the picture that well, but when Marshall said he found it incoherent we went back and made all sorts of changes and cut things out. There was some kind of joke about Annie living with this guy in California and I didn't feel and Ralph didn't feel it was enough to justify what occurred at that point. So I spent four weeks shooting all kinds of other scenes—and never used any of them; we used the original.

[*People milling about on the sidewalk as Alvy walks out of a store and moves toward the foreground.*

ALVY (*into the camera, to the audience*) I miss Annie. I made a terrible mistake.
A couple, walking down the street, stops as the man talks to Alvy.

MAN She's living in Los Angeles with Tony Lacey.

ALVY Oh yeah? Well, if she is, then the hell with her! If she likes that lifestyle, let her live there! He's a jerk, for one thing.

MAN He graduated Harvard.

ALVY Yeah. He may— Listen, Harvard makes mistakes too, you know. Kissinger taught there.
The couple strolls away as an older woman walks up to Alvy.

WOMAN Don't tell me you're jealous?

ALVY Yeah, jealous. A little bit. Like Medea. Can I show you something, lady? (*He takes a small item from his pocket.*) What I have here . . . I found this in the apartment, black soap. She used to wash her face eight hundred times a day with black soap. Don't ask me why.

WOMAN Well, why don't you go out with other women?

ALVY Well, I tried, but it's, uh, you know, it's very depressing.]

EL: Keaton's singing "Seems Like Old Times" is such a showstopping number. Did you always have that in there for her to sing?

WA: I always had that in. I knew she was great and this song would be beautiful in the movie.

EL: I don't think we've ever talked about the famous fashion look of hers that came out of that picture.

WA: That's just her look. That's the way she dressed. She was always an eccentric, creative dresser. And the costume lady would come to me and say [*sort of whispering*], "Don't let her wear *that.*" And I'd say, "I think she looks great. She looks absolutely *great.*" Of course I did let her wear it.

EL: Was it her suggestion? Did she say, "Let me do this"?

WA: She didn't do it in a formal way. I had had the experience over the years in theater and movies of these *adorable* actresses coming in to work looking like a trillion dollars, then getting into the costume provided for them and looking awful, like my mother's friends, you know? I used to do *Play It Again, Sam* on Broadway every night and there were seven or eight girls in the cast, including Keaton. Some very beautiful girls would show up and knock your socks off and they'd go into their dressing room and they'd all get into their costumes, what was chosen for them—

and they'd look terrible. Then after the show, they'd take them off and get into these wool caps and short skirts and they'd go out looking like gangbusters. So I always had great faith in the actresses wearing what they want to wear, particularly when someone was proven, like Keaton, who always knocked everybody out with the way she dressed. She just wore her clothes and then everybody wanted to wear them.

EL: Well, *Annie Hall* seems a good segue to *Manhattan*.

WA: *Manhattan* was something that Gordon and I talked about in the Hamptons during the filming of *Interiors* at dinner a number of times; we used to eat dinner together all the time. And I talked about doing a wide-screen picture and the thought was not to do a war picture or a typical large-screen picture but to do an intimate romantic picture with a wide screen. We wanted to work in black and white because that had a Manhattan feel to it.

I had bought Michael Tilson Thomas's recordings of Gershwin overtures and I kept hearing them in the shower every day and thinking, God, a scene would be great set to this, or a scene would be great set to that. And I started working out the story with Marshall Brickman.

It was not going to be Gershwin, though, when I started. When I first wrote it, the first music you heard over the opening was Bunny Berigan doing "I Can't Get Started," because that was playing several times every night at Elaine's [*the famous Manhattan celebrity-filled restaurant*] on the jukebox. And we fade in on Elaine's. And then when I did that montage at the beginning, [*film editor*] Sandy [*Susan E.*] Morse said, "I just see *Rhapsody in Blue* here." So I looked at it with *Rhapsody in Blue* and said, "Yeah, of course that would work beautifully." Then I said, "Then we should just do all Gershwin. We'll get the New York Philharmonic and just do all Gershwin." And we did.

It was a romantic picture, beautifully photographed. It was fun to work with Mariel [*Hemingway*]. She was a wonderful person and a terrific actress.

EL: I remember I was with you when you were mixing an earlier film in that old dump of a place on Broadway. I went out of the room for fifteen or twenty minutes and when I returned you looked at me as though I was the poorest sap in the world and said, "You know, you just missed *Mariel Hemingway.*"

WA: [*Smiles*] She came to meet me. She and her girlfriend came up. I had wanted to use her—I had seen her in *Lipstick* [*1976*]—and I had to meet her live once just to verify that she was right. And she popped by for a minute and we all said hello to her.

She was a wonderful, cheerful kid and a terrific actress. Towered over me.

[*Manhattan (1979) is the story of Isaac Davis (Woody), a TV writer whose wife (Meryl Streep) has left him for a woman. He now is involved with Tracy (Hemingway), a sophisticated but very sweet seventeen-year-old who loves him. He adores her but feels there is no future for them. He meets Mary (Diane Keaton), the mistress of his married best friend, Yale (Michael Murphy), a college professor with aspirations to write a book. Ike falls for Mary but then when Yale decides to leave his wife, Emily, for her, she breaks things off with Ike. Tracy, moving on with her life, has made plans to go to England to study and just as she is set to leave, Ike realizes too late what he has given up.*]

EL: There is the realization that Ike has at the end, that he had been crazy to give up Tracy for the supposedly intellectual and worldlier Mary.

WA: I just thought it was a funny idea that the guy was adored by this young woman who has so much purity and is so decent and he blows it.

One of the criticisms of that picture that became not popular but was mentioned more than once was, "Who are these people? I don't know any of these people. These are not New Yorkers as I know any New Yorkers." And I can't argue that necessarily; that may be a completely valid criticism. But for some reason, the picture had enormous resonance, and success, all over the world. I was as surprised as anyone.

It may be completely true that these are not real people, just as the depictions of Manhattan I've offered up are not necessarily real in the sense that they're naturalistic. But obviously there was something about the people in *Manhattan* that resonated everywhere—France, Japan, South America.

EL: Was there ever much comment about the age difference between Ike and Tracy?

WA: Not the critics but some people were annoyed about that. To me, I gave that about as much credence as I gave the criticism of my relationship to Soon-Yi. If two people are happy with each other, they're happy. Anyhow, it seemed like a good plot contrivance—and it was.

Speaking of Soon-Yi, it is ironic that my marriage to her, which was seen by many as so irrational, to me is the one relationship in my life that worked, and here it is many years later and we're happy, with two great kids. [*Woody's wife, Soon-Yi Previn, is the adopted daughter of André Previn and Mia Farrow, who were divorced in 1979. The next year, Woody and Mia began a relationship and she appeared in every one of his films over the next dozen years. She adopted an infant daughter, Dylan (now known as Malone Farrow), whom Woody coadopted two years later. They also had a son, although they were not married and never lived together. The relationship ended when Woody and Soon-Yi became involved in 1992.*]

EL: What was the genesis of this film? You've told me that you wanted to do a film that celebrated Manhattan.

WA: Conversation with Marshall Brickman. I wanted to show the city the way I felt about it. We'd chat and I said something like, "Wouldn't it be funny if I liked this really young girl and if Keaton was this major pseudo-intellectual?" And he would envision a scene and start to ad-lib it and I'd take it from him and carry it farther and he'd take it back from me and carry it even farther—the way people collaborate. We'd joke with each other and he'd play a character and I'd play a character and eventually the story emerged.

EL: Did you have any of the problems with this one like you did with *Annie Hall* or did this one come together easily?

WA: No, no, no, I had problems.

EL: What were some of them?

WA: The usual problems that minor writers have [*laughs*] and that is the end—the very, very ending, those couple of shots were always the same. But there was a missing climax where I went to the guy's classroom and confronted him [*Ike and Yale are both involved with Mary*], that was never there. I didn't have a good end to the picture. I remember Marshall's wife saw it—I'm not sure if they were married then—and she said, "What's missing is some kind of scene where you pay off that problem."
[*After Mary tells Ike that Yale is leaving his wife for her, Ike goes to Yale's classroom and confronts him. Along one wall are several full human and ape skeletons.*

In *Manhattan*, Yale (Michael Murphy) and Ike (Woody) argue in a classroom about their mutual attraction to the same woman. The skeletons just happened to be in the room used for the shot and Woody ad-libbed dialogue: "You know, someday we're gonna—we're gonna be like him!"

After some back-and-forth about Mary and who should have been forthright with whom, they get to the heart of the argument.]

YALE Well, I'm not a saint, okay?

IKE *(gesturing, almost hitting one of the skeletons)* But you—you're too easy on yourself, don't you see that? You know, you . . . you—that's your whole problem. You rationalize everything. You're not honest with yourself. You talk about . . . you wanna—you wanna write a book but, but—in the end, you'd rather buy the Porsche, you know, or you cheat a little bit on Emily, and you play around with the truth a little with me, and—the next thing you know, you're in front of a Senate committee and you're naming names! You're informing on your friends!

YALE *(reacting)* You are so self-righteous, you know. I mean, we're just people, we're just human beings, you know. You think you're God!

IKE I—I gotta model myself after someone!

YALE Well, you just can't live the way you do, you know. It's all so perfect.

IKE Jesus—well, what are future generations gonna say about us? My God! *(He points to the skeleton, acknowledging it at last.)* You know, someday we're gonna—we're gonna be like him! I mean, you know—well, he was probably one of the beautiful people. He was probably dancing and playing tennis and everything. And—and— *(pointing to the skeleton again)* and now—well, this is what happens to us! You know, it's very important to have—to have some kind of personal integrity. You know, I'll be hanging in a classroom one day. And— and I wanna make sure when I . . . thin out that I'm going to be well thought of!

(The camera stays focused on the skeleton, its full form shown now, as Ike leaves, then Yale.)]

EL: Let's talk a bit about *Radio Days*, which has always struck me as one of your most personal films.

WA: A purely pleasurable, self-indulgent thing. I wanted to do a whole movie of scenes based on memories of songs of my childhood, like Artie Shaw's "Begin the Beguine" and Bing Crosby's "Pistol Packin' Mama" and "Mairzy Doats." It was that kind of nostalgia; self-indulgent pleasure that one gets re-creating one's childhood atmosphere. You know, somebody puts twenty million bucks in the bank—whatever the budget was, fifteen, sixteen million—and you get a chance to re-create your childhood, or a facsimile of it. It really isn't my childhood exactly, but there are many aspects of my childhood that I've put in for fun, that I remember.

EL: Like some of the home life.

WA: Yes, some of the home life mirrored my home life because we always lived with other relatives. That's what the evenings would be like. They'd be listening to the war news on the radio and my uncle and my father or my aunts and my father were playing gin rummy and my mother would be knitting and the radio would be on and you'd get reports on how the war was going on the seven o'clock news or the nine o'clock news.

In between they would listen to all these shows, which I remember as incredibly wonderful, but they're not. A lot of times I get together with people my age and someone will say, "Radio was a much better medium than television because television's so insipid and radio, you had to use your imagination." Then someone will come out with packages of those shows and I'll listen to *The Shadow* and other old radio shows and they are *quite* god-awful. Except for Jack Benny, who holds up brilliantly. What comedy writing, and what a performer he was.

EL: So it's the reverse of movies you didn't like when you saw them in the theater but do like when you see them on TV. Here's stuff you loved on radio but disappoints when you hear it decades later.

WA: You hear it again and you realize just how awful it was. But Benny! Someone gave me a wonderful tape of Jack Benny and his guest star was Ernst Lubitsch and it was just a wonderful, funny, funny radio show. Just as funny as could be.

[Radio Days *is a story about the power of imagination and memory. Woody narrates but does not appear in the film, which is a combination of a boy's oddball family stories and childhood yearnings held together by music and voices from the radio in the early 1940s. Just as what the boy hears fires his imagination, the people behind the radio voices have their own incongruent lives and yearnings.*]

EL: Was the sexy substitute teacher in *Radio Days* based on anyone real?

WA: No. Totally fabricated. First of all, no teacher who ever crossed the threshold of P.S. 99 ever looked like anything that you'd find outside of, you know, an aquarium. With a substitute teacher there was a breakdown of discipline. It was like a vacation for the day. So that part of the scene did happen. But you never got a really good-looking teacher.

EL: Even though it was only a forty-minute subway ride away, midtown Manhattan must have seemed like another world compared to Brooklyn.

WA: Right. It was a very pleasant trip. You'd buy the paper and get on the train and thirty-five, forty minutes later you're there. You were in Manhattan in twenty minutes but you had to get uptown to Forty-second Street before it started to matter.

But the difference was simply amazing. Brooklyn was nice. And you can tell that now as it's getting its refurb. The houses for sale in Park Slope and on the waterfront there are absolutely gorgeous. But it didn't matter. You were in Brooklyn and it was *fine*. But when you crossed over into Manhattan, it was an *explosion* of everything that you only knew from Hollywood movies. Because when we went over—especially at *my* age—you could only *walk* on Park Avenue or Fifth Avenue or Times Square or wherever you were, but you couldn't go inside those places. The only thing that took you inside the apartments and the penthouses and the night-clubs were the movies.

And so when you went into Manhattan you knew when you saw the houses on Fifth Avenue, on Park Avenue, that if you were to pan by, there would be some incredible love affair going on in apartment A, and in apartment B there'd be a songwriter writing the next Broadway show, and you'd pan to the next apartment and there'd be some young model who had just come to New York and was falling in love with someone and was going to take acting by storm. You bought into all that stuff that you saw when you were a kid. So it was all the difference in the world.

EL: The other day you told me that your father used to bring you into town and give you a guided tour as you walked, describing the buildings that used to be there. How old were you when that started?

WA: It was during World War II, so I was six or seven. He would take me from the train station on Avenue J in Brooklyn and we'd ride into New York. I'd go to the Automat, I'd go to the Circle Magic Shop, which had a big arcade downstairs. We'd go to the arcades on Forty-second Street—my father loved to shoot the rifles. It was *dazzling*. Rarely we went to a movie, *rarely*.

EL: Did you know he was a cab driver during that period? I'm reminded of the poignant scene in *Radio Days* when the kid gets into a cab and is startled to see his father is the driver and his father is clearly embarrassed.

WA: No, I didn't. That anecdote was not 100 percent true but almost true. Whenever I'd ask my parents what he did, I would get a different answer because he often switched jobs. So they'd always say, "Your father is a big butter and egg man." "Your father works in the city." "He's in business." I could never get a straight answer.

In the course of that time he'd owned a store that was a sort of grocery store, and he'd worked at all these other jobs. He once was a bookmaker, for [*the mob boss*] Albert Anastasia, actually. He also had worked in and run a pool hall.

I was coming out of the movies one day with my friends and a cab goes by and my father was at the wheel, with the taxi driver's hat [*laughs*]. It didn't bother me at all. I thought he was a bit embarrassed by it. I said, "What are you doing?" And he said, "Ah, I'm just doing this for a friend."

To me, it was all the same. A cab driver was no different from a bank president. I had no negative feelings about it.

EL: There is that nice dramatic shift when the kid is being chased by the parents to give him a spanking and they are interrupted by the radio bulletin of the little girl who has fallen into a well.

WA: Now, I made that up. We *had* listened to a similar story on the radio, as had many American families. That was a tense thing. And I was chased around the house many times. And I did dye my mother's coat. That was true.

All that stuff about going out with my aunt when my sister was being born—none of that was true. I went out with my father when my mother was in the hospital. We visited her just after she had given birth and my father took me into Manhattan. Maybe we went to a movie or to a war museum like the kind that was in the movie—battleships and guns. And he bought me—it wasn't a chemistry set, actually it was an FBI fingerprinting set. He always bought me stuff—I was spoiled.

I was very scientifically inclined as a young boy. My parents had to put me in the hospital for a couple of days for allergy tests. It was very unpleasant and I hated it all. I had always wanted a chemistry set but they thought it was dangerous to be around chemicals. But I guess my father felt so guilty about my suffering and having to be in the hospital that the day I got out they bought me a $40 Lionel chemistry set, which was quite a top-of-the-line thing.

It's a typical example of taking bits and scraps of my childhood that really never happened as they appear in the movie, or even close to the way they appear in the movie, and using them for a certain value but not autobiographically so.

So when you see *Radio Days*, my aunt takes me into town with her boyfriend and I watch them dancing, but none of that ever happened. I never went anywhere with my aunt and some boyfriend. Those relationships didn't exist. That was pure drama for the story. Yes, I was chased around the house, but it had nothing to do with that kid's falling down the well—Kathy Fiscus, or whatever her name was. [*In 1949, three-year-old Kathy Fiscus fell into an uncapped well in the Los Angeles suburb of San Marino. Radio bulletins kept a horrified public mesmerized for three days while rescuers worked in vain to retrieve her alive.*]

I'm relying on information in my life, but that's why I say it's not autobiographical. It's much more exaggerated to make the story better.

EL: I wasn't thinking of an exact parallel.

WA: But people do.

EL: Yes. But you're saying that you take some things that are true but then you make something completely different out of them. Like you pick a flower and then some others and after a while you have a bouquet. Here you have an anecdote and then you add a bunch of other things and then you have a screenplay.

WA: Right. Nor, incidentally, did I live with my grandmother and grandfather. I stayed with them only once. We practically always lived with relatives, but it was an aunt or an uncle. My grandparents lived down the block in another house with other aunts. So it's a conglomeration of some things.

EL: So in the case of *Radio Days,* you took the music that evoked the period and you tell a story about an important time in your life, but you were a kid and you're relying on what you recall of your facts and fantasies as a kid.

WA: It's atmosphere, that's really what the fun of the movie was. It's not a big heavy plot movie. It's a movie of anecdotes and the atmosphere of what the kids did when I was younger—went to the beach and looked for German submarines.

EL: Did you ever see one?

WA: I never saw a German submarine. The truth of the matter is, we used to look up for aircraft because all the kids were encouraged to do that. You could buy games that showed the silhouettes of the Axis aircraft so that you could identify them. When I lived in Long Beach [*on Long Island, a few miles east of Brooklyn*] we'd go on the beaches after school every day—not with binoculars like in the movie—and it's conceivable that one day we might have looked out at the water and said, "Gee, what if we saw a German submarine out there, or a German battleship out there. What would you do?"
But we did scan the skies. That was a fairly popular thing.

EL: Did you do it because you were worried or because it was fun?

WA: We did it because we wanted to participate in the patriotism of the day and it had a kind of official patina to it and we felt we were doing our job to foil the Axis, and maybe we would see a German plane and [*laughs*] could report it. People were encouraged to do those things; I'm sure people were encouraged to go to the beach and look, though I don't remember that particular propaganda. I do remember collecting tinfoil. [*Metals were recycled for the war effort.*] That was major.

EL: At that age did you care a lot about music?

WA: Yes, the popular music of the day. I had records—the breakable kind of 78s—and a Victrola that was very important to me. I go back to those where you screw in the needle and wind it up.

EL: You had one in your room, didn't you?

WA: Yes, I had one as a very young boy. I was eight when my sister was born and I remember my record player antedating that by a lot. I remember anti-German records during the war—1941, 1942.

EL. What else do you remember about the music?

WA: The music for the most part was quite good. On Saturday nights I could turn on *The Hit Parade* and you'd hear Benny Goodman and Frank Sinatra and those kinds of people. Or *Make-Believe Ballroom.* They'd have good songs by good people.

I didn't play an instrument with any seriousness. I started and stopped the violin.

EL: Going back to your father for a minute, it sounds like you had a very pleasant relationship, at least when you were making those trips to Manhattan.

WA: Yeah. It's one of those things where you hear older people saying, "I was happy but I didn't know it." Or "I was poor but I didn't know it." And this is true. From where I sat, there was never a question of missing a meal or that the rent wouldn't be paid or I wouldn't have clothes. My relationship with my father was always better in a friendly way than with my mother. My mother was always a disciplinarian and made things work. My father I could talk to about baseball and gangsters and all those things that interested me.

EL: Did he ever talk about working for Anastasia?

WA: No, not then he didn't, because it was not something to brag about at the time. He had worked for him before I was born and it raised a question about whether my mother was going to marry him. He worked for bookmakers and he had to spend every summer at Saratoga at the racetrack and take bets and pay off bets. And my father loved it because he got, you know, a per diem and nice money and it was a very pleasurable job. Then his father told him he was going to wind up bad if he kept pursuing that. I found out about it later in life.

EL: Sounds interesting.

WA: Yeah. You know, my father had a fairly interesting life. He joined the navy at sixteen and quit school and when he was in Europe he saw the world—he was in Russia and all over Europe, and present at executions, and a bomb hit his boat, or his boat exploded, off the coast of Florida and everybody had to swim for it and only about three guys made it. My father was one of them. It was a news story at the time.

He was an expert at duckpins—small pins, small bowling ball—and played the New York State champion, Mel Luff. And he was a fine pool player. I played with him later and he was much better than me. And he had been mascot for the Brooklyn Dodgers. He grew up in Brooklyn when it was all farmland. When World War I ended his father bought him this fabulous automobile and he drove all over Europe in it.

So he was a colorful character, in that sense. His father was apparently a bright, cultivated guy who had season tickets to the opera and would take the boat to Europe so he could go to the racetracks there.

EL: And your grandfather lost his fortune in the Depression?

WA: The Depression wiped him out. He had many movie theaters, including the Midwood Theater in Brooklyn, and lost them all. And then they were poor, poor.

September 2005

Woody has finished editing Scoop—*though he will later make a few tiny corrections—and I'll see it in the next couple of days. In the immediate time ahead, he will try to sort out the idea for his next film, but that will be difficult because he is not certain where it will be made. London provided unanticipated pleasure and he expected to make a third film in a row there, but the critical and financial success of* Match Point *has brought about other interesting possibilities.*

EL: I'll wait until I've seen *Scoop* to quiz you any more, but is there an observation you'd like to make about it before we move on? I'm particularly interested in how your ideas for films may be changing.

WA: I'm in it because it's a comedy, and because it's a comedy it's automatically lighter. Because it's lighter, I have a tendency not to get as involved as a viewer. You know, there was a time when I was younger and I was involved in comedy and I thought, Oh, this is funny, *this* is funny, *this* is funny. But I don't feel the same now. It was fun to do *Match Point* and I was very involved as a viewer as I was making the film. I loved the fact that I wasn't in it, I loved the fact that it was serious, and when it did come out, it had a good feel for me and good substance and I had a feeling of pride in it. Whereas in a comedy, and especially a comedy that I'm in—which automatically makes it kind of silly because I'm a silly comic, I'm a lower comic [*he pauses*]—I find it hard to get interested in it.

It's possible to do comedies of interest and substance, but those are the ones that have a greater serious content. *City Lights* has that kind of content, and when Chaplin blends his pictures, however clumsily, with more seriousness, they become more substantive. Bernard Shaw did that in his plays. There's more *seriousness* in

Pygmalion, it isn't just a bunch of laughs. And *Huckleberry Finn.* But when I'm in comedies, they tend to be comic in the tradition that I enjoy playing and feel comfortable in, which is light and frivolous. But now I feel I'd be better off doing serious pictures without me in them.

EL: In your early films, like *Take the Money and Run* and *Bananas,* was there pleasure in doing the comedy with you in it?

WA: Yes, I got pleasure out of it, and part of it was that it was so much fun to just get into the movie business and make movies. I kept thinking, Oh, wait until the audience sees this. And it was fun to make jokes and have them laughed at. But even then, I felt in my mind, hopefully this would be a stepping-stone to the more serious things that I enjoy more. Because I myself—and I'm going only as a viewer—enjoy more serious things. I know this is always read as "Oh, he hates comedy." But of course I *love* comedy and if I'm surfing through the television channels and, say, the Marx Brothers or Bob Hope comes on, I always pause and always watch and laugh and enjoy it. But the things I like to watch the most are serious things. I enjoy watching *A Streetcar Named Desire,* or *The Iceman Cometh.* That's how I feel about it.

EL: When did you start to notice the shift from feeling, Gee, it's great to be in the movie business and the audience is going to enjoy this?

BELOW LEFT: Recently dead ace reporter Joe Strombel (Ian McShane) escapes from the boat to the afterworld long enough to tip off neophyte reporter Sondra Pransky (Scarlett Johansson) about the identity of a killer. Strombel appears in *Scoop* in a magic Chinese box used by second-rate magician Sid Waterman, aka Splendini (Woody), from which Sondra was supposed to disappear.
BELOW RIGHT: Sid and Sondra just before she goes into the box.

WA: I felt it on this last movie [Scoop] most acutely because I'd just come off *Match Point,* which was a pleasure to do, and I got a very positive feeling watching it after I was finished. I felt, Yes, this is a nice film. If I had made a career of doing films like this, I would feel better about myself.

And then I had this amusing idea, which I *thought was an amusing idea, Scoop,* and I thought, I should do this because it's a funny idea. The idea that a reporter would be hot on a story even after he dies was funny to me. So I did it, but in retrospect I might have been happier myself if I had chosen a melodrama. Incidentally, this goes back to funny concepts not scoring. *Scoop* proceeds laugh by laugh but the concept—which is witty—counts for little. [*Woody is Sid Waterman, a second-rate magician known as Splendini, and Scarlett Johansson is Sondra Pransky, a novice American journalist living in London who volunteers to step into Splendini's Chinese box during a performance. She is meant to vanish but instead encounters the ghost of Joe Strombel (Ian McShane), a recently deceased ace reporter who has managed to temporarily slip off the boat to the afterworld and tip Sondra off about the aristocrat Peter Lyman (Hugh Jackman), whom he believes is a serial killer. Sondra contrives to meet Peter but in the quest to unmask him falls for him instead, with dangerous results. Sid pretends to be Sondra's father to help her investigate the story, and the film is full of banter between them (Sondra: "Oh, you always see the glass half empty." Sid: "No, I see it half full. Of poison!") and comic remarks to others by Sid (at a fancy garden party he tells other guests, "I was born of the Hebrew persuasion, but I converted to narcissism").*]

EL: You said you had to write three scripts in twelve weeks for this one.

WA: Yes. I had an idea, which I don't want to give away, but I knew I was going to be making the film in England. Then I found out from people after I wrote the script that this kind of phenomenon does not occur in England. Then I wrote another script that, as I've mentioned, people thought some things about the character were going to seem too autobiographical—though they weren't.

EL: You said the third script, *Scoop,* put together a couple of ideas you had in that collection you have in your desk drawer.

WA: Yeah, the idea of the reporter coming back. And I had the murder idea of folding it into somebody else's oeuvre [*he chuckles*], his résumé. [*A man who commits a single murder makes it look like the work of an uncaptured serial killer.*] And those are two totally separate ideas.

EL: How much had you written on each of those ideas?

WA: Nothing.

EL: Just your little note.

WA: Just a note saying, "This would be a funny idea—the guy's such a dedicated reporter that he cannot resist the story even though he's dead. This [*the copycat murder*] would be an interesting way to commit a crime."

But I've done that before. *Zelig* comes to mind. I always wanted to do a period documentary and I had an idea about a guy who becomes whoever he's with. But *Zelig* was never meant to be a documentary when I started to write it. I remember the first few pages were about a guy who worked at public television, and it gradually happened in contemporary time as a realistic story. Then I thought to myself, This would be a very good period documentary. So it was a conflation of two things.

EL: Do you know yet where you're going to shoot your next film?

WA: No, I don't know yet. I'm waiting to find out, and that will dictate what I write.

EL: What will determine it?

WA: It will be dictated by the origin of the money. If the British people give us the money to make the film, the condition usually is that we shoot it there [*for tax benefits for the backers*]. If it's a French co-production, then we'll shoot it in France. Sometimes you raise money and they don't care where you shoot it, in which case, I don't know—I might shoot it here [*in New York*]. But the ideas that I have in my notes are quite different. I have an idea for Barcelona. I have an idea for Paris. I have an idea for London. [*He is laughing now.*] I have an idea for New York. But they're all different. And I'm waiting to pounce. I'd like to pounce tomorrow, but I probably won't know for about four weeks [*the end of October 2005*], in which time I'll finish *Scoop* and just noodle. I mean, I could write a play, or maybe try and write a piece for *The New Yorker.* I'll fill the time.

February 2006

EL: I watched *New York Stories* the other day, which I hadn't seen for some time, and in *Oedipus Wrecks* [*see page 21*], your portion of it, there's that scene after you've had dinner with Julie Kavner and she's wrapped up the leftover boiled chicken. And you go home and although you hadn't expected to enjoy yourself, you start to reflect happily on the evening—

WA: [*Remembering now*] Oh, right.

EL: —and you unwrap the chicken and hold up a leg. It was a scene you considered reshooting but a major reason you didn't was that the leg had great gobs of chicken jelly hanging from it and you know you couldn't duplicate that. I throw this out as a reminder to prompt any recollections of the film.

WA: It was fun to make that film. We were working with a very limited budget and we had a very short time to shoot it, but it was only a short story. And short-story films notoriously don't do well at the box office.

EL: Yes, it's a point you've made before, that it's a series of peaks—the audience goes up, then has to start with a new one, then a third.

WA: They don't like that and I understand it because I don't like it myself. Every ten years, someone gives it a try in the face of all of that. And it doesn't work. Then no one gives it a try for another ten years. But there's always some angle: You'll have seven great directors doing the seven deadly sins. Or someone will get [*Federico*] Fellini, [*Luchino*] Visconti, and [*Vittorio*] De Sica and do three great Italian tales of sex. [Boccaccio '70 (1962). *Mario Monicelli did the fourth sequence. All parts were loosely adapted from Boccaccio's* Tales of the Decameron.] But it doesn't work. On *New York Stories,* I was working with Marty Scorsese and Francis Ford Coppola, two great directors. I sandwiched myself in there to get, you know, acclaim by association.

Ironically, it's a good medium for me, short films, because I've written sketches many times in my life and I can write short things, and many times I have ideas that are amusing but don't develop into any kind of story. I could do a film tomorrow if there was really any point to doing six or eight short stories of my own.

EL: Had the idea for *Oedipus Wrecks* been around for a while or was it one you came up with for the film?

WA: I had that idea among many other short ideas and there were times when I was groping for ideas for a movie and I would think that maybe I should do two or three stories about a certain theme.

I think that one of the only successful short story compilations in film history was *Everything You Always Wanted to Know About Sex,* and that had a different makeup to it because it was based on a best-selling book. Maybe it was one person doing those ideas. They weren't stories you had to get emotionally invested in. These were all trivial little sketches. You could laugh at them and might even think, Great, I've had my six minutes of this, now I'd like to move on to another one. So for whatever reason, that one worked.

ABOVE LEFT: Every child's nightmare comes true in *Oedipus Wrecks*. Woody plays Sheldon, whose mother, last seen entering a magician's Chinese box for a disappearing/reappearing trick, instead reappears in the sky over Manhattan and kibitzes with passersby about her son's failings.
ABOVE RIGHT: Sheldon is further traumatized when his aunt (Jessie Keosiam) and mother (Mae Questel), fresh from seeing *Cats* and loaded with souvenirs, interrupt a meeting with partners in his law firm, making their entrance to the beat of the tom-toms in Gene Krupa and Benny Goodman's rendition of "Sing Sing Sing." ("Ominous," Woody said, red-faced with laughter, when he first saw the music playing with the scene.)

EL: Back to *Oedipus Wrecks*. Sven Nykvist [*died 2006*] shot it. This was just on the cusp of digital effects getting really good and you had so much trouble getting the mother in the sky right.

WA: Now they're incredible, but then you had to do these things the hard way. Any time I made films with special effects prior to digital technology I really had to labor because I never had any money for experiment and no flair for it, either [*laughs*], but now I can do it much better. I still don't have the money, it's still expensive. I know it cripples the front office when I come in and need some of those effects.

EL: I remember a couple of things you said at the time you made *Oedipus Wrecks.* One was when you were laying in the music and cut in Gene Krupa on the tom-tom in "Sing Sing Sing" as your character's mother and Aunt Ceil come barreling around the corner in the law firm office. It's a funny sequence and you were laughing as you saw it for the first time.
[*Sheldon, Woody's character, is in a meeting with partners at the law firm where he works. A secretary nervously interrupts to say his mother has come to see him. The partners are not pleased but he leaves. The tom-tom starts as he looks down the empty hallway and then around the corner come two short elderly ladies with* Cats

paraphernalia, obviously having just gone to a matinee. There is comedic menace in their stature and walk, and dread on Sheldon's face, as Benny Goodman's clarinet starts the melody.]

WA: I laugh a lot of times at jokes when I write them and also when I see them on the screen. And sometimes I'm borne out by an audience. But not all the time. I consider myself a typical audience that way. If I find something funny, generally there's a good number of others who will.

EL: The drums are so comically ominous. And Julie Kavner is wonderful.

WA: She's great. She's a huge talent.

EL: I'd forgotten that Larry David is in it. [*He plays the stage manager.*]

WA: Yeah, he's been in a couple of things. *Radio Days.* He was a funny guy around town. I didn't know him very well. But he was a funny guy. And had a good look.

EL: George Schindler, who played Shandu, the magician, was very convincing. He was a real magician, yes?

WA: Originally I had Wallace Shawn in there. He's one of my favorite actors and I've used him many times since. He didn't have the flair of a real magician, though. I got a real magician and it made all the difference in the world in terms of having a true feeling for it.

EL: You use magic a lot in your films. In the early 1980s Diane Jacobs wrote a book about it.

WA: Yes. That was insightful of her. She was proven prophetic—someone steps off the screen [The Purple Rose of Cairo], someone doing a magic trick, like Maureen Stapleton [*died 2006*] in Interiors. Many cases of it. [*Among them: his character's mother appears in the sky in* Oedipus Wrecks; *magical herbs allow a woman to become invisible in* Alice; *the dead rematerialize in* Match Point; *a character offers advice from the grave in* Scoop.]

EL: Anything more on *Oedipus Wrecks*? Mae Questel as the mother was terrific.

WA: When my sister saw her, she really laughed. She said she looked like our mother. Mae was the voice of Betty Boop. I think we used her as Betty Boop in *Zelig.*

EL: Do you remember the germ of the idea for *Alice*? [*The film is a meditation on memory, magic, marriage, daydreams, boredom, and the oddities of attraction. Alice Tate (Mia Farrow), a woman long ignored by her wealthy husband (William Hurt) and whose once strong conscience has withered, suddenly finds companionship with an attractive musician (Joe Mantegna). She consults an herbalist in a ramshackle office in Chinatown who gives her a concoction that makes her invisible and allows her to spy on her husband being unfaithful. Finally faced with a choice between the escapist life she has lived and what she most values—a life of responsibility—she finds rejuvenation by being a good mother.*]

WA: I wanted to do something about a rich Upper East Side lady—because I always like to write about rich Upper East Side people—a rich Upper East Side lady like the kind I used to see when I took Dylan to school. I would see these mothers in sneakers and running suits with a Blackglama sable or mink coat over it and I always got a kick out of that. Now, there are people that resent that kind of thing. I'm not one of them. I am amused by it, affectionately. There is a line in *Alice* that I don't exactly remember but it is about if the kid doesn't get into the right preschool he won't get into the right college. That whole world interested me.

And I remember at that time friends were going to a quack doctor in Chinatown, sucking up these herbs and paying a fortune for them. They could have been dangerous, but they certainly weren't helpful. Did I tell you the story about the cat's whisker in the eye?

EL: Tell me again.

WA: I always find that stuff just total nonsense. So I was having an eye problem of some sort and I couldn't get rid of it. It just went on and on and I took all sorts of

RIGHT: The Greek chorus in *Mighty Aphrodite*, led by F. Murray Abraham. FACING PAGE: The chorus advises Lenny (Woody) not to try to find the mother of his adopted son.

medicine. Finally my friend said, "I'll buy you a session with this doctor and I guarantee he will get rid of it."

I said, "I'm not going to Chinatown."

And she said, "He'll come over to your house and he will cure you. What do you have to lose? Give him one session and if he doesn't cure you, then no harm."

So I said okay and the guy comes over to my house and he's got a pussycat whisker. And he puts it in my tear duct and he leaves—and of course it had *zero* effect. When I told my eye doctor, he said, "Don't ever let *anybody* put *anything* in there! You could get an infection. God knows what could happen."

And it occurred to me when I was writing *Alice* that this Upper East Side woman hears from her friends about this man who works wonders, and goes downtown and gets all these potions—and then I thought, What if they really *were* magical potions? I thought it would be a likeable story and maybe it was to some people.

EL: It's funny when Alice goes down at the end and the doctor, played by Keye Luke, is hurriedly packing to leave town, supposedly to do further study. [*Luke played the Number One Son in all the Charlie Chan movies. He made 185 films in a career that stretched from 1934 to his death in 1991. Alice was his last picture.*]

WA: Yes, I'm sure that it's the inevitable fate of these guys, that sooner or later they have to skip town because somebody blows the whistle on them.

EL: You have a Greek chorus in *Mighty Aphrodite* [1995], which gives it a magical aspect of another sort than *Alice.* Where did that idea come from?

WA: I'd always wanted to do a Greek chorus film. I originally thought of doing it on my short story—I can't remember the title, the one where the guy is dating the girl and then falls in love with her mother . . .

EL: "Retribution."

WA: "Retribution." I was going to do that with a Greek chorus. I thought it would make a good story. But then I didn't want to do one of my stories as a screenplay, and a couple of years later I remember thinking about Dylan when she was adopted, she was so lovely, I was thinking, I wonder who her mother and father were. And then I thought there was a story there someplace about an adopted kid whose adoptive parents liked the kid so much that they thought, Gee, her mother was probably very nice. And then you go find her mother and you fall in love with her. That was my first thought. Then I thought, You find her mother but her mother's not very nice at all. And then I thought [*he smiles*], That's got a Grecian feeling to it: the more you know about a child's provenance, the worse the situation gets. And I thought I should do that with my Greek chorus. Then the idea occurred to me for the ending, which really made the idea for me, that she would have my child and I would have her child and neither of us would know it. The whole thing came together as a Greek story and I did it with the chorus. I put it together years before I made it.

[Mighty Aphrodite *is the story of what happens after Lenny (Woody), a sports-writer, and his art-world wife, Amanda (Helena Bonham Carter), adopt a baby boy, Max. Because Max is an attractive and smart kid, Lenny can't help assuming the parents are as well and he sets out to find them, despite woeful warnings from the leader of the Greek chorus (F. Murray Abraham) and comic comments from some of its members. ("I see disaster. I see catastrophe. Worse, I see lawyers!" one of them says. "Don't be such a Cassandra," she is told. "I'm not such a Cassandra," she replies. "I am Cassandra.") But Max's mother turns out to be a porn actress and hooker named Linda Ash (Mira Sorvino), who despite her occupation and rough edges is very sweet. Without telling Linda that she is Max's mother, Lenny tries to get her to change her life. After Amanda tells Lenny she wants a divorce, he and Linda have one night together. But Amanda returns, Lenny's efforts on Linda's behalf pay off, and they lose track of each other—until one day in a toy store they bump into each other. Lenny is with Max, and Linda is with her winsome daughter. Each admires the other's child without realizing they are the parent.*]

EL: Written out and put in a drawer or just in your head?

WA: No, I didn't write it out, but the movie came off. Mira helped because she is a very smart girl and a very good actress.

EL: You said the funny, squeaky, high-pitched voice she used for the part was good for taking the edge off the profanity and lightening up the story.

WA: Yes, because whenever you have someone doing such an extreme voice, you're out on a limb with it. But she was able to bring it off. I'd look at dailies and think to myself, Looks good to me. I hope I'm not going to get killed with this but it looks good. And I hired the choreographer, Graciela [*Daniele*], who did my musical, and of course she did a great job on the chorus.

EL: You shot the chorus in Italy or Sicily, didn't you?

WA: We shot it in Sicily, in Taormina, in an amphitheater, and then we planted them in New York in certain places. We were there in February and the crew had to take their shirts off, because it was so hot and the sun was so blazing.

EL: The film does have an ironic feel and, as you say, a Greek sensibility.

WA: I've had Greek organizations and Greek people writing me ever since then thinking I'm an expert on Greek theater.

I visited Athens recently and saw the theater and I must say, of all the things that I saw, what took my breath away the most was to stand at the Acropolis and look down and see the theater. That's the place where *Oedipus* opened and *Medea*. The original cast was down there playing those parts.

EL: *Deconstructing Harry* [1997]. How did you conceive of that?

WA: I haven't seen it in a long time but I remember the idea clearly. You'd see a guy who I could play—a New York Jewish writer—and you would watch the guy and learn about him, but learn about him through what he wrote. You'd see his short stories and excerpts from his novels and that would tell you about him. I thought that was a funny idea and had a certain cleverness to it and it would give me a chance to do a number of short little comic pieces that wouldn't sustain for a

Mariel Hemingway, one of Harry's ex-wives in *Deconstructing Harry,* tries to stop Harry (Woody) from taking their son.

whole movie but can be funny in short stories. I can do the sketch about death coming for the wrong guy and the sketch about being out of focus. I just needed some mechanics to hang the stories on.

[*Robin Williams plays an actor who suddenly goes out of focus—not because the camera lens is off but because he actually is corporeally unfocused—and whose selfish solution is that his family wear corrective glasses. The film is about how art can be transcendent but the artist who creates it (Harry Block, a writer played by Woody) can be ruinous to those in his life. "You expect the world to adjust to the distortion you've become!" complains one of the six psychiatrists Harry has consulted. The action flips between reality and fantasy, between Harry and his lengthy roster of aggrieved ex-wives (three), ex-lovers (dozens), and relatives, and enactments of their thinly disguised portrayal in his novels and stories. The cast includes Kirstie Alley, Richard Benjamin, Judy Davis, Mariel Hemingway, Amy Irving, Julie Kavner, Julia Louis-Dreyfus, Tobey Maguire, Demi Moore, and Elisabeth Shue.*]

EL: You were able to use Mariel Hemingway again.

WA: Yes, she stopped by and said she would love to do something, and I said, "I have a picture planned—there's not an elaborate part for you, but I could always find something." She's a very fine actress. I wish I had something significant for her. I feel she's not used enough in a significant way. She always delivers.

EL: And Billy Crystal.

WA: Yeah, it was great. I got a chance to work with Robin Williams and Billy Crystal, two guys who have appeared together so much. They both were wonderful. They both came in and Robin did his thing beautifully. It really worked. I knew he'd be funny doing it. He was very nice to work with. And Billy, too, who played the Devil. They're just two very gifted guys you can give stuff to do and know you're going to get 100 percent and more out of; they're going to contribute.

EL: I like Harry's characters coming to honor him. And also the notion of a writer who can do the work no matter what else is happening in his life.

WA: That part was me. I could do that. I know people think the film is about me and I think that is funny because the film's not remotely about me. I thought when the picture was over that I would say, "Oh, yes, this is definitely me," and not go through the usual dance where I'm saying, "It's not me, it's not the way I work, I've never been blocked, I've never kidnapped my kid, I wouldn't have the nerve to act like that, I don't sit home and drink and have hookers coming over to the house all night." If I was being honored by an old school—which I wouldn't be—I probably wouldn't show up. Apart from the ability to write anytime, there was nothing in the movie at all that was me, but the path of least resistance was to say yes. I've given up trying to say no.

EL: What about the genesis for *Celebrity* [1998]?

WA: The idea came to do a film on the concept of celebrity. Everybody was suddenly a celebrity, every plastic surgeon and model and athlete. I thought it would be fun to fool around with.

EL: The notion of celebrity was also a large part of *Stardust Memories*.

WA: Right. A lot of odd things happen to you when you're a celebrity. I mean, a girl doesn't come up and say, "Sign my left breast." But they do say, "There are people that the Russians are locking in nuthouses, can you help them?" Or "Can you help me with this?" And as I've pointed out to people, *Stardust Memories* preceded John Lennon getting shot, because I felt there was that ambivalent feeling between the audience and the celebrity. The audience worships the celebrity and on the one hand cuts the celebrity much more slack than the celebrity deserves, merits, or earns. On the other hand, the audience loves it when the celebrity is denigrated and they get an enjoyment of saying, "Oh, you should have read so-and-so about this movie. He really crucified him." They have an ambivalent feeling, and that's the same ambivalence that that crazy guy had toward John Lennon, or that crazy person felt toward Jodie Foster. They idolize them and they're also dangerous.

EL: There was a spate of several films starting with *Husbands and Wives* and going through *Mighty Aphrodite, Celebrity,* and *Deconstructing Harry* in which the actors' dialogue is often raw and profane. Some people have said that these pictures reflect the turmoil in your life that surrounded your breakup with Mia Farrow. [*A complicatedly made film using a variety of cinematic techniques including a handheld camera and choppy cuts between characters that add an unsettled edge,* Husbands and Wives *details the disintegration of a marriage that seems perfectly sound and the rehabilitation of another that in the first scene is declared to be over. Gabe and Judy (Woody and Mia Farrow) arrive at the home of their good friends Jack and Sally (Sydney Pollack and Judy Davis), who cheerfully say they are divorcing. Gabe and Judy are at first shocked, then Judy becomes furious. A handheld camera follows the action, giving the film the jumpy feel of a documentary, and that sense is enhanced by the narrative by an unseen observer and interviews by what is assumed to be the director of a film within the film. The characters all become involved with other people: Judy introduces Sally to Michael (Liam Neeson), an editor, who falls for her, to Judy's unhappiness because she desires him. Jack becomes involved with his aerobics instructor, Sam (Lysette Anthony), whose beauty is matched by her lack of intellectual depth. Gabe, a novelist who also* *teaches at Columbia University, teeters toward involvement with Rain (Juliette Lewis), one of his students. (In a private moment at her twenty-first-birthday party in her parents' penthouse, she asks him to kiss her and he, smitten, says, "Why is it that I'm hearing $50,000 worth of psychotherapy dialing 911?") And in the end, it is Jack and Sally who are reunited while Gabe and Judy divorce.]*

WA: *Husbands and Wives* was written two years before things happened with Mia. There's no correlation. I was experimenting. I felt that with the documentary style it should be open, sexually and cinematically.

EL: *Curse of the Jade Scorpion* [2001].

WA: I let down an exceptionally gifted cast. I had Helen Hunt, who is a superb actress and comedienne. I had Dan Aykroyd, who I always thought was just hilarious. I had David Ogden Stiers, whom I've used many times and he always comes through. Elizabeth Berkley was wonderful. And it was successful abroad, not so successful here. But I, from my personal point of view, feel that maybe—and there are many candidates for this—but it may be the worst film I've made. It kills me to have a cast so gifted and not be able to come through for them. They put their trust in me.

[*Set in 1940, Woody plays C. W. Briggs, a self-confident ("I'd hate to have me after me"), wisecracking insurance investigator, who, under the spell of a nefarious hypnotist, conducts a series of robberies of which he has no memory and thus no realization that he is the thief he seeks.*]

EL: Where did you go wrong?

WA: I think I went wrong in playing the lead. I looked but I couldn't find anyone else who was available who had any kind of comic flair. But I was not right in that picture. I would have been better off if I had less laughs and had a straighter, tougher leading man. So I think I sank everybody in that picture. And I felt it as I was seeing dailies every day. I didn't know how to get out of it. I couldn't figure it out—it was a complicated thing. It was period and I didn't have a lot of money. I was dependent on locations that Santo [*Loquasto, his production designer*] had made brilliantly but we couldn't go back and shoot in them because it would have been too expensive to redo his work. We couldn't just simply say, "Let's just get another actor and shoot it over."

So for me personally I have great regrets and embarrassment because people trusted me, and took their jobs for no money. The picture was successful abroad. Perhaps in translation or with the goodwill toward me that many countries have I dodged a bullet or got by with it, but I don't have a good memory of it. It was not successful here.

EL: Bob Hope could have played your part very well.

WA: Oh, yes, but I would have written it much differently as a Bob Hope movie. I would have written it with the glib facility of Hope and the scenes would have been subjugated to the one-liners. It would have been a vehicle for Hope to breeze through with that wonderful quality he had. I made it much more fleshed out or realistic than he would have done it—even though it was not realistic at all.

EL: Do you remember when the idea came from?

WA: Yes, I had that idea thirty-five years ago. The idea is a very good one, I think. I just screwed it up. The guy is hypnotized and he is a criminal and also the guy hunting for the criminal. I should have done it more seriously—not as a serious film, but I trivialized it with my presence and so the movie was not good.

EL: That's a pretty harsh assessment. Do you have the same criticism about yourself in anything else?

WA: Yes, I feel if I play in a sophisticated kind of film I wind up playing the kind of New York neurotic guy you've seen many times, who's, let's say, as bright as I am in normal life, which is not [he laughs heartily] record-breaking. But if I play someone like Danny Rose [the talent manager he plays in Broadway Danny Rose], who's less articulate than Alvy Singer, I get rid of the patois of a certain class and certain kind of subject matter about relationships and sophisticated New York things that are intellectual—or should I say pseudo-intellectual or psychoanalytic? And when I do neither a sophisticated character nor a lowlife but something in the middle, like Jade Scorpion, where I'm not playing my regular character, the film becomes trivial, it becomes silly because I can't bring it off. In Take the Money and Run, you laugh and yes, it's an okay little piece of nonsense for a first effort. But I can't do that now. So the film seems trivial to me because I had to play a silly character and you don't get interested in the people because they're not believable, they go joke by joke. It's hard to write good films and accommodate my character. It's always been a problem. That's why I'd just as soon keep out of my movies in the future and then I won't burden myself and I won't burden the audience and I'm free to do any movie I want and not have to face the problem of creating a good story and one that also has a funny part for a limited actor—me.

EL: Hollywood Ending [2002]. You've said it mystifies you that audiences did not find it as funny as you do.

WA: It's not that—it's that they didn't show up. I think if they came in to see it they would have found it funny, but they didn't come to see it. I thought it was quite funny. It is a funny picture with a funny idea, executed funny. I was amusing in it.

[*Woody plays Val Waxman, a once-prominent director whose films have fallen from favor. He is given a chance to resurrect his career when his ex-wife, Ellie (Téa Leoni), persuades a studio executive who is also her fiancé—to let him direct a New York melodrama. But just before shooting begins, Val goes blind from hysteria and tries to fake his way through the picture with the help of his agent (Mark Rydell) and Ellie, whom he wins back. The film ends with Val's effort viciously panned by every American critic but hailed as a masterpiece in France. Where, of course, Woody is revered.*]

EL: Téa Leoni stands up to you really well.

WA: Téa Leoni—again, sensational. Beautiful. Wonderful actress, a wonderful sense of humor. I don't think I let her down. She looked great in the picture, *was* great in the picture. And I was amusing with her. I was so confident I took that picture to Cannes, the first time I ever did that. I've sent pictures before, but I went on opening night and felt, Oh, everybody's going to love this and the French will particularly love it because the ending teases the French. And it was successful but nothing big—in France.

EL: Was that a new idea?

WA: No, it was an idea that had been around for years. I had kicked it around with Marshall Brickman. It was an idea that was not applied to a film director but to other things originally.

EL: *Melinda and Melinda* [2002].

WA: *Melinda and Melinda* was an idea I always wanted to do and I mentioned the idea to Peter Rice [*of Fox Searchlight, who financed and distributed the film*], who I liked working with. I had a couple of conversations with him on the phone and he wanted to do a film with me. I said I wanted to do a comic and a serious version of the same story and he loved that idea. They didn't like the idea of working the way I work—that is, not seeing the script, not knowing the plot, not knowing anything about it. But he was willing to do it, much to his credit, I think. Again, it was a film in which the dramatic story interested me the most. All the heat and passion was in the dramatic story.

[*Over dinner, two playwrights (Wallace Shawn and Larry Pine) argue whether the essence of life is tragic or comic. The film then cuts between drama and comedy as the writers embellish the story of a woman who unexpectedly shows up at a dinner party thrown by friends, and whose influence eventually leads to adultery,*

Radha Mitchell played tragic (left) and comic (right) versions of a woman's story in
Melinda and Melinda, with an appropriate look for each.

*though differently in each version. Radha Mitchell is Melinda, who in the drama
(the hosts are the wealthy Laurel, played by Chloë Sevigny, and her alcoholic actor
husband, played by Jonny Lee Miller) is a bored wife who shows up bedraggled and
skittish after she has left her physician husband for a photographer and lost her
children in the ensuing custody case. After a bout of depression that landed her in a
mental ward buckled into a straitjacket, she now is struggling with life. In the
comedic version, she is an unmarried blithe spirit who captivates her neighbor
Hobie (Will Ferrell), an out-of-work actor married to Susan (Amanda Peet), a
maker of independent films, who leaves him for another, fabulously wealthy man.]*

The comic story was fine because Will Ferrell is a funny guy and Amanda Peet is
great—she's beautiful and sexy and also *quite* funny. Quite a wonderful actress.
And they did a terrific job. But the comic half never interested me as a writer as
much as the other half of it. The other half of it was where my heart was.

And I got a chance to discover Radha Mitchell. We were originally going to work
with Winona Ryder and Bob Downey and I couldn't get insurance on them. The
insurance companies are very prissy and sticky and gave us a hard time. We were
heartbroken because I had worked with Winona before [Celebrity] and thought
she was perfect for this and wanted to work with her again. And I had always
wanted to work with Bob Downey and always thought he was a huge talent. Then
the actors got upset with us, like we're the ones who made the decision. But I felt
we're the ones that got screwed every bit as much as them. We couldn't get bonded.
The completion bonding companies [*who provide insurance for the investors that
the film will be completed within the budget and in a timely fashion*] would not
bond the picture unless we could insure them.

I wouldn't have thought of Will Ferrell because he's such a broad knockabout comic, but then there was something in him that I thought was sweet and vulnerable and I thought, Yeah, this guy could probably act this and be very sweet. And Radha I saw in something and thought, This girl could be terrific in this picture. And she came through for me in spades. And Chloë Sevigny I'd always wanted to work with, and she exceeded my hopes in that part.

I had just seen Chiwe [*Chiwetel Ejiofor*] in *Dirty Pretty Things* and everybody loved him, including me, so I was thrilled to get him for this.

I had a good time making the picture but in retrospect would have liked to make a picture just of the serious part. Exactly my feelings after I saw *Crimes and Misdemeanors*.

The film was a nice little conceit. I think they broke even on it or made a couple of dollars. It wasn't a blockbuster, I might say [*he smiles*] in understatement.

EL: Where did the idea for *Anything Else* [*2003*] come from?

WA: I've always had that idea. I think it came off fairly well. Jason Biggs was in the movie and he was another actor who people thought was playing me—and I was *in* the movie, playing a different part! I thought it came off and it surprised me that it didn't do better. I thought it had everything—there was a good story between Jason Biggs and Christina Ricci . . .

EL: And Stockard Channing.
[*Jason Biggs is Jerry Falk, a comedy writer hopelessly ensnared by Amanda (Christina Ricci), his enchanting, smart, emotionally spontaneous, lying, manipulative, and all too often unfaithful girlfriend, whose behavior is directed not by meanness but because she just can't help herself—her passion turns on and off as easily as a faucet, which makes her all the more appealing to Jerry, or at least drives him to sexual distraction. Naturally, the relationship is in trouble and it is not aided by Amanda's flighty chanteuse of a mother (Stockard Channing), who (along with her piano) has moved in with Jerry and Amanda, further cramping an already small apartment. Although Jerry gets no help from his useless agent and his uncommunicative analyst—each of whom he is as unable to leave as he is Amanda—he finds a mentor in David Dobel (Woody), an older schoolteacher and comedy writer with a flair for large words and a deeply ingrained paranoia. Dobel shows Jerry the way off the emotional merry-go-round that has stalled his life and career and onto a path of self-reliance and what will certainly be success. (The business arrangement Jerry has with his agent—a sliding scale that slides only in the direction of the agent—is remarkably similar to Woody's with his first agent.)*]

WA: Yes, the cast is wonderful and I thought it was an interesting story and full of good jokes and full of good ideas. Somebody said it summed up everything that I always say in movies—they were saying this positively—and maybe it did and that was a negative for me. I don't know. I had screenings of it and people seemed to love it. Again, it was one of those pictures that nobody came to.

You know, a lot of it is the luck of the draw with someone like me. I'm review-dependent. You hit a guy who likes the film and writes a good review of it, it might possibly do business. The exact same film, if that reviewer's sick that day and the other critic on the paper doesn't like it, then it doesn't do business. There are many, many people making films who are *not* review-dependent and it doesn't matter what anybody says about them, they have an audience. I have only to mention *Spider-Man.*

With me, it depends who's writing the review. But I did think *Anything Else* was a funny movie. I thought it was a good movie. I was crazy about Christina, and Jason was adorable, and Stockard Channing is always a really strong actress.

EL: Dick Cavett told me at least thirty years ago about the night the two of you were at Trader Vic's in Los Angeles in the 1960s and you said to him over dinner, "You know, I don't have enough time, no matter how long I live, to write all the ideas I have." Do you still have a limitless supply?

WA: I have a lot of ideas. I still have the same bag—actually I've taken them out of the bag because the bag tore [*laughs*]—but I've got the same stuff. In the cutting room I still have a bag and I throw ideas in and then when it comes time to do something I dump the paper thing on the bed and a billion papers of all kinds fall out and I go through them. It's very tedious and I put the best, most promising ones aside. Sometimes I'll see one and I'll think, Oh, this would make a funny idea, and I do it.

EL: Do you cull the ideas from time to time? Do you throw stuff out as the years go by? Or is it once they're in there, they've made the cut?

WA: I only throw ideas out once I've done them.

2

WRITING IT

Summer 1972

Woody is filming Sleeper *in Los Angeles and outside Denver. This film is in many respects a step up from the demands of his first three—*Take the Money and Run, Bananas, *and* Everything You Always Wanted to Know About Sex. *The first two are a series of jokes strung together, and the latter is a series of short sketches, though the beginning of his interest in style as well as comedy is particularly evident in one of the segments.* Sleeper *is a full narrative film, albeit one with many jokes and sight gags, in which Woody's character emerges for the first time as the hero rather than a loveable loser. One day while he waited for a scene to be set up for shooting, we settled in a room in the hamburger-shaped futuristic house where Miles Monroe (Woody) finds brief shelter and talked about the problems inherent in comedy, and about the evolution of the character he writes for.*

WA: Pacing is always a problem. There are very few great comedies and even the greatest have *languor* in them. There's no way out. There are moments you tolerate. Once in a while you hit on something like [*the Marx Brothers'*] *Duck Soup*, which has practically not a dead spot in it. If you were asked to name the best comedies ever made, and you named [*Charlie Chaplin's*] *The Gold Rush* and [*Buster Keaton's*] *The General* and a half dozen others, *Duck Soup* is the only one that really doesn't have a dull spot.

EL: What are the problems with *Sleeper*? [*See page 4.*]

WA: *Sleeper* is like three-dimensional chess. On one level you have a story that you want people to believe enough but not so much that it's a problem. You want an abundance of verbal jokes and an abundance of visual jokes. It's tough. Bob Hope's movies are almost all verbal jokes. Keaton just had to worry about his visual jokes. Chaplin's movies, for the most part, are all visual jokes. I've tripped myself up many times on both verbal and visual jokes.

EL: You have such admiration for Bob Hope, and there are times I can hear his inflection in your delivery. How are you similar?

WA: Hope and I are both monologists, and as characters we both think we're great with women, and we play as both vain and cowardly. Hope was always a super schnook. He looks a little less like a schnook than I do; I look more schnooky, more intellectual. But both of us have the exact same wellspring of humor. There are certain moments when I think he's the best thing I've ever seen. And I do him all the time. Sometimes it's everything I can do to not actually mimic him. It's hard to tell because I'm so unlike him physically and in tone of voice. You'll see the similarity in his older movies, like *My Favorite Brunette.* Hope had those sort of snotty one-liners that I always liked. [*Woody delivers a Hope-like line when he and Diane Keaton, dressed as doctors, attempt to kidnap what's left of the all-powerful Leader—his nose. When they encounter suspicious guards, Woody taps one on the chest and tells them with perfect Hope false bravado, "We're here to see the nose. I understand it's running."*]

EL: But doesn't so much of the humor rely not on the writing but on the delivery?

WA: Yes. The hacks who would do *The Ed Sullivan Show,* say, and kill the audience and then disappear, faded because there was no believable character behind the stories and jokes. Their lines were funny on paper and people were laughing at the lines because they aren't bad. But at their best, jokes are a vehicle to present a character.

When I started out, I thought just the opposite. I just wanted to go out and do my jokes because I felt that was what the audience was laughing at. But [*his manager*] Jack Rollins kept saying to me, "You have it backwards." I didn't know the first thing because I was totally oriented as a writer. I thought, If S. J. Perelman goes out and reads "No Starch in the Dhoti, S'il Vous Plaît" [*one of his many* New Yorker *stories, called "casuals" by the magazine*], they're going to howl. But that's not what it is at all; it's that the jokes become the way for the person to display a personality or an attitude. Like Bob Hope. You're laughing not at the jokes but at a guy who's vain and cowardly and full of false bravado. You're laughing at character all the time.

EL: How has your view of the character you write for changed over the past few years? Or has it?

WA: I guess that like everybody else I have a limited view of myself, whereas somebody outside me can alert me to a dimension that I wouldn't embrace automatically. Naturally for my first movie I stayed with my safest stuff, which is stuff I know: abject humility. [*He laughs.*] I was very timid in that picture. But there was

Miles Monroe (Woody) and Luna Schlosser (Diane Keaton) encounter guards while they try to kidnap what remains of the Leader in *Sleeper.* "We're here to see the nose," Miles says in perfect imitation of Bob Hope's false bravado. "I understand it's running."

no way I could have been anything else. I had never made a film. I was never the star of a picture before. When I met [*the late* New Yorker *critic*] Pauline Kael after she saw *Take the Money and Run*, she said, "We *want* you to get the girl at the end. We don't want you to fail. You have a different conception of yourself." Kael was saying that I have a masochistic view of myself, that I should think of myself more as a hero and that people should identify with me because I say funny things, in a positive way. And I believe she was right in that in *Sleeper* I'm coming out aggressively a little bit, and I'd like to continue to do that and see what happens. I'm just beginning to feel my oats to a degree and feel more confident. I have to think of myself as learning all the time. I can't think that I'm a guy who does surreal comedy and that's all I'm going to do. I feel that over the next couple of years I should experiment with various styles of comedy.

EL: Do you have a clear idea of the character you're writing for?

WA: There is no conscious molding of my character whatsoever. I never think, Well, he wouldn't do this. In nightclubs and films I do what I think is funny and it's 100 percent instinctive. I just know I wouldn't shoot a guy and put him in the freezer. I just do what I do and apparently a character emerges. Beyond that, it doesn't mean anything to me. I just want to be funny. And if in addition to being funny a point can be made, that's fine.

I've no interior judgment of the character that comes out. I can describe it only in terms of what I've heard: contemporary, neurotic, more intellectually oriented, loser, little man, doesn't get along with machines, out of place with the world—all that crap. I can see certain parts of it, but I never thought to myself at the beginning, I'm going to make myself a loser and a little man. I don't think you can try and do anything. You do it and that's it.

I'm sure there was no calculation with Chaplin, even though people would say, "Well, the moustache represents vanity, and the oversize shoes this, and the walk that." I'm sure what was going through his mind was, Hey, I bet this will be funny: I'll wear these big pants and these big shoes and a moustache and I'll look silly.

It's so accidental, so contingent. In the making of a film so much of what you planned on doesn't work the way you thought it would, and in the editing room you make new discoveries all the time. I think if you don't allow for that you become one of those literal film directors who you give a script to and they shoot the script exactly. I'm not saying I just improvise. But the experience of making a film happens when you *make* the film, it's not in the *writing* of the film, whereas a play is 95 percent in the writing.

EL: Jackie Gleason's writers often talked about their work as "feeding the monster," that their job was to supply material for his persona. Would you ever want writers to do that for you?

WA: I wouldn't mind having a couple of writers who could feed the monster because that would leave me free to do other things. I wouldn't mind knowing there were a couple of funny guys who were going to write a really funny comedy for me, and I knew that I was going to shoot it or, say, Herb Ross [*who directed* Play It Again, Sam] was going to direct it. Then I would know I was going to appear in a funny picture and that would take care of one aspect of my career. Then I could write a kind of dramatic picture or something offbeat that interests me more. But I feel at this point I have an obligation to make films and not be incredibly indulgent with them.

[*In years to come, he will become more indulgent (and confident) and make whatever sort of film—a drama, a musical, a comedy—most appeals to him at the time. It is the difference between the concerns of a neophyte filmmaker and one who has established a worldwide reputation.*]

EL: There is a theory that humor is often disguised hostility. Is that true with you?

WA: I've found that if I'm really hostile about a subject I don't write anything funny about it. If I wrote something about the Nixon administration [*this was during President Richard Nixon's administration*], it would come out hostile without being funny. My wellspring of humor may be different. I know if I wrote something on Ingmar Bergman or Kafka, both of whom I adore, it would come out funny without hostility toward them.

Humor is enormously complicated and it's very hard to come out with any generalized truths. I think what makes up comedy, like a chess game or a baseball game, are a million psychological knowns and unknowns. If something makes you laugh, it's funny. That's more profound than you think.

EL: You admire dramatic films more than you do comedies, but isn't it harder to write a great comedy?

WA: There's no question that comedy is harder to do than serious stuff. There's also no question in my mind that comedy is less valuable than serious stuff. It has less of an impact, and I think for a good reason. When comedy approaches a problem, it kids it but it doesn't resolve it. Drama works through it in a more emotionally fulfilling way. I don't want to sound brutal, but there's something immature, something second-rate in terms of satisfaction when comedy is compared to drama. And it will always be that way. It will never, never have the stature of *Death of a Salesman* or *A Streetcar Named Desire* or *Long Day's Journey.* None of it, not the best of it. If you take *School for Scandal* and *The Frogs* and *Pygmalion* and *The Country Wife* and *You Can't Take It with You* and *Born Yesterday* and *The Front Page* and *Modern Times* and *Duck Soup* and *The General*—and that's some of the best of the crop—they'll never have the impact of *The Seventh Seal* and *Potemkin* and *Greed* because there's something less satisfying about comedy, even though it's harder to do. Having said this, I'm talking for myself only.

The problem is, when you're doing a comedy it's okay to worry about the photography, but voraciously coming up on your tail is that monster that you've got to be fast and relentlessly funny. I don't mean a joke every second. You could be doing a comedy that had a joke every five minutes, and not a gag but character humor, but you've got to keep the rhythm going or the ground rules you laid down in the first five minutes, the deal you made with the audience to hold their interest and be funny, is violated. And because of that, it's very, very difficult and frequently just impossible to do the kind of things that are interesting to me.

EL: So what does interest you?

WA: What's interesting to do is some of the more schmaltzy kinds of stuff. All the dramatic kinds of things that are done by Bergman and [*Michelangelo*] Antonioni. Great mood stuff. Serious directors have the most fun. *Cries and Whispers* has lots of close-ups and the color is printed down. That's not appropriate for comedy. Mostly the good-looking stuff is stuff without laughs in it. That's why the most fun I've had with anything is the Italian sequence in *Everything You Always Wanted to Know About Sex*, because I didn't have to think about anything except what is the best shot I can make with the camera. [*The sequence, titled "Why Do Some Women Have Trouble Reaching an Orgasm?," is about a woman who can climax only in fashionable and expensive public settings.*] I didn't have to worry if it was dark or if it was moody, or if someone was half shadowed or half blocked, because it contributes to the joke—I'm satirizing that style of shooting.

June 1974

Sleeper is greeted with very good reviews and a large audience. It is a breakthrough movie for Woody in that although there are many jokes, it also is a narrative with a comic relationship between his character and Diane Keaton's. He is now working on his next film, but he is wrestling with three competing ideas, one of which is easy to write but requires no stretching of his talent. Whatever advance he made with Sleeper, Woody wants to advance further, yet he is also unsure of what the audience he is developing will accept. The first film he talks about—the relationship picture—will eventually become Annie Hall (1977). The second—the "flamboyant" idea—is Love and Death (1975).

EL: You've been writing for a few months but don't yet have a script for your next film. What's the holdup?

WA: I want to do a departure film. When I set out to do my next movie, I wanted to do a real-person film—comedy but a real person. Not a guy who wakes up in the future or a guy who is a bank robber or a guy who takes over a Latin American country. I want to do one where I play me, Diane Keaton plays her, and we live in New York, with real conflict in our relationship, as opposed to too flamboyant an idea.

I wrote this idea and I read it and I liked the first half but not the second. So I rewrote it and I got a completely new idea and used much of that for the first half that I already liked, and then I didn't like *it*. Then I got a third idea, which became further out and I used much of the first half that I liked—and then *that* didn't work for me.

So I've finished three things and now I'm kicking ideas around.

EL: Is one looking better than the others?

WA: I've finished thirty-eight pages of a new idea I've called *Love and Death.* [*A Napoleonic farce melded with twisted Dostoevsky. Woody plays Boris, a Russian peasant with a philosophical bent who with his great unrequited love, Sonia (Diane Keaton), sets out to kill Napoleon.*] But the problem is this: it's easy for me because it's flamboyant; it's not real at all. It tries to be very funny—funny in the way one reads an S. J. Perelman essay. It's just crazy, manically funny. It's been one of the most pleasurable experiences in that sense; I've got scenes that just one after the other Hope should do—it would be a better movie than if I did it. But I feel it is not what an audience would most respond to, so I don't know yet if I'll complete it. I keep working a couple of hours a day on it and then take a few hours and try for another idea. I'm sure it will all end in a flash. What will happen is either I'll finish *Love and Death* or work out this new idea. I'm a very fast writer, really. It will take me four to six weeks to finish the script.

I don't know if I'm doing the right thing or not in the sense that I might write a real story and people will laugh at it but I'll get the same reaction in certain quarters that I got with [Play It Again,] *Sam:* I expected something a little farther out, more imaginative. The thing I'm working on fits right into the type of film people expect of me.

EL: But you want to move beyond the expected, don't you?

WA: Yes, I'd love to get the real thing, because that would be the biggest departure for me. I think audiences have hooked into me personally now, so I don't want to do a comedy where I fade into the background in clever sketch ideas. I'd like to do a real story, but funny.

I'm sure, though, that once I start writing I'll think, What the hell am I doing here? I should be writing a crazy story, and I'll look at the first forty pages of the real

In *Love and Death*, Boris (Woody)'s father (Zvee Scooler) owns "a valuable piece of land. True, it was a small piece but he carried it with him wherever he went."

story and the first forty pages of the crazy story and I'll think to myself, There's no comparison in funniness; the crazy story's hilarious. The real story is funny, but funny only as you can be in real life. [*This is the first example of what Woody calls the lose-lose situation in which he would find himself trapped in years to come when trying to decide between ideas.*]

So if, hypothetically, I'm picking up a girl at my analyst's office who's another patient there, well, that could be funny, but I don't think it could be as explosively funny as that other kind of comedy—two Jewish computers who are tailors [*as in* Sleeper]. I don't want people to come out of the movie and say, "Well, where is all that inspiration, those imaginative ideas? That was just a movie that would really need George Segal or Dick Benjamin or Dustin Hoffman."

EL: Is it that you're trying to discern what the public wants, or is it that you are trying to determine what you can give them within your range?

WA: I just don't want to run out and do scripts I would have done two years ago because I'm trying to advance and not simply repeat, for my own growth. I always hope the public will enjoy the movie but I must never fall into the trap of doing anything but exactly what I want in an effort to be liked. Better to be disliked but good. Better to try to grow and fail humiliatingly than play it safe or worse, curry favor.

EL: If you don't do *Love and Death* now, is it an idea you'd like to try later?

WA: Yes, I would do that movie someday if I don't do it now. I know I'm going to work with Keaton in my next movie, whatever it is, so at one time I was thinking about those types of things that Tracy and Hepburn did because that would be fun. The problem is, you don't realize how old-fashioned they are now.

EL: How so?

WA: Naturally an audience is going to rock with laughter at *A Night at the Opera* and *Duck Soup,* the type of comedy where your tacit contract at the beginning is, "Listen, don't take me seriously. I'm just going to pull out all the stops and make you laugh. There are no heights I wouldn't go to or depths I wouldn't sink to to make you laugh."

But then there's another type of feeling, where you see a movie and it doesn't just appeal to you through the mind, you *feel* it in addition. You know, the guy calls for the girl and he's very funny waiting in the rain in front of her house, and it's hilarious. But it also has some feeling to it; you would like him to meet her. And it's not so plot-driven. And when they're not laughing they're still engaged and enjoying.

EL: How important is a plot for a comedy?

WA: Modern stuff is very non-plotty, and plot is dynamite in comedy; when you have plot in a comedy you're in great shape. When you're doing the kind of comedy, like *Bananas,* that doesn't have a plot, you're dependent on doing a tour de force. You have to be hilarious from the start and hilarious again and again; an hour goes by and you don't get any payoff from stuff you planted an hour ago. Then you have to be six times as funny at the end. Whereas if you get a premise going, a story, at the end you're cashing in on everything you've set up. I really labored to keep the

In *Play It Again, Sam,* by being himself, Allan attracts his great friend Linda.

ball in the air in *Take the Money* and *Bananas.* Did I make it? Only an audience can decide and each member decides for himself—or I should say he doesn't consciously decide. He watches his belly to see if it's laughing.

EL: Does one form lend itself to comedy more than others?

WA: All the accepted forms are great for comedy; that's why comedians work in them so much. So a comedy mystery is a great idea, as are comedy science fiction and a comedy Western. Hope did *Monsieur Beaucaire* [*comedic history*], *Paleface* [*comedic Western*], and *My Favorite Brunette* [*comedic private detective*]. The same with Jerry Lewis.

If you try to do character comedy where you're dependent more on people's psychological makeup and less on plot, it's harder. [Play It Again,] *Sam* was a character comedy. The laughs didn't come from plotting—Tony [*Roberts, who plays the best friend and is married to the Diane Keaton character*] is coming back from his business trip and I've got to hide behind the door. It comes strictly from the unfolding of a highly neurotic, bizarre personality caught in a situation [*by a believable though unexpected progression of character development, Woody's and Diane's characters have slept together*], but in no way a plot picture like *Some Like It Hot* or *Adam's Rib*. Where Diane's and my characters end up in bed is a plot moment and it is quite by accident. That's why even though it's an antiquated comedy, in a way it had a freshness to it. It was based more on character. [*He pauses.*] But will it always seem fresh? Probably not, because it lacks genius. [*He laughs.*] I mean it lacks a lot and also genius.

Late June 1987

Woody has transformed from a novice filmmaker to a celebrated one. Love and Death *was followed by an acting role in Martin Ritt and Walter Bernstein's* The Front [1976], *then the Academy Award–winning* Annie Hall (*Best Picture, Best Director, Best Screenplay, and Best Actress for Diane Keaton*), *the drama* Interiors (1978), Manhattan (1979), *and* Stardust Memories (1980).

His films since 1982 are A Midsummer Night's Sex Comedy, Zelig, Broadway Danny Rose, The Purple Rose of Cairo, Hannah and Her Sisters, *and* Radio Days—*a popular skein, with the exception of the first. He has just finished shooting* September—*not once but a second time, with rewrites and a partially different cast. It will not prove so popular. He also is preparing to film* Another Woman. *He has shown me the first draft of the script, which centers on Marion Post, a woman in her fifties, whose feelings are so intense that she must either smother them or be drowned by them.*

At the beginning and the end of the script, Marion talks about the sensation one gets when looking at the stars. In the first, she recalls what her father said about peering through the Mount Palomar telescope in California when Marion was eight months in the womb: "They were bright and of numberless multitude. There were millions of stars. They gave you some perspective on the pointlessness of life and our own insignificance in the scheme of things. It's funny—you know it's aimless and yet in order to live you're forced to sell yourself a bill of goods."

At the end of the draft there is this description of the present: "The stars were coming out now, too, although they were harder to see amidst the lights of the city."

In recent years Woody had become a father and echoes of a child, or of a child not had, are at the heart of the script. In one scene, Marion sees a pregnant woman and flashes back to the abortion she had when she was much younger.

"I liked the idea of a child," she says in an argument with her then husband, "but the personal aspect was too much."

By the end of the script, Marion can no longer escape her past and her feelings, as she has for all her life.

"I was past fifty now," she says, "and it was time to leave certain notions behind."

Woody was fifty-two when he wrote the script. As I read it, I can't help notice what to me are parallels between Marion's feelings and his own that he has described to me over the years. Although he almost always denies that there is a directly personal aspect to the characters he creates, when I ask him about Marion he answers, "I put all I felt about turning fifty into Marion. It took me at least a year to get over it."

We will have many more conversations about this movie as it is filmed and edited, but when we next meet, two months later, we talk a bit about September, *which will soon be released but still has no title. He quickly gets to the point of why he made the movie, and also why he made it not once but twice.*

EL: You often reshoot part of a picture, but here you redid the whole thing.

Leonard Zelig's ability to become whomever he is with (an Indian, a black man, an obese man) is comic on the surface, but the message of *Zelig* is that a person who wants to be liked so much that he accepts the views of whoever he's with can be led to fascism.

WA: I couldn't have reshot any other movie I've made. I was just lucky on this—six characters, one set. I'm thinking of calling it *September*—I want a title that doesn't promise much. That's my confidence. I try to take a soft sell, nonpretentious approach, like one-word titles.

[*Of the twenty-two films he will make between 1987 and 2006, only four*—September, Alice, Celebrity, *and* Scoop—*will have one-word titles. But seven will have two words and nine will have three. Which leaves only two*—The Curse of the Jade Scorpion *and* Everyone Says I Love You—*that a purist might consider lengthy.*]

EL: Like *Zelig* [*in which Woody plays a character so wanting to be accepted that he becomes a chameleon man who mirrors whatever group he's with. Leonard Zelig is seen in the background in newsreel footage of people as diverse as Babe Ruth and Hitler*].

WA: *Zelig* had lots of titles, many of them 1920s expressions: *Cat's Pajamas, Bee's Knees.* I had a title derby with my friends over dinner. We'd shoot titles down. The only fun was the next person's contribution. That was very unproductive. Finally I shot several titles and ran them through with the film. The second I saw it with *Zelig* I knew.

EL: It looks like a complicated movie to have shot.

WA: No, not really, easy filming. *Zelig* was fun to shoot. We didn't have to set up for elaborate lighting, just shoot. But there was a lot of work in postproduction. We ordered TV equipment and did all the newsreel footage on cassettes. We had hundreds of thousands of feet of Nazi footage and other historical things.

EL: What about reshooting?

Zelig (third from right) among the crowd at a Hitler rally as he realizes what his desire to fit in has led to

WA: Scenes in the white room [*in which the psychologist Eudora Fletcher (Mia Farrow) interviews Leonard Zelig (Woody)*] were done over and over. The joke was that I had a portable white room in a suitcase. We used studio space all over New York and Queens. I shot it nine times. Some of the dialogue was ad lib, some was written out.

A clever idea I couldn't bring off was that I start to act like Mia, and for the first time in her life she sees herself in me and changes her life. I shot it but couldn't get it. So much additional information had to be given for that to work. It was a rich view I wasn't skillful enough to bring off, so I restricted myself to a simpler version.

EL: Was it always meant to be a "documentary"?

WA: I first thought it would be a contemporary movie. A guy who worked for WNET [*the Public Broadcasting Service television station in New York*]. But then I thought it would be better as a cultural phenomenon. I've always liked the documentary form. People thought I was satirizing *Reds* because I had interviews with witnesses, but I had them in *Take the Money*. [*He shrugs.*] They're standard documentary fare.

EL: *September* is a film in play form, in part about how people cope with their pasts, and in part about unrequited love.

WA: That was an interesting notion to me for a long time, an idea that I'd always kicked around: a traumatic incident will happen in one's life [*a young daughter confesses to killing her mother's apparently abusive lover, but it was likely the mother who committed the act*], and there are kinds of personalities that just simply get wrecked by it and never recover—and there are other kinds of personalities for whom it just washes off them.

EL: You have three youngish people and an older man, each in love, but none whose love is returned by the object of their desire, and two parental characters who are blissfully content with each other.

WA: I thought it was interesting that Diane, Lane's mother [*Elaine Stritch*], is able to sail through life and nothing really bothers her. She has a sense of humor, a lot of energy, she was pretty at one time. Now, Lane [*Mia Farrow*] is floundering, as is this other woman [*Stephanie, played by Dianne Wiest*]. Yet Lane's mother comes in with a new husband at this late stage of life. And he's not a jerk, he's a physicist; it's not as if she's wound up with some theatrical agent or bookmaker. The guy's an intelligent man and she's able to cope with life. She has enough humor—or has enough lack of feeling for people—to shut off; she's selfish enough to get through life without being hurt. Whereas Lane is shattered and will never recover from that.

EL: Do you have any thoughts about the characters' backstories? Is Lane telling the truth about the killing? Did she kill her mother's lover or did Diane really do it and get Lane to admit to it?

WA: I assume what Lane said happened, happened. I assume the mother was involved with a lover and got into a drunken squabble or something and the guy was a bad guy and she wound up shooting him.

Then probably she called her lawyer hysterically and he came over and said, "Look, the thing to do is say this story because nothing will happen to the kid but you would be in serious trouble." And this is what I assume happened in the Lane/Diane relationship.

But the interesting thing to me is not the story itself; that's why I never bothered to show it in flashback or write the film about that. What interested me only was the responses, the long-term responses.

EL: What do you think are those long-term responses?

WA: I think Lane flounders and never finds herself. She does her best to survive, but it's always rough going for her. She's too hurt and damaged to ever really find anything special and she never has really a great life. I think that Dianne Wiest goes back to her husband and lives out her years in a kind of functional, mechanical marriage. As for the guys, I think Denholm [*Elliott, the widower*] remains lonely. And that Sam Waterston [*the aspiring writer*] goes home thinking he had met somebody nice but that nothing is going to happen. Nor will his dream about taking a summer off from his job and writing a book come true.

I think everybody's going to have a tough time except Lane's mother, who manages to sail through these things. She pays a price for it, perhaps, in terms of having a generally unpleasing image to other people. She is crushed only by getting older, so although she suffers a certain amount, it is her own selfish feelings, her shallow feelings, that have gotten her through. She was clearly a playgirl and never really worked. She loved to party and go to nightclubs and get her name in columns and was in modeling and fashion but never did anything very serious. And when it came time, she left her husband and gave Lane a very unpleasant life and thought only of herself. And so she's able to survive.

January 1988

Shooting on Another Woman *is finished, and while Woody edits it he is also putting the finishing touches on the script of* Oedipus Wrecks, *which will be filmed in the spring, and is thinking hard about what to write as his movie to be shot in the fall. He has had a few days off for the New Year holiday. We quickly turn to his writing.*

EL: Have you settled on a story yet?

WA: I'm not settled on the idea but what I usually do is give myself an indulgent period of a couple of weeks where I do nothing but let my mind roam freely through all the ideas I have noted down and anything else that comes to mind. I just sit and completely indulge myself and think of anything from bleak dramas to musicals. Then I start to home in on something. Very often it comes down to a choice between one of two things and much time is spent agonizing over which one to do. And no matter which one I choose, I feel I should have chosen the other one. Especially when you start to do it and as it goes from fantasy to reality it's not as wonderful. The other one is always looming in the back of my mind and I think, If I had done the one about the cowboy, gosh, I could have done this and this and it would have been so perfect. But if I had done that one I would have seen that the one about the penthouse was better than the one about the cowboy.

EL: So you've spent your mini-vacation just free thinking?

WA: Yes. Today, these last three days, I've not been in the cutting room, I've been indulging myself. One thing I've just been toying with—and I don't know that it would ever happen or I'd want it to happen—but one thing I've been toying with is doing my play *Death* and playing the lead. [Death *is the German Expressionist story of Kleinman, an everyman bookkeeper roused in the night by a vigilante party looking for a serial killer, who turns out to be Death. Woody played Kleinman in what became* Shadows and Fog (1992).] It could be an extremely interesting offbeat kind of comedy. It's not the usual me and New York and romances and stuff like that. And it's about a subject that's very interesting to me. It would need a significant rewrite and development. But it sort of languishes in its present form, read by very few people. It's an interesting idea, it could be a very funny idea. So I thought about the possibility that that might be it. I've got to do a comedy next because I've really extended the amenities of Orion [*the financing and distribution company for his films at the time*] by first doing *September* and now doing this one.

EL: And you need to be in it as well, don't you?

WA: Yeah. So since I have to be in something I thought to myself, There's the light kind of comedy, the Hope-Crosby kind of comedy. But I don't really want to do that, it really doesn't interest me very much right now. And I can't get a musical together right now because I don't have enough time. And I didn't want to do my blacklisting idea because I think it would be expensive. Bobby [*Robert Greenhut, then his producer*] was telling me to try and stay away from a period piece if I could at this point because it would be a lot of extra money. And I've been in one black-listing film [The Front (*1976*)].

Then there are the kinds of picture I could do and would do, those in the ball-park like *Hannah*—where it's basically a contemporary New York picture and it says something about relationships. I might want to do something like that. It's possible. But I thought to myself that this other thing [*the adaptation of* Death] might be offbeat and an interesting concept. It's a natural cinematic kind of thing to be dealing with a homicidal maniac and trying to catch him. It has a natural ominousness and tension and it's a funny predicament for me to be in. And if it comes off, it will have a certain classic quality. That is to say it's not a contemporary, social, middle-class comedy; it has a certain classic feel to it—sort of a metaphor for a universal predicament. I made a case for the possibility of doing it as a film. And tomorrow I'll make a case *against* it and *for* something else.

EL: How long will this go on?

WA: This will go on for a couple of weeks because there's nothing I can do right now anyhow. I'm going to be editing *Another Woman*. And then it will hit me with conviction: Yes, *do* this, or No, definitely don't do it, do that other one you're thinking of. And once that happens—let's say that happens within the next two weeks, three weeks—once the decision is made what to go ahead with, then I start structuring it.

EL: When, if you're editing all day?

WA: When I come home at night a little bit, on the weekends, when I'm walking or sitting around, I'm thinking of it. So when it comes time to write, I'm almost ready to write. Maybe one week's time of not writing and I'm ready to write because I've been doing a lot of thinking about it and imagining it beforehand.

EL: You've told me that you don't get ideas from dreams, but do your dreams influence what you write?

WA: Not dreams, but something in my subconscious. When I was working on two pictures at once I was having a very hard time. I had decided to do *Zelig* and *A Midsummer Night's Sex Comedy* simultaneously. The plan was I would shoot a scene from *Zelig* and if that was a good location we'd shoot a scene there for the other film. And we almost did it that way. There were some things that overlapped, certainly in the reshoots. But I was finding it very hard to do emotionally. It was not hard physically. That was nothing. It was very hard because you don't realize that your entire core, your essence, engages on one idea and it doesn't let go. It's very hard to get rid of that and then go over to the other idea because there's an enormous obsession with the first one. Marshall Brickman said to me at the time he always felt that when you're working on something, you're working on it even when you don't know it—when you're eating, when you're walking down the street, when you're asleep—you're working on it even though you think you've pulled away from it. It's always cooking; I've found that to be an accurate observation.

If I'm sitting somewhere for ten minutes unoccupied, my mind just clicks into it. I can't help it. I come home and I'm thinking about it. It just works that way. I even try to think about it when I get into bed to go to sleep.

I never like to let any time go unused. When I walk somewhere in the morning, I still plan what I'm going to think about, which problem I'm going to tackle. I may say, This morning I'm going to think of titles. When I get in the shower in the morning, I try to use that time. So much of my time is spent thinking because that's the only way to attack these writing problems.

EL: Tell me more about the shower as a good workplace.

WA: I've found over the years that any momentary change stimulates a fresh burst of mental energy. So if I'm in this room and then I go into the other room, it helps me. If I go outside to the street, it's a huge help. If I go up and take a shower it's a big help. So I sometimes take extra showers. I'll be down here [*in the living room*] and at an impasse and what will help me is to go upstairs and take a shower. It breaks up everything and relaxes me.

The shower is particularly good in cold weather. This sounds so silly, but I'll be working dressed as I am and I'll want to get into the shower for a creative stint. So I'll take off some of my clothes and make myself an English muffin or something and try to give myself a little chill so I want to get in the shower. I'll stand there with steaming hot water coming down for thirty minutes, forty-five minutes, just thinking out ideas and working on plot. Then I get out and dry myself and dress and then flop down on the bed and think there.

Also, to go out for a walk is a help. I used to do that more often before I was known. I remember [*the playwright*] Abe Burrows [Guys and Dolls] telling me that Robert Sherwood [The Petrified Forest] used to walk around New York City writing his plays in his mind and speaking them as he'd walk the streets. I used to love to do that. But I don't do that as much anymore because I get recognized and it breaks my concentration. It's annoying and it can even get to a point where someone says, "Hey, can I walk along with you for this block? I've just got to tell you this." That's happened to me a number of times. I can't concentrate. I get intimidated.

EL: Bobby Greenhut told me that once when he was working on someone else's film and they were setting up a shot near your apartment building, he looked up at your terrace and there you were, pacing.

WA: I go out on this terrace a *lot*. One of the best things about this apartment is that it's got a long terrace [*there are several hundred feet of space*] and I've paced it a million times writing movies. It's such a help to change the atmosphere. It's a liberating thing for me.

EL: Once you've done the pacing, do you write down what you've thought?

WA: I don't have to write it down after I've thought of it. My outline for a movie rarely takes up a single page. Usually I lose interest in the middle of writing the outline. I write, you know, "Alvy meets Annie. Romantic scene. Flashback to when they met." I'll write like eight of those and by the time I get to the eighth or ninth I'll have lost interest because I know the story so well I don't really have to be doing this.

EL: Did you always have these aids to creativity or have they developed over time?

WA: I learned by observing. If I went out and took a five-minute break to get the papers or a prune Danish or something, when I got out on the street I was so full of renewed vigor that I thought, Hey, I'm going to stay out on the street, I'm not going to get the papers and come right back to the apartment. I'm going to take a nice walk around Central Park or around the city.

The same thing with the shower. I'd be sitting there for two hours and nothing would be coming and I'd decide to take a shower because I had to go downtown later. I figured, I'll take a break and come back to it later. Then in the shower I'd suddenly find an unblocking of energy—a terrible phrase, but I don't know what else to use. So it happened accidentally. Now I do it on purpose.

EL: How do you keep your focus when the writing or the thinking it out is going slowly? With me and most writers I know, that's when we start looking to see if the pencils need sharpening.

WA: One thing that may have been helpful to me over the years is that I came up as a writer in a certain sense in the most brutal circumstances. This was taught to me by Danny Simon. [*Danny Simon (died 2005) was Neil Simon's older brother, with whom Woody was paired by NBC in the 1950s. "Danny took me out of fantasy and into reality. Suddenly I was in a situation where you had to come up with one or two sketches every week. You had to show up in the morning and write them. We were getting a lot of money and the stuff had to be delivered," Woody said in one of our earliest conversations. "Everything I learned about comedy writing I learned from him."*] So I quickly learned that writing doesn't come easy, it's agonizing work, very hard, and you have to break your neck doing it. I read many years later that Tolstoy said, in effect, "You have to dip your pen in blood."

I used to get at it early in the morning and work at it and stay at it and write and rewrite and rethink and tear up my stuff and start over again. I came up with such a hard-line approach—I never waited for inspiration; I always had to go in and do it. You know, you gotta force it. So I could always do the writing and rewriting because I'd force myself. I found a million little tricks over the years to help get through that unpleasant time.

EL: You talked once about Paddy Chayefsky, who said that a writer between projects wants to kill himself. Is that the case with you?

WA: When you finally think, This is the idea I'm going to commit to, it's such a pleasure. Then comes the time when you're structuring the idea and that can be difficult or not. But when you actually sit down to write, I mean then it's like eating the meal you've spent all day in the kitchen cooking.

EL: What are some of the million little tricks you've found?

WA: Always setting myself something to think about for the project at any given free moment: When I go into the shower in the morning; when I go to sleep at night; when I'm waiting for an elevator. Somebody told me years ago about a major league pitcher who always wanted to be a pitcher. When he was growing up on his farm his father told him, "Whenever you're sitting around pick up a stone and try and hit a blade of grass with it, try and hit a twig with it. Make use of every moment." And that sounds very logical to me. So I've always tried to do that. I always have a problem to think out.

Also I've always tried to be very, very wary of all the traps that take you from writing and not to fall into them. So many things turn out to be an excuse not to do

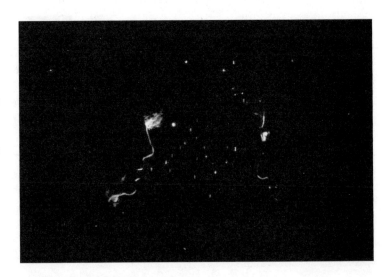

Woody credits cinematographer Gordon Willis with "artistic genius" and says, "He introduced me to the beauties of darkness photographically." This shot from *Manhattan* of Mary and Ike in a moonscape at the American Museum of Natural History in New York shows them only as dark silhouettes.

that unpleasant task of getting up in the morning and being alone all day and thinking with no good results and going to sleep not having thought out your problem.
You know, it's such an unpleasant business, that part of it.

Another thing that helps me a great deal is to hear myself state the problem
aloud because it suddenly takes it out of the realm of fantasy in my mind and makes
it concrete. I'll call up Mia and say, "I want to speak to you about some problems."
Now, these are problems there's no way she could solve, because how is she going
to say, "No, work on this one" or "Work on that one"? She doesn't have the faintest
knowledge of what I've been thinking for the last days. But I'll stroll along the street
chatting with her, and just hearing myself say it is a big help.

You also have to be wary of this little Sartrean trap where you're presenting your
problem to someone and you've already made up your mind what you want to do
and you're just getting that person to agree to it. You present the problem in such a
way that they agree to it even though seemingly you've laid down both sides of the
argument quite objectively. It's tricky. That's where 90 percent of everything fails, is
in the writing. It doesn't usually fail in the acting and it doesn't fail in the directing.
It fails in the writing.

Gordie [*cinematographer Gordon Willis*] and I used to talk about this all the
time. If you have a good script and you shoot it in a stupid way, badly lit and badly
shot, you can still have a successful movie. That's been proven a million times. You
see films that are just miserably made, ranging from amateur filmmakers to [*Luis*]
Buñuel, where the writing is so fine that it works even if things make no sense.
Whereas if you have bad material, if the writing is not good, you can shoot the eyes
out of it in every way and most of the time, no matter what style you bring to the
film, it doesn't work.

EL: There are moments on the set when you're sitting still and looking down at
the ground. Are you working on problems then as well?

Between
shots during
the filming of
Match Point

WA: I'm usually letting air blow through my mind then. There *are* certain things that refresh me. One is to turn on the television set if I'm at home to some sports and watch two innings of baseball or a basketball game. That kind of thing is necessary for me. It really relaxes my mind tremendously. And on the set, too, I need relaxation time. But if it's going to be more than ten minutes or fifteen minutes, I try to go back to the camper because there's stuff to do—answering phone calls or dealing with things that have come up. That has to be done, too.

November 1988

I want to spend part of this conversation in Woody's apartment talking about what he has read that has influenced him. He takes me to the downstairs bedroom, where he does much of his writing lying on the bed. The walls are red. Over the fireplace is a picture of Marilyn Monroe autographed in pencil. On the tables beside the brass double bed are piles of books. The table on the left is stacked with those he has recently read (there are many volumes of poetry among them as well as a paperback on the last Vatican Council); the table on the right holds those still to be read (the Bible and books on linguistics). Because Woody has so long held Ingmar Bergman's work in high regard, I start by asking for his response to some of Bergman's writing.

EL: Bergman writes: "I've a strong impression that our world is about to go under. Our political systems are deeply compromised and have no further uses. Our social behavior patterns—interior and exterior—have proved a fiasco. The tragic thing is, we neither can nor want to, nor have the strength to alter course. It's too late for revolutions and deep down inside ourselves we no longer even believe in their positive effects. Just around the corner an insect world is waiting for us— and one day it's going to roll in over our ultra-individualized existence. Otherwise I'm a respectable social democrat."

WA: I don't take a great view of institutions. I do think the salient feature about human existence is man's inhumanity to man. If you were looking at it from a distance, you know, if we were being observed by space people, I think that's what you would come away with. I don't think that they'd be amazed by our art or by how much we've accomplished. I think they'd be sort of awestruck by the carnage and stupidity.

EL: Bergman: "If I see a cloud in the sky, I think the world is coming to an end."

WA: I'd love five out of seven days like this [*today is overcast*] and maybe two conventionally nicer days.

EL: Here's Bergman on writing his scripts: "I wrote my films not really understanding what I'd written. Then I shot them, and they meant certain things to me. But what they meant—that I didn't really understand until afterwards. Long afterwards. If my relationships to my own products are so odd, it's because often when I'm writing and shooting a film I'm inside some sort of protective shell. I hardly analyze what I'm doing or why I'm doing it. I rationalize afterwards."

WA: That sounds like a great intuitive artist. I think I'm more in control than that on a cerebral level and less in control on a competence level. So I start off knowing what I'm doing and what I want to do and because I'm not competent at it, it turns out to be something different [*laughs*] and I'm surprised by it.

EL: How about this? "The importance of the dreary in art mustn't be underestimated."

WA: I happen to find dreariness very beautiful. I see it in Martha Graham. A lot of people when they see *Radio Days* laugh at that early scene where I say, "I remember my childhood as so beautiful" and we cut to Rockaway and it is a rainy, wave-tossed day. I meant it completely straight, but more often than not it gets a laugh.

EL: You've talked several times about always hating school and being largely self-educated. Do you just follow what interests you?

WA: It's an eclectic kind of education. I read a little philosophy, some history, some novels, next year you go back to something else. But there's no pattern to it. I started with novels. That's what interested me first, American novels: Hemingway, Faulkner, Steinbeck. They were contemporary but their heyday was in the 1920s and 1930s.

EL: What prompted your interest in linguistics?

WA: One of the drawbacks and pluses, but more a drawback, of being an autodidact is that you read eclectically in an effort to have a rounded education. In autodidactic people it seems there are surprising gaps in very, very conventional places. So maybe I've read a couple of books on semantics and linguistics, but it's capricious. In talking with me for a while, if you hit on six of the subjects I've taught myself about, you'd think I'm literate. But then suddenly you hit something that every college kid knows, and because I'm self-taught, it's a gap in my learning and I don't know it. And it can be a simple thing.

For example, my grammar is terrible. Just terrible. There is a mass of corrections from *The New Yorker* all the time. They are forever saying, "You can't say this. This is not good English." And [*film editor*] Sandy Morse is forever correcting my English when I write a narration. Saul Bellow, when I gave him his lines to say in *Zelig*, said, "It's all right if I change this, isn't it? Because this is grammatically incorrect." I just have no grammar at all and that's something fundamental you learn in school. There are many things like that.

EL: Do you regularly read poetry?

WA: I've been rereading a lot of poetry recently. I still have many of the same favorites I've always had.

If you had spoken to me years ago, I would have said poetry is like giving a guy a piece of paper or a canvas and he slops paint on it and says, "Yeah, that's what de Kooning's doing and Kandinsky's doing. I could do ten of these a day." He doesn't get it. You want to say to him, "That's not what they're doing. You're just splotching paint. You think they're splotching paint but they're not."

Well, that's how I was with poetry. I've always liked it, but the more I learn about it, the greater I find Yeats and the more I can really appreciate him. There's a number I appreciate very much. Everyone I know appreciates Eliot, of course, because to me he's the great city poet. But Yeats is astonishing, given what one tries to do in poetry, tremendous. Like Shakespeare. I've always loved Emily Dickinson and William Carlos Williams and Robert Frost and E. E. Cummings. I love Philip Larkin.

I think that had I been better educated, I could write poetry, because a writer of comedy has some of that equipment to begin with. You're dealing with nuance and ear and meter, and one syllable off in something I write in a gag ruins the laugh. And that's all done with feeling. Sometimes an editor will correct something in a story and I'll say, "Can't you see that if you add just that one syllable, the whole joke is ruined?"

Also in jokes, in actual one-liners, there's something succinct, you do something that you do in poetry. In a very compressed way you express a thought or feeling and it's dependent on the balancing of words. Now, you don't do this consciously. For example, "I'm not afraid of dying. I just don't want to be there when it happens." In a compressed way it expresses something, and if you use one word more or less it's not as good. Maybe if I experimented I could find a better way to say what I wanted to, but basically that seemed the way to do it. And you do it instinctively. You don't count it out or anything. And this is what the poets are doing. They're not working their meters by the numbers, they're feeling.

EL: Didn't you once tell me that it took time for you to appreciate Shakespeare?

WA: I've gotten to appreciate Shakespeare's *writing* much more. It's his writing that I find beautiful and genuinely superior. Not so much the plays but the *words* of the plays. They're written so beautifully. I don't find any of his comedies funny, but the speech is so magnificent, it's so gorgeous, that you're overcome by it. But I find the plays dumb and bumpkin-oriented and aimed at the groundlings. The serious plays have some really beautiful moments, but often they're not constructed at all well. But you sit through them because the language is so elevated.

EL: You often have jokes that play off philosophy, for instance in *Love and Death.* Do you read much of it?

WA: Philosophy was something I was interested in without knowing I was interested in it. I took to it right away and the fact that Harlene [*Rosen, his first wife. He was twenty, she seventeen when they married in 1956; they divorced in 1962*] was studying it was very stimulating to me. Not enough for me to go to school and study it, but any time in my reading I inadvertently came across philosophical texts, they had extra interest for me. If I had my education to do over, I would probably go to college and probably be a philosophy major.

EL: Which philosophers speak to you when you read them?

WA: The most exciting can be the German philosophers, although it's pretty exciting when you first read Plato. It's fun in an artistic way. The same thing when you read Nietzsche. It's fun. Hegel I find boring and you have to slog through it. But in the end, what kills you is down deep, the ones that make the most sense turn out to be rationalist, pragmatic philosophers who are basically more dull but it's very hard to argue with them. In the end, much of Bertrand Russell makes much more sense, resonates much more deeply with me, but he's not nearly as much fun or as exciting as, say, Camus, Jean-Paul Sartre, or Nietzsche—the ones who are more dramatic and concerned with life-and-death subjects and talk about them in very lurid ways.

EL: How about German Expressionism?

WA: German Expressionism was something I liked even as a boy. When I used to go to the Museum of Modern Art, the room that always captivated me the most was the room with the Kirchners and the Schmidt-Rottluffs and the Noldes. It was just something I always identified with. I loved it.

EL: What about literary critics?

WA: I've just finished George Steiner's study of Dostoevsky and Tolstoy [Tolstoy or Dostoevsky: An Essay in the Old Criticism] and that sent me to reread *The Idiot,* so I'm in the midst of that now. The Steiner book was fun to read. It is a comparative study done as only certain teachers can do. Steiner is one. Isaiah Berlin is another. There are certain guys who are just great teachers. William Barrett is another, the classic being *Irrational Man,* because he has that knack of popularizing a subject so a mental cretin like me can get it.

EL: This is a rather abrupt lowering of the brow, but in the tribute to Bob Hope that you narrated for the Film Society of Lincoln Center, you say that after seeing Hope and Crosby on camelback singing, "Like Webster's Dictionary, we're Morocco bound," that "I knew immediately what I wanted to do with my life." It's a great line, but how true is it?

WA: Of course, that was when I was very young. When I was a little kid, I loved comedy and I loved Bob Hope and Groucho Marx. I grew up with that. Right up until my teens, I tried to act like Hope and make the jokes and snap off the one-liners effortlessly. But then as I got a little bit more literate and older—seventeen, eighteen—I wanted to be in the theater or in show business in some way. My interest was in writing drama. I wanted to write for the theater and I didn't think of writing comedies. I thought I wanted to write what Ibsen wrote and what Chekhov wrote. I knew I had a comic talent because I was already getting paid for it. And I kept succeeding in comedy and always longed to make a jump over to serious work. It's always been a frustrating obstacle for me. Not to mention I was too cowardly to leave what was bringing me fame and fortune and risk writing what might not be drama but soap opera.

EL: Does that mean you view your ability to write comedy so well as a bit of a curse?

WA: I never thought succeeding at comedy was a curse. I thought, This is very good, because I'm writing these comic things and I'm becoming a performer. It all puts me into position to do what I want to do ultimately, and ultimately what I'd like to do is some heavy, dramatic things—as a writer, as a director. I never thought there'd be any additional obstacle whatsoever.

EL: You've written so many films, is it a challenge to constantly come up with names for characters? Some names seem to crop up again and again. For instance, Ceil—the name of your mother's sister.

WA: People have asked me for years how I get my names and I always tell them that when I'm typing my script I go for short names because I don't want to type so much. I used to use Louise a lot because I could type it with facility. But there's practically always a Blint and a Gray, Mr. Gray, Mr. Blint; always. And always an Abe or a Ceil. Never a Priscilla or a Murgatroyd.

EL: When were you exposed to Chekhov and other "serious" writers?

WA: It was the very end of high school when I started going out with women who found me illiterate. I thought those girls were so beautiful: no makeup, silver jewelry, leather bags. I'd take one of them out and she would say, "Where I'd really like to go tonight is to hear Andrés Segovia." And I'd say, "Who?" and she'd say, *"Andrés Segovia."* And I just wouldn't know what she was talking about. Or one would say, "Did you read this Faulkner novel?" And I'd say, "I read *comic* books. I've never read a *book* in my life. I don't know anything like that."

And so in order to keep pace, I had to read. Hemingway and Faulkner really interested me right off; not Fitzgerald as much. Then I started reading plays. And as soon as I was writing comedy, I remember saying to Abe Burrows [*a relative by marriage—Woody's mother's brother wed Burrows's father's sister*], "I want so much to be a television writer."

And he said, "You don't want to be a television writer your whole life, do you? That's not your ultimate goal?"

And I said, "Of course. Why not?"

And he said, "You should think of the theater. If you have a talent and you want to write comic dialogue, you should think of the theater."

And I said, "Well, maybe the movies. Don't all the guys in the theater want to get into the movies?"

And he said, "No, it's just the opposite. All the screenwriters in California would love to get a play on Broadway. That's what they all want to do."

In those days a screenwriter was nothing, just an anonymous name whose work was butchered. And a playwright was a big deal. And so I started to go to the theater a little bit. I was about eighteen.

September 1988

Woody has recently returned from a lengthy trip to Europe including Scandinavia. Before he left he said he expected to do no work on a script he had half completed: "Generally there is no break in writing like I'm taking with this vacation. I might put a script in a drawer for a week but this is eighteen days." To his surprise, he finished the script by writing every morning on, the stationery of the various hotels where he stayed, then folding the pages and putting them in his coat breast pocket. As the trip progressed, the scratch pad–sized paper of the Grand Hotel in Stock-

holm was folded together with the long, rectangular sheets of the Villa d'Este on Lake Como; the wide, pure white, gold-embossed stationery from the Gritti Palace in Venice; the smaller, barely engraved paper of the Hotel Hassler in Rome; various telex forms; and several sheets of lined paper ripped from a school notebook bought on the street in Copenhagen. By the time he reached London, his pocket bulged as though he had a loaf of bread in it. Finally his assistant Jane Martin convinced him to stash the work in the hotel safe rather than cart it around, if only to avoid spilling soup on it in a restaurant, so each day pieces of the small, elegant, blue Claridge's stationery were folded in half, piled on the heap, and locked away before he went out to wander the streets.

By the time he returned to New York, he had the first draft of what is tentatively titled Brothers *but will eventually become* Crimes and Misdemeanors.

EL: Before you left, you told me you were only going to write a review of Bergman's autobiography for the *New York Times Book Review* while you traveled. What happened?

WA: Yeah. I had half the script done before I left and I figured I'll do the second half when I come back and I'll do the Bergman piece while I'm there, because I'm not going to really be able to concentrate and work, I'll be too distracted by the traveling and the new places.

Pages of the manuscript for what became *Crimes and Misdemeanors*, written in a series of hotels while Woody vacationed in 1988

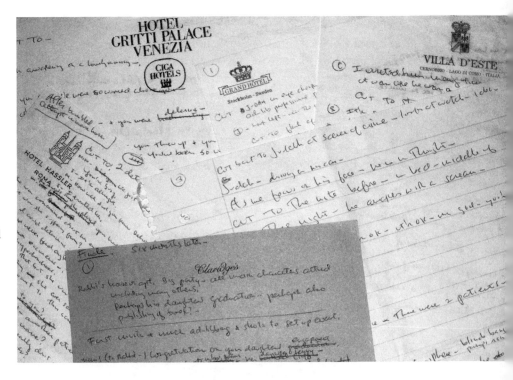

But that wasn't the case. I wasn't able to get the script off my mind. I was able to do a few hours' work each day and so it was just fine.

EL: Did you write the Bergman review?

WA: [*He laughs.*] No. I'm not good at book reviews. I find it hard to review a book because it's a different kind of writing, and because I wouldn't review a book and knock it. Unless it was written by, you know, someone I couldn't stand. I mean if one of those fundamentalists, if [*televangelist*] Jimmy Swaggart wrote a book, then I can express myself comically. But someone like Bergman whom I think is so great, it's just a spate of encomia. Know what I mean? I wouldn't be able to write anything funny about that.

EL: Let's talk about dialogue for a minute. Some critics found the dialogue in *Interiors* to be stiff. What do you say to that? [*The film is about the troubled family dynamics of three sisters, their obsessive-compulsive mother (who commits suicide), their father, and the free-spirited woman he marries after his wife's death.*]

WA: After *Interiors,* months later, I was sitting home and suddenly thought to myself, Gee, did I make this mistake? Because of my exposure to foreign films, in my ear for dialogue, was I really writing subtitles to foreign films? When you see, say, a Bergman film, you're reading it because you're following the subtitles. And when you read it, the dialogue has a certain cadence. My ear was picking up on subtitle-style dialogue and I was creating that for my characters. I worried about that. It's something that I never really resolved clearly. I don't know.

EL: Do you think you write more formal dialogue for a dramatic film?

WA: A few people who like my films very much have said that to me. And I'm not sure if that's true and I have a blind spot, or it's not really true. It's just that I get serious people to play it and they never give it the loose feeling that I give it when I act in my films. I'm loose and streety. So far in my dramatic films none of the characters are streety. Maybe that's one reason.

At the end of Crimes and Misdemeanors, *Cliff (Woody), a failed documentary maker, and Judah, the ophthalmologist/murderer (played by Martin Landau), sit on a piano bench at the wedding of the daughter of Ben, the blind rabbi (played by Sam Waterston). The scene provides a chance for Cliff to sum up his (and Woody's) feelings about the randomness of life. Woody had hoped for Waterston to do it, but by the time he had rewritten the scene, Waterston was in Russia on another project. Driving home after a screening of the film, Woody feels it works with him doing the lengthy solo speech because of his training as a monologist, and because "I feel that my films are such a personal statement that I'm shameless about moralizing in the end. It's like the old Sid Caesar show joke among the writers. Sid would sum up a sketch and say, 'If there's one thing I've learned . . .' Maybe all the writers were nice Jewish boys brought up to have a little idealistic lesson at the end as a summary."*

EL: This film takes on some pretty big issues. [*A successful ophthalmologist (Landau) who is regarded as a pillar of the community takes a mistress (Anjelica Huston) who becomes increasingly demanding that he leave his wife. He promises to but doesn't and eventually the mistress threatens to expose his financial impropriety with a charity. Desperate to keep his place in society and his family intact, he asks his less successful brother, who has underworld connections, to rid him of the threat. A murder is arranged and at first the doctor is racked with guilt. But in time he realizes he has gotten away with it; he accepts that in what he sees as a godless universe, there will be no consequences and so resumes his comfortable life.*]

WA: Something I've always been fascinated with and have dealt with in other films of mine is this Tolstoy crisis—he came to the point in his life when he just couldn't figure out why he shouldn't commit suicide. Is it worth living in a godless world? The head says no, but the heart is too scared to take action to end it.

EL: There is seldom any swearing or raunchy language in your films. Is that a conscious decision you've made?

WA: It's a fifty-fifty line. There's part of me that grew up with an automatic cleanness about my pictures. They've always been clean because my influences when I grew up were Chaplin or [*George S.*] Kaufman and [*Moss*] Hart, Cole Porter. Listen, even *Another Woman* is a PG picture. We were lucky we didn't get a G.

EL: But in *Crimes and Misdemeanors* you use the word "asshole."

WA: The original line was, "Every line of human kindness sticks a shaft up God's ass," but [*laughs*] I couldn't go through with it. It's just the brutality of the language.

EL: Len Maxwell [*a comic who performed many of the skits Woody created as a young writer*] once said of you: "Anybody who says, 'I wafted gently over to her' doesn't need to use 'fucking.' "

WA: The truth is I would use whatever language was required to get the effect I needed. So far nothing I've done has required language other than what I used.

EL: There's an incident in the film where Cliff loses the only copy of his manuscript. I've noticed you never make a copy of your work as you're doing it.

WA: I've been sending an only copy for twenty years to Studio Duplicating. I never, ever make a copy, ever. Of anything. And I've sent them over there sometimes very cavalierly. I should get a little Xerox machine in the house here and just run the thing through for ten minutes. I should. I'm just too lazy.

As for Cliff losing his manuscript, I know someone who worked for years on a novel, a major novel. He had his manuscript in a suitcase, it was at a hotel in Boston, I think, and the suitcase was stolen. It was an only copy. It shattered him. He was never able to write again. He could write television jokes and stuff, but not another book. Sad.

EL: Have you ever lost a manuscript?

WA: Someone wanted to make a television series out of *Acres and Pains* or something by S. J. Perelman and I wrote a script. I was just starting as a comic, I was about twenty-five years old and I just idolized Perelman. I was going with Louise [*Lasser*] at that time. It was when Mickey Rose [*his childhood friend and collaborator on* Take the Money and Run *and* Bananas] lived in New York. And the three of us went out and I had the script with me. It was the only copy. I had to deliver it someplace that night. And there was a fire in Times Square, in the Times Tower, in which a few firemen died from smoke inhalation.

There were six thousand people in the street and I'm watching the fire and then I go on with my evening. Two hours later I realize I lost the script. And I came back to Times Square and there it was on the curb, all walked over, in the manila envelope. [*He laughs.*] Isn't that incredible?

EL: The guy with the suitcase should have been so lucky. What happened to the proposed series?

WA: It never got off the ground. The producers felt that my script was too prosy and they wanted it in dialogue. They were schleppers. They didn't know what they were doing. It was actually fine.

EL: Do characters change much after you've written the script?

WA: I'm writing the movie as I'm making the movie. A lot of times I'm sitting there with [*casting director*] Juliet Taylor and she'll say something to me about a character I've written—say, Peter in *Hannah*. After a lot of conversation about who to cast, she said, "What about Max von Sydow?" And suddenly [*snaps fingers*] the idea rings a bell and it's great. And the part [*a painter devoted to art*] was then tailored for him. He became considerably older and very angry. The same thing happens when we find a wonderful location. Suddenly the scene is changed for that because the visuals are good.

The movie is never written in advance. It's a general idea but clear enough to work out the budget.

June 1989

The Manhattan Film Center, Woody's editing and screening room in a swank residential building on Park Avenue. Formerly a bridge club, he bought the space in 1979 after Manhattan *was released.*

Woody learned a month ago that Brothers *is not available as the title for the film and he is searching for another. For a while he settles on* Anything Else, *but that title will not be used until 2003. Another thought is to have something to do with crime in the title:* High Crimes and Misdemeanors *catches his attention, but then he feels it sounds too much like Gilbert and Sullivan.* Crimes and Misdemeanors *sounds interesting for a brief while but then is rejected (temporarily, as it turns out).*

*Sometimes titles come easily—*Hannah and Her Sisters *and* Broadway Danny Rose *are good examples—but usually the search drags on. This film is proving the most difficult of all.* Brothers *so neatly summed up the varied relationships of the characters that he is at a loss. There are several conversations about the title over many days but without success. His film editor, Sandy Morse, is with Woody as he sits at the wooden desk outside the editing room.* A Matter of Conscience *is suggested.*

"I don't like A Matter of . . . ," he quickly says, then adds, "There's no one word that means the human condition, like 'fandango,' is there?"

He starts to free-associate.

"Dr. Shenanigans. [A laugh.] Decisions. Decisive Moments. Make a Killing. Crimes and Vanity." The phone rings. It's Bobby Greenhut, producer of the film. After a minute Woody says, "I guess you don't like The Lord's Prayer. *Do you think it puts too much of a burden on the film?"*

After he hangs up he takes a legal pad and divides a page into sections. He wants to make a connection between eyes and God and success. Yesterday I repeated for him a quote from Aeschylus: "Success in men's eyes is God." He was intrigued but now he laughs as he says, "I can hear it now." His voice becomes pompous. "The title is from Aeschylus." He writes down prospective titles under the proper headings on the legal pad.

Good and Evil	**Eyesight Group**
Acts of Good and Evil	*The Eyes of God*
Moments of . . .	*Windows of the Soul*
Scenes of . . .	*Visions of the Soul*
	Dark Vision

Hope	Choice
Glimmer of Hope	*A Matter of Choice*
Hope and Darkness	*Choices in the Dark*
Faint Hope	*Decisive Points*

He fills the bottom of the page with doodles as he thinks. Empty Choices *is suggested.*

"That'll send them away with a big sneer on their face. Split Decisions. *Those titles always sound like those other pictures—too commercial. Jeff Katzenberg* [then chairman of Walt Disney Studios, whose Touchstone Pictures financed and distributed the film] *was saying over lunch that you couldn't have three worse words than* Dead Poets Society. *Plus it got bad reviews, but it's through the roof."* He pauses. "The Eyes of God, The Sight of God." He shakes his head. *"It's a little much to ask for the shopping mall people to come and see."*

January 2000

Sweet and Lowdown *has recently been released;* Small Time Crooks *will come out later in the year. Woody and I meet to talk about his films of the past several years, beginning with* Manhattan Murder Mystery *(1993).*

The ending of a picture is sometimes a problem for Woody and he will rewrite or reshoot it. In Manhattan Murder Mystery, *a satisfying comedy, he and Diane Keaton are Larry and Carol Lipton, a middle-aged married couple who get caught up in investigating a woman's disappearance, which Carol soon suspects to be a murder. Larry, nervous and anxious by nature, wants nothing to do with her sleuthing. Carol's doggedness draws the interest of their handsome and recently divorced friend Ted (Alan Alda), and when Larry suspects there is a romantic interest developing between Carol and Ted, he reluctantly joins the hunt.*

With the murder solved and Larry and Carol out of harm's way, the two walk down the avenue talking about all that has happened. It turns out there was no romantic spark between Carol and Ted. Larry says dismissively of him, "Take away his elevator shoes and his fake suntan and capped teeth and what do you have?" And Carol, without skipping a beat, answers, "You." Moments later the screen snaps to black.

I ask Woody about the ending.

WA: The joke originally came in the middle of the script but I didn't film it. Then it floated back in. I didn't think it would have such a good impact. I thought it was a nice joke but not that great. After I first cut the movie I realized it would work there, so we went out and shot it.

EL: There are nods to a couple of acclaimed films, especially the ending in the hall of mirrors that echoes Welles's *Lady from Shanghai.* There's also a bit of Hitchcock's *Vertigo.* In one of the scenes a bus passes and it has a poster for the rerelease of *Vertigo* that coincided with *Manhattan Murder Mystery.* Was that on purpose?

WA: I was told afterward that *Vertigo* did a bus thing. I'd seen the film once and never concentrated on it. It's so slow at first. I don't like it although I know it is worshiped by Hitchcock fans. Still, I was part of the group that funded the restoration and rerelease because it's important to preserve films like that, but it's not a personal favorite of mine. The appearance of the sign in any event is pure coincidence. I've yet to notice it to this day.

EL: *Manhattan Murder Mystery* is the story that was part of the first draft of *Annie Hall,* then was put aside, right?

WA: Yes, it's had a strange history. I developed this idea years ago and decided that Marshall [*Brickman*] should write it and direct it and I'd be in it. He got sidetracked in the writing and it didn't work out. So I said, "Look, you can keep the script and if you can sell it elsewhere, it will be yours." But he didn't. Then it just lay dormant. Then years later I said to him, "Why don't we fool around on that script? Why don't you give it back to me and see if I can write it?" I really knew what I wanted to do with it. He agreed and I did a version for me and shot it and that was that. But we collaborated on it in the planning, which for me—and for him and for any writer—is the tough part. The actual writing of the thing I like to do for myself because I want to write dialogue I can say; I don't like to say somebody else's dialogue.

EL: Did he come to the set when you made this? I've never seen him around when you shoot.

WA: Marshall never comes to the set. As a writer, he's wonderful to work with. He's so smart, so funny. Some of the best memories I have are times I worked with him writing a film. We'd sit in my living room and talk for an hour, an hour and a half. Then one of us would say, "Come on, let's go for a walk" and we'd take a walk around and get some fresh air and keep pitching ideas. Then we'd go to dinner together and talk over dinner and sometimes come back to my house. There was a heavy social component, but we were working all the time. He's very companionable, witty, and creative, wonderful to work with.

EL: But you are the one who actually writes out the script?

WA: Only because it's a time-saver—and I have to say the lines. I don't make notes. I'll just retain the ideas. We sit and talk endlessly about the thing, talk it all out—he says, "First you write your story and then you write it down," and I agree completely. When I go to write it down, the work's been done by both of us and I can write it down in three weeks, two weeks, because all I'm doing is writing down all the work we both did. He could just as easily write it down.

The last time I worked out dialogue with a collaborator was on *Sleeper* [*with Brickman*] and two guys pitching lines always takes twice as long.

EL: You used a new collaborator in Douglas McGrath for *Bullets over Broadway*.

WA: Doug is someone I knew socially [*he is married to Woody's former assistant Jane Martin and is the director of* Emma, Company Man, Nicholas Nickleby, *and* Infamous, *as well as a screenwriter*] and someone I thought it would be fun to collaborate with just for the pure enjoyment of it. I had no other reason. I showed him several ideas of mine, all of them good, and said, "Which one of these strikes you as most fun to work on?"

And he said, "The one where the gangster turns out to be the playwright."

And I said, "Really? Because that's last on my list." I had a political idea that I thought he would warm to, and one of those personal ideas where he said, "Ah, it's another of those films where you talk to the audience." So I said, "All right, you want to work on that one, we'll work on that one." [*Bullets over Broadway demonstrates that artists are born, not made. John Cusack, a decent, dedicated young playwright, pours his soul into his art but discovers that he will never be an artist.*]

EL: Is it any different working with him than with Marshall?

WA: We worked much the same way as I do with Marshall. He came over to my house. We chatted, planned, structured. Then he went off and I wrote the script down and made the movie. It worked out very well.

I don't usually like to collaborate now, but I like my collaborators personally and every five or six years or so you get lonely in the room and you want to have another human being for the fun of it, and Doug seemed like a very good choice because he's creative and witty and a friend.

EL: You said *Bullets* [1994] was one of three ideas you had. Was it generally worked out in your head before you talked with Doug or did you still have to sort out much of it?

WA: I remember when the idea came up of bumping off Olive [*the no-talent actress girlfriend (Jennifer Tilly) of a mob boss (Joe Viterelli) who puts up money to back a play so she can be a star*], that's when I knew I was going to go ahead with that story. [*One of the boss's thugs (Chazz Palminteri) is assigned to keep an eye on Olive during rehearsal. Despite all appearances, he turns out to be the true writing talent, and his suggestions make the play work. He kills Olive rather than let her acting kill the play.*]

I remember saying to Doug, "You know where this is going to go? He kills her and the play opens and it's a big hit and the gangster becomes the toast of the town. And a few months down the line he's dying to be a gangster again because the people in show business are such sharks and are so awful that they're worse than the clear-cut killers that he's dealing with. They double-deal him behind his back, they don't return his calls, they manipulate him because show business is so awful"— and that was where I was going with it. But when I wrote the thing, I didn't go there because that was too much of a new beat. The film ended where it ended and this would be an odd appendage. So although it sounded great, its natural end was where I ended it. Doug asked where it disappeared to, but it was adding another fifteen minutes. It meant starting up again.

Incidentally, the business with the gunshots [*the gangster is gunned down backstage during the opening performance by fellow gang members who realize he killed Olive, and the audience thinks the offstage shots are for verisimilitude*] was an idea I got from the cracking of the Indian nuts on the soundtrack of George S. Kaufman and Moss Hart's wonderful movie satire *Once in a Lifetime.*

EL: Your training as a magician taught you a lot about misdirection, and you used that well in this film.

WA: I frequently use misdirection in scripts. For instance, until it happened, the audience did not have the slightest idea that I was going to hook up with Julia Roberts in *Everyone Says I Love You.* Hers was a separate story from mine. [*There are several story lines in* Everyone Says I Love You. *Joe Berlin (Woody) is divorced from Steffi (Goldie Hawn) but the two remain close friends, to the extent that her new husband, Bob (Alan Alda), a wealthy Park Avenue liberal, treats Gabe like a family member. Gabe and Steffi's kids have easily bonded with Bob's. Lane and Laura (Gaby Hoffmann and Natalie Portman) are adorable East Side schoolgirls; DJ (Natasha Lyonne) is more savvy and the film's narrator. Skylar (Drew Barrymore) is a perfect debutante, while Scott (Lukas Haas) is proof of the randomness of life: he is a flaming conservative. Skylar is engaged to Holden (Edward Norton) but then meets Charles Ferry (Tim Roth), an ex-con on the make for whom Bob and Steffi, always in the vanguard of liberal causes, host a party. Gabe becomes entranced by Von (Julia Roberts), who is unhappily married and whose most personal thoughts shared with her psychiatrist are overheard and made known to Gabe, who thus is able to say and do everything she hoped for in a man (an idea Woody had toyed with using before and did to a lesser extent in* Another Woman). *Everyone in the film breaks into song at one time or another, but intentionally with the polish of someone in the shower rather than of someone in a musical. The film was lusciously shot in New York, Venice, and Paris.*]

Writers do it all the time and I do it, too, to throw the audience. In *Manhattan Murder Mystery* when Keaton and Alan Alda are at the wine tasting, I wanted you to think they were developing a crush on each other. Then they see the lady [*who is supposedly dead*] on the bus, and Keaton and I set off after her.

EL: That worked well, as does the idea of the gangster having the real writing talent while the John Cusack character, as earnest and devoted to his craft as can be, simply doesn't have it. It's the kind of twist you wrung out of *Purple Rose of Cairo.*

WA: I did sneak in the gangster being the writer. I always feel that my years doing magic help me in those situations. I'm very deceptive when I have to be; I know how to draw on the little deceptive wrinkle in magic that makes something seem as innocent as can be. I often use little subtle things that throw the audience off, where they just don't have a clue where I'm going. It's the exact same principle that you do in a magic trick where you do something that throws the audience off. Say later on I'm going to have to go to my wallet in some way; half an hour before that I might sit down and go to my wallet several times, and so when I do it later, it's been done and now seems innocent.

So the first time the gangster says something he gets up and says, "That line, it's gone to my head. It's stupid writing," you don't for a second think that he's a writer in any way. The thing becomes full-blown when he shows up at the nightclub and says, "Sit down." Then it tumbles forward very fast.

EL: Is there much pleasure for you in seeing a film finished pretty much in the way you envisioned it when you sat down to write it?

WA: I enjoy the process of writing the stories and mounting them on the screen. I can look at my films with complete objectivity and think, This film is better than that stupid comedy that is making a fortune, but now let's compare it to *The Bicycle Thief.* Then reality sets in. I can see when I'm good or bad and I don't think I overpraise or overcriticize my work.

EL: *Bullets* is very much about the difference between *wanting* to be an artist and *being* an artist. Do you see yourself as an artist?

WA: I have a very realistic view of myself. Some people think it's too much or even fake humility when I say I haven't made a great movie. When I dramatize my observations of life, they say it's cynicism. But in neither case is it either. I'm telling the truth. I don't see myself as an artist. I see myself as a working filmmaker who chose to go the route of working all the time rather than making my films into some special red carpet event every three years. I'm not cynical and I'm far from an artist. I'm a lucky working stiff.

May 2005

Woody is preparing to go back to London to film Scoop, *at present untitled. He is not in* Match Point *but will appear in this one, as will Scarlett Johansson for the second film in succession.*

We are in his screening room at the Manhattan Film Center, in the dark avocado green velour swivel chairs that have been there for years. Next to us are cabinets filled with the records, mostly of music from the thirties and forties, that he draws on to score his films.

Almost everything is as it has been for twenty-five years. The one thing that is different is his enthusiasm for Match Point. *He rarely shows any for a film when it is finished, but he is happy with everything about this one, including the script.*

EL: Why did it work so well?

WA: I think it had to do with a few things. One was that I was not confined to comedy. I could do what I wanted to do. I didn't have to think, "I'm doing a film but it has to be a comedy," or "I've got to be in it." I had no restrictions, so I could do the film I wanted to do. I wrote, I thought, a good script. And I was able to bring it off. I had all the resources.

EL: There are two brutal murders in the film, but you show neither the shooting nor any blood. Why?

WA: It wasn't about either the killing or the blood, so I didn't feel there was any necessity to just blast people away in front of you. It wouldn't have added anything. I was very lucky on this picture. Everything that usually goes wrong on a movie went right here. There are things that often give you a hard time—getting the right actors, having to compromise certain roles, getting the right weather every day— that just worked. Every decision that was made on the picture, not just by me but by everybody, just worked. I don't know if I can ever repeat it or make a film as good.

EL: Paul Kaye, who played the real estate agent renting the flat to Jonathan Rhys-Meyers, has about the only funny lines in the film. Did you write the scene that way?

WA: That's the perfect example of every person in the film making a contribution. I wrote it very simply, not funny at all. But he was ad-libbing all over the place and ad-libbing in character and he was funny. Not one actor came in, read the lines, took the money, and left. Everybody made something out of their part.

EL: Time moves from season to season smoothly and with little exposition. For example, the two weddings in the same church tell us that months have passed without your having to do any exposition.

WA: My instinct for telling the story was that I could do that, that it didn't require any more than that. I just felt [*snaps fingers*], This is all information, get it quickly and move on.

EL: Do you think being in a city other than New York made a difference?

WA: It's always fun to see a new city, but I wasn't doing the kind of film where I could exploit the city as much as I wanted. I could exploit London a certain amount, but if I had been doing a romantic movie, I could have done it in the way I exploited Manhattan in *Manhattan*. But here there was a real narrative story to tell and I couldn't indulge myself very much on sightseeing.

EL: This film came out just as you saw it in your mind. But how about other films—*Purple Rose of Cairo*, for instance?

WA: Yes, that's one of my films that came out as I envisioned it. Not that I ever see it.

EL: You once told me that you got stuck after you had the notion that a character comes off the screen.

WA: The inspiration I had was that a character [*played by Jeff Daniels*] comes off the screen, but I couldn't follow through. I wrote fifty pages and gave up on it and put it away. I only came back to it when it dawned on me that the real actor is troubled by this. So he comes to town and the girl [*Mia Farrow*] falls in love with him as well as his character from the screen and is forced to choose, and chooses the real one and he hurts her—that's what made the story for me. But until then I had fifty pages where the guy comes off the screen, and I had some fun with that but that was it.

EL: Reality always gets you in the end.

WA: My perception is that you are forced to choose reality over fantasy and reality hurts you in the end, and fantasy is just madness.

EL: What a choice.

WA: Yes, like life it's a lose-lose situation.

EL: When you're writing are you able to transport yourself into the fantasy?

WA: I transport myself in very easily. You get into the story when you write something. You get into it in a pleasurable way. It's hard to explain, but it's the kind of thing I imagine a graphic artist has when he or she formulates a collage or works on a painting. You want to return to it and build it up. It's a pleasurable feeling.

EL: When you did your stand-up, did you write out your routines?

WA: No, I never wrote them out. I'd have the idea for a joke and I'd write two lines—the routine would be, say, car joke, then mother-in-law, whatever, that blended together in a narrative. I'd practice it a couple of times at home, then I'd get onstage and I would edit live onstage. I just knew that I had done the watch joke and everything was fine. [*"Pardon me a moment while I check the time," he would say, pulling out a pocket watch. "They're pretty punctilious about time here and I can hear the band padding in behind me." He held up the watch, the face toward the twelve hundred people in the audience. "I don't know if you can see this, but it's a very handsome watch." He brought it down and looked closely at it. "Has marble inlay," he continued, still looking at it. "Makes me look Italian." He paused. "My grandfather, on his deathbed, sold me this watch."*] But I knew instinctively that the audience right then didn't want to hear the joke about the sled and the elephant, that I should cut right to the business where the girl goes to my apartment, for example. And I made the edits right there live as I felt them.

When I wrote, I always started off with a longer monologue—but not deliberately; I just thought, This is going to be *great*. Then I got onstage and I realized, Oh, God, if I say that now, I can feel that they're not going to laugh, even though they've laughed at the last six jokes, this is not the one to go to. When you're in the line of fire, your body tells you where to go. You just know what you're going to die with.

It's very different if I'm sitting home and I write something and I imagine an audience. But when I watched my sketches at Tamiment years ago [*a camp in the Pocono Mountains of Pennsylvania, a couple of hours from New York, whose owners hired some of the best New York writers and performers to create a new show each week for their one thousand guests*] I was there with a live audience and a dynamic occurs that is not possible in a closed room. You just know what to do and what to cut and you feel the electricity in the air in some way. In a Broadway theater, with the audience there tittering or buzzing, I can know absolutely with lead-pipe accuracy what's going to play and what's not. You sense the reality of the moment unfailingly—well, not unfailingly, but rarely failingly. You can still screw up. Of course, grasping it when you're amongst the audience and not at home writing it means often that it's too late.

EL: Can you feel the same thing on a film set?

WA: No, there's no audience. There's a bunch of technicians, each guy worried about his own job, doing stuff. You're just trying to grind out that moment.

EL: What about the actor you're playing off?

WA: When you're playing the scene—when I'm with Diane Keaton or Scarlett or whoever—once you're into the scene, you may have written that she'll say, "Come on, let's get out of here," and you may have written, "Yeah, we've got to get out right away because they're coming back soon," and then she says, "Come on, let's get out of here." And you just know, because you're living the scene at the moment, that it's better to say, "Hey, what's your rush? We've still got two minutes to go through this desk and look at the papers." Because writing in my bedroom, it's one thing. On the set with a person, it's a different feel; you're in a reality that you're not in when you're writing it because you react differently and more accurately.

EL: The first thing I learned from you, thirty-five years ago, is the importance of the straight line. If you don't have that, then nothing else is going to work, no matter how funny the punch line. So do you think about what the funny situation is and then go back over the steps to get to it?

WA: This is one of the things I learned from Danny Simon. You can't cheat and give yourself straight lines that will accommodate your punch lines. If I've got a wonderful idea for a joke, I can't allow a straight line that's illogical or not quite real to precede a joke. The joke needs a true straight line—something the person could actually say. You have to be spartan and cruel about your straight line so that when you make your joke, it's coming off an absolutely honest line, not a line that has helped you slightly by its wording to get to where you want to go. So when you're writing the thing, you have to start not with the joke but with what the person would say under the circumstances. So if the person would say, "That's my parking space, I've been waiting for an hour," you've got to get your joke off that. You can't have the person say, "I just bought a car this morning. It's fifteen feet long, and I need fifteen feet for my space" only because you've got a great joke if someone would say that. You can only go where the straight line honestly enables you to go.

EL: Do you get the punch line first or does the joke suddenly appear out of a straight line?

WA: It all comes at once. The joke consists of the punch line and the straight line. You don't think of a free-floating punch line. Sometimes you'll think of a funny idea and maybe you're lucky and once in a while you can think of a way to backtrack and get there gracefully. But particularly if you're writing dialogue, what you have to write is people talking like they talk in life—but funny, if you're writing funny dialogue.

There's another kind of dialogue, which is great and harder, and that's character dialogue, where there's no joke at all but the dialogue is written so it can be played funny by a funny actor. So, obviously, if you're reading a Bob Hope script, it's full of jokes. One character will make them, the next guy'll make them—Hope makes them better, but everybody can say them, they're jokes. Whereas—again, reducing this to very simple terms—if you're writing a Jackie Gleason *Honeymooners* sketch, and he's saying, "*I'll* tell you where the thing is," there's no punch line anyplace; what's funny is the *guy*. If you did those lines, it would mean nothing. But because Gleason is doing them they're funny because they're character funny.

EL: Alan Alda comes to mind as someone who does that in your films.

WA: Alan is a perfect example of a guy who can take material that has the potential to be funny but is not funny in anyone's hands except an extremely skilled performer, and he'll make it sing.

EL: Do you ever laugh at your stuff when you're writing?

WA: Yes, all the time. And it often bears [*laughs*] no resemblance to what the audience laughs at. I'm hearing a joke for the first time when I write it or when I say it. I'm in the room and I write the joke or say the joke out loud and it's coming from my unconscious, so I'm hearing it and I laugh at it like a stranger.

EL: Do you often speak the dialogue before you write it?

WA: Sometimes I will. I remember when I was first writing with Danny Simon decades ago, he always did it. It was a very good habit. I'm a little lazy, but he had tremendous discipline that way, and he always acted everything out so there was never any question that it would play. And it always did. Some things read well, but when you get them on their feet with actors they don't.

EL: Was someone taking notes when he was playing the material?

WA: We'd both be in the room and he'd be walking around and would say, "Darling, I'm home from work. . . . No, don't give me that fish" and we'd both burst to the typewriter to get the joke down. I act out a lot of stuff, but I rely on hearing it in my head a certain amount because sometimes I'm too lazy to get off the bed and pace the room or because I'm writing fast. Sometimes I can get away with that because I'm experienced, sometimes I can't. Sometimes I'd be better off speaking it.

EL: Are you more inclined to speak aloud the material you write for yourself or do you hear that so well you just do it with material for others?

WA: I do all the material, all the parts. I do the straight line and the punch line.

EL: When you're writing a more dramatic piece as opposed to a more comedic piece, is there anything different in what's going on as you write it? Are you thinking in another way? Do you enter the scene in a different way?

WA: It's not the same for me, because for me, comedy just flows and I feel in control and I have that feeling that a musician feels who can play. I feel that I've set the rules. It's immaterial to me what's gone before, what other people do, what other people think, what's accepted. Whatever I want to do that I think is correct I do instinctively and it's for the most part served me well over the years. Not unfailingly, but reasonably well. I've been able to earn a living at it my whole life.

So I just feel if I want to do a movie where someone comes off the screen, if I want to do a pseudo-documentary, whatever I feel at the time, I do. I'm not afraid to set the style—not consciously, of course. With serious stuff, I'm more at sea and I flounder more and I don't trust myself. I'm not as comfortable, I guess, because in comedy you hear the laugh and you know that they're laughing. Whereas when I do a drama in the theater, I don't know if anyone's liking it or not liking it. They're watching it, but when it's over they may be bored numb or they may be thinking, God, that was a wonderful experience. I have no idea. With comedy, you know right away. They're just laughing too loud and if they're not, you're in trouble.

EL: When you're writing drama, are you transported into those characters as well?

WA: Yes, that part's the same. I write it, I get into it. But I don't feel as secure. I'll write a scene and think, Nobody's going to laugh at this scene. Is it going to be worth presenting to anybody?

In *Melinda and Melinda,* the comedy part of it was not a problem for me in any way. You know, the guy likes the girl, he's downstairs and he takes her out and he's jealous, he's nervous; it's just simple as pie to me. But the dramatic part, I'm hoping when I write it—I'm having fun writing it—that it is going to have the effect I want. I got lucky in that film. I got an actress [*Radha Mitchell*] who said the material the way I heard it in my mind's ear, so I felt good about that. But I don't know what the effect's going to be when you just look at ten straight lines in a row. I don't know if anybody's going to enjoy it or get with it or be moved by it or get caught up in it—or think, Hey, when does this end so we can eat?

With comedy, it's just much easier for me. When anybody talks about how much harder comedy is, they don't mean harder, they mean rarer. It's simply that comedy comes naturally to some people and dramatic material comes naturally to some people. And I just feel that I will always be able to make audiences laugh more than Ingmar Bergman can. If we each had to do a dozen comedies, mine would be funnier, I would make the audience laugh. Quite the opposite, of course, in a serious film.

If you can do comedy, it's not hard. If you can't do it, it's impossible. The same with drama. Arthur Miller could do drama, he had a good feel for it. Tennessee Williams had a wonderful feel for it. For me, it's more work. It doesn't come as naturally, though I enjoy it more as a spectator. I enjoy a Bergman film or *The Bicycle Thief* or *A Streetcar Named Desire* or Chekhov. And so naturally I have an impulse when I go home to want to write something with that seriousness.

Now, my genetic gift or [*laughing*] whatever it is that I have goes in a different direction, and so I have to work to try and write something serious, and I haven't been as effective with it over the years as I have been with comedy. But it doesn't mean that I intend to stop trying. And I think with *Match Point* I was reasonably successful, maybe the most successful I've been with dark material.

EL: Critics have sometimes written that you'd rather play Hamlet than the parts you've played.

WA: I'm not a comedian who wants to play Hamlet. I haven't the slightest interest in being a dramatic actor. I mean, if the opportunity came along and I thought I could do it, I would do it, but I'd never write myself anything dramatic to play and I have no big yen to play anything serious. It's different for me as a writer.

I was lucky. I've had a talent for comedy that's enabled me over decades to sustain myself. I've worked in all the mediums—prose, television, radio, stand-up, Broadway, movies—and I've performed in England, Europe, and the United States. I've gotten laughs in France with my dreadful French. It's just something I can do. And it isn't that I don't appreciate my own gifts, that I don't value my comedic ability. People jump to the conclusion that I do comedy but I hate it, or that I feel drama's great and comedy's nothing. But that's never been the case. I always find comedy wonderful and I always enjoy doing it and I always enjoy writing it. But I have a personal preference and put a greater value on a successful dramatic piece than on a successful comedy piece. It's purely personal. I'm not trying to convince anybody of anything when I say this. But as I've said, when I spend my 50 cents at the movies—or $50 now—I enjoy a wonderful dramatic movie more than a comedy. Naturally, I don't want a mediocre drama over a good comedy but given equal quality I prefer one to the other.

EL: Years ago you said you stopped doing *New Yorker* casuals because you worried that if you kept doing those, all you would have in the end was several collections of essentially the same thing. You said that you want to write novels when filmmaking becomes more arduous than you want it to be.

WA: I stopped writing casuals and I did write the novel, but I didn't like it [*the result*], so I've gone back to writing casuals. At least I learned that it's not as easy as you think to write a good novel no matter how much time and energy you put into it. But I was true to myself in trying. That is not to say that I won't try it again at some point.

EL: What was the novel about?

WA: I eventually used a certain amount of it in the movie *Anything Else* [*a tale of modern love in which Jason Biggs falls for sexy but flaky Christina Ricci, whose affections are mercurial*]. There were many funny things in the book but it wasn't really good enough, probably because I hadn't grown up as a literate person. I didn't read when I was younger. I wasn't encouraged to read, so I did not grow up knowing what the novel is. At fifteen, I could probably have directed a movie—I mean, I had enough instinct then. It was like the feeling I had about how to get it up on a stage in front of people and make people laugh. It wouldn't have been polished, but I would have known what to do. Whereas with a book, it's not baked into me, I didn't absorb literature in the same way as I absorbed movies or had comedy built into me. So when I finish a manuscript I have to show it to people and ask, "Is this a book? Is this a novel?" It wouldn't surprise me if a person said, "You have not written a novel. You have a good outline for a novel" or "This has the makings of a good short story."

But with stage or movies or nightclubs, I make the rules. I'm the one who decides because I just have a feel for it and I have utter confidence in my own feelings about these things.

EL: Who read the novel?

WA: [New Yorker *writer and editor*] Roger Angell read it [*in 2001*] and a couple of friends of mine, and they all pretty much had the same criticism of it, which I didn't really need more than one person giving me. I would have accepted it from any one of them. [*Former* New York Times *film critic*] Vincent Canby asked me if he could read it. They were very kind to me, and very helpful, but I could see that I just didn't pull it off. I always have tried to gamble for high stakes and was perfectly willing to strike out, which I did. I didn't want to write a mediocre novel that gained some popularity because I was a show business person. I wanted to compete in the big leagues with a real book, and I failed. But maybe I'll try again with a fresh one.

EL: How did you feel when you gave it to them? Did you really have no sense of whether it worked or not?

WA: I had no sense.

EL: How disappointing was this?

WA: Not very. I just like to work, so I did the work and I would have preferred if it was terrific. I put in a lot of time. But when a film of mine fails or something I write strikes out or I send something over to *The New Yorker* and they send it back and say, "This is not up to your usual standard," I'm never really very disappointed. To me, the fun is working on it. On the other hand I'm not that thrilled when the opposite happens, when I have a success, which has happened to me many times and has been no big deal. Of course, it's very nice if a picture opens and it's very successful. It's nice for the people who put the money up and it's nice for the studio, but I found early on that it didn't have an enormous effect on my life.

After I had my first successes, which I needed to get established, it didn't mean much to me. Not that I'm an ingrate. I'm thankful for my luck, but to me, no success or honor bestowed on me can alleviate my genetic gloom. Believe me, it's my loss.

EL: Can you ever say, "I'm satisfied with this"?

WA: Yes, I can do that with a movie. I can say, "This turned out to be a good movie." I don't really know how people have responded to the film because I gave up checking years ago, but if they liked it, great. If they didn't like it, it doesn't mean much to me, not because I'm aloof or arrogant but because I sadly learned that their approbation doesn't affect my mortality. If I do something that I feel is not very good and the public embraces it, even wildly, that doesn't make my personal sense of failure feel any better. That's why the key is to work, enjoy the process, don't read about yourself, when people bring up movies deflect the conversation to sports, politics, or sex, and keep your nose to the grindstone. Apart from the cash—we're so overpaid—the so-called rewards are all vanity and take time from your creative work. Plus, they can lead to delusions of grandeur or mistaken feelings of inferiority.

November 2005

Match Point has garnered consistently good reviews and press. It has opened in France and Switzerland, and when it opens the next month in the United States, New York Times critic A. O. Scott will write: "This is a Champagne cocktail laced with strychnine. You would have to go back to the heady, amoral heyday of Ernst Lubitsch or Billy Wilder to find cynicism so deftly turned into superior entertainment . . . it is the film's brisk, chilly precision that makes it so bracingly pleasurable. The gloom of random, meaningless existence has rarely been so much fun, and Mr. Allen's bite has never been so sharp, or so deep. A movie this good is no laughing matter."

Scoop *is virtually finished and Woody is on to his next idea.*

EL: You said today was a great day. You wrote four pages of a script.

WA: Yes, I got four pages written on a script and everything else worked out. I had plenty of time to work my clarinet, and time to do a parent/teacher meeting at school with my kid, and I was able to do my treadmill. Everything fell in.

EL: Can you talk at all about the new script? [*It will become* Cassandra's Dream.]

WA: No, except to say that it is again a very serious, dark script.

EL: And it looks like it will be done in London next summer?

WA: That is my guess. That is where it looks like they will consummate their financing.

Wherever it is, it will be done in the summer because the kids are out of school then. I wish I didn't have to consider the kids' school because then I could do pictures when I wanted to do them. For instance, I have to do a Barcelona picture in the summer [*of 2007*] and it's hot in Spain in the summer. I'd rather have been able to shoot in the spring.

EL: Let's talk a bit about the women in *Interiors*. [*See page 89.*] It's an interesting group. One's a real artist, another wants to be a writer in the worst way but writes only *in* the worst way, and the third is great-looking but vapid.

WA: I don't remember the picture well. I remember being out in Long Island filming it in the wintertime and liking the Hamptons in the winter—finding that nice and moody.

EL: There is a refrain in our conversations by you about your films: "I don't remember the picture well."

WA: It's not that my memory fails me, but I made them over the years and I've made thirty-six, thirty-seven movies and I haven't seen them since they were made. *Take the Money and Run* was 1967, '68, and it's been what? Almost forty years. So I don't remember it. Obviously if you ask me something about *Match Point*, I can tell it to you because I just saw it. And there are individual incidents I vividly remember about *Annie Hall* or *Manhattan* or *Bananas,* but I don't remember the movies well. I just remember that when I was shooting *Bananas* I was in the mountains of Puerto Rico at night and a bug crawled on my leg [*laughs*] and I let out a piercing shriek. I remember going in my spare time with Diane Keaton to the one movie house they had in San Juan and it leaked, so when it rained you'd have to find a seat that it wasn't leaking on.

I think I've mentioned this before, but it struck me as so true that I bring it up all the time. Tennessee Williams said, "When you write a script, you transcend it. It's a pity you can't throw it in a drawer. But you have to go and make it." And I feel the same way. When I write the script, it's over for me. It's a shame I have to go make it. Then once I've made it, it's really over. I have absolutely no interest in it.

EL: Didn't you buy a house in the Hamptons after *Interiors* was done and then almost never stay in it?

WA: One night.

EL: You spent *one night* in it?

WA: [*Matter-of-factly*] Yeah. I was in the Hamptons in the dead of winter, January, and it was empty and cold and the beaches were desolate and gray, and it was great for me. I loved it. So I thought to myself, Gee, I could get myself a house on the water here and just stare into the ocean and listen to waves. It's perfect for my personality.

EL: Where was the house?

WA: I searched and found a house in Southampton, and it was beautiful. It was the closest house to the water in Southampton and maybe all of the Hamptons. It was a great, large house and I put a lot of work into it. I had construction people there and architects and I made it incredibly beautiful—I'm talking about landscaping, the trees and everything. And I went out and I furnished it beautifully. The whole house was just drop-dead beautiful.

And after a year's work I went and spent my first night there. And then I thought, Hey, this is not for me.

EL: Why?

WA: I don't know. It just wasn't for me. I guess I am a creature of the pavement, of Madison Square Garden, of the restaurants, of the bookstores—you know, the streets. The sound of the waves drove me nuts. And I could hear the admonishing voice of my mother when I was a child, saying, "You *know* you don't like the country. You *never* liked the country. You don't like to be away from the *city*."

She said that many times over the years, and I always would say, depending on my degree of enthusiasm at the time for whoever I was going away with, "Oh, don't worry, I'm going to like this. This is different. This is great. The beach is not the country." Or "This is the *nearby* country."

But in the end, she was right because I just don't cotton to it. I like to get up in the morning and walk out into the city streets and navigate my way through the city and come back at night in the city and hear the traffic outside, not waves lapping.

EL: It's remarkable to me that you would spend a year on it, put in all that time and money and energy and thought into it, and then know in one night that you didn't want it.

WA: Well, the creativity of doing the house was fun, because you get to choose colors and furniture and decorate and reconstruct and all kinds of wonderful things. It's like writing or filmmaking—the work is the best part, not the results. But then, when I went there, maybe, *maybe*—at that time I was dating Mia—she said to me, "You're crazy, we're going to stay here, you've got to just tough out the first couple of nights." And she was perfectly supportive, but she wasn't insisting, "You've *got* to do it." She was saying, "The place is beautiful and it's fine."

Maybe things would have changed. I don't know. But I was irritable about being out there and didn't like going to sleep at night and [*he laughs*] hearing waves. I like to hear buses and sirens.

EL: When you drove onto the grounds that first day, was there a sudden sense of foreboding?

WA: [*Seeming amused by the memory*] I didn't have a sense of foreboding at first. I went up there, you know, full of brio, and walked on the beach and went in the house and went out of the house [*laughs*] and went in the house and went out of the house. [*Still laughing.*] And then I started getting that feeling that I used to get when I went up to the country with Mia. Mia had a beautiful place in Connecticut, she still has it. I would get there around one o'clock and I'd think, Yes, it's very pretty, and I'd walk around the grounds, which are capacious—sixty-five acres, seventy-five acres. It could be a gray wintry day or a spring day. And then I'd go into the house, and come out of the house, and go into the house, and come out of the house.

Now the light starts to fall and it's dark and you can't really go out of the house because it's pitch black and if it's wintertime it's seven o'clock at night and *black*, coal black outside, everywhere you look.

And I'd think, Gee, if I'm in the city I could go up to Elaine's, I could go to the movies, I could go for a walk and there are ten thousand things to do, and I could see a million people.

And here—she had some neighbor friends, but you've got to get in a car at night and do those country roads; they're fifteen, twenty minutes away on those country roads. You come back home at eleven o'clock and it's dark on those roads.

I used to say to her, "What are you going to do if you're asleep there, what if a car pulls up at three o'clock in the morning and somebody gets out—or more than one person gets out—what are you going to do? You're in the house, the house is utterly accessible, the windows are open. You can't lock everything every night."

And she said, "You're crazy. Everyone goes to sleep here and no one thinks about it. I feel more frightened in the city." And probably pound for pound, the city is more tense. But not to me. It may be completely imaginary, but I feel in the city, while it may be statistically more dangerous, I have some options. I can maneuver a little bit. I have some plan that may or may not work, but at least I have some plan. Whereas out there, you are dead meat.

Also, by seven-thirty, eight o'clock at night, there's nothing to do there. It was completely boring. Yes, we had chatted in the afternoon, we talked, we walked, you know, had dinner later at seven-thirty or eight, so it's nine, nine-thirty. What do you do?

Someone with a more rural temperament would say, "Well, I sit by the fire, I read a book, I listen to music." [*He starts to laugh again.*] I'd rather put a bullet through my head. I mean, if that's my option, I'd just as soon do that.

I just want to do it in the city. If I'm going to read a book, I'll read in my apartment and I'll listen to music in my apartment. I don't have to be, you know, in the dead black of nowhere.

EL: [*Laughing*] So to go back to Southampton for a moment. There you are on the beach. You go in the house, you go out of the house, and then at some point in that afternoon or evening—

WA: Toward the evening.

EL: —you suddenly say, "Oh, my goodness . . ."

WA: "This is not for me." And the next morning we got up, had breakfast, drove back to town. I called my accountant and said, "Sell the house."

EL: *Really* not for you.

WA: Not for me. [*He shakes his head, then speaks slowly.*] Not. For. Me.

EL: Did you have to change much of the design of the house you used for *Interiors*?

WA: Yes. It was a very pretty house and I thought we made it very, very beautiful. But the owners did not think so. When they came back they were *mortified.* Not that we had done anything wrong; they knew we were going to change it. But they were mortified at how we made it. I thought it was quite beautiful. There were owners of antique stores in town who told us after the picture came out that there was a big run on country antiques, French, English, and American country antiques. Of course, we restored the house to the way it was.

EL: Anyway, the three distinct women and the relationship between them is an interesting way to tell the story.

WA: Yeah, I was trying to make the picture interesting from that point of view. I was trying to show that it was poignant to be full of feelings and not have any ability to express those feelings, what an awful feeling that must be for someone [*Joey, played by Mary Beth Hurt*]. And yet that didn't save the person who was more gifted in the family [*Renata, Diane Keaton's character*]. And the third sister was very superficial and that wasn't the answer to anything [*Flyn, played by Kristin Griffith*]. And the only hope was that there would be some kind of a new life for Mary Beth Hurt, that she dies and gets reborn [*Pearl (Maureen Stapleton), Joey's new stepmother, pulls her from the ocean after she's walked into it in despair on a stormy night and gives her mouth-to-mouth resuscitation*]. I think I could do that film much better now, much better. In fact, I know I could. But I did the best I could at the time.

EL: The other day you said that from what you've learned over the past thirty years that you'd make it less poetic, and that you'd bring in the conflict from the start.

WA: There are a number of ways to approach it. There are a number of wonderful things I failed to exploit. It's a shame because it's a wonderful idea that I just wasn't fully up to. I got some of the juice out of it but nowhere near what it should be.

EL: The E. G. Marshall [*died 1998*] character, the father, is someone who is also rescued, or is trying to be rescued.

WA: Yes, the figures were very vivid. Here was a guy who had lived with this woman, Eve [*played by Geraldine Page, died 1987*], for many years. He had stayed with her loyally because she had been mentally unbalanced and had stayed with her because of the kids, and had put in his time and he was an extremely decent father. Then he reached a point where the kids had moved out and he did not want to have to put his glass down on the coffee table in the exact same place. And he was entitled to that. It was a saintly life he had lived prior to that.

All these characters are good characters and their conflicts are good, but I didn't milk it skillfully enough.

EL: Maureen Stapleton is able to throw off the deaths of her first two husbands as an aside over dinner.

[**ARTHUR** (*Sipping his wine*) Pearl's husband was something of a chef.
PEARL (*Touching his arm*) Hm. He was an amateur chef. Actually he was in the jewelry business. My first husband, may he rest in peace. Adam, my second, was an orthodontist.
RENATA (*Making a face*) How many have you had?
PEARL (*Sipping her drink*) Two. Adam had a massive coronary. Rudy was an alcoholic. (*To Arthur*) Would you like some more gravy?]

Whereas it would have been such anguish for Eve to have described that.

WA: Right. Maureen was full of life and full of vitality. And I think you would be hard put to find Geraldine Page acting better in anything she's ever done than she did in that film. I don't say that because of me; it wasn't my doing. She understood the character.

EL: When she picks up that lamp and says, "I have to point out one thing. This really belongs in the bedroom, because it's too insignificant a piece for in here. The shade is just wrong against all these slick surfaces," her obsessive perfectionism makes me cringe. She's completely believable.

WA: Oh, yeah, I based all these people on people I've experienced in my life, and that is what they do. I may have exaggerated a bit for dramatic purposes, but it was true to life.

Woody was much influenced by the films of Ingmar Bergman when he made *Interiors*, as seen in this shot of the three sisters played by Diane Keaton, Kristin Griffith, and Mary Beth Hurt.

EL: You once told me there is a lot of you in Eve.

WA: People always look for me in the movies, in my characters. For instance, Pauline Kael mentioned that she thought I was in the Mary Beth Hurt character because I'd given Mary Beth these tweed jackets to wear and I wore tweed jackets. I didn't think that at all. In fact, in real life I was extremely lucky compared to Mary Beth's character. I had some kind of talent—it may be minor, but it's some kind of talent to express myself—and Mary Beth Hurt was full of feeling and had no outlet whatsoever. I thought I was closer to Geraldine: a kind of disciplinarian, obsessive, wants everything just right, controlling things, making things perfect; trying to be tasteful and restrained and furnish the room with just the right amount of furniture—that was *her* obsession. I might choose to furnish a room the same way or I might choose to furnish a room by cluttering it, but it's a deliberate effect.

So I saw myself in her and probably imagined myself as emotionally fragile as she was. But I'm not.

EL: You're not going to put your head in the oven like she did.

WA: I did empathize with her a great deal. I did think, Gee, I'm someone who suffers that deeply and through the grace of God or lucky accident, I'm not a candidate for shock therapy. I've managed to avoid it, but *just*.

EL: If you suffer that way, then how do you stay away from the despair that drove her to suicide?

WA: I think I've burned over a low flame of depression my whole lifetime. I haven't had the kind of depression that people call "clinical" or makes you commit suicide. But I have had a kind of low-level depression, like the pilot light's always

Geraldine Page as Eve, the compulsive, controlling mother in *Interiors*. Of all the characters in the film, Woody identifies most with her.

on. Over the years I've worked out a million little strategies to get around it: work-ing strategies and relationship strategies and distraction strategies.

EL: What are the relationship strategies?

WA: I've been able to have some close, supportive friends and I've had a couple of relationships with, for me, some very good women. And I've had a lot of little tricks to distract myself, to keep myself working. My lack of participation in things or my attitude is frequently seen as aloof, when it's not aloof. It's depression. [*He laughs.*] But my inability to participate in some things, my lack of interest in read-ing about myself or reading my reviews, or not caring if my film makes money or not, or caring if the audience likes me or doesn't like me—it often seems like I'm being aloof, but it's not that at all.

When I'm confronted, of course intellectually I say, "Well, I'd rather my film made a lot of money. I'd rather my film was loved by everybody." But you can see in my behavior that I don't do anything to bring that about. I make the films. I never care about their fashionableness, their commerciality, their relevance, their depth, their superficiality. And when they come out I never have a big party and enjoy the opening, although sometimes I'm forced to go and show support.

You know, *Match Point* is going to come out here [*in December 2005*] and I'll go through the motions of going to a premiere in California and a premiere in New York because, you know, DreamWorks paid money for the film and they want a lit-tle cooperation and I'm not an idiot, I'm not a monster. So of course I'll participate. But if they didn't beg me to, there's no way in the world that I would. It's certainly something that *I* wouldn't do.

Scoop, I've already finished and I'm writing the next one and I have hardly any interest in *Scoop* anymore. I'm going to color-correct it and mix it, but as soon as possible I won't lay eyes on it again. Just like *Match Point*, which I *like*.

EL: One of your strategies is to do a film a year because it allows you to invent a world that you can inhabit for that amount of time, that you're happy to go to for nine or ten months.

WA: Yes.

EL: So with *Match Point* well on its way and *Scoop* virtually done, have you now moved your mind and your imagination, if not quite your furniture, into this new one?

WA: Yes, yes. I'll pop into the office tomorrow or the next day to check one last reel of the dupe negative, which the laboratory screwed up on *Match Point*—they had a little problem getting the color right on one reel. So I'll pop in, look at it for ten minutes [*the length of a reel of film*], and say [*snaps fingers*], "Fine."

Then I'll run into the next room and I'll shave a few frames off two scenes in *Scoop,* which is all I want to do at this point, and we'll give it over to sound effects and they'll take a couple of weeks to do all that. And then I'll color-correct it and get it mixed. But I'm home working on something else at this point.

EL: It seems you transfer from a film as easily as you were able to move in and out of the house in Southampton.

WA: Yes, but I want to tell you an interesting thing. Emotionally, I have to wait until the project is basically finished. The physical details that I have to do with *Scoop* now are trivial. I couldn't have begun this picture that I'm writing now, or any picture, while I was emotionally invested in *Scoop,* while I was immersed in it.

EL: Earlier you told me the difference between the physical and the emotional demands of making a film, which you learned firsthand when you made *Zelig* and *A Midsummer Night's Sex Comedy* simultaneously.

WA: Yes. Everybody who anticipated a problem beforehand anticipated it would be a physical problem. But shooting two films at once, from a physical point of view, was in no way a challenge. It was a piece of cake. But I regretted it after I started because I had a tough time pulling out emotionally.

So I could be shooting *A Midsummer Night's Sex Comedy* in the barn where I was shooting on the Rockefeller estate, and we might figure out that this would be a great place for [*production designer*] Mel Bourne to build a little set so I could do a couple of interviews for *Zelig.* It's a wonderful time-saver. I'm right there and you're always looking for those things anyhow. And from a physical point of view, nothing. Gordon Willis and I got up, we put those cameras away, we took the old camera with old lenses and did the shots.

But mentally, I had a tough time washing away one picture and getting into the next one.

EL: It seems from what you say that the moment you finish whichever film you've spent the past year on and have decided on the next one, it's almost instantaneous transferal, like the magician's Chinese box in *Oedipus Wrecks* or *Scoop.*

WA: Yes, I'm on to the next one. The pleasure is in the doing. I'm having fun now. I get up in the morning and get to my script.

EL: When you're living in that world, it's great.

WA: Yes, and it will be fun—and this varies from film to film—it is fun for a period of time. When I was doing *Bullets over Broadway* or *Radio Days,* I woke up every morning and was with these characters in costume all day long and they were colorful and they were singing songs and acting amusingly.

When I was doing *Match Point,* I'd wake up in the morning and there were Jonathan Rhys-Meyers and the beautiful Scarlett Johansson, and I spent time with them all day long and we joked and we tried to make things very serious when there was a serious scene and sometimes we laughed very hard after it was over or before we did it because of the tension of doing it or the embarrassment of doing it or just the fun we were having, the malicious fun we're having pretending to be so heavy-handed.

I do that for a period of time and I take the footage back and I sit down with my editor in the cutting room and I order my tuna fish sandwich and the thing takes shape and it's very pleasurable. It's like doing the house in Southampton. It becomes an aesthetic and pleasurable thing. And then it reaches a point where it's basically finished. All you need is a couple of decisions here and there. And then [*he snaps his fingers*] you put it out and the people like it or they don't like it. And I'd just as soon not hear about it. I made the movie and it's over with. It comes from my depressive personality not to celebrate a success or get a spear through the heart if a picture fails.

Years ago when *Manhattan* opened in New York—it was much heralded before it opened—I did not go to the premiere at the Ziegfeld Theater and the big party at the Whitney [*Museum of American Art*] after, I got on a plane and went to Paris a few days before. So people think, He doesn't care, or He's too aloof, or He's snooty or arrogant, but as I said, that's not it. It's not arrogance, it's more like joylessness. It doesn't thrill me. It just doesn't really mean anything. [*He smiles.*] But Paris thrilled me.

I'm trying to explain how I feel and I can see why it gets misunderstood: There's no honor that a human being can give me that would mean anything to me. For me to get something that means something to me would require a different universe. [*He gives a small laugh.*] I know this is seen as either eccentricity or aloofness or "he thinks he's above it all." But I'm not above it. I'm either below it or at least to the side of it [*laughs harder*].

EL: Why is that?

WA: Because awards are dust gatherers; they don't change your life, they don't affect your health positively or your longevity or your emotional happiness. The places that you want fixed in your life or helped, the adjustment and comfort you need, are not addressed by the greatest honors in the world.

So the entire world standing at the grave of Shakespeare and singing his praises and making him an institution larger than life on the planet doesn't mean a thing to the Bard. And it wouldn't have meant a thing if he was alive and at the opening of *Hamlet* [*he begins to laugh*] and had a toothache [*laughing hard now*].

You have a small amount of comfort from science and technology. It obviously doesn't have all the answers, but it has a couple of things that help. It does help to be able get the Salk vaccine and sunblock. But all the rest—the philosophers, the scientists, the other stuff—is all . . . [*He trails off.*]

[*His comments remind me of something he said to me in the late 1980s, while film-ing* Crimes and Misdemeanors: *"Why not opt for a sensual life instead of a life of grueling work? When you're at heaven's gate, the guy who has spent all his time chasing and catching women and has a sybaritic life gets in, and you get in, too. The only reason I can think of not to is, it's another form of denial of death. You delude yourself that there's a reason to lead a meaningful life, a productive life of work and struggle and perfection of one's profession or art. But the truth is, you could be spending that time indulging yourself—assuming you can afford it—because you both wind up in the same place.*

"If I don't like something, it doesn't matter how many awards it's won. It's impor-tant to keep your own criteria and not defer to the trends of the marketplace.

"I hope that somewhere along the line it will be perceived that I'm not really a personal malcontent, or that my ambition or my pretensions—which I freely admit to—are not to gain power. I only want to make something that will entertain people, and I'm stretching myself to do it." But he is not really bothered if audiences aren't entertained: "In fact, I'm used to it."]

EL: I'm still curious. Once you start to write, it's fun because you've thought the story through and blocked it out in your mind before you begin to write it down. The hard part really is the thinking through it. So when you were transitioning from *Scoop* to this new one—as recently as a couple of weeks ago you said you had three choices of what to write, depending on where you were going to shoot. You had a Barcelona story, a London story, and a Paris story—were you thinking through each of these during that time?

WA: Yes, I think in the cracks all the time. I never stop. I don't need peace and quiet to think. I can be in there playing pick-up-sticks with my kids and participat-ing with them fully and kissing them, but trying to work out a problem in my mind at the same time.

When it comes time to write, I need some space. But when I sit down to eat, the mind is always working. I enjoy the work. I get into bed at night, I watch the end of the basketball game, I'm exhausted and I can hardly turn off the light, and in the minute or minute and a half it takes to go out [*laughs*], I think about the story. [*He pauses as he thinks of an exception.*] Never during sex, though—I'm not *that* dedi-cated.

EL: And you remember it. Often people lose those last thoughts.

WA: [*Emphatically*] Oh, I remember it.

I remember many years ago when I would read books on playwriting. Danny Simon advised me to read some, and I read some others on my own. And I read one, I believe it was written by John Van Druten, who wrote *Bell Book and Candle* and that other wonderful play *The Voice of the Turtle* [*as well as* Cabaret]. And he was talking about how you didn't have to write down ideas—he wasn't talking about the kind of writing where you keep a notebook and six years later you refer to it—because if they're real, they stay with you. And I found that to be absolutely true. I don't work off an outline. So when I go to sleep at night and I get an idea, I remember it.

I liked *The Voice of the Turtle* very much. [*The film, directed by Irving Rapper, is the story of Bill, a soldier in New York on a weekend pass. On Friday he goes to Sally's apartment to pick up her friend and his date, Olive, who suddenly thinks she has a better offer and concocts an excuse to ditch him. Sally, an aspiring actress, is nursing a broken heart but goes with stranded Bill to the French restaurant next door. Afterward it's pouring rain and she innocently tells him to sleep on the couch, which he does, but only with restraint on both their parts. (The play and film were considered daring and sophisticated for their time.) By Sunday night, their future together in the uncertain post–World War II world is set. The film was released in 1947; Woody turned twelve that December.*] That was the kind of thing I grew up on, that kind of sophisticated comedy. I don't consider it a great play by any means, but it is the kind of thing that molded my image of the theater and of New York, of a kind of Upper East Side apartment that had a restaurant downstairs that you'd go to right near it, come back upstairs, and sophisticated women wanting to be actresses in this case and a guy who was on leave from the army, and who was going to bed with whom. It just played right into my fantasy of what life in New York would be. I was impressed with it because Eve Arden was in it and I always loved Eve Arden.

EL: Me too. I was a big fan of hers growing up. It was wonderful to see her every week on *Our Miss Brooks*.

WA: Yeah, we all loved her. You're younger, so you remember her from that.

I came this close to using her [*his thumb and forefinger are nearly touching*]. I hired her. She came to New York for costume fittings. She was playing the Zoe Caldwell part in *Purple Rose* [*the Countess in the eponymous black-and-white film within the film*]. At that time I was thinking, My God, I'm working with *Van Johnson* and *Eve Arden*! Whoever thought? I'm playing the outfield with Joe DiMaggio and Babe Ruth! [*Laughs, then pauses.*] But then her husband died and she pulled out and I was very fortunate to get Zoe Caldwell.

EL: Not to belabor the point, but were you thinking of all three ideas at once, not knowing which you were going to do?

WA: I had three ideas that I knew upon reflection would prove developable, and I was anxious to get to work on one of them. I conferred with my sister [*Letty Aronson, who now produces his films*] and she said, "I really think we should proceed thinking it's going to be London even though it isn't definite at the moment; that seems to be the high probability."

EL: And how long from then, when you started to put your mind to it, were you able to begin writing? It sounds like within a couple of weeks.

WA: Yeah, but with obsessive thinking. That is the worst part. That is when I get all my ailments and I get my acid reflux and I get my physical exhaustion. Writing is a joy, but waking up in the morning when the structure's not coming is a horrible thing. You get up and you have breakfast and you know you are going to go back into your room and start thinking about where this goes. It's like writing a symphony. The theme begins here but it's going to resonate three movements later, and if *this* is wrong, *that* is going to be terrible.

It's funny: in a chess game I can't see [*laughing*] one move ahead, you know? But when I'm writing a script—and it can be a fairly complicated one with lots of characters—I can see far ahead and work out my problems. Now, I don't always get it right on the first draft, and I have to make readjustments early in the script because I haven't gotten to the later parts of the script gracefully. That is okay. Until then, it's very, very unpleasant. And the day that I start to write is exhilarating for me. I can't explain it. I have so much energy; I'm almost manic in my conversation. I can just bounce along the street and walk places fast, do things like I'm twenty years old.

EL: It seems this is one of the few times that you spring out of that narrow emotional band you operate in.

WA: Yeah, because most of the writer's work is tough. Even my little kids, they're five years old now and six, they say [*he uses a childish voice*], "Daddy's going inside to think."

And I say, "When you go to the circus, what am I going to do?"

[*He uses the childish voice again.*] "You're going to *think.*"

And they come into the room and there I am on the bed like this [*mimes lying on his side and staring into space*] and I'm in there thinking. And then I go eat lunch, and I'm thinking at lunch. Then I go back in there.

EL: No paper or pencil?

WA: No paper or pencil, no.

EL: How's Soon-Yi with this? Did she quickly learn to adapt to it?

WA: She just thinks it's one of the mysteries of how I work, that lots of my effort goes into thinking. She's always amazed because she thinks I'm such a fast writer. But she makes the same mistake that most people make. They think the writing is the writing. As Marshall Brickman pointed out, the *thinking* is the writing; the writing is the writing down. If nothing comes after a month, I say to myself, This idea was not meant to be.

Sometimes I have obsessional problems about two ideas where I write two weeks on one and find it tedious and then am pulled to the other and find that the same. The hard part is getting the ideas that work and getting them in order.

EL: As a writer, I admire how easily you're able to move into the new house that holds the next idea.

WA: Yeah, because I'm through with the last one and it doesn't hold my interest anymore. When I screened *Scoop* with you the other day, fifteen minutes in I thought, Ach, am I going to have to sit through this thing *again*? I have to sit through it when I mix it, and when I color-correct it, and do the DVD, and the dupe negative, and after all that, I don't want to see it again. And I don't.

EL: Let me return you to *Interiors* because you said you have friends and mental tricks you play to keep you from falling into despair, but not so terminal as happens with the Geraldine Page character.

WA: Yeah. I have my various distractions. I lose myself in sports; I do exercise every day. My sense of discipline in general—to *practice* the clarinet, to *get* on the treadmill, to *get* in the room and write—all that stuff helps. It helps militate against giving oneself over to the horrid gloom of reality.

EL: When you talked of *The Voice of the Turtle,* there you were in Brooklyn not liking school, not reading that much. It's interesting that this caught you and grabbed your attention.

WA: The fantasy of sophistication gripped me early. Why, I can't tell you. When I was a very young kid, it was not the pirate pictures I liked or the cowboy pictures, which *thrilled* my friends. I fell asleep at them. What turned me on at the *youngest* age was when the credits finished and the camera panned the skyline of New York. I imagined people in these Park Avenue and Fifth Avenue houses, involved in their lives, with their butlers and their valets and their breakfast in bed, dressing for dinner and going to nightclubs and coming back late at night. Supper clubs, cocktails, piano bars. That world for some reason, I don't know what it is, clicked in for me, and that's what interested me.

EL: When you were talking with your neighborhood friends, were they puzzled or amazed that you were reading plays like *The Voice of the Turtle*?

WA: Well, teachers were amazed in school because my references were sophisticated references. I wasn't literate, but my references were witty. What I made jokes about at the youngest ages, before I really knew what I was talking about, were Freud and martinis, things like that, because I was emulating the witty patois of films that I saw, who I wanted to be, what I identified with.

It's possible that I have a built-in gene for wit—those pictures I'm describing have a certain amount of wit in them. But they are sophisticated, they are divorce comedies, they are comedies of popping champagne corks and witty remarks. And there is something about that that enticed me as a really young person.

I always thought my friends were square as could be. I mean, I liked them and we did stuff, and I'm not saying I didn't go to see *King Kong*. I liked the Marx Brothers or Chaplin, but what I got really interested in were pictures like—this preceded me by a little—*My Man Godfrey* [1936]. Pictures at a later date that would have been mother's milk to me as a child are *Unfaithfully Yours* [1948] or *The Philadelphia Story* [1940].

I still love them. If I'm watching television and I switch to a channel and there are people entering a nightclub, I'm hooked. I've had Santo [*Loquasto*] re-create that for me several times.

February 2006

EL: How are you doing on the new script, the one for London this summer?

WA: Let me explain. This is a bit complicated. I'm not a good writer, but fortunately I'm a robotic writer. So I finished mixing and all the other things on *Scoop* and my situation was, I was going to do a film for London this year and Barcelona next year. So I sat down and wrote a film for London. And at the last minute, there was a switch to Paris. The London film did not firm up right, my management did not want to get involved with some of the financing. So the London thing came apart at the last second, and I mean the *last second*. I had written the script and completely rewritten it meticulously because I had made a big change in the rewrite; I had worked like a Trojan on it.

Three days later, it fell through. Then suddenly a very good situation in Paris came along. The film could be made from June to August, so it would work for the kids and give the family a new venue to explore. The only thing missing was a script. This was the beginning of February and it didn't leave much time. It had to be conceived, written, budgeted, cast, and so on. I'm down to the last two pages now. Tomorrow I'll finish it. Then I'll have a little grace period. I'll type it this week. Then I can fondle it for a week or ten days before I give it in. But it was quite a little race to the finish line.

EL: Did you use the Paris story you referred to earlier?

WA: Yes, but there is a difference between having the story and a script. Even though you have the basic idea, it takes a while to get it all thought out. The film may turn out to be terrible, but if it is, it's not because I had to write it in a hurry.

EL: Is it a drama or a comedy?

WA: It's a romance.

EL: Are you in it?

WA: No, it's too much of a strain on me in the writing stage. I can only write a certain kind of film when I'm in it. When I sat down to write *Match Point*, it was refreshing. I never had to think, What's the part for me? I just wrote scene after scene.

EL: Some of the themes of *Match Point* are in *Crimes and Misdemeanors*, in which there *is* a Woody Allen character. How did the writing of these two scripts differ, having you in one and not the other?

WA: In *Crimes*, nobody had any interest in my aspirations [*those of Cliff, the obscure documentary filmmaker*]; they were only interested in success. My part of the picture was for comic relief. The real story of *Crimes and Misdemeanors* is Martin Landau's.

EL: Who gets away with murder.

WA: There were a lot of people who felt that Marty was haunted and he had to keep telling the story like the Ancient Mariner. But that was not it *at all*. He was in no way haunted. He was just fine. He realized that in a godless universe you can get away with it and it doesn't bother him.

EL: How does *Crimes and Misdemeanors* stand in your estimation?

WA: It was okay, but it was a little too mechanical for me. I think I was working too hard, whereas *Match Point* just flowed organically. I just happened to have the right characters in the right place at the right time.

EL: You also were fourteen years ahead in terms of experience. When you were writing *Match Point* were you thinking, I've dealt with this subject somewhat before in *Crimes and Misdemeanors* but I have these other things I want to say?

WA: No, I was saying that I want to obey the story and if you obey the needs of the creation of the piece of fiction, the meaning reveals itself. And for me, naturally, it's going to reveal itself in a particular way. Years ago Paddy Chayefsky said to me, "When a movie is failing or a play is failing"—he put it so brilliantly—"cut out the wisdom." [*He laughs.*] Marshall Brickman said it a different way—I told you this before—but just as cogently, just as insightful: "The message of the film can't be in the dialogue." And this is a truth that's hard to live by because the temptation is to occasionally take a moment and philosophize and put in your wisdom, put in your meaning. I did that in *Match Point* to a certain degree—they're sitting around the table and they're talking about faith being the path of least resistance. But the truth of the matter is, if the meaning doesn't come across in the action, you have nothing going for you. It doesn't work. You can't just have guys sitting around making hopefully wise insights or clever remarks because while they're saying these things the audience is not digesting them the way the author intends—"Hey, did you just hear that Shavian epigram?" They're looking at it as the dialogue of characters in a certain situation: "He's saying this because she's thinking this and he wants to get on her good side. . . ." They're watching the *action* of the story. When you lose sight of that, and we all do—I certainly do—you think you're making your point, you think you're infusing your piece with wisdom, but you're committing suicide. You're just militating against the audience's enjoyment.

EL: But *Match Point* fits into a long-standing theme of yours, that in a godless universe the only check you have on yourself is your own morality. No one else is going to punish you if you're not caught.

WA: Interestingly, I read an article someone sent me that a Catholic priest wrote about the movie. It was very nice, but he made a wrong assumption. The assumption was: if, as I say, life is meaningless and chaos and random, then anything goes and nothing has any meaning and one action is as good as the next. And it immediately leads someone with a religious agenda to the conclusion, Well, you can just murder people and get away with it if that's what you want to do. But that's a false conclusion. What I'm really saying—and it's not hidden or esoteric, it's just clear as a bell—is that we have to accept that the universe is godless and life is meaningless, often a terrible and brutal experience with no hope, and that love relationships are very, very hard, and that we still need to find a way to not only cope but lead a decent and moral life.

People jump to the conclusion that what I'm saying is that anything goes, but actually I'm asking the question: given the worst, how do we carry on, or even why should we choose to carry on? Of course, we don't choose—the choice is hardwired into us. The blood chooses to live. [*Laughs.*] Please note as I pontificate here, you're interviewing a guy with a deficient denial mechanism. Anyhow, religious people don't want to acknowledge the reality that contradicts their fairy tale. And if it is a godless universe [*he chuckles*], they're out of business. The cash flow stops.

Now, there are plenty of people who choose to lead their lives in a completely self-centered, homicidal way. They feel, Since nothing means anything and I can get away with murder, I'm going to. But one can also make the choice that you're alive and other people are alive and you're in a lifeboat with them and you've got to try and make it as decent as you can for yourself and everybody. And it would seem to me this is so much more moral and even much more "Christian." If you acknowledge the awful truth of human existence and choose to be a decent human being in the face of it rather than lie to yourself that there's going to be some heavenly reward or some punishment, it seems to me more noble. If there is a reward or a punishment or a payoff somehow and you act well, then you're acting well not out of such noble motives, the same so-called Christian motives. It's like the suicide bombers who allegedly act out of noble religious or national motives when in fact their families get a financial payoff, revel in a heroic legacy—not to mention the promise of virgins for the perpetrators, although why anyone would want a group of virgins rather than one highly experienced woman is beyond me.

Anyhow, I disagreed with what the Catholic priest wrote, but I didn't engage him. He was very nice; this was not a hostile thing he was writing. He was imputing to me a point of view and was trying to refute it. But he was refuting a point of view that I do not hold with what I feel is a preconceived religious agenda—and

Harry Block has muddled his relationships with almost every living person in his life, but his characters gather to honor him in *Deconstructing Harry.*

the film can't honestly be read to imply I'm saying anything goes and that's fine with me.

I saw another piece written by a priest-philosopher at St. John's University, who thought the film was perhaps the most [*laughs*] atheistic film ever made. But he was very nice, very complimentary. His point of view was more lenient toward me because he felt that over the years the fact that I constantly espouse an atheistic and hopeless and godless and meaningless universe means I am saying that the absence of God in the universe matters. And I feel that he's right, I *am* saying that it matters. I said that explicitly in *Crimes and Misdemeanors.* To me it's a damn shame that the universe doesn't have any God or meaning, and yet only when you can accept that can you then go on to lead what these people call a Christian life—that is, a decent, moral life. You can only lead it if you acknowledge what you're up against to begin with and shuck off all the fairy tales that lead you to make choices in life that you're making not really for moral reasons but for taking down a big score in the afterlife.

So the film inspired a lot of talk in that area and I'm glad. I'm glad it wasn't regarded just as a suspense murder mystery, which, mind you, I'm not knocking. I love those as much as or more than anybody as a movie viewer. But I had hoped to use *Match Point* to at least make one or two points that are my personal philosophy and I feel I was able to do that.

EL: What do you think happens with Jonathan Rhys-Meyers [*who murders his pregnant lover, played by Scarlett Johansson, and her elderly neighbor*]? The same as with Martin Landau?

WA: Yeah. I think he's in a situation that he's not delighted with. He's married to a woman he's not passionate about. He's a son-in-law who likes the easy life he's married into but is claustrophobic working in the office. His wife is already saying to him that she wants another child.

He has no thoughts about the crime. He's got what he wanted and he's paid the price for that. It's a shame that that's what he wanted. I can see down the line that he won't be content in that marriage and maybe he'll be on such a good financial footing that he'll leave her.

EL: You've invented so many characters now. Do they stay with you? Do they come visit you? Do you think of them? When you sit down to write, do you think, I've written this guy, I have to write somebody else?

WA: Yeah, that happens sometimes. It's not a pleasurable thing. I'll get an idea and realize I'm redoing something I've done before and it's going to be repetitious. Sometimes I don't realize it at the time; sometimes I'm blinded and I don't see it until the movie comes out and someone else points it out to me.

EL: In *Deconstructing Harry* there's the scene at the end where all his characters lovingly come to honor him. Has that ever happened to you? I don't want to make this too literal, but have you ever had a visitation from a delegation of your characters?

WA: No, because I don't see the films, I forget them. My characters are full of screwups. I think about, you know, Chekhov's stuff and Bergman's stuff and Tennessee Williams's stuff, and that gives me pleasure; other people's movies and plays. But I don't think about my stuff. These pictures we're talking about, I haven't seen some in thirty years. I remember incidents in the making but I don't remember dialogue from them or scenes or characters.

EL: The characters and performances in *Shadows and Fog* were terrific. [*The story is both a farce and a metaphor. An inept group of vigilantes drafts Woody's cowardly clerk to join in the hunt for a vicious killer, who turns out to be Death. The film takes place at night and, as Woody says, "once you get out in the night, there is a sense that civilization is gone . . . the city is just a superimposed man-made convention, a function of one's own inner state."*]

WA: Oh, the people are great. I mean, I think I did a good job directing it, and Santo's [*Loquasto*] sets are beautiful. But the picture is in the writing, and people weren't interested in the story. You know when you're doing a black-and-white picture that takes place in a European city at night in the twenties, you're not going to make big bucks. Nobody liked the picture.

EL: You told me that Eric Pleskow of Orion looked like he had been hit by a mallet after he saw it.

In *Match Point*, Chris (Jonathan Rhys-Meyers) has a wealthy and loving wife but the price he paid was murder.

WA: He was always trying to put a nice face on things and was always a gentleman, but you could tell by the [*laughs*] tremolo in his voice that he was disappointed.

EL: It was shot so well. Was there any pleasure for you in that?

WA: Carlo [*Di Palma, the cinematographer*] won an award for it in Italy. It just looked great. There was pleasure in the way it was photographed, and in making it. Again, I make these films to amuse myself, or should I say to distract myself. I wanted to see what it would be like making a film all on a set, outdoors being indoors. And setting it during one night and having all these characters and this old European quality to it. The hope always is that others will enjoy it when I'm finished. Like *Everyone Says I Love You*. It fulfilled that desire that keeps me working, that keeps me in the film business. I do all my films for my own personal reasons, and I hope that people will like them and I'm always gratified when I hear they do. But if they don't, there's nothing I can do about that because I don't set out to make them for approval—I like approval, but I don't make them for approval.

EL: It seems to me that your films hold up. They're not of a time.

WA: *I'm* not of a time. That also costs me. I've never used the music of the time and I've never written about subjects that were on the minds of people at the time. *Match Point* was a subject that has no time sense to it. It's about luck. And if it's a good picture, it ought to be good a hundred years from now. And if it's not, it won't hold up. Pictures like *Munich, Brokeback Mountain* [*both recently released*] are pictures that very much reflect problems and attitudes of a time. And in a certain sense that is very important and enjoyable for an audience. I can see why they like that because I like it, too. They're very well made films and they reflect problems that are on the minds of people. Whereas the problems my movies reflect could by chance be on the minds of people or not, but they never are social or political issues. They're always psychological issues or romantic issues or existential issues. So no matter how events change they'll always be what they were. If it's a bad picture, it will always seem a bad picture. And if it's a good picture, it won't seem dated. What's wrong with any picture of mine is not that it's been affected by time. It will always be [*starts to laugh*] that they were no good then and they're no good now.

EL: Did you write *Deconstructing Harry* pretty easily? [*See page 51.*]

WA: It was episodic, and it was easier to write episodic than to construct something tightly. Tight construction requires real craftsmanship. I can do it, but it's more sweat and it takes more time. When you're writing episodically, you know, Harry's bouncing down the road and I'm free to involve him in whatever incidents I want.

EL: It's actually a very sweet movie.

WA: I think that picture was well received. I don't know if it made any money, but I think it was nicely received. [*Its U.S. box office gross was around $11 million, a little more than half the budget, but with foreign rights, TV, and DVD sales, it probably broke even or made a bit.*]

EL: Does it rank highly in your regard?

WA: No, not high, but I didn't dislike it.

EL: *Sweet and Lowdown* is a much modified version of *The Jazz Baby*, which you wrote about thirty years ago but didn't film. [*Sean Penn is Emmet Ray, an itinerant jazz guitarist with more than a passing resemblance to Django Reinhardt, whose playing is heavenly but whose sweet and low-down personality is warped by self-absorption. "Such is the ego of genius," a slumming socialite (Uma Thurman) who takes up with him notes. "Must get used to it." The best woman in Emmet's life is the mute and long-suffering Hattie (Samantha Morton), whom he of course loses. The music is also a star of the film and is a jazz lover's delight.*]

WA: Right. I was going to play in *The Jazz Baby*, and so it would have been lighter. I would have brought a lighter sensibility. Thank God I didn't play it because it's much, much better the way Sean did it. Sean is a billion times the actor

I am and a hundred times deeper and more complex and more interesting. He made the picture an interesting story. I would have made it amusing in spots, but he infused it with some impact.

EL: Did you see him in the part as you wrote it?

WA: No, not at all. I wrote it and wondered who to get. I had reservations about working with Sean because he had a reputation for being temperamental and difficult. [*Casting director*] Juliet [*Taylor*] and I both agreed that he's a fabulous actor and there was no question that he would do wonders for the part. Then I checked up on him and the last couple of people who worked with him said he's not a bad guy. So I met him—I'd met him before but briefly—and I found him very, very nice, and as so often happens, what you hear about someone doesn't bear out. I had a great experience with him. He was creative, he contributed to the part. When he came up with ideas, if I was unresponsive to them for any reason—and not always, most of the time they were good ideas—he didn't push the point. When I came up with ideas he was always ready to try them. I could criticize him without him having any insecurity at all. But again, when I direct great actors or actresses, I rarely have to say anything.

Here was a guy who never played the guitar and we gave him some lessons and I didn't have to cut away when he played. I could go right to his hands.

EL: Had you seen Samantha Morton before? [*As Hattie, Emmet's mute girlfriend, she steals the movie.*]

WA: Juliet showed me some tapes and I said, "I think that girl is the one we should follow up on." We brought her into the cutting room and she was a delight.

Samantha Morton as Hattie, the mute, mistreated girlfriend of Emmet Ray (Sean Penn) in *Sweet and Lowdown*.

I feel good about that picture. Musicians have told me that's how it was. Guys would get in their cars and go across the country and have no money and play a job. They'd play the clubs and be invited to parties afterward. I feel I captured that with some reasonable truth. The picture looked good, and the relationship between Sean and the mute girl was an interesting one, I thought.

EL: It took thirty years to get it made. Was it an idea you thought of a lot during that time, or did you go years without thinking of it?

WA: There was nothing burning about it, but I always knew it was a good idea. I always wanted to do something about a self-centered, egotistical, highly neurotic genius guitar player.

EL: Was Hattie always meant to be mute?

WA: At first I thought of making her deaf because I think it is ironic that he could play so beautifully and she couldn't hear it. But there were too many problems.

The next day we meet again. Yesterday Woody said he was two pages from the end of his new script [Cassandra's Dream], *and I ask the obvious question.*

EL: So did you finish the script?

WA: Yes. Now I have to type it up and fondle it. It will take me about three days on and off, listening to jazz, then I'll give myself a day's rest and start to nurture it [*he moves his hands as if molding clay*]. It's much, much easier to finesse it than starting with a blank page. Going from zero to this is the hard part.

November 2006

Cassandra's Dream *is edited, and Woody, pleased with the outcome, has screened it two or three times for friends to get their opinion. It is the story of two brothers (Colin Farrell and Ewan McGregor), one a London garage mechanic and compulsive gambler playing for bigger and bigger stakes, the other trying to avoid the trap of spending his life working in his father's grungy restaurant by investing in a get-rich-quick hotel scheme in California. They both love sailing and have put what little money they have toward a boat,* Cassandra's Dream. *But Farrell's winning streak stops and he is in deep debt. The brothers hope that their wealthy uncle (Tom Wilkinson) will loan them the money to pay off the loan sharks and invest in the hotel scheme. When they approach the uncle, he agrees to help, then surprises them by saying he needs something from them. An associate is going to testify against him in an embezzlement investigation, and slowly the boys realize to their horror that their uncle wants them to commit a murder. Eventually they do kill the witness and are not suspects. But Farrell's conscience drives him to distraction and he says he is going to turn himself in. McGregor sees their dreams vanishing and persuades his brother to spend a day sailing, like they did in more innocent days. McGregor intends to get Farrell drunk and then give him a drug overdose, but he cannot bring himself to do it. During an onboard scuffle Farrell accidentally kills McGregor and then, in sorrow, himself.*

EL: You now have a second drama you're satisfied with. Has this built on the confidence you gained from *Match Point*?

WA: Yes. I feel that I could do dramatic films now with the same confidence that I had when I was rattling off comic films, and I feel people will now accept them. I mean, *Match Point* made more money than any film I've done in my life. So I'll probably do a certain amount of them.

EL: Is *Cassandra's Dream* an idea you've had for a while?

WA: I had written a play for the Atlantic Theater [*in New York*] and one of its aspects was a guy was waiting for his uncle to come. He had worked for him and wanted to borrow some money. There was the same kind of dynamic that his uncle was coming and a lot was riding, though in the case of the play he had quit working for the uncle and had had a bad experience because they were both in love with the same woman and the uncle wound up marrying her.

Then it occurred to me, what if the uncle came and beat him to the punch and *he* needed something, he was the one in trouble? You think someone can help you, and they come and say, "Guess what? I've got to talk with you. I'm really in trouble." And the story grew out of that. I wrote the play four or five years ago. I also had the mother who idolized her brother, the boys' rich uncle.

EL: What made you decide to do it as a film?

WA: As a play, you do get the moment where there is the reversal and it's the uncle who needs something. But you can't show all the action onstage. The guy had to go after the person causing the uncle problems and kill him, and then gradually it developed into two brothers who need help.

EL: Did you have the title *Cassandra's Dream* from the start?

WA: That emerged as I was doing it. I'm *shocked* by the number of people who say to me, "Who's Cassandra?" I'm not talking about submentals but well-read, bright, sophisticated, college-educated people.

EL. There are several twists in the script. Were they all there, or did some come as you rewrote or during shooting?

WA: It was a good idea and a good script. It's harder to get a good script than it is to execute it. I usually know where I'm going and I write the whole thing out. Then when I'm rewriting, things occur to me that get embellished. For example, when they go to kill him at his house and they're waiting in his apartment, that was not in the original. Then I got the idea to be in his apartment, and then for someone to come home with him and screw up their being able to kill him. Then I wanted a spectacular climax. One idea we all worked on was for the guy to go back to Brighton to visit his mother. He takes a walk on the boardwalk that gives me a visual of Brighton at night, which I don't have in the film; it's only in daylight. Then he gets into that amusement park with the thrill ride that turns upside down on the track and the brothers get in the car behind him and while he's upside down, they shoot him in the back of the head.

But it was a little too Hollywood for me. I wanted the story to be more realistic. For someone who had never committed a murder, this was pretty acrobatic. Then when the cost of it came in, it was prohibitive—it meant taking the pier over at night and making a lot of walking following shots—and I breathed a sigh of relief because I was already thinking to myself, I should not have gone here. This is not consistent with the tone that I want in this movie. Economics intervened to save me, short of my saying, "I made a fool of myself, this is not a great idea." Also, I couldn't have shot the murder live because everything's moving too fast. We'd have had to use some process. If Steven Spielberg or George Lucas wanted to do this, they could make it look like a trillion dollars and make it seem like it happened. I couldn't afford to do that.

So the office told me, "We know this is going to break your heart, but we can't do it." But they didn't break my heart. I said, "Okay, I'll live with it," but [*laughs*] when I got outside I flattened against the door and said, "Thank God, you saved me from making a fool of myself."

EL: I found myself looking away from the screen during the murder scene in *Cassandra's Dream* just as I did in *Match Point,* because the moments are so intense.

WA: I think that's because in both pictures I take the time to develop their characters, their parents, their family, their feelings, so it isn't like a genre picture where the plot itself is the star of the picture and the characters are cardboard cutouts.

You want these things to be about people and that's what I always feel makes it interesting. Even in *Manhattan Murder Mystery*, I wanted very much to show Keaton and I coming back from the hockey game, like everybody else on a Saturday night in New York coming back from an event. They get the papers, they get lox and bagels, they go up in the elevator, they meet a neighbor. It's happening to real people.

That's what was wonderful about *Bonnie and Clyde.* They [*director Arthur Penn and writers David Newman and Robert Benton*] took the time to develop the characters—their needs, their love life, their aspirations—so when things were happening to them, you were involved.

I didn't want to see the murder in *Cassandra's Dream.* I notice that's a theme of my movies going all the way back, and it's not conscious. I always have my sex off camera, and I always have my real violence off camera. It's not that I can't do violence, because in my first picture, *Take the Money and Run*, I got machine-gunned and I fell on the floor and I let my leg spastically twitch the way Ingemar Johansson's did when he was knocked out [*by Floyd Patterson in 1960, in their second heavyweight title bout*]. It was so real. But for some reason, unconsciously I eschew it. In *Manhattan Murder Mystery* you never see the dead woman, she's behind something. In *Match Point* you don't see the shootings. The same in *Crimes and Misdemeanors.* And in this, you hear the shooting but the camera goes off behind the hedge [*on Cheyne Walk, by the Chelsea Embankment*]. I don't know why. I'm not ashamed of it, I'm not shy about it, I have no problem with it.

Someone else doing *Crimes and Misdemeanors* could have a brilliant murder scene. Alfred Hitchcock or Martin Scorsese—a guy knocks on the door holding flowers and she answers it and what ensues is a minute and a half of brilliant cinema. The only explanation I can give is that for me, because I'm more writer than anything, all that stuff becomes material for me to make my points on, to talk about, to philosophize over. I'm not interested in the killing itself. The killing takes place

The ever-hopeful small-time crook Virgil Starkwell, back in prison at the end of *Take the Money and Run.* In an earlier incarceration he had nearly escaped using a fake gun carved from a bar of soap, but rain turned it to bubbles just before he was free.

so guys can talk about guilt and God. In a picture as trivial as *Manhattan Murder Mystery,* it takes place to give me and Keaton a chance to pop off the jokes, whereas in *Psycho,* Hitchcock, who could have not shown that murder or done it in some discreet way, instead showed it in an iconically beautiful way.

EL: How long did you leave in the footage of you being machine-gunned?

WA: I had it in through a number of screenings. It led to my trick ending where you think I'm dead and Janet Margolin and our kid come out to the cemetery and they say a few words. Then the camera was on her feet as she turns and walks away and then you hear, "Psst, psst," and you see her feet turn around and walk back. I had a good dramatic instinct but insufficient experience to know how to utilize it. But my instincts were in the right place, and later I would use them more wisely.

It was an attempt at a theatrical ending, but the audience was not ready for me to be machine-gunned. I mean, I was soaked in blood. A. D. Flowers, who did the effects for *The Godfather,* put the squibs all over me.

So I floundered around for an ending and had six million tries and finally tagged on what I could to float the picture.

[*Early in the film, Virgil tries to escape from prison by holding a guard hostage with a gun he has fashioned from soap and colored with shoe polish. He marches the guard to the gates and is nearly out, but it is a rainy night and at the last moment the guard sees that the gun has turned to bubbles. At the end, Virgil is sentenced to eight hundred years in federal prison but at the trial tells his lawyer confidently that with good behavior he can cut his sentence in half. The film closes with him being interviewed in prison as part of the continuing documentary, airily avowing that "crime definitely pays. It's a great job and you're your own boss and you travel a lot."*

"How do you manage to spend your time in prison?" he is asked. "Do you have any hobbies?"

"I do," he says. "I've been doing a lot of stuff in shop. I'm very skilled with my hands." He produces another soap gun and asks, "Do you know if it's raining out-side?"]

WA: I hadn't earned my dramatic ending with the picture.

3

CASTING, ACTORS, AND ACTING

February 1973

Preproduction on Sleeper *(see page 1) is under way. Like most of us if given a choice, Woody prefers to work with people he knows and trusts, and to that end he is building a more or less permanent crew and group of principal actors. He makes every major decision and many of the smaller ones, but his comments on the aspects of planning are kept to a minimum. Part of his reticence is shyness, part because he simply does not like to have much to do with most people (a feeling that will not change much over the years). Though he is not overtly rude, his silence and detachment can be disconcerting. He does not recall ever interviewing alone someone up for a spot in the crew or cast, "because I find it hard to encounter a person. I can't really learn about them if I do it alone because my head is swimming at the time," so a colleague generally asks questions while Woody sits quietly and listens. (Over time he will become more relaxed but still a bit removed.)*

He is looking for an actor to play the Leader, a character whose picture abounds in the film but who has no lines. Woody is in his bungalow on the lot of the old Culver City Studios in Los Angeles, where Gone with the Wind *and* Duel in the Sun, *among hundreds of other movies, were shot. The bungalow, meant as a star's dressing room, looks like the residence for a small, lower-middle-income family (and is sometimes used for exterior shots in films). A few daisies grow in front, and a foot-high white picket fence surrounds the flower bed. Inside is a kitchen, a small room with a desk, and two larger rooms, one filled mainly by a pool table, the other furnished with a couch, a record player for Woody's jazz collection, and a Moviola for editing film. Clark Gable used the bungalow, with different furnishings, as his dressing room for* Gone with the Wind.

Woody sits on the edge of the pool table and watches while Elizabeth Claman, his assistant for the film, greets each prospect for the role of the Leader. She makes sure the name on the list is that of the actor and asks how tall they are. Each looks puzzled but answers.

"Thank you, that's all," she says.

"That's all?" several ask, some peering at Woody.

After each actor leaves, Woody assesses him. He falls into the problem of liking each one better than the last. (He will make choices more easily as the years pass.)

"It's like the Marx Brothers," he says, crossing off yet another name the way Groucho and Chico rip up a contract clause by clause in A Night at the Opera. *"We need one with a little more gorgiositude, but not too much." (He started adding "-iositude" to the end of adjectives twenty years earlier, during his TV writing days, when he saw a book entitled* The Essence of Negritude. *"It was a serious book," he explains, "but I thought the title was funny.")*

After musing awhile about each actor he shakes his head in frustration and says softly, "Fellini just pulls them in off the street." Then he looks up to see the next hopeful.

A few days after he has chosen the cast, Woody gathers the actors who will play the doctors in the anti-government underground around the pool table; they have only their lines, not the full script, as is his custom. After they read the scene aloud a few times, Woody asks them to do it once again, "if that's all right. I want to play everything as realistically as possible and—I'll forget this, I know—keep it going at a good clip." (After this film, he will cease rehearsing even this small amount.)

"Ambivalence is the death of comedy," he tells me after the actors leave. "In silent-film style, they are cartoon characters: they fight one another and the next frame they're up and okay. Actors want to complicate characters, give them ambivalent relationships. You want to look at a character and immediately know that's a good man or a bad man. Chaplin's style was to play against other characters. You see him coming down the street and swinging his stick, and you know immediately what's going to happen."

The only thing in filmmaking that is sure is that there are no sure things. Often what looks good during filming doesn't, for some mystical reason, look good on film. And what looks good on film may look terrible when cut into sequence. So Woody is working on several slapstick routines and is putting particular effort into inventing a walk that will make him look like the robot he pretends to be in Sleeper. Over a period of days, whenever he has a moment, he practices and varies it. Finally he decides to film a few versions in black and white to see how they look on the screen.

"I can walk wry," he says after performing one that makes those watching him laugh. He tries another version. "Specializing in puckish walks." People laugh again. He smiles but shakes his head. "I can't believe a man of my intelligence has to walk funny to make people laugh."

September 1987

Woody is casting parts for Another Woman. He and Juliet Taylor are in the screening room of the Manhattan Film Center in midtown Manhattan, Woody's combination office and editing rooms. Plush avocado green swivel chairs line the walls. On a riser beneath the projection window is a sound control panel, the beige-and-black loveseat Woody sits in, and two more of the plush chairs. Behind the chairs along one wall is Woody's collection of records of music of the thirties and forties, and on a countertop by the records, slightly out of place for this room, there is a Japanese sake set. Casting is an uncomfortable process for the actors as well as for Woody. People are scheduled every fifteen minutes, a dozen or so in all. Word comes that the first is there.

"Let's get started," Woody says. "I can't bear that that woman's waiting out there."

"It's only been thirty seconds," Juliet says, laughing.

The young woman, one of several for the part of the youthful Marion, Gena Rowlands's character, comes in. Woody has a picture of Rowlands rolled up in his hand to consult as he looks at them. They don't see her picture. Woody takes what will be his place, in the middle of the room and out of sight as one enters from the small anteroom. As soon as the person enters, he starts walking to greet them. He says to the young woman (and will say virtually the same thing to everyone else), "Hi, this is for a film that starts shooting October 13 and goes through Christmas or New Year. Juliet thought you might be right for one of the parts, and today I just want to see how you look. I can let you know very soon, within a couple of weeks."

The young redhead is nervous. She stands still and answers, "Okay." Woody looks closely at her for a couple of seconds and then says, "Okay, thank you." She shakes his hand and waves to Juliet on her way out.

As an actor reads with Juliet, Woody listens in a chair at the other end of the room, his right hand an awning over his eyes, the casting call sheet and pictures in his left hand covering the rest of his face to the base of his eyes. ("Hiding," he explains later. "Just hiding.")

Standing in his spot awaiting the next person, he whistles the New Orleans jazz tune "Spicy Advice" and taps his right foot in time. Another girl comes in for the part of young Marion. Woody goes through the same spiel as for the redhead. "I wanted to see your face," he adds, looking closely at her.

"Well, here it is," she says.

"Thanks for bringing it."

The next hopeful will read a scene. "I don't normally read people," Woody says. "We generally know them from other work. It's awful having to read. I could never get a job as an actor if I had to read. The problem with actors is, when they come in and just stand around talking, they're fine. Then they start to read and they shift into third gear. Then they don't talk like a real person."

The actor comes in, and Woody tells him, "This is just a guy at a party—not boorish or anything, just a regular person."

After the actor leaves, Woody says to Juliet, "He was pretty good. He didn't immediately lapse into two hundred years of lessons. The question is, could he do it when the lights are on and everyone is there? But I've always thought that if you can do it at a reading, you can do it anywhere. There's nothing more unnatural than coming into this ghoulish room, people looking at you, the sake set out . . ."

"Remember," Juliet asks, talking about Woody's first few films, "when you used to sit in the back of the room in a rocking chair while [assistant director] Freddy Gallo or [associate producer] Jack Grossberg asked the actors questions? Those were the days when you would have been happy to sit behind a screen and just listen."

Woody smiles and says, "One-way glass would still be ideal. You can look with-out interruption."

.

Six months later, there is an amusing casting session as Woody searches for the right actress to play the part of his character's mother in Oedipus Wrecks. *As he waits for the candidates to arrive, Woody says, "I used to cast faces, and whenever Gordie [Willis] and I were not sure of the actor's ability, we shot in single so you couldn't get hurt." (If none of the takes was good enough, he did not have to reshoot with the other actors in the scene.)*

The first hopeful of what will be a string of elderly women who look like they come from old-world Brooklyn arrives. She takes a seat and Woody explains the part.

"Be contemptuous," he tells her after she reads the first lines. "He's your son and you love him, but be contemptuous right from the start."

To another: "You love him, but he's a worm. Be very contemptuous of him and very suspicious of the woman he's brought home. Have nothing but slow, steady contempt for him."

One says: "It's hard to be contemptuous of you."

"You'll grow to," Woody responds quickly.

Another, after listening to direction, finds a personal context: "So talk out of the side of my mouth like Uncle Julie? Uncle Julie's an uncle of mine."

Woody: "So I'm going to know him?"

To each he will say, "That's very good. Now, try it a little slower." Or "A little more contemptuously." Then "Good, very good." And "Very good. Now, just for amusement, read it with contempt for your son."

After the last applicant leaves he says, "You know where this movie is going to resonate? Israel. It's going to be the Gone with the Wind *of Israel."*

October 1987

With shooting on Another Woman *under way, Woody makes a comparison between American and European male actors as we talk in his apartment.*

WA: It's hard to find just men. Not a gunslinger. There are a few. Sam Waterston in *September.* Denholm Elliott. But American actors, who are as great as any in the world—De Niro, Nicholson—are not bland. They're so charismatic. We breed heroes: John Waynes and Humphrey Bogarts and Jimmy Cagneys and we don't have many regular people like, say, Fredric March. Our film history is mythology, whereas in Europe a lot of it is adult confrontational, a realistic story where you need a man. Our actors are too charming and beautiful and charismatic: Wayne, Brando. I learned this the hard way, by casting. When I need a regular fifty-, fifty-five-year-old I can't find him. Dustin Hoffman is closer.

Sam Waterston is the constant in *Interiors, Hannah,* and *September.* He is a regular man. In America, we have these very, very special kinds of people as actors. Robert De Niro is very special. He's one of the greatest actors in the world, and so is Jack Nicholson. These guys have very special qualities. But just to find a very fine actor who can play a simple advertising writer is a very, very tough thing. We've had some in the United States. I think George C. Scott [*died 1999*] is a great actor who can be believable just as a regular man. He doesn't have to be sexy or a gunfighter. I think Dustin can play a lot of things. He's a wonderful comic actor, too. He's so gifted. So Sam is a guy I've relied on at times for a guy next door, for a regular, recognizable human being who is not a cowboy and you don't get the feeling he carries a gun or beats up people. He is one of the few people out there.

Women don't have that problem. With so many gifted actresses around, it's a pleasure. I want Jane Alexander for the sister-in-law, and Max von Sydow as her husband. He has the right level of coolness. Blythe Danner as Lydia. John Houseman [*died 1988*] as Marion's father. I need a younger man with a voice like his for early on. [*Houseman suggests David Ogden Stiers to play the father as a young man.*]

EL: Max von Sydow did wonderful work in *Hannah and Her Sisters.* His intensity shot off the screen. [*He plays Frederick, a passionately committed artist with a cold personality, who is involved with Hannah's beautiful sister Lee (Barbara Hershey).*]

WA: Max is so good, the crew applauds. That never happens for an actor. His gift is so large, it's universal. Whether he plays sophisticated or unsophisticated, it doesn't matter.

Max von Sydow as the fiercely artistic painter Frederick in *Hannah and Her Sisters*

In *Hannah,* Michael Caine's part [*Elliot, Hannah's husband, who falls for Lee*] wasn't written for an Englishman. But there is no American actor who could be a regular man who is an accountant. American men are dangerous and potent. Michael has the James Mason approach. He loves to work and never stops. He gets a great kick out of playing a CIA agent or a comic role.

EL: Sometimes you've hired actors who haven't worked out, usually, you would say, because of deficiencies in the writing rather than their performance.

WA: Yes. Chris Walken is one of my favorite actors. I used him in *Annie Hall* and I was dying to use him again. I think he's a great, inspired actor. He was in the first version of *September.* After a couple of weeks of working we were very friendly, we ate lunch together every day, but we couldn't get copacetic on what to do. He was uncomfortable with certain things, and I didn't feel the ways he was doing certain things were right for the character and he was feeling awkward doing them other ways. So we talked about it and he basically decided himself that instead of his making concessions and my making concessions, we'd work on something else down the line. I said, "Are you sure? I'd be happy to reshoot all your scenes and we'll approach them differently." It's happened before to me.

EL: Michael Keaton was first cast in the movie star role in *The Purple Rose of Cairo* that Jeff Daniels eventually played. What happened with him?

WA: Michael Keaton was right out of the 1980s, not the 1930s. People are always trying to figure if it was more than that, but that's all it was. I loved him in *Night Shift* [1982]. I thought he was absolutely terrific. I'd love to do something with him, but that wasn't the piece. I'd look at dailies and he was fine, but you got no sense of a 1930s movie star from him; he just was too hip. But I find him one of the funnier, one of the inspired young guys.

EL: You were able to hire Denholm Elliott for *September.* I know you've long been a fan.

WA: I wanted to work with Denholm for years. At one point I wanted him to play the father in *Interiors* [*E. G. Marshall played the part*], but I didn't want it to be an English person. I've always thought he's great. I've seen him in a number of films. I saw him play Krogstad in the Ibsen play *A Doll's House* [1973] and in a Clive Donner film before *Pussycat* [Nothing but the Best, 1964]. He'd always been outstanding. But you could never find him. He was living in Ibiza and he had no phone, he had to be called at a bar at a certain time of day. I finally tracked him down, and asked, "Can you do an American accent?"

And he said, "Absolutely. Would you like me to do it?"

I said, "Yes."

And then he recited "Hickory Dickory Dock." But it was totally British. [*Woody says "HICKory DICKory DOCK" in an English accent, then he starts to laugh.*] I'm on the phone to a bar in Ibiza and he's saying "Hickory Dickory Dock" and the accent is totally English.

I said, "Well, thanks very much."

And he said, "Well, are you going to hire me? I'd like to know."

"Let me think about this," I told him. And I talked to Juliet Taylor and said, "I just can't do this. I want an American to play that and he just can't do a convincing American." But I was so thrilled that he was available for *September*. I've wanted to work with him for years.

EL: Let's talk about *September* [*see page 16*] for a moment. During shooting you replaced Christopher Walken, in the part of Peter, the advertising copywriter, with Sam Shepard. Then after you looked at the first cut, you shot the whole film a second time, with a substantially different cast. In the first version Charles Durning played Howard, the widower neighbor, but it was Denholm Elliott in the second. Shepard was replaced by Sam Waterston. Jack Warden was brought in to play Lloyd, the physicist husband, and Elliott took over the neighbor role. The mother, Diane, was played by Maureen O'Sullivan [*died 1998*], but she was replaced by Elaine Stritch. What prompted so many changes?

WA: When I set out to write this I had Maureen in mind for the mother and Mia and Dianne Wiest for the daughter and her friend. I think if I was casting this cold I would think of Mia for either of these roles. But because I was thinking of Mia and Maureen, I just automatically thought of Mia as Maureen's daughter. [*Maureen*

Denholm Elliott in *September*. Woody had long wanted to work with him.

O'Sullivan and Mia Farrow are in fact mother and daughter.] It never occurred to me any other way because it was going to be Maureen and Mia, and Dianne for the other one. But if from the start I knew it would be Stritch, Mia, and Dianne Wiest, I don't know, I might have finished writing the thing and gotten together for dinner with Mia and Dianne and said, "You guys have read this. Do you have any feelings of how you want to divide this up?" Because I think they're both wonderful actresses. Mia's a real actress. Obviously in the same year she can play that silly cigarette girl in *Radio Days* and play this. And Dianne is a great actress, no question about it. She can do the same thing. She played Aunt Bea in that other thing [Radio Days] trying to get the husband, and here she's doing something very different. So I would have been happy to let the women give me input about who plays whom. But because it was conceived for Maureen, too, it just never occurred to me that Maureen's daughter would be Dianne.

EL: How did Maureen O'Sullivan see her part?

WA: Maureen is ballsy and bawdy and full of stories with punch lines, but with this she was a little trepidatious in that she felt, Gee, it's such a big part, can I do it? She had just recovered from a bout with pneumonia, which later laid her low again. She was a little concerned about that but not so concerned that she didn't want to do it. She was fine. She had a real interesting quality. But she would have had to be available for another ten weeks of work.

EL: So what happened?

WA: After seeing what I shot I wanted to do it again. I brought the idea to Mia and she said, "Well, my mother will never be able to do it again. She's in the hospital with pneumonia. And she has a commitment to do something else that she might not be able to do because she's not well." Then Sam Shepard was in California for something he was committed to and Charles Durning had something else. I thought maybe I could wait for everybody, but really, I couldn't, because I had a set that was standing. One of the reasons that this movie was a cinch to make is that it was one set and it cost us nothing to go back in and use it again.

So I switched around the cast. Denholm had seen the Howard part being played. I deliberately did Jack Warden as a little off center in terms of a physicist. I've met some physicists and not all of them are guys with steel-rimmed glasses and elongated foreheads. Some of them are cigar-smoking kinds of guys in leisure suits and they're absolutely brilliant. So I wanted to do that kind of physicist rather than an academic.

EL: What difference did you get in the part of the mother?

WA: Maureen, because she's older than Elaine Stritch, was more vulnerable and less in charge. You felt sorrier for her. And that's good. That's why I think this thing could be played as a play in different ways. She had a very good interpretation of it, a very good natural quality for it. You thought, Poor thing, she's living on past delusions. And you felt, Oh, God, she was once pretty but that is past, and she drinks and she's unsure of herself. Stritch has a stronger presentation and Maureen has a much more vulnerable presentation, a completely different quality.

EL: Is there something inherently more difficult with drama than comedy? You had a huge cast in *Radio Days* with no turnover, and here was a piece with a half dozen characters and four out of six changed.

WA: It may be coincidence, but there is some truth to that. A comedy is looser, it's rougher, it's not as varnished and finished a product. You don't have to be as perfect in a certain way. In a serious piece you're requiring the audience to go along with you and become emotionally involved and care, and you can't suddenly have somebody break that reality by giving a bad or unreal performance. So the best thing to do is cast wonderful people. But even when you do cast wonderful people, once in a while, either because of my inability to direct them well or connect with them or their inability to grasp this particular role even though they've done fine ones in the past, for some reason it doesn't come together. So your choice is to leave in a less than perfect performance or to make a change. And I always feel obliged to the people who are putting up the money for the film and for my own artistic integrity and to everybody involved to make the change. But in the course of my life, I've done seventeen pictures or something [*that is, in the course of his career to 1987*]; I've changed very few people.

In a movie like *Hannah* or *Annie Hall* or *Bananas*, somebody can come on and the level of depth and sensitivity in their performance needn't be that high. It's people talking fast and bright and quipping and falling and running around and you don't notice the imperfection so much because it's razzle-dazzle and jokes and silliness. But when you're doing something where the camera's close and it's quiet and people are doing longer speeches or longer emotional things and you're trying to suck the audience into that, everybody's got to be good.

EL: You have Gene Hackman in this film [Another Woman]. When he did one of his scenes, I was four feet from him and his performance was literally electrifying— I could actually feel something in the air.

WA: It's reserve power. You feel that he's cruising at eighty miles an hour and being brilliant and that if he felt like stepping on the gas there's still another three hundred miles an hour he could do. You feel the depth of his power. When he's yelling it's not just surface; you feel it go all the way down through him.

March 1988

Woody is shooting Oedipus Wrecks.

EL: Mia Farrow is in everything you write these days and have written for some years. Looking at the variety of parts she's played, she's clearly very versatile.

WA: You can write anything for Mia. She's that kind of actress. She's more of a classic actress, but she can play a little songstress or a dramatic mother. [*Diane*] Keaton can do that, too, to a large degree. But Keaton has a very, very spectacular personality of a certain sort and is very enjoyable on the screen. The plus of that personality is that it's unique and a tremendous gift. And the drawback—and I don't think this is much of a drawback—is that that personality isn't always easy to lose if you want to submerge it in the character. She was always very good at that, though. She has a very wide range, too. But because she has such a special personality, she would not have been able to play an Italian woman so easily, if at all, because she has too much of herself that's so strong. But there are a lot of dramatic things she can do. She was sensational in *Baby Boom* [*1987*].

Mia grew up with a father who was a director [*John Farrow*] and a mother [*Maureen O'Sullivan*] who is an actress and was acting at a very young age. She was very successful on television in that thing, uh, that very famous series [*he pauses a few seconds*] . . . *Peyton Place* at seventeen years old. And then she did some films, at least one of which was enormously successful, *Rosemary's Baby.* And she went away to England and did a number of Royal Shakespeare shows and then didn't work for years. She just retired and stayed out in the country with the kids. Then she came back. So she's a totally professional actress. You can have her play a mother or a gun moll or give her a song to sing and she can do it. I think there are probably a lot of people like that, but they never get their shot.

EL: Because she has such range, do you conceive parts for her?

WA: When I originally conceived of this movie I envisioned her in the lead. But I don't have to think about her so much because there's always a part for her. Perhaps it's more of a strain on her than it would be on, let's say, one of Bergman's actresses, because I would guess that almost everything he would do would fit into quite a heavy dramatic category. He's found a number of great actresses and he can always count on them and they can always do it.

But the range I've been trying to do is very wide. I'm not saying successful but wide. And so it puts a little bit of a strain on Mia because one year she'll have to play Tina [*the moll in* Broadway Danny Rose] or the cigarette girl in *Radio Days*, and then the next year it will be something quite dramatic.

When we began *Radio Days* we had no idea what we were doing in terms of her character [*a nightclub cigarette girl with a high, Bronx-accented voice who becomes a sophisticatedly spoken radio gossip personality*]. We didn't know what voice she should use or anything. The first scene of hers we shot for *Radio Days* I did about thirty-five takes of it and she did thirty-five different voices and I looked at them all and picked one and that's the one we used for the picture. And of course [*he laughs*], that scene never made the picture. And when she turned into the other girl, the gossip columnist, the day that we shot it she did a half dozen versions of that for me. We only picked the one we were going to use as I started editing.

EL: You seem able to ask her for unlimited retakes.

WA: I feel that I can do those things because she's so close to me. I can do that with Keaton, I can do that with Dianne Wiest. These are women I've worked with now a number of times and I'm friendly with and they like me and we're all in it together. But an actress like Gena [*Rowlands*], I don't know so well. I'm sure if we did two or three pictures and got friendly, then we could make any kinds of demands on one another, as friends do. But I have hesitations with Gena because I just don't know her well enough, and I don't want to intrude on an area that she might not want me to, so I have to be cautious. But with Mia, it's absolutely nothing. I just call her up and say, "Gee, what we did yesterday was just terrible. Let's do it again today," and "This was awful, and let's try this." She has a great attitude.

EL: Do you think she's changed much as an actress since she began to work exclusively with you?

WA: She's had a change in her life in this sense professionally: she was used to being in the commercial film world. In the commercial film world you get as much money as you can get. You get the highest billing you can get. You try and get the best parts you can get. You're as good as your last box office. It's an ugly, silly world, I think. And here, when I first met her, I said, "This is a completely different world where you're working not for the money or the billing but just for the fun of working. Just forget about all those other considerations completely. Just don't think about money, don't think about billing, don't think about egos." And she had no problem. She said, "Fine, I couldn't care less what I get, and I'm ready to work." And so in the long run, of course, that turns out to be even better for you. You forget about all that silly stuff and you just work.

The first movie we did together, *A Midsummer Night's Sex Comedy*, was not a hit.

But it didn't mean anything. If that had been done in the commercial world, so to speak, it would have been a setback for her or for me that it didn't make any money. But we just put it out and those that liked it liked it and we went on to the next film, *Zelig*. And that one was very successfully received. Then we just went on to the next one. As I said, we're not in the traditional world of hits and flops, or money or deals or billings solely determining the financing of the next picture. We're in the world of strictly working and trying to do your best. Mia would be completely willing to play a backbreaking lead in a film and work at it for four months and shoot every day and be perfectly happy the next time to do a ten-line part, if that's what there was, and then go on to the next one. And that's good for her and it's good for me.

EL: How did *Sex Comedy* come to be made before *Zelig*? Hadn't you written *Zelig* first?

WA: I had just finished the script of *Zelig* and I was waiting a couple of weeks to have it budgeted and I thought to myself, While I'm waiting, why don't I write something? And this little idea occurred to me. I thought it would be fun to get some people in a country house and just celebrate summer, and make it very beautiful, with butterfly nets and badminton courts and picnicking and butterflies. So we set this up. We just budgeted eight or ten weeks for it. Then, as you know, I had tried to overlap the shooting of the films and ran into some problems. We finished it before *Zelig* because there was a weather requirement in it.

I wrote it for Mia, knowing she would play the part of the psychoanalyst who treats Leonard Zelig. She was very nervous playing it because it was the first time she was working with me. She said she would disappoint me. She was a little nervous. Sort of shaking, as a matter of fact. I calmed her, but I can be a little abrupt sometimes. I often make the wrong assumption that the actor's going to be secure. I think, You've got the part. I think you're great. I would not have called you or hired you if I did not think you were great. So I can say to you, "Oh, God, that was terrible that last take you did," and you can say to me, "Jesus, these lines you wrote, nobody can say them." It goes without saying that we respect each other and we're working together and it's a free and open conversation and I'm going to be very critical and you can be very critical. Mia had nothing to worry about. I knew she'd be wonderful in it. It never occurred to me she'd disappoint me. So I didn't think to myself, Oh, my God, darling, are you upset? It just never occurred to me.

EL: Has an actor ever gotten mad at you on the set?

WA: José Ferrer got a little bit angry with me during *A Midsummer Night's Sex Comedy*. I had a wonderful time with him. I thought he was a total delight in every way. But once I bothered him for a line reading fifteen times, and finally he said to me [*in a good Ferrer imitation*], "Now I *can't*, you've turned me into a *mass* of terrors." And I thought to myself, My God, you're *José Ferrer.* How can I turn you into a mass of terrors? You're this wonderful actor and all I'm doing is saying, "No, that's not really the way I wanted, do it again." So I guess I'm insensitive, because I just take it for granted that they should take my requests for granted.

EL: Have you thought about expanding the character you play?

WA: No. If anything, I've retreated. I feel that I couldn't be in a dramatic movie because people would laugh. And that I understand. There are a lot of parts I can't play. The next movie—not this little one [Oedipus Wrecks] but the next movie [Crimes and Misdemeanors]—I'll be in because, you know, contractually I've got to be in some.

EL: But within your range, as you put it. Do you find that narrowing?

WA: It's not narrowing, it's what it's always been. It certainly doesn't expand. I can play some versions of what I am, a New York character. And there is a little variation within that. I can play serious moments in a comedy. People will accept that from me. But not in a serious film. Perhaps I have some small range within myself. I would be believable as a college teacher, for example. I could play someone who worked up at *The New Yorker* magazine, or worked in a fairly literate circumstance. And I could be believable as a bookmaker in a Damon Runyon story. I could also be a guy who bets the horses, and be a certain kind of urban rat or lowlife—a squealer, or a sportswriter, or a bookmaker, that kind of thing. But it's a small urban range. I could never, nor would I want to, play a really serious character. I mean, it would just be laughable. If I were in *Interiors* or one of the husbands in *Cries and Whispers,* it would just break up everybody. They'd never stop laughing. But if it's clearly a comedy and I'm making the audience laugh, and then there's a turn of events that's sad or dramatic, I can play that convincingly. But to start out serious, the audience doesn't want to see that. The audience is waiting for me to say something more amusing. And they should be, because that's what I've represented myself as over the years.
   Also, the audience doesn't want that from me in this sense: Bob Hope, Charlie Chaplin, I want to see them do what they are known for doing. It's the same reason that I don't want to see Marlon Brando playing a certain kind of role because it's not as much fun for me. When Robert De Niro played *The Last Tycoon* [1976], he did it well because the guy's a born actor. But it's more fun to see him do things like Jake La Motta [Raging Bull] and *Taxi Driver* and *Mean Streets.* He's a superb sociopath on the screen. Of course, he's going to do everything he does great, but it's not as much fun for the audience to see him in a part that constricts him.

EL: Do you do anything to get in shape for acting?

WA: No. To me it's like falling off a log. It's not acting. You could turn the camera on now and I could play my part. That's the beauty of having no talent. I stay within my small range. There's absolutely no acting required. I'm not doing anything different now than I'm going to do when they turn the camera on. The stuff that I do as an actor is the easiest stuff in the world for me. I'm not saying it's great, but that modest thing I do is achievable without any effort by me at all. As I said, I'm capable of a dramatic moment in a comic film. When I was in *Danny Rose,* I had to walk down a hallway at night and I realize that my act is leaving me and I have to respond to it. It's a nicely acted moment, I think. But it's the easiest thing in the world for me to do. I have this tiny range and I know what I can do. That's reflected in the parts I write for myself.

I show up in the morning, wearing my clothes from home. That's what I did on Broadway [*during the run of* Play It Again, Sam]. I'd go right out onstage and play that character and there wasn't a false note in the character because I had completely protected myself going in: I had not written a word that I couldn't say as natural speech. And if by any chance I *had* made a mistake, I changed it.

EL: Which helps explain why people feel you are the character you play.

WA: Yes, people think the fictional person I've created is me. It isn't. It just talks like me and dresses like me [*laughs*], that's really what it is.

When I was in *The Front* [a *1976 picture about the 1950s anti-communist film and television blacklist, written by Walter Bernstein and directed by Martin Ritt. (Both men were blacklisted, as were several cast members.) Woody plays Howard Prince, a restaurant cashier whom a blacklisted childhood friend persuades to "front" for him by turning in the friend's scripts as if they were his own. Howard at first basks in his newfound fame but eventually takes a brave stand against the life-wrecking injustice of the blacklist*] and speeches were written for me, I was always able to put them in my own idiom. I tell every actor who works with me not to worry about the dialogue, to say it just the way he wants to say it. I know that will guarantee a certain credibility on the screen. A lot of actors say, "Your words are much better than what I would say." And they're not, really. What they say would have a lot more impact on the audience. But they don't trust themselves to do it.

EL: You seem very relaxed when you perform. Are there any actors who would make you nervous if you were playing opposite them?

WA: If I found myself tomorrow in a movie with great performers I didn't know—Meryl Streep or Jack Nicholson, say—I wouldn't be so relaxed and free. I wouldn't want to cramp them or put them off or do anything that would bother them. I would do my best, but I wouldn't be totally at ease acting with them. It would be like playing jazz with Coleman Hawkins.

EL: In this film [Oedipus Wrecks], there is a scene after you've come from the surprisingly pleasant dinner with Julie Kavner. [*Woody's character, Sheldon, is beset by his mother, who vanished in a Chinese box during a magician's trick and reappeared as a giant specter in the sky over Manhattan, kibitzing with pedestrians and chiding Sheldon for taking up with a beautiful WASP (Mia Farrow) rather than a nice Jewish girl, which Kavner's character happens to be.*] You read her note and then you open the foil-wrapped chicken she's sent home with you. The moment requires you to act introspectively. You pick up the leg and smell it and as you do, "All the Things You Are" plays. Did you know you were going to use that song as you were doing the scene? It seems timed so well to the music. And were you acting with music in mind?

WA: I knew I would be doing some sweet music, but I wasn't timing myself to it. I was just acting, like any actor would. I pick it up and I know I've gotta smell it and make it romantic-looking. I'm [*laughs*] pretending. I'm not thinking at the time that I'm the character and I'm not thinking, Oh, God, I love her. I'm not living the character. I know I'm pretending. I'm thinking, Okay, I've waited enough time. I've dropped the letter and now I'm standing there and this is going to get boring if I don't move now, because I've dropped the letter but it seems enough time to notice the chicken thing. I'm aware: Keep it like this; don't be too feminine about it. I'm not thinking motivation; I'm thinking mechanics.

January 2000

In the past several years Woody has made Husbands and Wives, Manhattan Murder Mystery, Bullets over Broadway, Mighty Aphrodite, Everyone Says I Love You, Deconstructing Harry, Celebrity, *and* Sweet and Lowdown. *The preproduction work on* Small Time Crooks *is under way as we talk at the Manhattan Film Center.*

EL: Let's talk about some of the actors you've worked with recently.

WA: I love Jack Warden. [*He appeared in* September, Bullets over Broadway, *and* Mighty Aphrodite.] He's a wonderful actor who's got a big range. He's totally believable in the most serious parts and hilariously funny. I love John Cusack, I think he's great. I'd love to work with him again. I loved him when I first worked with him in *Cries and Whispers*. [*He pauses and laughs at his slip.*] *Shadows and Fog*—I should be so lucky. And I loved him in *Bullets over Broadway* [*he was a student in the first, and a would-be playwright in the second*]. Cusack is one of those guys like Liam Neeson and Michael Caine, incapable of a graceless moment in front of the camera. You give Cusack junk to do and it sounds beautiful, he makes it sound real. And the same with Liam, he's amazing that way. We tend to take Michael Caine for granted because he's been great for so many years.

EL: John Cusack brought a wonderful combination of artistic bravado and then the sinking realization that he really isn't an artist to the role of the writer in *Bullets*.

WA: He is one of those actors who make everything great. Chazz Palminteri [*who plays the hoodlum who is really the artist*] I had never heard of and Juliet Taylor said, "You've got to meet him. He's coming out in a movie called *A Bronx Tale* that he wrote." And then Chazz walks in the door and I think, This is the character I wrote. Just get a contract out quickly and sign him. Joe Viterelli [*the mob boss*], I saw him in a movie and said [*approvingly*], "Who *is* this guy?"

EL: It seems you gave more direction to Dianne Wiest [*playing the Broadway diva*] than anyone I can think of in all your other films.

WA: I had to play a lot of that to show her. She kept saying, "I can't do this. You've got to get another actress, I can't do this." And I kept saying, "Are you kidding? You're the greatest actress in the world. Where am I going to get another actress like you?"

I wanted her to camp it up more than she was. To show her what I wanted I came flouncing in and said, "Oh, *God!*" And I did the scene. And she said, "Really? You want it that broad?" And I said, "Yes."

But in her hands it hardly looks like the way I did it. She got an Oscar for it.

EL: There's that wonderful recurring line when just as Cusack starts to talk she very dramatically tells him, "Don't speak."

WA: When I was writing I remembered the scene in *The Rose Tattoo* when [*Anna*] Magnani knows that her husband has been killed and she played that so dramatically. She truly was the greatest actress in the world. And I thought it would be funny if Dianne did it. The more she did it in the movie the funnier it was. Mary-Louise Parker as the girlfriend was terrific.

And I was lucky to get Rob Reiner because it was a small role [*Sheldon Flender, a bohemian*]. He made it memorable. He's perfect at doing a coffeehouse kind of Russian intellectual chess-playing communist. Also, Jim Broadbent [*Warner Purcell, an ever-fatter leading man in the play within the movie*] was a find. Juliet said I had to see him and he was so funny. When I saw him I thought he was hilarious. And Jennifer Tilly [*Olive O'Neal, the no-talent actress*] was so funny improvising. And of course that other genius Tracey Ullman [*actress Eden Brent*].

EL: Lysette Anthony in *Husbands and Wives* was a casting surprise to me because she's British. But she sounded completely American.

WA: You meet her and she has an overwhelming British accent. Then she reads and it's a dead-on American accent. She didn't need any coaching. Very beautiful. Very nice.

EL: You've told me that *Mighty Aphrodite* was tough to cast. Why?

WA: I did a lot of casting on that picture. I went to England to look at people. I was looking for someone to play the chorus master [*for the Greek chorus that offers warnings and commentary*] and Juliet and I had meetings in our hotel with all the peerage of the Crown. I'm reading these lords and sirs one after the other. They were all great but none of them had the delivery I wanted, so I finally went to an American and the person who seemed best to me was F. Murray Abraham. It seemed like he had enough Shakespearean authority but spoke like a Brooklyn guy. I looked at a lot of English women before I cast Mira [*Sorvino as the sweet and daffy hooker who is the mother of the child adopted by Woody's character*], and a lot of American women, too.

EL: As I understand it, she had read for you in New York but it took her showing up for an appointment with you in London, dressed in character, for you to realize she was the person you were looking for.

WA: It shows you how little foresight I can have. Like with Sylvester Stallone. I was making *Bananas* [*during 1970*] and asked the casting people to send me a couple of gangsters, and they sent Stallone and another kid and I said, "This is not what I meant. Not tough enough." And the two kids said, "Please, Mr. Allen, give us a chance, let us make up." They came back in sixty seconds and I realized what a schmuck I was. So when Mira happened to be in England and asked if she could come by, she walked into the hotel suite with the boots and the short skirt. The

Woody did not hire Mira Sorvino to play the sweet hooker Linda Ash in *Mighty Aphrodite* at her first interview, but when she came by in a costume she devised, he cast her on the spot. Her performance earned her an Oscar.

minute she walked in I thought she was perfect. She looked appropriate for the part of a hooker without being too vulgar. [*He laughs.*] Frankly, I couldn't figure out how she got past the house detective. Then she read, not in the voice, but her acting was so good and convincing without the voice. [*Her character's voice is heavy Brooklyn lightened by helium and thus made comic—which softens the coarseness of her vocabulary, making it almost naive. She won an Oscar for Best Supporting Actress.*]

EL: She was a revelation to me. I love her voice.

WA: Part of the credit for taking the edge off the profanity in *Aphrodite* goes to Mira. She brought a lightness to it, she played it like such a cartoon. That voice was all her. I had some uneasy moments about it during shooting, which I didn't share with her, though I thought, My God, if they don't buy in to the voice, I'm really in trouble. But I bought it and I went by my instincts and it turned out I—or should I say she—was right.

She had the voice from the first day. She's very meticulous about building a character, much more so than I am. She had a lot of moments when she wanted to be alone to think about her character. She had worked it out very carefully and very intelligently and I didn't have to give her very much help at all. She's smart and she's talented. I'd work with her again if I had the right part for her because she'd make me look good again.

EL: Which other parts gave you trouble?

WA: I had a tough time casting the wife [*of Woody's character*] until I got Helena Bonham Carter. She was someone I had just seen in those bonnet pictures. She's a wonderful actress. Since she stepped out of those and into things like *Fight*

Everyone says they're Groucho Marx at a New Year's Eve party in Paris at the end of *Everyone Says I Love You.*

Club [1999] and *Women Talking Dirty* [1999], I think she's greater than ever. Juliet suggested her. She came in to read. Also did a very good American accent. And she was just right. She was beautiful and she was classy.

EL. Let's talk a bit about *Everyone Says I Love You* [*see page 96*]. You'd wanted for years to do a musical, and when you did, it was a sort of homemade version because the actors sing in regular voices, not like trained singers, although of course you had those great dancing and singing numbers by real pros.

WA: Julia Roberts was great. She's a wonderful actress and terrific to work with. I *did* have to lean up to kiss her, of course, which is one of the, you know, annoying things in life.

Drew Barrymore was sensational as well [*as a debutante*]. At first I was worried about casting her because she had this trailer park image; Drew doesn't have the image of the Upper East Sider in the sense that Gwyneth Paltrow does. But Drew was available and I heard from everybody who had worked with her that she is so talented and so dedicated that she'd make it work. She came in and I liked her very much. She read wonderfully and I figured [*he laughs*] we could cover her tattoos. And she *was* superb.

EL: Edward Norton was new to me. [*He plays Drew Barrymore's preppy boy-friend, who, joined by a chorus of dancers, breaks into a rendition of "My Baby Just Cares for Me" while buying her an engagement ring at Harry Winston.*]

WA: Edward Norton was a discovery. He came in with a million guys who I didn't know, but the second he read the part, as far as I was concerned, he had it. No one had read it before with any reality or conviction. He was like a real person doing it. I never told him it was a musical.

EL: [*Incredulous*] You didn't tell him he'd have to *sing*? Did you tell *any* of the actors?

WA: [*Completely blasé*] It never occurred to me to tell anyone because I wanted to do a musical paying no regard to whether people could sing or not. I called him a couple of weeks later and asked, "Can you sing?" And he said, "Yeah, I think I can sing a little."

When I was making it, the people in the music department were saying, "They can't sing!" And the distributors were saying, "They can't sing!" And I kept saying, "Yes, I *know,* that's the *point.* If they sing like they do in the shower, like regular people, that's the idea. I don't want Edward Norton to start singing and sound like Pavarotti." I wasn't casting for singers. I was casting for believable actors. And some could sing—Alan Alda, and Goldie Hawn, a beautiful singer. Only Drew said, "I can't sing. I'm tone-deaf, I can't do it." So I said, "Okay, in your case we'll dub you," and we got one of Soon-Yi's friends to dub her in that one song in the picture. Tim Roth [*who is English*] had to sing with an American accent, and Dick Hyman [*who wrote the original music*] kept saying, "He can't sing! He can't sing!" and I kept saying, "It's *okay*"—unless it's like caterwauling and becomes punishment.

EL: The scene at the end with everyone looking like Groucho Marx is one of my favorites. And then there is that elaborate and touching scene on the quay with Goldie Hawn [*who plays Woody's character's ex-wife, though she, he, and her husband are close friends*].

WA: My Groucho is in the genes, the family genes. I lucked out that Goldie was available. She is one of those people who can do it all. You want someone to dance, Goldie can dance. She can sing, as I said. You want someone to improvise, she can improvise. She can act, she can do the joke. She is very authoritative and talented. At first I thought to go with one of my cronies, like Judy Davis, but Judy was pregnant or something.

EL: That scene by the river seems really complex, not only for the exposition that brings your and Goldie Hawn's characters back together but for her dancing in midair. How complicated was it to do?

WA: It was cool but not punishing when we filmed on the quay. I was over there the other night, having dinner, and I was looking down at it from the window of the Tour d'Argent, and thinking of how Carlo [*Di Palma*] had lit it. He had days to light that thing. We had rented every light in France. Notre Dame was lit and the other side of the Seine was all lit and this side was lit. We must have had five hundred lights. Normally it is lit, but that was quite amazing.

EL: *Deconstructing Harry* was originally called *The Worst Man in the World.* You've said that Harry Block, the character you play, is "a nasty, shallow, superficial, sexually obsessed" writer who barely fictionalizes his life and his work and richly earns the enmity of those who once loved him. People who are prone to look for autobiography in your work had a referential field day, even though people who know you realize how different you are from Harry.

WA: Yes, he's a New York Jewish writer—that's me—but he's a writer with writer's block—that immediately disqualifies me—who is willing to kidnap this kid, something that I lack the courage to do; sits home and drinks; has problems in his life; has hookers come to his house every night; his mother had died in childbirth. It just wasn't my life. It was a fictional character I made up. I tried to get somebody else to play it—I tried to get *everybody* else to play it. But I knew if somebody else played it they'd say it was me anyway. Still, I thought it could be played better than I could play it. I first went to Robert De Niro. I went to Dustin Hoffman. I went to Elliott Gould. I went to Albert Brooks. I spoke to Dennis Hopper. I couldn't get anyone to do it for one reason or another. One person wasn't available, one person wanted too much money, somebody else didn't want to play it because he thought he was too young. Finally, maybe less than two weeks before shooting, I said I'd play it.

EL: Were you happy with Elisabeth Shue in the film? [*She plays the gorgeous patient of Harry's psychiatrist ex-wife (Kirstie Alley), with whom he starts a romance.*]

WA: She was an actress I had liked very much. She was fortunately available and she was terrific. She was a very good, believable person to idolize me. She had met me in the elevator—in the movie. She was beautiful and sexy and a fine actress.

EL: *Celebrity* has two actors in it who themselves were being heavily celebrated at the time you made it, Charlize Theron and Leonardo DiCaprio.

WA: Charlize Theron has screen humidity, as I like to call it. It comes from within. She's great-looking and has a lot of justified confidence. She knows how to present herself. Add up her looks and confidence and talent and you have a winning package.

Leonardo DiCaprio is not a flavor of the month. Apart from being good-looking, he's a tremendous actor, an actor up there with the best of them—De Niro, Pacino—a great natural. He's real and full of intensity and a great improviser. His instincts are beautiful. [*His voice becomes rueful.*] I make the first DiCaprio film after *Titanic* and it didn't make a dime [*laughs*]. I was coming off *Everyone Says I*

Charlize Theron demonstrates what Woody calls her "screen humidity" in *The Curse of the Jade Scorpion.*

Love You and *Deconstructing Harry.* The musical was popular in Europe and especially well loved in France, and it was hard to follow.

EL: How does the script for *Sweet and Lowdown* differ from its first, uproduced incarnation, *The Jazz Baby,* as far as the key characters?

WA: The style of telling *The Jazz Baby* was anecdotal hearsay about a guy. The structure was the same. Some of the character traits were the same. The jazz musician lead was a pimp, but it was different. It was much less amusing—not that this is a laugh riot—and much more masochistic. The impression you get from the original was that the musician was so self-destructive and it's so sad. You've got a big ladle of masochism, of Germanic Emil Jannings masochism. It needed some spirit to it. We had to go find a guy who looked like Django Reinhardt. Not so easy.

EL: One thing I remember from reading *The Jazz Baby* many years ago is the relationship between the mute girl and the egocentric guitar player that was played out so well by Samantha Morton and Sean Penn.

WA: Samantha Morton sat in this very room. She could only lose the job. The minute I saw her in *Under the Skin* [1997] I knew I wanted her.
"I would like you to play this like Harpo Marx," I said.

And [*he starts to laugh*] she said, "Who's Harpo Marx?"

And I said, "*Harpo Marx*, the Marx Brother that doesn't speak."

And she said, "Who are the Marx Brothers?" [*Not only that. Twenty years old and from a small, rural English town, she told* Variety *that after her agent informed her that Woody Allen wanted to meet her, her response was, "So who's Woody Allen?"*]

I realized how old I was. I told her she should see the Marx Brothers because she would like them, and I hired her and she went back to England and she did see the Marx Brothers. The next time I saw her was on the set. She did a perfect impression of Harpo Marx and I had to explain to her, "I don't want you to really *act* like Harpo Marx, but that's the general idea I'm going for, that mute character. As opposed to Johnny Belinda."

EL: She stole her scenes without ever saying a word.

WA: People kept saying to me, It's so hard for a young actress to act without speaking. I answered yes, but I was thinking to myself, Not really. It's something that an actress can really sink her teeth into. There's not an actress out there who wouldn't want to play a mute or a blind person because you have something that you can play. [*Morton received an Academy Award nomination for Best Supporting Actress.*]

EL: Was Sean Penn your first choice for the part?

WA: He was Juliet's first choice. I thought about other people because often Sean is not available. He had told people he wanted to work with me, and then every time I would send something his way he would say, "No, I want to be with my kids, I just did two movies, I can't afford to work with you, I owe money." I tried him for at least two other films; I don't recall which, but Juliet would know.

I thought of but never contacted Johnny Depp for the part. Nicolas Cage's name came up as well.

EL: There were reports at the time of difficulty between the two of you.

WA: As I said before, my relationship with Sean Penn was wonderful. I'd use him again in a second. I think he'd work with me again. We never had a moment that wasn't civil. He always knew his lines—he may have studied them five minutes before he came to the set but he always knew them. He was wide open to suggestions. And as I said, he had his own suggestions; if I liked them, great, if I didn't like them, he never made a stink about it. He also offered me a part in a film he planned to direct, so it was a very positive experience for both of us.

EL: Did he have any problems with the part?

WA: There were certain scenes, as with any actor, but I felt that most of the time he brought his genius—and it *is* genius—to the acting. Ninety-five percent of the time he made everything sing. He learned all the guitar fingering, he could play those songs, as I said earlier. I heard him play "Limehouse Blues" slowly while he was waiting to rehearse and he was amazing. He's devoted. His ability as an actor carried him through to what a musician should be.

There were just a couple of scenes he didn't get to my liking and I shot them over and over and we came back two weeks later and came back two weeks after that.

EL: What was the problem?

WA: He just wasn't getting the comic nuances the way I heard them in my mind. I've always said if you scratch the surface of a scene that's not working, 99 percent of the time it's the writing. Once in a while it's the acting, once in a while it's the directing, but almost always it's the writing. So my feeling is, I was saddling him with material that if he wasn't getting, nobody would have gotten.

EL: What were the scenes that required so many reshoots?

WA: Most noteworthy was the one in the poolroom with the two hookers. That originally was in a hotel where one of the johns was fighting with a girl and Sean has to intervene on her behalf because he was managing the girls. That scene didn't work out well, so we went back and shot it again, and shot it again, and I rewrote it each time. Finally I changed it to the poolroom. But he was always ready; he never said, "Hey, what's going on here? I've done this scene three times." And he always gave me more than I dreamed of. When you get an actor to do those lines the way he does them, it's a treat.

EL: In *Small Time Crooks* you played opposite two great comediennes.

WA: I was working with Tracey Ullman, who is a great, great, great talent and that really helped. And Elaine May's an iconic American comedienne. I really surrounded myself with great talent.

EL: You and Elaine May both worked the nightclub scene in the sixties, and Jack Rollins managed Nichols and May. Were you friends then? Are you now?

WA: Elaine's path and mine would cross occasionally in the sixties because [*Woody's second wife*] Louise [*Lasser*] was playing in a thing called *The Private Bar* in Greenwich Village with Peter Boyle and Elaine was the director. I was right across the street at the Bitter End. I think she and Mike [*Nichols; Nichols and May teamed up in 1957 and were a seminal comic act*] were tremendous talents. I'm not a social friend of Elaine's, but we've always been very friendly and seem to like each other though our paths rarely cross. I saw her more when we each had a one-act play as part of *Death Defying Acts* [1995] because we would be backstage together either commiserating or kvetching. [*Their relationship with director Michael Blakemore was not easy. Woody's piece was* Central Park West. *David Mamet provided the third of the plays.*]

I named the character May when I wrote it and Elaine was the first choice, as was Tracey. Zero problem with Elaine. She shows up on time, she knows her lines, she can ad-lib creatively and is willing to. If you don't want her to, she won't. She's a dream. She puts herself in your hands. She's a genius, and I don't use that word casually. It's in her voice.

Tracey's also a massive comic talent—limitless in her ability. Two hilarious women.

EL: How was it acting with Diane Keaton in *Manhattan Murder Mystery* [*see page 93*] after, what, a dozen years or more?

WA: I thought there was real chemistry between Keaton and me. I really feel that in that kind of relationship, in that kind of equation, we'd always be great together. You know what's interesting? I wrote that for Mia, then everything fell apart and Keaton stepped in to do it. She is such a strong comedienne, such a vibrant comedienne, that the whole emphasis shifted and she became the funny one. If Mia had been in it, I would have been the funny one because I'm a more naturally comic person than Mia. But that equation is always great where Keaton has the mad lust to follow the guy and do all the things and I'm the one saying, "Take it easy." She's such a great maniac.

EL: You worked with Anjelica Huston again in this, in a far different role than she had in *Crimes and Misdemeanors*.

WA: I was lucky to get to work with Anjelica because she is one of those actresses who make everything real and project intelligence, and I needed someone who projected intelligence. Some people just do it. Jodie Foster does. Great talents. I'm very lucky.

There was a scene that was cut out of the picture where I kissed Anjelica but she had to sit on the sofa [*laugh*] and then I walked by and kissed her [*bigger laugh*] because if you think Julia Roberts was tall, [*with Anjelica Huston*] it was like kissing, I don't know, Kareem Abdul-Jabbar.

EL: This is a circular way to ask about comic performers, but a psychiatrist who interviewed you wrote that you are childlike in your makeup. Does he have a point? Do you see yourself as childlike?

WA: I can see why I might be perceived as childish rather than childlike. I'm also more at home with kids because I don't trust adults. [*He laughs.*] Not that I trust many kids. And I can't stand pets—any kind. But this doesn't answer your question. Maybe my social awkwardness makes me seem immature. I have my phobias and general anxiety about many things—dinner parties, meeting people, traveling, [*laughs*] the shower. I've always struggled with life's trivia. Maybe the psychiatrist you're referring to is not that far off.

EL: Do you think this affects you as an actor, especially as a comedian?

WA: It's a little bit of a conundrum. When you start out as a comic you are childlike. Many comics remain childlike their whole life, and many of them remain physically youthful into old age. If you look at Jerry Lewis and Milton Berle [*died 2002*] now, they're like kids, the way they behave. So comics are childlike and they are suing for the approval of the adults. Something goes on in a theater when you're fourteen years old and you want to get up onstage and make the audience laugh. You're always the supplicant, wanting to please and to get warm laughs. Then what happens to comics—they make it and they become a thousand times more wealthy than their audience, more famous, more idolized, more traveled, more cultivated, more experienced, more sophisticated, and they're no longer the supplicant. They can buy and sell their audience, they know so much more than their audience, they have lived and traveled around the world a hundred times, they've dined at Buckingham Palace and the White House, they have chauffeured cars and they're rich and they've made love to the world's most beautiful women—and suddenly it becomes difficult to play that loser character, because they don't feel it. Being a supplicant has become much harder to sell. If you're not careful, you can easily become less amusing, less funny. Many become pompous. You can think of some, I'm sure. If you're lucky you grow up in the roles you play, like Robin Williams, for example. He grew with success.

A strange thing occurs: you go from court jester to king. It's very hard unless you work at retaining your perspective. Someone like Chaplin really had that problem. He was torn. He could play the "little fella," but really who he had become was the consort of kings and queens and the guy who now fancied he had statements to make about capital punishment and fascism, and so he was no longer very funny. In fact, I think he was quite awful in those films.

It becomes unbecoming to see guys sixty, seventy years old walking on the sides of their feet [*laughs*]. An interesting problem.

EL: How much has this affected you?

WA: I think it has affected me to a certain degree. I used to sit with my girlfriend in the Thalia and the New Yorker theaters when we would see a foreign film on a

Friday night and I was twenty years old, and I would think while they were changing films, My God, I could get up onstage here and just fracture these people. They would think I'm so funny. I could make jokes and just fracture them. And they later proved to be a great audience for me in clubs. Then over the years you gain a certain amount of success—financial success, critical success, personal success—and you try to elevate your work. And that's where I'll strike out in my most embarrassing ways. Sometimes I make it, but I often strike out. I can't go out tomorrow and make a series of films like *Take the Money and Run* and *Bananas*. I expect more of myself and the audience does, too. They want to hear my observations on something. It's very hard to keep that in balance and not become a pontificating ass. And so when I try and do a serious film, I can easily fall—and have fallen—into that trap where I become a blowhard, and that's when I have my most embarrassing failures.

April 2005

Woody has recently finished Match Point *(see page 24). It is the first of three pictures in a row he will make in London, followed by one in Barcelona. The direct cause of filming away from New York is that the most favorable financing deals for his films are in Europe, but also these are cities he is comfortable in, and the chance to work with European actors and crew members is an agreeable one to him.*

EL: *Match Point* is one of the few films you've not made in New York. How was it making a picture in London rather than your own neighborhood?

WA: *Match Point* was great, absolutely great to do. I didn't think it would be, but it was fabulous. First off, the weather was great because it was London in the summer, so it's cool. You don't have any of the drop-dead heat you have here. Two, because it's London you get a lot of gray skies, which is very pretty for photography. Three, they have a huge pool of wonderful actors and actresses who are happy to play small roles, and every little role of *Match Point* is beautifully played. It is really a treat. And because they don't have the same union setups we have here, there is a much freer way of working. I don't mean exploitive, but a lighting stand-in for someone can pick up a megaphone and direct traffic for a moment. It's like student filmmaking in the best sense of that word. Everybody does everything. They just don't work in the regimented way we work here. For example, when we go out on the street in New York we have a million ADs [*assistant directors*] doing crowd control. There, they don't do any crowd control. Sometimes somebody will look in the camera and they'll do another take. It's a very loose, easygoing thing. It's just great. I had a wonderful time. And I made one of my better films. For me to say that is something.

EL: Any other differences between London and New York?

WA: To an American ear, the English sounds so great. The English actors are wonderfully trained. They sound like a million bucks when they do your lines. I wasn't making an American picture in London, I was making a British picture, it was a British story. The picture I'm going to do this summer [Scoop] is more about Americans in London.

EL: How does European financing differ from American?

WA: Doing films in Europe looks like it may be a good thing for me because in the United States, for one reason or another, they want participation. They say, "Look, we're not just the bank. We want to be in on the casting, we want to read the script, we like to know what we're getting"—and I can't work that way. These businessmen in the United States fancy themselves creative mentalities, and they're the opposite. They adduce for proof financial success in movies, and the financial successes they have are almost always questions of luck. They do a number of films and some of them work and most of them don't work, and they really feel they're making creative contributions when they're only obstacles tolerated by creative people not in a position to tell them to get lost. They don't know the first thing about writing, or about directing, or acting, yet they want to be in on it. But in Europe, they're not used to studio systems and nobody there fancies himself an expert.

EL: Scarlett Johansson is your newest find.

WA: Scarlett's just a wonderful actress. I was a great fan of Scarlett's from *Ghost World* and *Lost in Translation*. But she was not the first person I took for the part. I thought because of the way the money was raised for the film we had to use European Union actors, so I cast the film with all English people and I cast the wonderful British actress Kate Winslet. But as we got closer to shooting, and I understood this completely, she just felt that she had been working for so long and neglecting her kid by going from one picture to another, that she wanted to spend time with her family, so she bowed out. I wrote her a note saying, "Believe me, my highest priority is not filmmaking, either, no problem at all. Maybe someday we can work on something else."

By that time we had hired so many British people that my sister [*Letty Aronson, his producer*] pointed out that we had fulfilled our contractual obligation regarding British tax requirements and we could use an American. We sat around and talked and thought Scarlett Johansson would be great, and Juliet found she was available. She was just no-nonsense. I sent her the script on Friday afternoon and by Sunday night she was committed. She came, did her costume tests, showed up on the set;

the first day we did a very hard scene and she did it brilliantly. She's a wonderful actress. Over the years I've worked with Keaton and Wiest and people who have been sensational. And many people I've worked with briefly were wonderful: Helen Hunt and Téa Leoni and Christina Ricci and Radha Mitchell, one after the other. Now I've lucked out with Scarlett.

EL: How much did you have to rewrite to change the character from English to American?

WA: I had to do a little rewriting, but that only helped us in strengthening the premise.

EL: Scarlett's character, Nola Rice, starts off as pure confident sexuality, but as the story progresses she slowly builds up a hysterical, demanding quality. Was that easy to get?

WA: Scarlett has such a built-in likeable quality that I really had to work on her so the audience wouldn't get mad that she gets done in. I had to be very careful there. I could have cast any number of actresses where the audience would think, I'm on his side, but with Scarlett, she has so much personal charm and humor and vulnerability, I had to make sure that when he took care of her, it was okay with the audience—that it was not like killing Mary Poppins.

EL: This is a lot different from when the Martin Landau character arranged for the murder of the Anjelica Huston character in *Crimes and Misdemeanors*.

WA: Yes. Anjelica is a taller person and she's older and she has a different quality totally, a much more commanding presence than Scarlett. Scarlett is a younger, more vulnerable actress. Anjelica was a grown woman when we did that picture, probably in her thirties, and Scarlett wasn't even twenty. Just different personas.

EL: Scarlett's character really begins to turn darker in the scene outside the office where she yells, "You lied!" and is almost out of control with rage and hysteria.

WA: She's great. She just turns it on. She's a wonderful actress. The first scene I worked with her, she had flown the night before and arrived in London in the morning. She came right over to the pub and I had no rehearsals or anything. [*It is an intense scene with Jonathan Rhys-Meyers (Chris), who has become obsessed with Nola.*] She plays a little bit drunk, and the first takes were great. I was blessed. It was like everyone was from an all-star team.

EL: What is it about Scarlett's look that is so effective?

WA: She's sensuous. She's got a wonderful face full of character, and pretty of course, and a wonderful body, and the sum total you can't quantify in the way you couldn't quantify it with Marilyn Monroe—you can only talk about it, but you never get it. Everything comes together: her personality, her voice, her look, her eyes, her weight, her lips, everything comes together in a way that the whole is greater in some way than the sum of the parts—and we're talking about some pretty great parts. It's a combination of nature and nurture, but mostly nature; it's all those genes. It's the same with any star. You could pick any at random, whether it's Nicole Kidman, or Marilyn Monroe, or Julia Roberts. Something magical happens.

With men, you look at those old movie stars like William Powell and Humphrey Bogart and Edward G. Robinson, these guys were not, you know, great-looking guys in the conventional sense. But for some reason everything came together with Bogart and everything came together with George C. Scott. They had sex appeal without being gorgeous. Scarlett has sex appeal and *is* gorgeous.

EL: Did you know much of Rhys-Meyers's work?

WA: I saw him in *Bend It Like Beckham* and I knew he was what I wanted. I also knew he'd be good, but I wasn't prepared for how good he was. I already knew how good Emily Mortimer [*Chloe, the daughter who falls for Chris*] and Brian Cox and Penelope Wilton [*her parents*] were.

Matthew Goode [*Chloe's brother, who brings Chris to the family*] was a discovery because I saw him on tape. I asked, "Who is this guy?" And people said, "Well, I don't know, he's a charming guy but I don't know if he can play this kind of dramatic thing. He can be amusing." But not only could he play it, he fleshed the character out for me beautifully, adding his own little idiomatic phrases and locutions. He did a beautiful job.

EL: There is more sexual intensity in *Match Point* than almost any other film of yours.

WA: There is sexual attraction but you don't see any real sex, any hard-core sex, and you don't see anybody get killed. The sexual intensity comes from the two stars. I put them in situations that are sexy to a degree; it's sexier when Jonathan Rhys-Meyers rubs her back with oil than to see two people making love, or when he throws her down in the rain. There's sexuality without showing any real sex. You get the idea. That's more fun. Real sex, you can see that all you want. It looks like pistons or a pneumatic drill but is rarely sexy.

EL: Did the actors understand their parts quickly?

Woody with Emily Mortimer between shots on *Match Point*. His only direction to her was not to play her character, Chloe, as sweet because, he says, she is innately sweet.

WA: I had no conversations with anybody. I had no conversations with Emily, Scarlett, Penelope, Brian, Matthew. They read it, they got it. Once in a while there was a question. Emily asked me one question when she first started doing her character. Her impulse to begin with was to play very sweet with him [*Rhys-Meyers*], and I said, "Don't do that. It comes out too sweet. You *are* sweet. Just do it plain and simple. It's built into you." That was the one minor piece of direction I had to give in the whole movie. And as soon as I told her that . . . [*snaps fingers*]. I once had to say to Brian Cox, "Can you speak a little louder?" And he laughed and said, "Of course, of course."

May 2005

EL: You've told me that when you're writing you transport yourself into the fantasy but that when you're directing you don't; it's all about filming that bit and putting it into the bank. How about when you're acting?

WA: I always lose myself as a character. I'm a very limited actor but I'm always into it. So if I'm playing a scene with someone and a fire breaks out or a plane passes overhead, I automatically integrate it. I'm there all the time. But I'm also watching myself doing it, even when I'm living it at the time. I was playing a scene [*in* Deconstructing Harry] with Kirstie Alley—she's a terrific actress and very funny [*although in this scene they are fighting*]—and she slapped a glass out of my hand and it broke, which was not in the script. But because she was in the scene, she just kept going. I reacted appropriately because I was in the scene as well. That's always the case for me. That's why I have no trouble making up dialogue as I go along. It's just easy for me. I could ad-lib a whole movie if I had to because it's really what I do as a writer. This is just something that comes easily to me. If it comes easily to a person, then it's no big deal—nor is it any guarantee it will be good.

EL: When you were shooting *Play It Again, Sam,* there is the scene in the bar where you down a shot of whiskey and have an elaborate reaction. The whole crew had to contain itself during the shot, and then exploded with laughter when Herb Ross called "Cut!" And you laughed as well. Did you know it was so funny?

WA: You make yourself laugh because the work is always a surprise to you. If I'm home writing a joke, I will get a funny feeling from it because it's a surprise to me—it's coming from my unconscious. The same thing with a take. It makes you laugh, too, because somehow it's just as big a surprise to you as it is to your lighting guy.

EL: Does it take you any time to memorize your lines?

WA: I don't memorize them. When I finish a script I'm on to my next film. I finished my script for this summer [Scoop], I gave it out two weeks ago, and I will probably never look at it again. Just before I shoot the scene I look at what the scene is and I say the dialogue the way I want to say it. It comes out the way I wrote it, or close to the way I wrote it.

EL: So it's stored away in your mind for easy collection?

WA: It's what I would say in that circumstance. I could write something, thinking of what the arguments are between the people in that scene, and then put the script away. If I rewrote that scene from scratch six months later or three months

Woody says of Scarlett Johansson that "every time I say something funny or that I think is dazzling, Scarlett effortlessly outscores me. I have a good chemistry with her because she is very bright, very quick, very funny."

later, I would write pretty much the same dialogue. It may not be in the exact order, but it could be. The same responses would be there in both cases. It's always been this way.

EL: Did you know Scarlett was going to be in the new picture [Scoop] when you sat down to write?

WA: Yes, because we had talked at the end of the last picture about doing something. I said, "You should do something where you are amusing because you're very funny." She kept herself available.

EL: You famously don't talk with actors on the set but you do with Scarlett, a lot. It seems that you have the easy and bantering relationship with her that you have with Diane Keaton.

WA: She falls into the category of those who always top me. It doesn't matter what I say, she comes back with a topping line. Keaton is that way, and my daughters Bechet and Manzie. Every time I say something funny or that I think is dazzling, Scarlett effortlessly outscores me. So of course to an old comic person like myself, I give that a lot of respect. I'm always amazed that she snaps back that quickly and that effectively. I have a good chemistry with her because she is very bright, very quick, very funny. And I think that she gets confidence—not that she needs confidence—from the obvious pleasure I get from her. She feels secure that I enjoy her so much.

EL: But you rarely socialize with actors, even her.

WA: Yes. Scarlett says I'm antisocial. [*He laughs.*] I'm not antisocial; I'm just not social.

Comedians gathered at the Carnegie Delicatessen tell the story of *Broadway Danny Rose.* From far left: Corbett Monica; Sandy Baron; Will Jordan; Woody's manager for fifty years, Jack Rollins; Howie Storm; Jackie Gayle; and Morty Gunty. As a young stand-up, Woody spent many evenings with Rollins this way.

EL: In *Broadway Danny Rose*, how much were you consciously doing a valentine to Jack and Charlie? [*Jack Rollins and Charles Joffe have been Woody's managers since the late 1950s and embody Danny's loyalty, as does Woody to them, although they don't have him over for turkey TV dinners at Thanksgiving, as Danny Rose does his clients. Danny (Woody) is the manager of performers on the furthest outskirts of show business: a balloon sculptor, a water glass melody player, skating penguins, a somewhat proficient hypnotist (he can get the subjects under; it's bringing them out of the trance that's still to be mastered), and Lou Canova, a singer with a single long-ago hit about indigestion, "Agita," for whom Danny wangles a comeback engagement at the Waldorf-Astoria Hotel. Lou, who's married, wants his mistress, Tina (Mia Farrow), a tough but entirely alluring woman with a haystack of teased blond hair, constant dark glasses, garish skintight apparel, and a streetwise, uncultured accent, who is the unsentimental widow of a mobster ("He had it comin!"), to be at the show, and Danny goes to New Jersey to fetch her. What follows is a Runyonesque adventure as told by a group of comics gathered around a table in a Manhattan delicatessen. Two stories intertwine: the unlikely romance between the selfish Tina and the selfless Danny, who for years is the only person who believed in Lou's talent; and the fickleness of Lou, who, sensing the big time at last, dumps Danny for a bigger-name manager. (Jack Rollins, who sat with Woody in his first years as a stand-up night after night at a similar table dissecting his performance and talking comedy, is among the comedians at the table in the film.)*]

First impressions can establish an actress in the mind of the audience, and "I take a lot of time in certain pictures to make sure that I've sold the actress to the audience the way I imagined her," Woody says. Four examples: Christina Ricci in *Anything Else;* Diane Keaton in *Sleeper;* Barbara Hershey in *Hannah and Her Sisters;* and Scarlett Johansson in *Match Point* (whom he recostumed and reshot three times to get the effect he wanted).

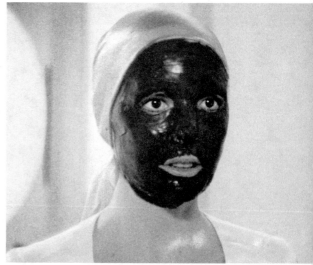

WA: I just knew that milieu very well. The impetus to do it was really twofold. One, that Mia wanted to play Mrs. Rao, Annie Rao, who we knew and would see up at the restaurant all the time [*Rao's, a popular New York eatery*]. And I wanted to play a different kind of character, not a neurotic, literate New Yorker. And one of the characters I can play, as I said before, is a lowlife. It just [*laughs*] comes kind of naturally.

EL: I recall only one short scene in the film where she's not wearing dark glasses. I think the only time you see her eyes in the whole picture is when she's just come out of the shower.

WA: She had a tough job doing that.

EL: It's really a hard way to sell a character.

WA: Yeah, but the glasses *gave* her so much character in the movie. But she had to act without using her eyes. And if you look at the shot, she's *incredibly* beautiful. It's one of the prettiest shots of Mia.

EL: There is an old axiom that the director has to fall in love with the actress through the camera so that the audience will as well. Do you agree?

WA: I take a lot of time in certain pictures to make sure that I've sold the actress to the audience the way I imagined her. I took a lot of time to do that with Christina Ricci in *Anything Else*. I did the same with Scarlett in *Match Point*. Three times I shot the scene when Scarlett meets Jonathan Rhys-Meyers at the Ping-Pong table. [*It is the first time the audience sees her, and the shot immediately establishes her beauty and dangerous sexuality, which are central to the story.*] I changed her hair,

I changed her costume, I changed the way I shot it, the cameraman and I talked about it. But it was very important for me to present the vision of her as I felt her in that character. So yes, a lot of work goes into that.

Of course, sometimes you don't have to do that, but other times it's important for the picture that the impact of one of the characters be made. Sometimes the effectiveness of the female character doesn't have to be so overpowering, but in those two films, among others, the leading women had to be very effective from the start. You had to show why Jason Biggs would be so obsessed with Christina and take so much from her, and put up with her sleeping around and living with her crazy mother and cheating on him all the time. I thought Christina had a kind of compelling, pretty, sexy quality and she could get a guy hung up on her. And the same with Scarlett.

But in *Scoop* she plays a semi-nerd. I devoted no attention to making her sexy. What little attention I devoted was so she would look like a potentially attractive college kid.

EL: Any others who come to mind?

WA: Keaton with green stuff on her face in *Sleeper*. Barbara Hershey in *Hannah*. You have to know why guys are attracted to her.

EL: Have you ever thought of bringing a character back?

WA: I've thought that you could do another story with some of them, but *Annie Hall 2,* I wouldn't want to do. I've had a lot of interest from other people in that over the years.

EL: Are you ever tempted to do it?

WA: No. And neither is Keaton.

EL: Julie Kavner as the interior decorator in *Alice* was very funny.

WA: She's the best. I've worked with Julie a number of times. She was my wife in the television movie of *Don't Drink the Water*. She never disappoints. She's always worried, self-effacing worried about how she's going to be—and she's always sensational.

EL: Let's talk about other actors you admire. You once told me that you want to write a movie for Hugh Grant. Let's start with him. In *Small Time Crooks* you cast him against type, or at least the loveable bungler he played in a series of movies, by making him a cad.

WA: He's an actor who I've always enjoyed. He was as good as I thought he would be. There was no doubt in my mind that he would be a great cad, because he's so charming and so skillful.

EL: Wallace Shawn is someone you rely on a lot.

WA: Wally is a very fine actor, very fine; not only funny but completely believable and credible. I've used him a number of times and he always comes through.

EL: You've used him since *Manhattan*.

WA: If it were the late 1930s or 1940s, Wally would be one of those great beloved guys who appeared in millions of movies and who you always got a positive buzz about the moment you saw him on the screen. You knew you were in good hands.

EL: Who haven't you worked with whom you'd like to?

WA: I've always wanted to work with Cate Blanchett. I thought she was great when I saw her in [The Talented] *Mr. Ripley*. She's great in everything she does. Reese Witherspoon.

EL: What about Dustin Hoffman?

WA: I've often said that Dustin Hoffman could have played the role I played in a dozen or so movies and played them better than I played them. But the guy is never available. He's always wonderful, but he's always working.

EL: Have you ever talked about doing a film together?

Wallace Shawn
(right), a favorite
character actor of
Woody's, in *Shadows
and Fog*

WA: He's evinced a desire. We talked about it once or twice, but we never could get it together at the same time. First of all, I could never pay him anything like he usually gets [*because of Woody's low budgets, actors in his films are routinely paid only scale, a few thousand dollars a week*], so he would have to be in a mood to work on the cheap. I never hit him when he was open. I remember calling him once on some project and he said that he had just scored a big hit and was finally earning good money after doing years of good work but struggling financially, and his management wanted him to do a couple of pictures in which he could earn some money, and I completely understood that.

EL: How about Jack Nicholson?

WA: I called him about *Hannah and Her Sisters* and he said that he had family commitments with John Huston—because he was going with Anjelica—to do *Prizzi's Honor*, if the picture went. If it didn't go, he would be available. The picture went, he won the Academy Award for it, and the guy I got to replace him, Michael Caine . . . [*He laughs.*]

EL: Won the Academy Award.

WA: Using an English actor was not my first choice. Because I wrote it for an American, I wanted an American. But I was very lucky to get Michael. Michael Caine, I've often said, is incapable of an unreal moment. He's just one of those actors who was born graceful in front of the camera and he's a truly, truly fabulous movie actor. I mean, he's got what you want for the movies, a complete ease and naturalness. Nothing ever seems like acting. It seems like he's talking all the time, you know, realistic talking.

EL: Who else fits that bill for you?

WA: Liam Neeson is a wonderful actor, also incapable of an unreal moment. I have worked with a number of great actors, but that's no revelation. Gene Hackman, I worked with him briefly, but to say he's a great actor is not news.

I've worked with a million people over the years and they've all been really wonderful. That's been my secret of directing actors: hire wonderful people [*laughs*] and take credit for their work. You hire Ian Holm and Gena Rowlands, what does it take to get superb performances out of them? Nothing. You just have to tell them what time to show up and provide the coffee and doughnuts. And that's what I've been doing my whole life, hiring people who can do it.

And they do it and they say to the press in their interviews, "He never spoke to me. The guy never talked to me the whole time I was there." Yes, because they were great. If they weren't, I'd have had to speak to them all the time.

And the reporter says, "You were so great in the movie." And he thinks, Well, it can't be that he never talked to them, or he's got this way of working that's brilliant and gets these great performances out of actors and it appears [*laughs*] as though he's never talking to them.

But the cold truth is [*still laughing*], I hire them, they're great. Michael Caine was great in *Educating Rita*, the picture he did right before mine. He's been great since then. He is always wonderful. I never had to direct him.

When I say "never," to be completely honest, once in a great while I will say to every actor or actress, "Will you seem a little more suspicious there?" or something like that. Maybe once or twice I'll venture something.

EL: There are some directors who need to impose their will on the actor.

WA: There'll be many times when I'll think to myself, Why is this actress yelling it so angrily? That's not what I had in mind when I wrote it. Then I'll say, "Could you do this slower and a little easier?" And the actress will. And she'll do it fine. And I'll say, "Great, thank you." Then when I'm putting the picture together I see that her way was the right way. Yelling it *was* completely correct for the character and completely in context and I was just married to the feeling that I had when I was writing at home, but her instinct when she read the script was better than mine. So having lived through that a number of times, I stopped correcting actors when they didn't read things the way I wanted unless I was 100 percent sure it was a disaster. But otherwise I found that their imposing their will on me worked better than me imposing mine.

EL: John Huston and Alfred Hitchcock come to mind as two directors who were really tough on actors.

WA: Well, I don't think the performances in Hitchcock's movies are ultra-special. Some of them are wonderful because the actors he used are wonderful. Cary Grant was a wonderful actor. So was Claude Rains.

John Huston, on the other hand, whatever he was doing, he was doing right. If imposing himself on the actors was how he got those performances, then I have to say that that was the perfect way for him to work, because the performances in Huston's movies are often superb, whereas in Hitchcock's they're often mediocre— although I love his pictures.

EL: You speak so highly of the actors you work with, whereas he is famous for saying that "actors should be treated like cattle."

WA: You know, for his kind of picture, I think instinctively he didn't want Marlon Brando's kind of depth and complexity. His are not those kinds of characters.

Instinctively, he knew what was right for him. But no, I wouldn't call Hitchcock a great actors' director.

EL: He had such a stylized heroine—cold and blond.

WA: He liked that and it worked for him.

EL: In your films, there's almost every kind of look imaginable in leading women—Judy Davis, Diane Keaton, Charlize Theron, Mia Farrow, Dianne Wiest, Scarlett Johansson.

WA: Yes, I don't have an obsession with one kind of look. I find Charlize Theron beautiful and Christina Ricci beautiful; one is a tall blonde, the other is a small brunette.

EL: In 1989, when you were making *Crimes and Misdemeanors,* you talked about the gulf between your Brooklyn childhood and what you'd become and you told me, "It's an amazing thing when I think back on the awful days in that little school, and coming home and sitting at the oilcloth-covered table, that one day I would actually be in a movie with Charles Boyer [Casino Royale] or direct Van Johnson. It's so unimaginable to me, and I guess you can say in a certain way that I get the full value of appreciation of all that's happened. Such an astonishing fact has retained its power to amaze me. Sometimes when I look in the mirror I'll see myself back there and I'll say, 'You're Allan Konigsberg from Brooklyn. Shouldn't you be eating in the basement?' " [*He laughs.*]
Yet almost any actress or actor in the world is happy to be in your films. Do you still have the same reaction? Do you ever think back to the days when you sat in the Midwood and Kent theaters in Brooklyn, that one day you would be able to get pretty much whomever you wanted to act for you?

WA: I didn't think that. I never think that. I always think, you give a person a part and they make whatever career move they think is right for them at the time. If I'm offering them a part and someone's offering them ten million bucks for another film, they take the other film. And if they think doing my part won't pay anything but it will showcase them in a way that will get them ten million next year, they'll do my picture.
But to this day I think to myself of the day we were shooting *Purple Rose* in the Kent and how I said to myself, I'm directing a film with [*laughs*] *Van Johnson* in it; I'm directing *Van Johnson.* I know I mentioned this earlier. Now, he in his wildest dreams couldn't have imagined how I felt about that. But if you had told me as I was prowling the streets of Flatbush as a kid—East Fourteenth Street and East Fifteenth Street—and looking in the windows of tailor shops and barbershops at the

cards they put up for the local movie houses and a card would say, "Such-and-such a picture starring such-and-such a person and Van Johnson"—if you had said to me, "You are going to be directing Van Johnson one day in a movie," I just would not have believed it. There were certain things from my childhood that were—I guess if something unimaginable in your childhood happens, it's amazing. It was not amazing to me that I was having dinner with Ingmar Bergman. It was a wonderful experience for me, but it was not amazing like that, probably because I became enamored of his films in my adult years. But when Mia and I took Eve Arden to dinner, I just couldn't get my mind around it. I thought, My God, Eve Arden, the wisecracking woman with the wonderful voice that I grew up on, who I thought was so funny when I was ten years old.

I first had that feeling in *Casino Royale.* I thought, My God, I'm in a movie with *Charles Boyer,* but it wasn't the same thing because I never met him. [*Pauses.*] And David Niven, whom I actually met. Niven was not a kind of local neighborhood icon of my childhood. He was someone I came to later in life and appreciated. But Van Johnson . . . I remember when I was making *Everything You Always Wanted to Know About Sex,* I interviewed Lon Chaney Jr. I thought, My God, it's the *Wolfman*! I mean, I'm sitting here in a chair and it's *Lon Chaney Jr.* So I never outgrew, apparently, certain childhood emotions about those people.

EL: Did you do silent comedy as a kid, either in front of a mirror or for your friends? How did you hone the skill?

WA: You don't. If you're funny, you do it. Verbal comics like Groucho Marx just have an automatic instinct to be funny physically—in his walk and when he dances or when he runs around and jumps on furniture. If you're funny, you're funny physically.

Woody as Mike Monroe seeking cover as a robot in *Sleeper.* While working out a comic walk to use he marveled, "I can't believe a man of my intelligence has to walk funny to make people laugh."

Marshall Brickman is a funny guy. So when he would demonstrate a joke, he would be physically funny. It sounds like I'm oversimplifying it, but if you're funny, it's not hard. If you can draw, you can draw. It's not a big deal.

EL: No, I understand. I remember watching you try out several different walks for your robot character in *Sleeper*. I just wondered if you ever worked out routines in front of mirrors or practiced them in any way—acted them out, so to speak.

WA: No, no, it's just instinctive. I could get an audience to laugh without talking—providing there are some props around.

EL: What's happening in your mind as you do physical comedy? Are you living what would be the dialogue so well that you're just reacting to the circumstance?

WA: No, you're not thinking. It's instinctive. If I'm sitting on the stage and a great-looking woman passes, I can get a laugh from the audience the way I respond to her physically. You feel it at the time.

EL: That's what I was getting at. For instance, in *Sleeper* you're sitting there as a robot and the guy's got calipers and he's yanking the heads off these other poor robots and you're next in line. Were you saying to yourself, What would I think if this were happening? Or are you just able to put that aside and have no intellectualization at all?

WA: Just automatically. I could play it now. The same thing that makes you funny verbally makes you do the physically funny things. People who are funny are funny and people that are not funny . . .

EL: Have to get another job.

WA: Actually, there are a lot of people who earn a living who are not really being authentically funny. In every profession there are a few really good ones. I'm certainly not putting myself in that category, just saying that in any profession, whether it's brain surgery or cops or comics, there are a few really good ones and the rest are, you know, basically workers who can do it but they're not inspired.

February 2006

In all our conversations, I don't recall Woody commenting on how he looks in a film, with three exceptions. He recently mentioned that he cut his nose while shaving the morning of the first day of filming on Take the Money and Run, *a scene with him in a cell in San Quentin. He says the cut is evident on the screen, though I have never noticed it in the many times I've watched the picture. I tell this to Woody. He is surprised; perhaps it is visible only on a movie screen and not on a TV monitor. He then tells me of another injury.*

WA: If you look at *Play It Again, Sam,* there is a place where I had my lower lip biopsied.

EL: I never noticed that, either. Only after you mentioned it and I looked carefully, could I see that your lip, from playing the clarinet right before shooting, is swollen in *Curse of the Jade Scorpion.* [*There is always a bit of a bump on his lower lip from so many thousands of hours of gripping the reed and mouthpiece.*]

WA: Yeah, I never did that again. It was terrible.

EL: I know *Husbands and Wives* is one of your favorite films, and it also was the last of thirteen films you did with Mia Farrow, many of which were in part tailored for her, for instance her pregnancy in *Another Woman* because of her real-life pregnancy.

WA: She is a wonderful actress. Any differences we had were personal. It was a pleasure to work with her. I found her very professional. I liked writing for her because I was aware that she could do things that she wasn't getting a chance to do—like *Danny Rose.* No one would have hired her to do that because they wouldn't have known she *could* do it and *wanted* to do it; I knew that because I had a personal relationship with her. She was always self-deprecating, telling me how bad she was going to be and then doing it much better than you had any right to expect.

EL: This goes back to something we discussed earlier. There were a couple of times when you wrote something special for Mia, but on the other occasions when you were writing did you think, What could she do in this? Or did you feel she could play almost anything you wrote?

WA: I thought she had a very good range, that she could play comedy, that she could play serious things. In *Another Woman,* a picture that was not overly lively, she was *very* good, *very* good. But because the picture suffered, she didn't earn the acclaim she deserved. She could do anything I gave her. She was game to experiment, like in *Radio Days,* when neither of us had the faintest idea about her character when we started. She could sing a song if she had to and it would be pretty effective. And she was very pretty, of course.

EL: Were there parts in other films besides *Zelig, Another Woman,* and *Danny Rose* that you wrote for her or to accommodate her?

WA: Yeah, I did write things knowing she would play it, and I was slanting things toward her, but I didn't have to slant very much because she could do them all well. It was a good experience to work with her. Now, it's possible, being fatalistic about it, that after all those pictures, it was too much already. I mean, thirteen pictures is a lot. I did a cluster of pictures with Diane Keaton, but eventually we stopped working together, for the most part. So maybe that was a blessing to the audience that we weren't going to work together because I do have a habit of getting into grooves and staying in them. But on a professional level I only have praise for her.

EL: Mia was going to do *Manhattan Murder Mystery,* then Diane stepped in. You said that you changed the roles a bit.

WA: Yes, as I said earlier, as soon as Diane took it over, because she is so over-whelmingly funny she became the comic center of it. Mia could play comedy and had a delightful comic sense. But I was a stronger comic than her. Keaton is a stronger comic than me; she just has the more magnetic and funny screen person-ality. I could labor all year and give myself a thousand funny lines, but when the camera hits her, that's what you want to see.

EL: You really believe that.

WA: Yes, absolutely. I see it all the time. I see it when I make films with her and I see it in other people's films—the film with Jack Nicholson and Amanda Peet,

The house of mirrors set at the end of *Manhattan Murder Mystery,* in a scene modeled on the ending of Orson Welles's *The Lady from Shanghai.*

Something's Gotta Give, and *The Family Stone;* when she was in that film with Meryl Streep and Leonardo DiCaprio about the dying kid [*Marvin's Room, 1996*]. She's just got something that works. People come away and say, "God, she's in her fifties and she's sexy," or "I didn't like this movie but I loved her."

I think that next to Judy Holliday, she's *the* greatest screen comedienne we've had. Now, she didn't choose to follow that up in a calculated way. She went in many different directions and didn't care about that, but had she wanted to pursue it specifically, she would have been every bit the giant comedienne Lucille Ball was or any of them. To me she's a much better screen comedienne than the ones that were touted in my youth, like Madeleine Carroll or Carole Lombard. They're fine, but she's superior. It's just she's never pushed it; it comes out in spite of her at times.

EL: What does she say when you tell her this?

WA: She thinks I'm crazy. [*Starts to laugh.*] First of all, she's very self-deprecating and very modest. And I have no credibility with her [*smiling*] because she knows me for the schlemiel I am. She lived with me and knows me intimately. You lose your credibility living together because your partner can't help but see that you're not just [*laughing*] a fallible human being but pathetic. But I've told her many times.

I had a wonderful time making *Manhattan Murder Mystery* with her. . . .

EL: You can see it on the screen.

WA: Because I love working with her, and she brings out the best in me and I bring out something funny in her, and there is chemistry between us, and I love doing this kind of old-timey Hollywood murder mysteries. This one was just that kind of thing. It had everything I grew up liking about those films—the sophisticated New York couple and the glitzy apartment and the sharp one-liners between them and the imminent danger. It had everything I had grown up loving in those wisecracking romantic murder mysteries. I loved playing it, I loved acting it, because I like to knock off those one-liners in those situations. I had a good plot and good surrounding characters, too. As usual, Alan Alda was brilliant as her would-be lover, and Anjelica Huston was great as ever. The plot worked out, and I was able to get a tour de force ending with the mirrors. [*The house of mirrors set in which the murderer is shot is an homage to Orson Welles's* The Lady from Shanghai, *which plays in the background.*]

EL: You didn't have that ending when you started shooting, did you?

WA: No. I couldn't figure out one for a long time but eventually figured one out and wrote it in. The murderer was originally a stamp dealer and I changed that to a movie house owner. Then I put in all that stuff about it being a broken-down movie house and you had to go backstage and see the mirrors. We built the set.

I just had a good time making that movie. And it came out very well. It's really one of my best movies. The only thing it suffers from is that it is a crime movie, a genre movie, but to me that doesn't make any difference whatsoever.

But I do think it's one of my best movies because everything in it works. The romance works. The danger works. . . .

EL: You said how much better the television version of *Don't Drink the Water* [*1994*] came out with you and Julie Kavner than the movie with Jackie Gleason and Estelle Parsons. [*Based on Woody's first Broadway play, produced in 1966 and made into a film in 1969. It is the farcical story of a bumpkin New Jersey family forced to take refuge in the American embassy in a communist country. He did not appear in the Broadway version but by 1994 was old enough to play the father.*]

WA: The original on Broadway with Lou Jacobi was quite funny, but the movie was ghastly. As bad as anything ever committed to celluloid.

What I did for TV was fine for what it was. The people were great. Julie Kavner [*as the mother*] was wonderful, Michael J. Fox [*the young diplomat who falls for the daughter*] was wonderful, and Dom DeLuise [*a priest who has lived in asylum for years*], I couldn't keep a straight face. I can hardly work with him, he makes me laugh so hard.

EL: *Celebrity.* You brought Sven Nykvist back and shot it in black and white. Some people said that Kenneth Branagh was imitating you. [*He plays Lee Simon, a journalist briefly brought into the circle of the celebrated.*]

WA: I had fun doing *Celebrity* but people were very critical. My own feeling is that they didn't like the movie and they were searching for a reason—not consciously but emotionally—and they pinned it on that. Because the truth of the matter is, Kenneth Branagh is very different from me as a natural personality, and even if he was imitating me, which he wasn't, *so what?*

EL: He was doing a New York guy and because you do a New York guy, people substituted one for the other.

WA: Yes, that picture will be judged much more objectively years from now, when people are not so interested in me—not that I'm in their consciousness—when they'll be able to look at that picture and judge it apart from whether Branagh is imitating me. I always felt I was lucky to get him. He did a job far superior to one I could have done if I had played it. He's a great actor. And I think that movie came off.

That movie was a look at celebrity in our society: the obsession with fame, celebrity, the perks that it brings, the power that it brings and the whole obsession with how people respond to it and what a cushy life it leads to. Celebrity also leads to some annoying things, but my opinion is that the perks far outweigh the negatives.

Getting back to Branagh, if I saw, let's say, *A Bronx Tale*—I liked it very much— and let's say that Chazz Palminteri in that movie was doing Al Pacino, I still would have liked the movie. I liked his persona on the screen, I liked the story; it wouldn't have bothered me. But Kenneth wasn't imitating, certainly not in the sense of Philip Seymour Hoffman re-creating Capote. But that became a very fashionable thing to say about characters in my films, that John Cusack in *Bullets over Broadway* was doing me and Will Ferrell in *Melinda and Melinda* was doing me. There were even people who said that Jonathan Rhys-Meyers in *Match Point* was playing the Woody Allen character. And I just smile and say, "Uh-huh" and move on. And these are people who *like* the movie. The notion that Jonathan was me could not be more hilarious.

I never mind or get upset if someone doesn't like a movie of mine, though of course I'd prefer it if they did. When I show my movies to people for a reaction, what I'd like them to say to me is, "I loved it," or "I started out liking it but then you lost me," or "I got bored in the second half." I like a simple reaction. But if they get into analysis of the film and what they feel is wrong with it, they lose me. It's very hard for anyone to figure out what's wrong with the film and why, and as the author or director of the film, you can always make a case against them. An example I always give is, when *Interiors* came out, people said to me that I didn't understand that even a serious film should have some humor in it and that it was too solemn, too serious. This is where it gets tricky. You can make the case there's no humor in *Persona*, the Bergman film, and it's a wonderful film. There's not much humor in *Macbeth*. There are many examples of works where there isn't a shred of humor and they're overpoweringly strong.

But the fact is, the person saw the film and found it too solemn and he or she is right for him- or herself. But the criticism that can be made of any film can be refuted from another point of view and, in the critical community, often is. So I'm not really interested in these analyses and discussions because I feel they're all rationalizations to justify an emotional response to the work. Two critics can see the same film and write opposite reviews and both are completely correct in their reasoning. So what do you have? Two conflicting intelligent points of view. So when I show my film to two or three friends in my screening room before I put it out, I'd like to hear their emotional response and not their cerebral analysis.

EL: I inadvertently skipped over *Small Time Crooks*. Michael Rapaport is someone you really like. [*He played a sweetly dumb small-time crook in the film. He also played a sweetly dumb boxer in* Mighty Aphrodite.]

WA: Yeah, I love him because he's not just funny, he's *true*. He's also incapable of a fake reading. He's real.

EL: He really can play a mug.

WA: He has a great mug persona. That was a trivial picture. A silly little picture. It does have some laughs in it because I was more skillful, the idea was clever, the jokes were clever, and playing a two-bit crook with grandiose ambitions was within my range. It's the difference between that kind of character and the insurance detective I played in *Jade Scorpion*. I'm not that guy, whereas I could easily play the cheesy little small-time crook. [*He plays Ray, a dishwasher ex-con with a get-rich-quick scheme to tunnel into a bank's vault from the basement of the store next door with the help of a couple of dim-witted cronies (Jon Lovitz and Michael Rapaport). His manicurist wife, Frenchy (Tracey Ullman), who happens to make addictively delicious cookies, settles into the shop to bake and sell them as a front for the tunneling below. All goes comically haywire with the robbery—they miss the bank—but the cookies are such a success that Ray and Frenchy become spectacularly wealthy, only to be swindled by a suave art dealer (Hugh Grant) who romances Frenchy. But Ray and Frenchy have the best revenge and a renewed marriage.*]

EL: When we talked yesterday about your new film [Cassandra's Dream], I asked if you are going to be in it and you answered, "No, it's too much of a strain on me in the writing stage. I feel it makes me write certain kinds of films when I'm in them."

WA: When I wrote *Scoop* I put myself in it because I felt, I haven't been in a film in a while, I should do it. But I really dislike the experience of having to make sure if I'm in it that there is a Woody Allen character. So I vowed that I wouldn't do that. And I won't be in the one I do in Barcelona, either, which is going to be a serious picture. Maybe never again. It limits me when I'm conceiving a project to have to think that there needs to be a Woody Allen character, because that immediately requires it to be a certain type of movie. I'm not going to be able to write *Cries and Whispers* or *The Bicycle Thief* and accommodate my character.

Now, if I have a brilliant idea that fits me like a charm and if it was the kind of picture that anyone casting it would say, "Oh, you've got to get Woody Allen to play this part," then fine, I would do it. But I'm not looking in that direction at this point. I'm looking to be not limited by having to accommodate anything, much less someone as constricting as myself.

EL: Is this something you were thinking about while you were doing *Scoop*?

WA: When I finished *Scoop* I thought to myself, What a nuisance. I'm wasting my time with this little comedy and I could be doing another piece of work like *Match Point*—another meaty thing. Why am I wasting my time with this?

Now, I wish I had come to this conclusion twenty-five years ago, but I didn't. And I don't know that I could have implemented it that easily because there was a fierce pressure on me from many people to do comedy. There was just no getting away from that. Now, it doesn't matter so much. My financing for the last two pictures came from abroad, my financing *this* summer's abroad, my financing *next* summer's abroad, and there's no pressure on me from those people to do anything but a good picture. Now also, fortuitously, with the success of *Match Point* financially, potential backers don't run for cover when I say I'm going to do a serious movie. They think, Oh, it's not a given that it's going to lose money. It's possible it could make some money.

EL: Do you think you'll miss acting?

WA: No, because I didn't miss it when I didn't do it and there have been times I went a couple of pictures—a couple of years—and it didn't mean anything.

EL: There's no sense of it being the end of one chapter and the beginning of the next one?

WA: I've been in films my whole adult life, almost, and I don't think there's anything about it that I would miss. I'm happy to do it as long as someone wants to finance me. But if tomorrow I couldn't get financing I would be very happy to write plays, very happy to sit home and try to write a novel and maybe under those circumstances try to write an autobiography or a memoir. I just like to work, to write.

One attendant phenomenon of a life in film is that the way the film industry has gone, it now is fraught with the bleak obligation to promote your film. Now it costs so much money to make and advertise a film that you can't just give them the picture and leave them holding the bag; you have to be decent and help a little bit. That entails traveling places and answering questions and being interviewed, trying to tell people how great your film is without seeming to say it's great. It's so silly. Often marketing people want to do ads that appeal to the lowest common denominator—although this goes as far back as when I first started and they said, "We're selling Fords, not Rolls-Royces." So there's a lot of the moviemaker's life I wouldn't miss.

As I say, I'm glad to do it. It keeps me distracted and occupied. But I could be distracted and occupied other ways. This is just convenient now. You don't have to be up early—I was talking with Marshall Brickman the other day and he's just had this success [*with the Broadway musical* Jersey Boys] and he was saying how great it is. The theater is fifteen blocks from his house and he gets up at a leisurely hour and strolls there and does rewrites and sees the fruits of his labor right away. That's a far cry from the cumbersomeness of the film, getting out there in the freezing streets with cameras at seven-thirty a.m. and filming and having to rope off blocks and stop traffic and create rain and do it day after day.

EL: What about acting in other people's films?

WA: That would be fine but no one ever asks me. I've always been willing to do it, though I wouldn't want to go to, like, Turkmenistan to act in a film. All the years I've been in the business I've gotten almost no offers and I've done almost all the ones I was offered: a film by Paul Mazursky, I did it [Scenes from a Mall, 1990]; I was offered *The Front* [1976], I did it; I was offered the [*Alfonso*] Arau film [Picking Up the Pieces, 2000], I did it. People have asked me for favors—I've appeared in a film of Stanley Tucci's [The Impostors, 1998]; Doug McGrath asked me to help out in a tiny part, I did it [Company Man, 2000]. To me it's not a big thing.

I'd love someone to come along and say, "I'm doing a film in New York and you'd be perfect to play the college professor or the shrink or the bookmaker"—or at this point Gramps, the loveable old linguistics philosopher [*laughs*]—"and we're prepared to pay you a lot of money to do this because you're really the best one for this. You're unique for it." That would be great. But it doesn't happen and it won't happen.

November 2006

Woody has completed the editing of Cassandra's Dream. *The cast includes Ewan McGregor (who's Scottish), Colin Farrell (Irish)—they both perfected lower-class English accents for their parts—Tom Wilkinson, and Sally Hawkins (both English). And there is a newcomer.*

EL: Hayley Atwell [*who plays the actress Ewan McGregor woos*] is new to me.

WA: You've never seen Hayley Atwell because it's her first movie. There were many women suggested for this part, but I wasn't comfortable with any of them. I kept getting batches of videocassettes with auditions by British actresses. Most were wrong for one reason or another, and then I saw Hayley's. To me, she looked beautiful in an interesting way. Her look wasn't commercial, it was just an interesting, beautiful look, and she could act. So we flew her into New York and she read for me, but she could have only lost the job, because I would never have flown her into New York if I wasn't certain I was going to hire her. Once I've flown somebody in, it's really that I'm going to hire them. They could blow it if they were nothing

Hayley Atwell in
Cassandra's Dream

like what I thought or were terrible—and that does happen occasionally, but not with people I fly in. There'll be an actor or actress I've seen in the movies and think, Oh, great. I have them come by and after they leave I'll be sort of shocked and say to Juliet, "I don't think they should be hired." But that rarely happens.

EL: Did it take a while to find your cast?

WA: The casting really was easy. I've been a big fan of Tom Wilkinson for a long time; we just had to work around his schedule because he had a pre-planned vacation with his family. Juliet suggested Ewan [*McGregor*], whom I didn't know very well. I had seen him onstage in *Guys and Dolls* and I liked him but I had only seen him in one movie, a long time ago. And Colin Farrell I didn't know at all. I had only seen him in the Terry Malick film and he had a beard. [*He played Captain John Smith in* The New World (*2005).*] They were both suggested to me. I met Colin for sixty seconds. He came to see me. "Hi," he said, "here I am. Okay, I guess you want me to go now?" I said [*laughing*], "Yes." He left and I said, "He's perfect."

I wasn't sure at first whether I wanted to go as old as they are or if I wanted two kids who are twenty-one years old, but I felt this would be a better story. Colin is really the real deal. And Ewan the same. Ewan could do anything. If you gave Ewan a vintage car, he'd get into it and just tear off. If he had to back up and make a four-corner turn on the next vintage car, he'd do that. If he had to pilot the boat, he'd pilot the boat. [*He laughs.*]

EL: There is the scene under that big tree where Farrell starts to twitch in reaction to what he realizes he is being asked to do.

WA: I'll get credit for direction there where these guys were in fact doing their own thing. If it had seemed wrong to me I would have stopped him, but it didn't. I felt, Hey, great. Look what they're doing to my script. [*Laughs.*] I'm a lucky guy.

EL: Sally Hawkins [*who plays Farrell's wife*].

WA: The English casting people were showing me this actress and eventually I figured I'd have to hire her because there was nobody better but I just felt we could do better. I asked them to show me just one more batch of people, and Sally was in there. The second I saw her on tape, there was no question she was right.

EL: Do any of the actors have that lower-class accent in life?

WA: I think Sally does. [*Pauses and starts to laugh.*] You know [*laughing harder*], I don't talk to them.

4

SHOOTING, SETS, LOCATIONS

Summer 1973

This is a brief down period. Sleeper is near its release, and Woody is about to begin writing Love and Death. *His reputation so far is for out-and-out comedies. His first two pictures,* Take the Money and Run *and* Bananas, *are essentially comic monologues on film: one verbal or visual gag piled onto the next without much regard for the film's artistic look. But with parts of* Everything You Always Wanted to Know About Sex *and in all of* Sleeper, *he has paid more attention to visual style and feels strongly that he must not simply make the same sort of film again and again. (A sense of the richness and variety of his films to come over the next three decades will begin with his next film,* Love and Death. *It will continue with the stark* Interiors, *then* Manhattan, *the rich black-and-white celebration of New York City and George Gershwin's music. To mention only a few of the wide range of styles and topics that follow, there also will be the documentary-style* Zelig, *the Depression-era reflection on fantasy and reality* The Purple Rose of Cairo, *the childhood memory* Radio Days, *the rough-edged* Husbands and Wives, *the musical* Everyone Says I Love You, *and the dramatic* Match Point.*)*

WA: I have to think of myself as learning all the time. I can't think, This is it, I'm a guy who does surreal comedy and that's all I'm going to do. Rather, I feel that over the next couple of years I should experiment with various kinds of comedy.

EL: It seems to me that your progress has been more instinctive and evolutionary than studied. Have you ever asked other directors for advice?

WA: A few. I talked with Arthur Penn before I shot *Take the Money*. But I read very little about filmmaking. I have no technical background even to this day. It's a mystique promulgated by the film industry that technical background is a big deal. You can learn about cameras and lighting very quickly.

Film courses aren't going to do it. It's what's in you. Someone who has something to say as a director will say it. He'll find ways. I'm surrounded by lots of expertise in my films. I can tell those guys what I want, and then go back the next day and do it over if I have to. You can't learn to shoot like [*Bernardo*] Bertolucci in two days—it's inborn. Still, it's his content—the style's a bonus. It's what you say, not how you say it. If you have an unfunny film, it doesn't matter how it looks; it won't make any difference. It's common sense when you look through the camera.

EL: The Italian sequence in *Sex* seems like a good example of your trying to do different things. You told me that Louise Lasser saw it in the script and when you said it had been cut in favor of a sequence about Onan and his wife that you wanted her to play with you, she argued that you put it back.

WA: Yes. She said she thought it was great, much more funny and stylish than what I had. And we started to talk. I saw the sequence shot in peasant style, totally. I saw it done in Vittorio De Sica style. It never occurred to me to do it as a contemporary Italian film. The premise is the wife of a guy in a small village can't have an orgasm, and they ask advice from a priest in the church. I saw it strictly as peasants in a little Sicilian village, and it would be shot in that black-and-white style of *Open City* and *The Bicycle Thief*.

Then she said, "No, no. I hear footsteps in a large corridor and I see Ferraris and that kind of thing."

And I said, "You're crazy; it can't work like that because those kinds of people wouldn't have that problem and they wouldn't consult a priest."

We argued and argued. And she said, "Why don't you do it with rich modern Italians?" And then all of a sudden the name Antonioni started flashing and I said, "Yes."

I tried to get Paula Prentiss and Richard Benjamin to play it [*they are married to each other*], and I tried to get John Cassavetes and Raquel Welch to play it, and those people and others were busy. Finally I decided to play it with Louise. And then I began to see it; I had more and more ideas. I really started to feel that piece. I just love it. Some of the shots there are very stylish. The shot right after I pull away from the wedding and she's by the Venetian blinds in the apartment waiting for me—it's pretty. The color is great. It looks like a satirical version of a Bertolucci shot. It's dark and there is a vase with some purple flowers and the slats are on the windows and the light's coming through. Some of it is very European. [*He laughs.*] Some of it is not as good. Still. [*Woody and Louise speak phonetic Italian while English subtitles play on the screen.*]

It would take us three hours to do one of those shots, but I never had anything to do except worry about imitating a certain style. If I did one of those shots in *Sleeper*—if Miles Monroe [*Woody's character*] is talking with Dr. Tyron [*a member of the underground*] and the camera goes behind the light and Miles is framed between two leaves of a tree—it's no good because it takes away from the comedy in the scene.

A good example is Mike Nichols's direction of a play on Broadway: simple, fast, clean, light, perfect. On the other hand, [*Elia*] Kazan's direction, something like *J.B.*, with the area lighting and pin spots, is what's fun to do, but it would murder comedy.

EL: Because the essential thing in comedy is to not distract from the laugh?

WA: A comedy has to have laughs to survive. There's no way out of it. It's not hard to get one or two, but it's hard to get ninety minutes of laughter at a quick

A scene from the Italian sequence in *Everything You Always Wanted to Know About Sex* with Louise Lasser, in which Woody reveled in being able to make satirical shots in a style he admires

I have waited so long for this moment.

go easy on my hymen.

enough pace that people aren't bored. It's so difficult that you try everything else. People are always saying that you should have some interesting characters who go with the story. And yes, you definitely want them, all that's wonderful—*if* the laughs are there. But if the laughs aren't there, then all that stuff doesn't mean anything. Whereas if there's no style but there are laughs, then you've got a good chance for a satisfying film.

EL: You managed to get a lot of plot and character quirks into *Play It Again, Sam,* though the film was directed by Herb Ross. [*See page 7.*]

WA: The thing to remember about *Play It Again, Sam* is that it is filled with laughs. All the character business and all that plot would have meant nothing if it didn't have an enormous amount of laughs. Also, it was a play to begin with, and in a play you write characters. Long after I'm dead people will be able to curl up in bed and watch *Sam* on TV and say, "Oh, that's a cute kind of story from the sixties," just as we watch *It Happened One Night* or that genre of films now. Not that I think *Sam* is very good—it's not. More likely they will curl up in bed and say, "What else is on?"

The kind of films I make, with the exception of *Sam,* and the kind of films Chaplin and the Marx Brothers made, are not the kind of films good for television or home showing. [*He was referring to his early comedies here; his films beginning with, say,* Annie Hall *are fine on television because they are not so reliant on laugh-out-loud jokes.*] I think you want to go out to a crowded theater; there's a lot of common anticipation there and it's a group experience. When you see them at home they don't hold your interest. I could see *Duck Soup* in a theater anytime more than *It Happened One Night.* But when I'm at home watching television, I need a story. Alfred Hitchcock mentioned this to me once. I asked him the difference between his television shows and his films and he said story is everything on television.

EL: Apart from *Sam,* your pictures are much more indigenous to film than to the stage.

WA: Yes. *Sleeper* and the sex film are basically me working as a comedian with material tailored for me. I have to be the comedian of *Sleeper.* The film is about a comedian, just like Groucho's films are about Groucho Marx. *Duck Soup* is not a film you can hire actors to play. What makes *Sleeper* funny is me, if I make it funny. Whereas *Play It Again, Sam* is a completely different experience. I wrote that and it's been played successfully by other people on the stage and might have been played better than by me. It's much more conventional, a more popular taste.

On the other hand, people have said to me, "Don't ever make that kind of film again—it's not your kind of film." After *Sam* I got letters from people saying, "Well, it looks like you've sold out now." But I wouldn't hesitate, despite what anybody said, to make another film like *Sam.* I want to mix it up. I don't think people should make a single kind of film. I think that's a mistake.

[*In 2006 he added:*] When I did *Annie Hall*, a number of people felt that I had sold out or made a terrible mistake because my type of film was *Bananas, Take the Money and Run, Love and Death,* that crazy kind of film. Anything less than a lot of crazy jokes, anarchic jokes, would upset them. I remember it very clearly with *Annie Hall* because it wasn't just strange goofy letters coming in the mail, it was people who were acquaintances. Charlie Joffe would say to me, "Gee, my friends wonder why you're wasting your time with that." Of course, that happened in *spades* when I made serious films. Bobby Greenhut used to report that people said to him, "Why would he want to make a film like *that*?" And [*director*] Joel Schumacher—a friend with my good at heart—said to me about *September,* "Why would you want to *make* a film like that?" I guess it's inexplicable to many people why I'd want to do something that's so far from what I'm recognized as doing all the time that I can't do well, and that there's no market for even if I bring it off. They have a point, but I always politely say, "I guess you're right," and go on doing what I'm doing.

Early September 1987

Woody's apartment. He is about to begin filming Another Woman *but has yet to make a crucial decision.*

WA: I'm still undecided whether to shoot in black and white or color. I had a long conversation yesterday with Jeff Kurland, the costume designer. He's vacillating but has the slightest tendency for color. He thought black and white would start the audience off with a slight distraction, and who needs it? Even one percentage point either way would make it worth doing it that way.

EL: Play out the problems for me.

WA: I could make an arbitrary choice to do black and white because I love it. On the plus side, some of the dream stuff would have a better feel, not quite as literal. On the other hand, black and white distances a bit. These are characters I want the audience to become emotionally involved with. I don't want to look pretentious—but that's my least worry. I'm trying to make the right decision for the material. I can envision the whole story [*see page 13*] more involving in color. But the only reason that's true is that black and white is a rarity now. In this day and age black and white has a weight on the material because it's different. I don't want people to come in and sit down and be distanced. I want them to sit down and watch, not sit down and say, "Gee, I wonder why it's in black and white." I want them to just come and watch the movie.

EL: I guess people feel a black-and-white film is too old fashioned.

WA: Yeah. Some segments of the audience just won't go to see black and white; they think it's inferior or you don't have enough money for color, or they just don't like black and white. Yet that's not the audience I want anyway. I figure I'm better off without them. They're no good with subtlety if something as elementary as that is a problem.

I'm working through a number of considerations about the look of the film. It has an autumnal tone; I could do black and winter gray clothes but shoot in color. That's okay in a studio but as soon as you're on the street or in a restaurant you get into trouble. You can't repaint the city; you have to film it as it is. On the other hand, it's easy for something like *September,* which was shot on a single set. I did use a certain color motif there and it worked out just fine.

You can control the look of a period film more—candlelight, antiques. A modern house has TV, telephones, that sort of thing. A period room is very different—Tiffany lamps or kerosene lamps. They have a poetry not found in contemporary rooms. Here I'm in a contemporary situation, so I'm not sure that working in color will make an effective contribution. Black and white could. But then in the first scene we see Gena Rowlands walking in black and white. It would be arresting but also distancing. It's hard to weigh those things.

[*Two weeks later, playing his usual Monday night gig with his jazz band at Michael's Pub, he sits down between sets and says, "I'm leaning toward color now. I'm not sure why and it's not final."*]

Two weeks after that Woody is location hunting in Sneeden's Landing, an upper-class community just up the Hudson River from Manhattan, days before the filming of Another Woman *commences. Cinematographer Sven Nykvist is in heavy wool pants and shirt with rolled-up sleeves, carrying a leather windbreaker over one arm. Woody is in khakis and a torn maroon jacket. At every stop Woody takes Sven aside and quickly explains the scene to be shot. Each is hard of hearing in his right ear, so whenever they talk they tend to circle each other to try to have their good ear closer to the other's mouth.*

At this moment they are looking at a house for the father of Marion, Rowlands's character, played by John Houseman. There is a small shed in back and beyond the lawn, some high grass and weeds. Sven takes off through the vines and around a tree.

"Is Sven looking for angles or a place to pee?" Woody asks.

Sven wants Woody to see something. "Angles," Woody says with resignation, "just my luck." He steps quickly through the brush to where Sven stands. After they confer a moment, Woody dashes out as fast as possible, then stomps his feet a couple of times to shake off whatever bits of wilderness have attached. His anxiety brings to mind a line from his stand-up act: "I am two with Nature."

Inside the house they move from room to room. The wallpaper in the dining room is too busy, but Santo Loquasto, the set designer, says he can fix it. Sven remarks on light streaking on part of the stairwell. He dislikes the contrast of white on the doorsill to the plum of the wall but does like the wall in the library-den. Woody sees a way to work the room into the film.

"We have the option of getting up after dinner and coming in here and looking at pictures," he says. He adds to Santo: "Get better books for the library." Sven leans against the door, looking at the light.

Woody says of the house, "It's bigger than I want but interesting."

Sven, equally interested by it, replies, "And we can make it smaller with bigger lenses if you want."

The large square window with leaded glass at the landing on the stairs casts a rich light that everyone remarks on. When the location scout and I are alone for a minute he says, "Don't tell anyone, but the red panels in that window are glassine left over from a commercial shot there some years ago."

Even though filming is imminent, the question of whether to use black and white or color remains unresolved. As the cars head back to Manhattan to look at a house in Greenwich Village as a possible set, the production manager is on the phone, arranging for a stage, cameras, drivers, and other personnel for a possible test shoot the next day. It is only after twenty minutes of walking through the house that Woody decides against black and white, because all the options and considerations he talks over with Nykvist and Loquasto are about color.

The car returning Woody to his apartment wends through Central Park and stops at the traffic light near the turnout for East Seventy-second Street. Late afternoon sun deepens every color: the bright green of the trees, the dense black of the road, the brilliant yellow of the taxi stopped in front of us. The angle of the sun is

Sven Nykvist, the cinematographer for Ingmar Bergman's most acclaimed films, and Woody's cinematographer for four pictures

such that the windows of the cab appear black; no one inside is visible. But then the right arm of a woman passenger comes up and rests on her head, high enough for light hitting the top of the cab to catch her brown skin and red nails. The arm is framed in the window in very rich tones. "Look at that arm!" Sven exclaims. "The car was empty and suddenly it's not!"

Woody smiles and says, "It's Buñuel's arm."

Late October 1987

Another Woman *has been in production for a couple of weeks.*

EL: Is this the film you envisioned?

WA: [*He lets out a little laugh.*] As soon as I heard Mia's voice in the first dailies I thought, Oh, this isn't the film I wanted to make. In your mind's ear, you hear it in a certain, absolute way. But so far it *is* the picture I conceived of.

EL: This is your first film with Sven. How did you two prepare to work together, so he knew the look you wanted and you could have his ideas?

WA: We didn't spend a ton of time on the look for the movie. It was osmosis in some way—location hunting, dinner, movies together, plus a couple of two- or three-hour formal discussions when we'd go through the script page by page. The two main decisions were, do we shoot in black and white or color, and would dreams and flashbacks be treated differently? [*No.*] Then we had mini-discussions at locations.

EL: Did you watch any films together?

WA: We saw three films. We watched them not out of research but to spend time together. We saw *Orphans* [*1987, directed by Alan J. Pakula*]. Then he saw *September* and *Radio Days*—which he already had seen—and I saw *The Sacrifice* [*1985, Andrei Tarkovsky*], which he did. We also watched *Fatal Attraction* [*1987, Adrian Lyne*] and *Someone to Watch over Me* [*1987, Ridley Scott*]. These all led to conversations of what worked. We're comfortable in conversation. Then once the film is under way I'll look at what the cinematographer has shot and it could go either of two ways—gorgeous or awful. But Gordon Willis, Carlo Di Palma, Sven—these are not guys who disappoint.

EL: I've noticed over the years that you have an aversion to blue. Why?

WA: I *always* prefer a warm picture. Blue is fatal. It's very tricky. I never used it with Gordon. It's too cold. This picture is kind of monochromatic. Yellow would crush. Maroon turns to mud. White was dangerous to Gordon. Sven said on [*Bergman's*] *Cries and Whispers,* it was a pleasure because a red picture is inherently warm. When the film was color-corrected and they took the red out of the faces, the walls kept the red yet left good skin tone.

EL: How much have you had to adjust to each other?

WA: Sven is quick—and wonderful, of course. The one point that we've had to learn to work together on is that after so many years of doing Bergman films he's so preoccupied with the actor. Shooting the actor is a big prerequisite from Bergman. You know, the actor, the actor, the light illuminating the face and making sure you're seeing the actor.

I'm interested in the actor, of course, but I have a bigger interest in the total frame. So in a scene like the one in which Gene Hackman and Gena are at the end of the hallway where he comes upstairs, Sven lit it more than I would have wanted him to and I never realized it while it was happening.

We talked afterward and I said, "Gosh, it's so light, so bright. I thought it was going to be dark up in that hallway, just light coming in through that end window. I picked that hall for the look."

And he said, "If that was the lighting we never would have seen the faces of the actors. It would have been a very pretty picture, but we wouldn't have seen the actors' faces."

EL: Where do you stand between Sven's style and, say, Gordon Willis's?

WA: I'm somewhere in the middle. Gordon is very devoted to the entire frame and is not worried about the actors' faces. He is worried about a completely different thing in his lighting. I love that and it's great. Sven has been trained or encouraged in the other direction. And I'm sort of in the middle of that. I want to see the actors' faces to a degree but I'm much, much more willing not to see them than Sven would imagine or Bergman would be. I'd be perfectly willing to do that scene where you didn't see the actors' faces and you just saw light coming through the window and they were dark and then as the camera moved in you saw their faces a little better. I don't want it ruinous, but I go much further than Sven is used to going. But that's the only thing we differed on. I don't mean we had an argument, but we had to discuss how we wanted to do those things. Everything else felt natural because I like to shoot long masters [*the scene filmed in one continuous shot*] with no coverage [*shots from other angles, close-ups of the individual actors, and shots over their shoulders of the actor each is talking with*] and so does he.

EL: That's the European approach, dictated, as you've said, in part because there's so little money for the budget and therefore less time to set up shots.

WA: Yes. Gordon's is a very American style. It's wonderful. He would have been sensational working with John Ford or someone like that. His shots are superbly lit, I mean like Rembrandt [*his films include all three parts of* The Godfather]. He just loves to paint with light. Carlo, on the other hand, is constantly in motion and is between the two of them. Sven likes to be in motion but not as committed to it as Carlo is, and Carlo is a very beautiful mood lighter. Gordon is probably the best technical cameraman in the world. Take *Zelig,* for instance—all those different lenses and old film stock.

EL: Sven is very mild-mannered, but I understand Gordon can have a temper.

WA: [*Laughing*] I've seen him so mad first thing in the morning he could barely speak. But he was never angry with me.

EL: Your first picture with him was *Annie Hall* [1977]. He seems to have been a great teacher for you.

WA: When I started with Gordon I had only done a couple of films. I had been trying to learn my way and improve myself. I was starting to think more in terms of the look of the film and I think you can see there's a slight improvement in *Everything You Always Wanted to Know About Sex,* and a much bigger improvement in *Sleeper.* Then in *Love and Death* I was working with Ghislan Cloquet [*died 1981*], the wonderful Belgian cameraman, and there was a big improvement there. I always wanted to develop graphics and not just shoot functionally.

I felt this is theoretically a Russian story and it should have some of the style of the Russian films to it—the big battle sequences and strange camera angles—and that would be part of the film. But it was still a comedy in the end. It was one of my funniest films, as I recall. I much prefer it to *Take the Money and Run* and *Bananas.* It's more integrated, it has a story line. But I always had a sense of structure even when people didn't think so, like in *Bananas.* They just can't see it because they think it's joke-joke-joke-joke-joke.

Anyway, by graphic I mean not just getting the information out there on the screen—our two-shot, your close-up, my close-up—with no sense of moviemaking. I did do that for my first couple of pictures because the only thing I could rely on was comedy. I knew I was funny and I knew my jokes were funny and I knew if I got them to the audience, they would laugh at them. To clutter them up with anything extraneous seemed self-destructive—and of course is, if you're doing that kind of film. Then as I gained confidence, I wanted to find more graphic, more cinematic ways of telling the story and not being so frightened to do anything that could stand in the way of the jokes. So after a while I got more and more interested in fooling with it and more risk taking for me. By the time I got to *Annie Hall* the lighting got darker because of Gordon Willis and I had characters doing lines offstage. It wasn't quite as on-the-nose filmmaking. I learned so much from him. I've been lucky because I learned a lot [*about editing*] from Ralph Rosenblum and I learned a lot from Gordon, and they're two masters in their fields.

EL: Is technique something you innately have, like a sense of style, or is it developed?

WA: Technique is something you learn. You know what it is? It's like throwing a ball or playing billiards or playing the piano, where all of a sudden you come to a point where you can do it. You cross that line of technique and you suddenly realize that you can actually do the thing. It's the same thing that happened with making films. I looked up one day and a certain technique had come from doing films and being interested in improving and working at it. And now I know what to do to make a film. A person could trust me with his money and I could make a film. He wouldn't have to worry that I was going to come back with everybody looking in the same direction or something.

EL: When did this breakthrough start?

WA: I noticed after *Annie Hall* that I started to get it. I could feel it right after that picture. It sort of consolidated itself on *Interiors* [*1978*] and when I got to *Manhattan* [*1979*], I just felt it completely. Then I think it took a leap forward when I got to *Hannah* [and Her Sisters, *1986*]. On *September* [*which is soon to be released*] I think it's even more advanced.

September is a picture that I think that I shot better than any before. I did it with more sophistication, because we were all in that house and the camera was moving constantly and there were tons of things happening off camera, which is a way I would never have shot in my early films. And now I feel that a certain technique has baked in and I don't think about it. I can walk onto a set and it happens quickly and instinctively. I don't have to know and don't even like to know particularly what I'm going to shoot that morning. I don't care about it. I go in and someone says, "Okay, the first scene we're doing is her entrance into the apartment." And I look around and it just becomes obvious to me what I want to do.

Now, to do a picture that looks like *Radio Days*, say, you've got to be very careful about planning the artwork; it's a lot about decor and art direction. But a film like *Another Woman*, you go around to natural locations and you find the best ones you can and you do a little painting or furniture changing so as to create consistency with a certain kind of look, but it's not a major art direction venture. That's not what the picture is about. The picture's about people, and people sitting in rooms talking and thinking.

EL: How did you and Gordon decide on shots?

WA: Gordon and I would come to a set and I'd tell him how I wanted to shoot it and most of the time he would be in agreement with me. But sometimes he'd say, "No, it's going to be very pretentious if we do that," or "It's going to look very tacky later," and he'd explain to me why he felt that way. And my feeling was that he was right, because he made sense. If there were times when I felt that he wasn't making sense—this was rare—then I would either shoot it two ways, or when I saw what we had shot and had reservations, I'd shoot it again. But his instinct is so good that in almost every case where he corrected me on something, it was a good correction.

Don't forget these are comedies and usually I know how I want to shoot them. For instance, in *Annie Hall*, I know when I meet Keaton I want to see us playing tennis and obviously I want it to be wide. And most of the time it was completely logical. But there were occasions when I'd say to him, "Hey, if we shoot Keaton this way, I'm going to be offstage when I do my joke." And he'd say, "That's okay, they can *hear* you" [*laughs*].

EL: Sounds like you had a good relationship.

WA: I had a very good relationship with him. It was a pleasure to work with him.

He was extremely meticulous. He needs that to do the kind of work he likes to do lighting-wise. At this point in my life I prefer a looser way of working. When I first started working with Gordie his meticulousness was helpful to me. It was good discipline and helped me learn. Then when you've absorbed all that, you want to break the rules and start to work differently.

A week later. Woody is filming in a restaurant in Greenwich Village. The crew sets up paraphernalia to block out the sun so the light on the street is flat; Woody doesn't want sunshine to interfere with lighting the shot. As they toil he says, "The sun is the bane of my existence. I hate it. I hate it in the morning when I wake up. I hate it in the summer. It's carcinogenic. I was walking through the park yesterday and there were people everywhere, rather like the [Georges] Seurat painting [Sunday After-noon on the Island of La Grande Jatte.] But it was ruined by the sun beating down."

As the lighting team rigs the shade, Sven says, "It looks like it should be so easy but it always gets complicated."

The light is not the only problem. The scene is a long one with Gena Rowlands's character and her sister-in-law, who asks for money, but the conversation sounds a bit off. "The problem," Woody says, "is getting these written words to sound like human conversation. I write everything with my own inflection, so if I were to do the lines they would sound totally natural. But for someone with a different cadence, it takes time to get it to sound right."

The Manhattan Film Center, a few days later. Woody and Sven Nykvist have come to watch the dailies from yesterday's shooting. Woody takes his regular place on the loveseat below the projection window, Sven and I and others are in the plush velvet chairs that line the sides of the room. The mood is tense. Nearly every day there have been problems with how the lab has printed the film, and there are worries that something will be wrong today. The day before, a Monday, the shots from Friday had too much yellow and red. "In Europe," Sven says, "we never send film for processing over the weekend because they change bosses and the shift in people means you always get the timing off."

WA: [*Slightly mystified that there has been such trouble with the lab*] We've always had good luck with DuArt. They know that I usually like warm tones and give it, but with these colors [*taupe and related subdued shades*] the red comes out of the walls.

SN: Every time I sit down to watch dailies I wonder, Shall I be ashamed? Ever since I was a little boy and starting out. But that's good.

WA: [*Rubbing his eyes, head back as if in prayer*] Please, oh, please, let the dailies be good.

The shots, made at a theater, are a disaster. They are at least an f-stop too dark even for Woody, who doesn't mind if faces are a bit obscured. In the first scene, with Sandy Dennis and Ian Holm, it's hard to tell who they are. The camera is far back in an attempt to show the stage. Woody says to Sven, "We should not be so bound by the convention of the theater. Start off and then cut back and forth to faces so we know it's Sandy and Ian."

In the third shot, an argument, there is not enough light on the actress's face. Woody wants to be sure her face is established in an earlier shot.

"Poor Sven," he says often as take after take is printed incorrectly.

Sven calls the lab and says he measured as much light on the actors' faces as in a regular studio. The lab manager tells him the shots were deliberately printed darker through a misunderstanding and offers to reprint them overnight.

Afterward, producer Bobby Greenhut, Woody, and Sven stand outside the screening room, plotting what to do. They have the frustrating realization that they will have to wait until the reprint comes back in the morning to decide whether or not to reshoot. Woody says, "I'd just like to have one day where we come in and the dailies are beautiful and printed right instead of getting clobbered every day."

Later, he points his right thumb and index finger to his forehead like a gun.

"Moviemaking," he says. "You go to all this trouble so a critic can give it three pineapples, or whatever."

October 1989

The Bleecker Street Cinema in Greenwich Village. It is the first day of shooting on what at present is called Brothers *but will become* Crimes and Misdemeanors. *The crew members, most of whom are veterans on many Woody Allen films, greet one another and talk of other first days, of things shot or not shot, and of times when the first day yielded no film. Today they will actually get something in the can.*

"It's like the first day of school," one says to me, "but we've all been held back with the same teacher."

"How many is this together?" one asks another. "Fourteen? It's time for a new group." They both laugh.

Bobby Greenhut and Woody stand on the street across from the Bitter End, where Woody performed as a stand-up, trying to think of the first shot of Manhattan. *They decide they started on page one in Elaine's. The talk turns to his night-club days.*

EL: Do you still see any of the people you performed with or were in and around the Village when you were doing stand-up?

WA: [*Folk singer*] Judy Henske is one of the few people I lost complete touch with that I wish I had touch with [*laughs*]. She got married and moved to Connecticut or Vermont and had a horse farm. She was great. She was very, very bright and very funny—I mean real bright and well read. She was this big kind of lanky brunette from Chippewa Falls, Wisconsin. That's where I got the name in *Annie Hall* from. Her father was a doctor.

I hung out a lot with her and we were close. Then she married some guy in the Modern Folk Quartet. I never saw her again nor heard anything about her.

But she was very bright. As a joke I looked for the driest, most unromantic book I could find and I got her something like *Pennsylvania Real Estate Laws,* one of those books that you buy in a bin. And she read it! She'd read anything that came her way. She always got the jokes. You could never get a reference by her—whether it was from Proust or Joyce, she knew it. She was a well-educated, bright girl. Keaton always reminded me of her.

January 2000

Preproduction on Small Time Crooks *is under way.*

EL: Is black and white or color a question this time?

WA: *Small Time Crooks* will be in color. Black and white is a pain in the neck these days, though every once in a while I like to shoot in it. The labs are so unsuited to black and white, and there are so many technical problems: static on the film; when you make edits they come out and you have to have the whole film coated because the temperature of the lamp melts the black-and-white stock going through the projector.

EL: I'm sure that *Everyone Says I Love You* [*see page 96*] was always meant to be in color. It seems the kind of film that you can saturate with different hues.

WA: Oh, yes. *Everyone Says I Love You* is one of those movies you can make look very rich. It's the realistic movies you can't. By realistic I mean taking place in the streets of New York. If it's musical streets, it's a different story. Or period. *Small Time Crooks* doesn't look like much. It's okay. Whereas you can make the musical look good because everything's so romanticized. I was lucky shooting in Venice because the few days we were there I had flat weather and it was in the dead of summer. Everything set in Venice was shot there except one little conversational scene we did in a mansion in the East Nineties in Manhattan. And everything in Paris was in Paris except the interior of the Ritz Hotel room. They wouldn't let us shoot there, so we did it at the Plaza here. I had originally wanted to call the film *Christmas at the Ritz* but they didn't want the Ritz used in any way—and these are people that like me. They couldn't be nicer to me at the Ritz.

The idea to do a musical had been floating around for years. I wanted to do a musical about rich people and the Upper East Side of Manhattan and I wanted it to be one of those old musicals, with families, but in today's Upper East Side it would be very different: a combination family from divorces and prior husbands and prior wives. I wanted it to be unabashedly about rich Upper East Siders because I thought that would make a nice atmosphere for a musical.

We were going to shoot [*the scene buying an engagement ring, in which there is an energetic dance number with a large ensemble*] at Tiffany's but they didn't want us to dance on the glass countertops. We said we'd put in our own glass and protect everything but they just didn't want dancing on them. They said we could dance in the aisles and take over the place but we went over to Harry Winston and they gave us complete cooperation and it was fresher.

EL: What about *Manhattan Murder Mystery*? Did you end up with the film you envisioned?

WA: It's one of those films that came out just as I envisioned it. I consider it a success. Great fun to make, just the kind of picture I loved to get lost in as a kid. I had a good climax scene with that scene from *Lady from Shanghai*. I was trying to get one of those tour de force scenes which I frequently leave out of my scripts and just say, "We'll find some tour de force scene," and then I say to Santo, "I've got to get some tour de force location." [*He laughs.*]

We shot a lot of scenes in the rain on the picture. There's no real sunshine in it. It looks like it's always raining in New York.

EL: You used Zhao Fei as your cinematographer on *Sweet and Lowdown*. My understanding is that he speaks almost no English. Was that a problem?

WA: Zhao Fei is trying to learn English. We're asking him to do the next film, but it depends on his schedule. People keep saying to me, "Get someone who speaks English," but it doesn't matter to me. Carlo Di Palma speaks limited English.

April 2005

EL: In general, how do you decide between filming in black and white or color?

WA: *Manhattan* was always conceived as black and white, as was *Celebrity* and *Broadway Danny Rose*. Every one I've done, my vision of each was in black and

Zhao Fei, whose limited English inspired Woody's creation of a similar Chinese camera-man to work with the suddenly blind director in *Holly-wood Ending*, dur-ing the making of *Sweet and Low-down;* Michael Green, who worked on many of Woody's films, is the camera operator.

white. It's funny how much is made of such trivia. People would meet me on the street and say, "When are you making your next film?"

And I'd say, "June."

And they'd say [*eagerly*], "Black and white? *Color?*"

So much is made of this. To me, whether a film is in black and white or color is of no import. Hundreds of the films you've loved in your life are in black and white, hundreds are in color. It's one kind of aesthetic you're using when you tell your story. If you use the reasoning that black-and-white films are somehow inferior, don't bother to look at *Citizen Kane* or *The Bicycle Thief* or *Grand Illusion* or any of the early Bergman films or *Treasure of the Sierra Madre* or *The Maltese Falcon* or *Double Indemnity*. There's a great beauty to black-and-white photography. There's a great beauty to color photography.

EL: When does Santo Loquasto get the script?

WA: I send Santo the script about the same time it goes to Juliet [*Taylor, the casting director*]. Then he has to work his magic. He really has a tough job because he has to do it for a budget. He's been with me for decades. He was a set designer and a costume designer for stage but he started off with costumes for me because Mel Bourne was doing sets, and then Mel finally went off on another project and wasn't available so Santo did the sets. [*Bourne did six films between 1978 and 1984, from* Interiors *through* Broadway Danny Rose.] It's amazing what I dump on Santo: this film is going to take place in the 1920s in New York, this one has to be shot all over the city. *Sweet and Lowdown* takes place all over the country—Chicago, New York, Atlantic City, California—but I never want to sleep away from home any night, so he makes it look like we were there. He's got no money and you look at the film and you see California, you see the studios with the palm trees, and you see traveling across the country and you see Chicago and the meatpacking and the cows. Santo's miraculous that way.

EL: Most directors get a script and have to answer two basic questions: "What's this about?" and "How am I going to tell it?" But not you.

WA: I can never re-create in real life what I envision when I'm writing a script. I remember when Bergman was writing *Winter Light* [1962] he went around with Sven to all these churches and said, "That's the light I want." Again, I'm not that dedicated. I want a certain light, too, but I don't do anything to get it. So I think to myself, I'd like a soft sepia light that you get just as dusk is beginning to fall on a summer's day. But I don't go to Central Park days before and wait and say, "This is the right time to get that light." If I've got the light that night, great, and if not, I rewrite the scene or find another solution.

[*During the filming of* Another Woman *in 1987, Sven Nykvist told me,* "Winter Light *is Ingmar's favorite. I changed my style of shooting with that film: there were no shadows except for the end, where it means something. I started using boards to get the right light. Then I realized that it worked for color, too."*]

EL: Shooting a scene requires a number of decisions in advance. selection of the lens, what f-stop, the color density, and so on.

WA: None of that is on my mind. I wouldn't know one f-stop from another. I know what I want and I can describe it. I have no idea how to get it. I have to tell the cameraman and he's got to try to get it for me. Now, I do make up the compositions of my shots. There are directors who don't look through the camera; they rely on their cameraman. I could never do that. I decide on the shot that I want and then the cameraman looks at what I propose and will say to me, "That's great," or "Wouldn't it be a little bit better if we didn't pan here but dollied into this part of it?" And I'll say "Yes" or "No" or "You're right," and then we'll talk for a minute. Then he'll light the scene in general, then I bring the actors in and tell them where to go, and they'll say to me, "Do I have to go there?"—although usually they say, "Fine." But once in a while they say, "Couldn't I go over to the fireplace and stand and then come over there?" And I usually say sure, and we make a little adjustment in the lighting. And then we shoot it. The cameraman knows the kind of lighting I want from discussions we've had before the film was ever shot.

EL: Is everything about the script clear to you when you look at it before shooting?

WA: Once I finish a script and have it typed, I may keep a script at my house and work on it because there's time before I start to shoot. But there comes a certain point where the actors want the script and they want it frozen so they can memorize things. Once I finish the *final* written version of a script I never look at it again; sometimes I don't even own one. So, let's say, three weeks or a month before we shoot, I freeze the script, at least to begin the picture. I see the scene the day I'm going to shoot it. It's completely clear to me; it doesn't matter what order I shoot it in. There's no advantage for me in shooting a film chronologically. I'm happy to shoot it all over the place like a jigsaw puzzle. But I will ask at times, "What is the last cut? What is the last shot when we shot the scene prior to this? I'd just like to remember for a second." If it was a close-up of an actress's face, for example, I don't want to begin this scene with a close-up of her face. But that's all.

EL: Do you think it makes much difference to actors whether a film is shot in sequence?

WA: No, I think they're professionals and they're paid to shoot out of sequence—that's how almost all movies are shot. Some actors think I intentionally start with a tough emotional scene, or I start with a given scene so someone can work his way in. But for me, it's wherever we start, we start.

May 2005

EL: Santo Loquasto has designed the sets for around twenty of your films. Does he show you drawings and mock-ups as he goes along?

WA: Yes, when we're going to build, because no one wants to go to the expense until we're all in agreement. He gets the script, and gets no budget, and is not allowed to find locations where we have to travel very far, because I like to sleep in my own bed at night. Once in a while he has to build something, but not too often because we don't have a lot of money to work with. But when he does, every detail is done, down to the stationery on the desk. When he did my one-act plays, *Riverside Drive* and *Old Saybrook* [2003] and *Central Park West* [1995], I talked to him about the set and we talked and talked and I had all kinds of ideas. Then he went away and [*laughs*] came back with something completely different that was wonderful and way beyond anything I had thought of or envisioned.

EL: *Shadows and Fog* required quite a set, twenty-six thousand square feet built from scratch at the Kaufman Astoria Studios in Queens. [*A dark and brooding place designed to look like an old Eastern European city with touches of the sets for classic Hollywood horror films. Damp cobblestone streets (faux stones coated with high-gloss polyurethane) lead into sinister dead-end alleys; a church looks not like a place of worship and refuge but rather a sinister prison.*]

WA: The biggest set ever built in New York.

EL: And there was all that fog [*actually a soy concoction that billowed from hidden oil drums*].

WA: Yes [*laughs*], and whenever anyone comes down with a cancer of any sort, they are convinced it was caused by that. We were all breathing it and the government environmental office checked it and it was deemed completely safe.

EL: Your sets usually require the look of contemporary life in a location.

WA: We find a place that works and then Santo makes every apartment in contrast to the others, so when you see two or three apartments in a movie they won't look the same. Even in the simplest apartments we get, Santo has work to do. He's got to put a fake wall here because the place is too big for a poor family, or a fake door, or soffits [*an architectural means to conceal a lighting fixture*] so we can get light.

EL: You had to build an elaborate set for *Purple Rose of Cairo*.

WA: We dressed an entire block and built the exterior of the movie house. We built all our facades on that block. The interior was a real movie house. Ironically, as I think I mentioned earlier, it was the Kent Theater [*in Brooklyn*], which was very important to me in my childhood because it was, as we always used to say, the last outpost. When a film left the Kent, it went into the archives, into the time capsule. And you would always hear the freight train in the Kent. You'd be watching a movie and you'd hear a freight train [*laughs*] go by for five minutes.

EL: About fifteen years ago we talked about your cinematographers, but I'd like to get a sense of how you feel about them now. You did eight pictures with Gordon Willis, starting with *Annie Hall*. What did you learn from him? And why did you choose him?

WA: He was the great American cameraman at that time and he had lived in New York and he was available. Someone brought us together and we had a nice chat in my apartment and decided we'd do the film together. We worked together very well. Gordie got me interested in shooting in black screen [*where there are no images on the screen and all the audience hears is the actors' voices, as in* Manhattan *when Ike and Mary are gradually seen to take a trip across the moonscape at the Hayden Planetarium*]. They used to call him "the Prince of Darkness." He introduced me to the beauties of darkness photographically.

We developed a vocabulary where I'd know that he'd never want to do a certain kind of shot, and he knew that I would hate something so he wouldn't suggest it.

EL: You once told me that Carlo Di Palma was as relaxed as you in setting up a shot.

WA: Carlo liked to work the way I do. Carlo was the opposite of Gordon in that Gordon has prodigious technique in addition to his artistic genius. Carlo was an absolute hunt-and-peck primitive. He would put a light there and look around and try something else, and put a light somewhere else, and somehow arrive at very beautiful lighting. He learned through no schools at all. He was the focus puller on *The Bicycle Thief* [*the crew member who adjusts the focal length of the camera lens*

Carlo Di Palma was the cinematographer for more of Woody's films than anyone else—eleven.

during a shot to keep the most important person or part of the scene in focus] and came up from there. Carlo had an artistic flair, a beautiful eye for color, a beautiful eye for composition, for movement, but he was a total primitive. It was very easy for me to work with him. He loved camera mobility and I loved that, too, at that point.

EL: Carlo captures so much character in how he shoots faces.

WA: He's got a prettiness to his work, so he makes the actors look pretty. Gordon can do that, too, but he's more concerned with the overall tableau. So if the tableau is beautiful, an actress can be three-quarters in the dark, you can just see a slice of her face and the girl may not be lit to her most flattering advantage, but the overall picture is so beautiful. Carlo was very flattering to the women he photographed, very cognizant of making them look good.

EL: What other difference between them?

WA: Gordon was very, very well organized. You got there, the lens boxes were off the truck, the lights were there. He really ran things [*snaps fingers twice*] like a guy who knew what he was doing. Carlo was like me. [*Laughs.*] He would come in in the morning and, you know, he was like what we used to say about the French government—that it was like a country run by the Marx Brothers. We'd sit there and think about what we were going to do that day.
"Do you know what scene it is?" I would say.
"No, do you?"
"Well, the sun's over there, but by the time we get there the sun will be *there,* so let's do this. Do you think this will be pretty?"
And I would design the shot and Carlo, like Gordon, would say to me either, "Your shot is very good" or "I would not do the shot that way, I'd modify it this way." It was rare that Gordon would say, "That's a terrible shot," although he *would* say

that. But usually it would be, "I think it would be better if we started with that and instead of ending the dolly there we do a little more." And Carlo would do the exact same thing.

EL: There are the shots in the scene in *Hannah* where you see the three sisters [*Mia Farrow, Dianne Wiest, and Barbara Hershey*] talking at a restaurant table as the camera circles three times, showing them individually and collectively. A friend who ran an advertising company told me that people copy that shot in ads all the time. What can you tell me about it?

WA: First I dollied around the table to set the shot up and I remember I thought to myself, Well, I can't keep going around and around. But it could be cut and go in closer and cut and go in closer the third time. Then as I looked at that to set it up, I thought, If they're talking naturally, there's no way I'm going to be on the right person all the time. And Barbara Hershey said, "So what? So you're not on the person who's talking, you're on the reaction shot." And I thought to myself, Well, Barbara [*laughs*], you're not only *pretty* [*laughs harder*] but it's a *very good* idea. You're right, it *wouldn't* matter, *would* it?

But you know, I was completely dissatisfied with that shot at dailies. I thought it was pretentious. Finally the "That's great"s prevailed. I guess I was wrong and not seeing something.

EL: Did it take long to set up?

WA: Over a weekend a guy in the crew made round track from rubber tubing for the camera to roll on so we could make the proper corner. Metal tracks are like the ones for Lionel trains and not exactly round. It took a while to light it, because you have to go all around the table. But once we did the first one, the next two were easier because they were tighter.

EL: Did it need a lot of takes?

WA: It was not hard. I don't like to do a lot of takes. It's not a precise shot and there were good actors in it—Dianne Wiest, Barbara Hershey, and Mia.

EL: You've had people talking off camera since *Annie Hall*.

WA: As I've said, Gordon taught me that. I remember we were setting up a shot when Alvy and Annie were breaking up and they were dividing up the books and I said, "Neither of them is on at the time. Is that okay?" And he said, "Yes, that's great, sure, there's nothing wrong with that at all." If he had said, "You can't do that, what are you thinking?" I wouldn't have done it. But as soon as I got his imprimatur, we always managed to do that in subsequent movies, and to this day I'll do it. In every movie there's at least one scene where nobody's on and there's just talking. I throw one in always in honor of Gordon.

I was recently on the treadmill and surfing channels and I passed *Anything Else* and it was that scene where Jason Diggs is on the phone to Christina Ricci and then he walks off camera and you just see the inside of her house.

EL: Are there things you do for your own amusement?

WA: There are a couple of kinds of shots we do in every picture. People are walking down the block toward the camera and then they get close to the camera and then the camera begins to dolly [*pushed on its wheels by a crew member*]. That's one. Another is where people are walking across the street and the camera is on the other sidewalk going parallel. There are certain clichés I've used over the years.

EL: Any new ones?

WA: Well, in the last couple of years—I've always done long takes—I've elaborated to *really* long takes. I don't mean these kind of tour de force shots that guys do with a Steadicam, where they go on forever. I mean the scene in *Anything Else* with Jason and Christina in the house with Stockard Channing, where people walk in and out and the combinations are complicated. Jason will go into the bathroom and you won't see him; Christina will come in and go out; then Jason; then Stockard; then Jason comes back; then we can't see anybody because Jason's behind a post. I've taken to choreographing a lot of that in recent years because I enjoy it and it saves me from covering [*making close-ups or reaction shots; the whole scene is completed in one take*]. I rehearse the cameraman all morning and do the complicated lighting and then break for lunch and come back and do the scene and we're finished with seven pages in five minutes.

EL: It's so different from the MTV notion of a cut every half-second that has pervaded films.

WA: I like to go as long as the scene holds without a cut. If you can make it hold, great.

EL: Carlo once told me that he learned about color from his mother, who was a florist. I'm thinking of the color that soaks through in his films.

WA: Yeah, and in his clothes. When Marshall Brickman met Carlo for the first time he said to me, "This guy should be the star of your movie," because Carlo was always so dashing and attractive and a peacock. When he would come into town to do those movies, there were eight trunks of clothing: the neckties, all the stuff. You can't believe it. I've seen pictures of him when he was younger—he was gorgeous. He had a wonderful flair for color, clothes. He was a very good still photographer, loved to go to the museums and look at paintings.

EL: He must have loved doing *Radio Days*, which is really colorful.

WA: Yeah, deeply saturated colors. That is the direction that I've gone practically my whole life of making films. Gordon, Carlo, Darius Khondji, Zhao Fei, all of them do that. The one who it didn't come naturally to was Sven, but he said afterward that he loved doing warm pictures.

Just today I was on the phone with the English art director of my upcoming film [Scoop]. It was the first time I ever spoke to her. She said she was surprised by the warm colors in *Match Point* because the art director, who she had worked with many times as an assistant and loved, had always used such cool colors. He did because that's a requirement of mine. I just like warm colors. It's a personal taste. I'm not saying there aren't cool-color films that aren't beautiful. There are. But personally, without making any pronunciamentos about film or color, I like deeply saturated, warm films, in the sense of what Matisse felt, that when you look at a painting, it should be like sitting down in an easy chair; a picture should be a comfortable chair for your eyes. So when you see work done by all these people we've been talking about, it is all very warm—and color-corrected in that direction, even more so. Sometimes the lab will call and say, "You really want it this warm?"

EL: But it sounds like your cinematographers all achieve that warm look differently.

WA: Yes, they all have different techniques. Zhao Fei [*the cinematographer for* Sweet and Lowdown] used so many lights you just couldn't believe it. Someone in the building shooting a TV show thought they didn't use that many lights on a television program. But if you look at the film, the color's just beautiful.

EL: That reminds me of the deeply yellow shirt Sean Penn wears a couple of times.

WA: We color-correct all that stuff in terms of yellows and red and emphasize those colors. We don't let the actors wear pale blue or stuff that's going to be tough to get warm.

EL: You figuratively took your graduate degree in cinematography with Gordon. After your eight years with him and you went to Carlo, were there new things you picked up with Carlo?

WA: Well, yes, their compositional styles are so different. Gordon would be great shooting a Kurosawa film, in that he loves actors dictating movement of the camera. And these really beautiful framed pictures that are not so easy to have mobility on and keep them lit the brilliant way that he likes. Because if you're composing a tied-off shot [*no camera movement, or a shot within a confined area*], you can light the teeth out of it. But if the shot's got to be over there and then move over here, you can't have lights over here making this beautiful and then go over there, then it really starts to get difficult. Carlo was obsessed with movement and would never like any shot that didn't have some movement in it and would compromise on the lighting for the mobility.

EL: Carlo must really have loved the handheld camera and all the movement in *Husbands and Wives*.

WA: *Husbands and Wives* was just a fun experiment. That was a picture that I wanted to be ugly. I didn't want anything to match on it or be refined or cut well. I wanted it to be an unattractive picture to see.

EL: When you were writing it, I assume you were thinking of shooting it this way. The look matches the subject matter.

WA: Yeah, I was thinking I wanted to make this picture just herky-jerky and unmatched and unrefined in every way.

EL: When you sat down with Carlo before *Radio Days*, did you have to explain what you wanted?

WA: I didn't have to say it at that point. He knew that I like great warmth all the time anyhow and that in a period film we're really able to lay it on with a trowel. And we had all these wonderful locations that are slightly distorted by memory, or heightened by memory, so you don't have to light it realistically, you can light it beautifully, so it came out good. We were out in Rockaway and whenever I'm shooting around a beach I wait for the flat days. If you get those gray days and the waves roll and the beaches are open, it's very pretty. I find beach shooting very beautiful and country shooting not as beautiful. I don't like to shoot in the country as much.

Of course, many people make the country look incredibly beautiful. In some of these English pictures and Stanley Kubrick's, it's to die, it's so beautiful. But my personal taste and favorite is to shoot at the beach on gray days.

EL: Carlo also shot *Everyone Says I Love You*. I noticed you did the dance numbers in master shots, as well as most of the other sequences.

WA: I did use masters. For example, "Makin' Whoopee" was shot in a hospital. I think Bobby Greenhut planned three days to shoot that because it was a musical number and there was a lot of dancing. But I never shot that way and don't shoot that way now. I shot that in one take, the entire song-and-dance number, which I did for practically everything in the picture.

When I see a movie, I want to see the dancers in front of me full length. I hate it when they cut to their feet. I hate it when they cut to their faces. I don't like angle shots. I want to see it the way I see it if I pay $10 and I go to City Center and the dancers are in front of me. You know, straight on. I later learned that Fred Astaire didn't allow cuts in his numbers either. That's all I wanted, straight on, simple, proscenium and no cuts. And I shot it in forty-five minutes. Graciela [*Daniele, who choreographed the Greek chorus in* Mighty Aphrodite] rehearsed the dancers and then we did maybe two takes and we were out of there.

EL: You talked for years about wanting to do a musical and you finally did it. But rather than an old-fashioned musical, this is more like one of your regular scripts with musical interludes.

WA: It was not like *Meet Me in St. Louis,* where everybody was very good. They were a modern family. The parents were limousine liberals who had their causes and went away for the summer to the Hamptons and girls from the divorce would come and be with their father. That was the milieu that I wanted to show. And I wanted to include psychoanalysis because that was one of the features of these people's lives: the Hamptons, Zabar's [*a fabled food emporium*], Frank Campbell [*a funeral home on Madison Avenue popular with the wealthy*] because death is also a part of this equation.

EL: Did you find any resistance to the end result?

Dance scenes in a hospital and at Harry Winston in *Everyone Says I Love You*

WA: I had a very good time making that film, but when I showed it to Harvey Weinstein [*then the head of Miramax, who distributed the film in the United States*], who had paid a lot of money for it sight unseen, he hated it.

EL: Why?

WA: He's usually very good with my films [Bullets over Broadway, Mighty Aphrodite, Celebrity]. Whenever I show him a film, he loves it. But with that film, he fell into that group of people who feel in a musical people have to be able to sing. But in the end he was very nice about it. And I was such a grouch. He wanted me to take out the one dirty thing, where they said "motherfucker," because then he could open the picture at Radio City Music Hall. And I just would not take it out. It's not how I make my pictures. So in the end he was a good sport and put out the picture nicely.

May 2005

We begin by talking about Match Point, *which Woody has recently completed and will soon debut at the Cannes Film Festival.*

EL: Were you on time and on budget?

WA: Yes, I was on time and slightly under budget. And everyone was absolutely panicked at the beginning that it was a foreign country and new people and it looked so tight, but we were under budget slightly and I had my little special effects in it and did all the reshoots I wanted to do as we went along, sparing no expense,

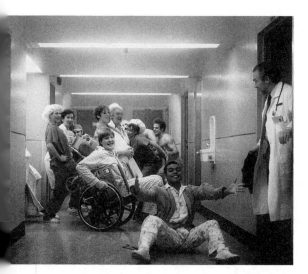

and I did my rain shots and whatever I wanted to do without thinking, and it still worked out. Now that's a tribute to the British crew and the British way of working.

EL: Were you able to use locations or did you have to build a lot of sets?

WA: The interior of the museum was built and the opera sets were built because you can't just come in and shoot at an opera.

EL: Was there anything liberating in working in London, in a completely new environment?

WA: It wasn't liberating. I always feel liberated. I only shoot in New York because I'm lazy and it's convenient for me. I like to eat at my favorite restaurants and sleep in my bed. And that's really the truth of it. I love going to London for a week to go to the theater and to see friends, but I was not looking forward to spending several months there. But it turned out to be such a great experience that I'm repeating it this summer.

I feel that I could make films anywhere. I've made them with crews in Hungary; I've made them with crews in Italy and France. As I've said before, not trying to be facetious, filmmaking is not rocket science. This is not the hardest thing in the world to do. You have your script, the crews all over the world work well. They're professionals, they're just as professional in Paris as they are in Budapest as they are in England as they are in New York or California. If you know how to do it, then it's not that tough. With common sense, you get it done.

If a big to-do is made of it, if it's a grand experience with temperament and craziness and it's an excuse to live your life a certain way, then it becomes a pain in the neck, beginning with the stars who come and want their masseuse and their makeup people and their political advisors paid for.

EL: I saw *Purple Rose* the other night. Gordon Willis got that harsh light you always talk about when you come out of a theater, the uncompromising light of reality.

WA: I deliberately wanted to come out to a very unpleasant situation for her [*Cecilia, the girl who loses herself in the fantasy of films, played by Mia Farrow*]. Gordon was able to do that. We had talked about that as a goal, to get that feeling— I described to him coming out of the movie theater and it suddenly being the real world in all its ugliness.

EL: We haven't talked about the black-and-white film within the film, the actual *Purple Rose of Cairo* in which the actors talk to the audience and the Jeff Daniels character leaves the screen and enters real life.

WA: The black-and-white portion was easy but what was hard to do was getting the look of the people in the film within the film to correspond to the people in the audience they were talking to. That took a lot of work, a lot of looking at it on paper. It was mathematically tricky.

EL: Were there any special concerns about making the film within the film?

WA: Well, when the film within the film covered the whole screen, or didn't correspond to conversation with anyone, there was no problem at all.

EL: Was that actual projection in the theater with the audience?

WA: I can't remember if we had enough room in the Kent to do rear-screen projection. I think we were just doing regular projection.

EL: *Radio Days* was the next Carlo Di Palma film. Again, a lush picture.

WA: As I said earlier, it's much easier, much easier to be lush and beautiful in a period film. I think all the period films I've done are quite pretty. Maybe the prettiest contemporary film I did, just simple prettiness, may have been *Alice*. But as far as my other films, it's usually the period films—not counting the black-and-white ones, which have their own kind of beauty, for me—*Sweet and Lowdown* is beautiful, and *Jade Scorpion* is very pretty and *Radio Days* and *Purple Rose* and *Bullets over Broadway*. You can be dealing in the past with cartoon-like costumes and amber lights and red velvet, and it just has a beautiful, nostalgic feel to it. Whereas in contemporary stuff, a guy walks across the street and, you know, there are parking meters and television sets and washing machines and garbage trucks and graffiti on walls—it's not as easy. But in period, if you're walking down a block, you pick a beautiful block where it looks like the houses are old and the lights are amber. In a contemporary movie, the lights are not amber. They have to look realistic.
Alice is the only one that I ever did where we stylized it so much that if you look at *Alice* and turn the sound off and just look at the color and the pictures, it's quite pretty.

EL: The family estate in *Match Point* is quite a pretty place, both indoors and out, with that great wheat field for the passionate scene with Scarlett and Jonathan in the rain.

WA: I didn't know how I was going to shoot that scene with Scarlett and Jonathan. That was made up at the time. It wasn't written in the rain or the wheat field. First it was written at night outside the house, in the garden somewhere. I

Chris (Jonathan Rhys-Meyers) and Nola (Scarlett Johansson) consummate their mutual desire in *Match Point*, even though they are involved respectively with a sister and brother waiting in the nearby house.

wrote it for night, but when it came time to location-hunt I said, "Ah, I don't want to go out to the country at night. [*He laughs at himself.*] Let's change the scene to the afternoon because I don't like to shoot at night and I certainly don't want to trek out to the *country* at night." So I made it in the afternoon and I was going to make it in the garden. Then I thought to myself, Well, we play a scene in the garden earlier, I don't want to go back to the garden. Then I thought, Maybe with her it shouldn't be that beautiful kind of sex, it should be raunchy. He gets her in the stable and he throws her down while the horses are there, and it's that kind of real dirty sex. And then people would say, "Ah, you don't want to do the haystacks, the haystacks have been done to death." I said, "Well, that's true." And then Sarah [*Allentuch, his assistant at the time*] said, "What about the wheat field?" Then I thought, Maybe the rain . . .

Once he threw her down in the wheat, it flattened it and it was the third take that I used. That was the take I moved in closer with the dolly, and by that time I was thinking, Make it sexy. Really do something with her. It's got to look sexier than it's looking. I don't want him to take her clothes off, but I want to get some raunchiness to it. And they progressed a little more and that's the take I used.

EL: By then they must have been pretty cold from their long drenching.

WA: They *were* cold. Jonathan was too gentlemanly to say anything but to bear it with male fortitude. But [*laughs*] Scarlett, you know, was all over me, in a funny way.

EL: The appropriate intensity of this scene is the opposite of one in *Hannah* with Michael Caine and Barbara Hershey that you decided not to use because in that case it was the wrong tone for the film.

WA: Yes. There was a wonderful sex scene with Caine and Barbara on a moored boat. It was wonderfully acted but it made him seem too nasty. I wanted you to like them. Showing him too aggressive was not what I wanted to do finally.

EL: Where did you develop your affection for long master shots?

WA: [*Quickly*] Laziness.

EL: You've said that before. Are you sure there isn't more to it?

WA: That's really what it is. I'd feel, I'm here, do I really want to shoot this scene? As [*longtime assistant cameraman and then camera operator*] Michael Green used to say to me, "Somebody else shooting that scene would take two days." He wasn't saying this as a compliment. But I used to feel, I am not going to shoot this scene with the three or four people in it and then shoot a pair of two-shots [*two people*] and a pair of two-shots and another two and another two and a single and a single close-up and an over-the-shoulder [*to keep part of one actor in the frame while another speaks*]—we'll be here all day today and all day tomorrow doing this scene. I don't have the patience or concentration. I can't stand listening to it so much. I design a shot and will get all the information in and we'll finish it and move on. And it's kept me sane over the years. That's why I've been able to work on so many films and I haven't got a great sense of tediousness.

EL: But it's not from any artistic value?

WA: No. You can tell the story any number of ways. You can tell the story in cuts [*interspersing different shots*] quite effectively and you can tell the story without cuts quite effectively. There are advantages both ways. If you're not using cuts, the actors get a chance to act five or six pages of script and not have to do it over. On the other hand, when you're doing the close-ups you can make them more effective than they really are and can make up for some mistakes that they've made. But I choose to come down on the side of the advantages of the long master because I'm lazy, and I justify it aesthetically by saying, "The actors get a chance to say six pages of script" and "You can make an interesting shot." But the truth of the matter is, Eisenstein among others—Hitchcock—didn't do the long masters. He did twenty million cuts and very brilliantly.

EL: It's a wonderful way to watch a film, just having the sense of being in the room as a long master plays out.

WA: There are many directors who will film a ton of material and cover everything and give it to the editor. You can't miss with that approach. But it often lacks personality and doesn't have any individual imprint.

What's funny is how often my use of masters is overlooked. So many people came up to me after *Bullets over Broadway* and said, "I loved you shooting all these long master shots," and I said, "I've been doing that in all my pictures for ten years, fifteen years." And they'd say, "You *have*?"

EL: Let's talk about camera operators for a second. You and the cinematographer decide what the shot should be and how it should be lit, but the operator and the focus puller are the guys who have to capture the movement and focus the way you want, often as actors are on the fly. Dick Mingalone was your camera operator for many years and Michael Green handled the focus before becoming the operator.

WA: Dick was a wonderful camera operator, as was Michael Green. I would always set up these elaborate shots and the last thing you want is a guy who, when the actors act, says, "I didn't get that. Can we do one more?" Of course, every once in a while every camera operator says, "That was my fault. We have to go again." But infrequently.

EL: I'm just amazed at how good they were because some of your shots are so complicated—they're just zooming in and getting the lens to the right stop and following the action. It's real choreography. Then they put that shot behind them and memorize the next one.

WA: Yes. I myself couldn't do that. I'm saying to them something like, "On Scarlett, and then when I say this, go to me, then stay on me for these three lines and then go back to Scarlett over there and then two lines later go back to me." And they do it. I'd find it a nerve-racking job, and especially when they've got to go on top of a building or in a helicopter or they're out in the freezing cold. It's a tough job.

EL: What are the pluses and minuses of shooting in, say, London, where it was all locations, and, say, *September* or *Shadows and Fog*, where you built a set and could control everything? Does being in a real place give a verisimilitude that you can't build?

WA: Yes, when I first started I only thought of shooting in real places. Then as I learned a little more I started to think and see that the art director is right, I should be building something because it will give me all the advantages and no one will know the difference. In general you have so much more control in a studio, but psychologically you can get bogged down. It's like going to an office. It's more fun to go into Central Park and make your shots and pull up stakes and go to Broadway and make a shot and then go someplace else.

As I said, I'm a lazy filmmaker. I don't like to go to grubby places or dangerous places. I don't like to work in excessive heat or excessive cold. Whereas other film-makers, they are so much more dedicated, they get a script or project in mind and they say, "Hey, I've gotta go to Afghanistan for two months." They'll go to Afghanistan, they'll build their own little movie theater there and get movies sent in, get some catering sent in, they'll live there.

[*He plays two people.*] "Going to make *Lawrence of Arabia* and you're out in the desert for two years?"

"Absolutely."

That's not me. I get the idea for *Lawrence of Arabia* and [*mimics crushing a piece of paper and throwing it away*]—right into the shredder.

EL: For a time in *Alice* you had scenes in India, but they were stock footage. I've always thought the film has a wonderful look.

WA: It's a tribute to Carlo and Santo, for the most part. It was a contemporary film that I wanted to make on the poetic side. Santo built the sets and also found wonderful locations for me, and Carlo lit them with that warm light, so it looks good. I was surfing through the television channels the other day and saw it and stopped for a second and turned the sound off and just looked at the picture for sixty seconds, not even, and I remembered many pretty things. I remember that apartment Santo built because we couldn't find an apartment; it is just bathed in light when you see it. [*There also was a very convincing translight—a painted screen—that made it appear that Manhattan was right outside the windows, ablaze in nighttime lights.*] There are some very good scenes in it. The Chinese actor [*Keye Luke*] was wonderful.

EL: The other day you told me that you always referred to *Danny Rose* as "the Italian movie"—

WA: [*Jumping in*] Because I saw that as a black-and-white Italian comedy. And that's probably why I made it in black and white. Because people said to me, "I don't know why you're making it in black and white because the characters, what they wear, they'd be so much better in color. You'd see their shirts and jackets. Why give yourself the headache of black and white?" But for some reason I saw it in black and white because I wanted to make a 1950s Italian movie. And Gordon Willis under-stood instantly. He said, "It just feels better to me in black and white, too."

EL: You have managed to make comedies look stylish. I watched a comedy on the plane flying in to see you that was completely in flat, bright light.

WA: Right, they don't waste their time with it—and maybe in a way they're right—because they're thinking, Why put a lot of time and effort into *that*? What we want to put our time and effort in is the jokes, the speed, the music. When Jerry Lewis does a brilliant bit, he wants it bright and lit. He doesn't want any artsy kind of nonsense competing with him. He doesn't want anybody in the audience to feel, Oh, there's some beautiful chiaroscuro. He wants you to see him doing his thing. Like Charlie Chaplin wanted it bright and right in front of you.

EL: Is that something he ever talked about with you when you were discussing doing *Take the Money*?

WA: No. I never talked about it with him but I observed it in his films. The cameramen he worked with gave him exactly what he wanted. If you see a Jerry Lewis picture or a Charlie Chaplin picture or a Buster Keaton picture, you will never see that beautiful lighting, the chiaroscuro and the shadows and depth and darkness and all that. Keaton's movies are beautifully photographed but not arty or pretentiously arty.

November 2005

EL: *Shadows and Fog* had to have a particularly stylized look to it.

WA: That was a tribute to Carlo. I knew when I did that picture that no one was going to want to see it—a black-and-white picture, an existential story set in Germany in the 1920s and shot in a studio. When [*Orion head*] Eric Pleskow saw it he said, "I've got to say, whenever I come to see one of your films I'm really surprised that they're all so different." He was groping for something to say. But again, it was

Woody as Broadway
Danny Rose

something I wanted to do and I hoped there would be enough people who saw it that studio people didn't bother me.

EL: There was a big change from *Shadows and Fog*—a black-and-white German expressionist comedy-drama—to *Husbands and Wives* [*see page 53*], with the camera moving all the time.

WA: Yes, I wanted to make a picture with no relation to beauty or any rules. I wanted just to do whatever I needed to do, like cut in the middle of scenes. It was one of those pictures that worked like a charm because I decided before I made the picture that it would be crude-looking and anything goes. I wouldn't care about cutting, I wouldn't care about angles, I wouldn't care about matching. And so we just shot it and if I was playing a scene with someone or someone was playing a scene and the scene was very good and then it got boring and then got very good again, we just cut the middle out [*claps hands*] and stuck them together.

EL: How about *Deconstructing Harry*?

WA: [*Long pause while thinking*] That was not a tough one to do. I remember cutting stuff out of that picture. It was too long.

EL: And *Bullets over Broadway*?

WA: Carlo really loved shooting *Bullets*. That's the kind of picture that he loved because it was period and color and the lighting doesn't become realistic, it becomes stylized like the period, so he could make that very beautiful. [*Pauses to think again*] And there were no big problems on that picture. The one thing I reshot was the scene in MacDougal Alley [*in Greenwich Village*] at the very end.

Jerry Lewis, here photographing Woody filling in for Johnny Carson on *The Tonight Show,* was interested in directing *Take the Money and Run.*

[There are many characters, some on the street, others at windows across the alley from one another.] I shot and moved the camera and moved the camera and moved the camera. And then I went home and thought, It's probably not going to work like that, I should just do it *[snaps fingers]* and cut it. And I did that and after I had gotten the whole company together again I went back to my original shot.

EL: You told me how surprised you were that *Hollywood Ending* was not more appreciated.

WA: Yeah, because to me, that's a very funny movie. It was one of my most successful ones in terms of an idea that was executed properly. The girl *[Téa Leoni]* was great in it. Of course George Hamilton *[as a studio executive]* is always wonderful, I've always wanted to work with him. *[He plays Ed, a Hollywood type who calls Val (Woody) "garbage" behind his back, then adds straight-faced, "But I don't mean that as an insult."]* I mean everybody in that picture was so good. And that Chinese kid *[Barney Cheng, as the translator for the Chinese-speaking cameraman Lu Yue]* that I found was so funny. And the guy who played the producer, Treat Williams *[the fiancé of Val's ex-wife, played by Téa Leoni]*. I just thought it was just such a funny idea and the whole thing came off and I played it and it was well done. I think if people had gone to see it they would have enjoyed it. But they didn't go to see it.

EL: You had trouble with Haskell Wexler and replaced him as cinematographer after a couple of weeks. Do you want to talk about why?

WA: It was a minor thing. It's funny, I was just watching an interview with Elia Kazan on television the other night and he was talking about *America, America*

George Hamilton and
Woody on the set of
Hollywood Ending

[*1963*], which is a *brilliantly* photographed movie because Haskell Wexler is such a great photographer. It's one of the most beautifully photographed movies. And he said, "I didn't get along with the cameraman. I would never work with him again. But he's great." And so I knew that he could be [*brief pause*] difficult. And I found him to be actually a lovely guy and full of energy and caring about the picture, but [*long pause*] I didn't get along with him. He was so—so dedicated, so fanatic, that he would bring me lists of changes that I should make in the script and never stopped bothering me to make shots. "Please, let's do this one just for me. I know you don't want to do it but do it just for me," he would say. And after two weeks of that, nobody could take it anymore. So we said, "This is not going to work out." But the guy is a genius cameraman, there's no question about it.

EL: How did you find Wedigo von Schultzendorff, who you brought in as the replacement?

WA: Someone had recommended him to me. They said he was just finishing a film and that I would like him and he was nice to work with and, being European, had a nice European touch. And I met him and liked him and he came in under very difficult circumstances—no preparation time or anything—and did a very good job.

EL: Yeah, it was a good-looking movie.

WA: But nobody came to see it. I don't know what will happen in the long run. I mean, nobody came to see *Broadway Danny Rose,* either, but now many people have seen it and it's many people's favorite movie of mine.

EL: There are a couple of people we haven't talked about. You used Vilmos Zsigmond for *Melinda and Melinda,* someone whose work obviously you liked a lot.

WA: Well, everybody's always liked Vilmos's work. I needed a cameraman to shoot *Melinda.* Carlo was either ill or not coming to New York at the time. Darius Khondji, who I had worked with [*Anything Else*], was doing a picture someplace. I was looking at the available list and I noticed Vilmos's name was on it. So I called him. Here was a chance to work with one of the all-time greats.

EL: What about Zhao Fei?

WA: Zhao Fei was wonderful, a major talent. We worked through a translator. The only trouble with Zhao Fei is that in China, there's no limit on time and money in making a picture, so he couldn't understand why Americans rush, rush, rush. He did not realize that we were spending $100,000 a day, $150,000 a day. In China, they go on and on, six or seven months, they get what they want. So it was hard for him not to say, "I need a hundred lights, I need this, I need that, why are we going so fast?"

And I'm not that fast. I've worked with people who took their time to prepare things, like Gordon Willis. But this was, you know, difficult. I did three pictures with him and I loved working with him. I think he made enough money on the three pictures that he decided to stay in China. Another thing, I don't think he loved coming here to do pictures, though he liked the money. I got along with him very well, communication was not a problem on the set. I just never speak to anyone.

EL: You used an example of him in *Hollywood Ending*, where you have a Chinese cameraman who speaks no English.

WA: Yes, I did, because I thought it was funny. If I wasn't a director who had a lot of credits, if I was a first-time director, I doubt the studio would have felt secure about using a cameraman who doesn't understand English. But they would with any number of directors who have done a lot of pictures.

EL: Years ago you told me how you and Sven Nykvist looked at a couple of films together before you shot *Crimes and Misdemeanors*. With Zsigmond and the others, did you have meetings beforehand about the look of the picture?

WA: Unless there is a reason dictated by the script, as I say, it's not rocket science. To shoot a picture like *Melinda* there are no special needs, really.

EL: You had two nicely separate looks, one for the comedy and another for the drama.

WA: But that was simple, that was a two-minute discussion. It was very quick and amiable.

EL: He's seventy-five years old and still going strong.

WA: Yes. He didn't look anything like I thought he would. I thought I was going to get a large, formidable, mad Hungarian. He was nothing like that. He's small, cheerful, pleasant, a smart guy. It was a pleasure to work with him.

EL: How about Remi Adefarasin, who did *Match Point* and *Scoop*?

WA: Remi is very sweet. He's a gentleman, cares very much about the picture, very dedicated. He's of the lighting school of Sven Nykvist where they just throw on a lamp someplace and in five minutes they're ready—and it looks good. You know,

Remi Adefarasin, the cinematographer for *Match Point* and *Scoop*, works out a shot for *Match Point* with Woody at the Tate Modern in London.

some guys make it look drop-dead beautiful with a thousand lights. Other guys make it look very pretty with nothing. It just depends on their sensibility.

EL: We were talking about ideas and influences for specific films a while ago and you said to come back to you again on it. Have any others popped into your mind?

WA: When I was doing *Purple Rose* I remember being influenced by [*Fellini's*] *Amarcord* [1973, *which takes place in the 1930s in a small Italian town*]. I remember the image of a town with a movie house and larger-than-life characters. I wanted to get that kind of nostalgic, melancholy feeling in it.

EL: For *Stardust Memories* was it also Fellini for all those wonderful faces?

WA: Yes. Well, the biggest thing about *Stardust Memories* for me was when I did the Judith Crist film weekend [*in 1973*].

EL: I remember.

WA: I thought, This would be such a funny idea. A guy was going away on a film weekend and everybody up there is asking me for autographs and asking me if I'll help them with this and will I read this and can I do this, and I'm completely out of my depth and over my head. I'm up there doing the best I can as a favor to Judith Crist, who I liked very much, and I thought that would make a funny movie. That was really the big inspiration for that film.

EL: But many viewers and critics were personally affronted by it because they thought by peopling the film with odd-looking Felliniesque characters you were saying that's how *you* felt about *them,* that they were sort of weirdos who wanted you only to make comic films, like they did Sandy Bates, the director you played.

WA: I tried to make the audience, as seen through the eyes of a guy having a kind of breakdown, as harassing. No one ever harassed me to that degree in life nor did I regard the audience with any contempt. If anything, I always assumed the audience was smarter than me, and never hesitated to use erudite or esoteric references in jokes, confident they'd get them. If I really felt like my audience were "weirdos," as you put it, I would never have depicted them that way and would have been much too politic to be that candid. Having said this, if the audience came away with an impression I was sour on them, then I failed to be clear—and of course what they came away with is more important than my inept attempts.

EL: This was probably your most misunderstood film when it came out and may still be.

WA: Yes. I wanted to make a stylish film. Gordon and I liked to work in black and white and I wanted to make a picture about an artist who theoretically should be happy. He has everything in the world—health, success, wealth, notoriety—but in fact he doesn't have anything, he's very unhappy. The point of the story is that he can't get used to the fact that he's mortal and that all his wealth and fame and adulation are not going to preserve him in any meaningful way—he, too, will age and die. At the beginning of the movie you see him wanting to make a serious statement even though he is really a comic-filmmaker.

Of course, this part is naturally identified with me even though the tale is total fabrication. I never had the feelings of the protagonist in real life. When I made *Stardust Memories* I didn't feel I was a much adored filmmaker whose life was miserable and all around me things were terrible. I thought I was a respectable

Woody cast actors with faces fit for a Fellini movie in *Stardust Memories* in order to give a sense of the distorted emotional state of director Sandy Bates (Woody).

moviemaker and the perks of success—as I said in my film *Celebrity*—actually out-weighed the downside. I was never blocked, conflicted much, or steeped in gloom—though I often played that character. I did it again later in *Deconstructing Harry*. That character is also a writer but nothing like me. Of course, the public doesn't know me—only the character I present to create conflict and laughs.

And so in *Stardust Memories* he sees the dead rabbit on the kitchen table [*eleven minutes into the story there is a scene in which Sandy's cook has laid out a rabbit to prepare for dinner. "How many times have I told you, 'no rabbit'?" he says with frustration. "I never want rabbit. I don't eat rodent. . . . It's furbearing"*] and as he looks at it the sight of death leads him to a series of thoughts. From then on [*another seventy-eight minutes*], the whole film takes place in his mind. It's shot in exaggerated form because it's in the mind. You see all the conflicts of his life with the woman he thinks of marrying, the other woman he was in love with, the new woman who reminds him of the first one. And you see all the downside of being a celebrity: you have no privacy, everybody thinks you can help them and that you're the answer to all their prayers when in fact you're not the answer to your own prayers. They think there's no limit to what you can do. Yet one can do very little of real significance. We all suffer and rage impotently about the human condition, even if we're successful. I exaggerate these problems and anxieties, drumming up all kinds of fictional uses for laughs. [*He pauses.*] It's no fun being a speck in space. That's really what it is [*laughs*]. That's what you are, a member of a failed species.

Anyhow, audiences at *Stardust Memories* thought, Oh, this guy is showing what idiots the members of his audience are. Of course, I didn't feel my audience was made of idiots at all. Of all the filmmakers around—and even as a stand-up comic—I was one who always gave the audience credit for being literate and at least as bright as, or, much more often, brighter than, I was. I never thought the audience was stupid or grotesque. I was always suing for their approval because, as I said, I thought they were smarter than me and more cultivated than me and more mature. The audience in the movie was just an exaggerated depiction of what somebody who couldn't appreciate his success might imagine under the pressure

of being a hit and yet still being unable to stave off life's tragedies or have a good love relationship.

But it was misunderstood. People took the path of least resistance and I can't necessarily blame them for that. If they pay ten bucks for a ticket, resistance is not the path they want. It's undoubtedly my fault that I wasn't clear enough in making my point.

EL: You were able to use all manner of cinematic wiles.

WA: Yes, I wanted to make it stylish. It's a dream film; the attempt is poetic. I'm not saying it comes off but the intent is poetic, so you're not locked in to a realistic story. You could certainly tell a realistic story about a guy who has everything and is unhappy but I was trying to do it on a more fantastic level.

I feel if you give the film a chance, there are some rewards in it. It's dense. But as with all films or books or plays, if you don't get hooked at the beginning then it doesn't mean anything and all my prattling about how well intended it was means zilch.

EL: In the end was it the film you set out to do? Were you satisfied?

WA: I haven't seen it in many years, but when I finished it I was very satisfied with it and it was my favorite film to that time. I don't know how I'd feel about it today. I know when I look back on my nightclub and television performances, I really don't like them very much. So I think if I look back on my films, while I might be pleasantly surprised here and there, for the most part I'd be very crushed.

EL: Where did you find all those actors with such unique looks?

WA: We were just stopping people on the street and putting them in the movie. If someone had a good face we gave him or her a red card with our phone number, and 99 percent of those who followed up with us we hired.

EL: This came out after you had done your first drama, *Interiors,* which led some people to complain that you were moving away from strictly comic films. It seemed you were having some fun with that notion of a filmmaker known for comedies who wants to make serious pictures.

WA: Look, I never took myself seriously. I thought it was a funny thing to make some jokes on my own desire to do drama, but what happens is people always think it's deeply autobiographically revealing when you use little experiences you've had. They're not autobiographical at all, in the sense that often they don't express your true feelings but go where the joke is strongest. As I've pointed out many times, there are great points in *Manhattan* and *Annie Hall* that express Marshall Brickman's view rather than my own. But people just don't want to know John Wayne offstage is any different than on.

Of course, the exact opposite of the dramatic question happened when I made *Curse of the Jade Scorpion, Hollywood Ending,* and *Anything Else* [*between 2001 and 2003*]. People asked, "Why are you making these light comedies?" [*He laughs.*] But you can never go by what people say. You have to make what you need to make at the time, and if people like it, you're lucky, and if they don't, you're not lucky.

February 2006

EL: Let's talk about *Alice* [*see page 48*], which came between *Crimes and Misdemeanors* and *Shadows and Fog.*

WA: *Alice* had a little style to it. I just intended it to be a fable. There might have been an amusing sequence here and there—like when she was invisible—but that's all. Now, whether it succeeds on that level or not I can't guarantee. I'm always working on a small budget and in limited circumstances, so I can't compare it to a truly stylish picture where these guys put a lot of time and money into the art direction.

I have no [*pauses*] particular regard for *Alice.* I don't *hate* it. I never think of it. [*Recalling*] Mia looked great with that red hat on; Alec Baldwin of course is always great. Bill Hurt, too. But it's a picture.

EL: I just watched *Everyone Says I Love You* and I want to ask you about shooting in multiple countries. You worked in Paris and Venice as well as New York.

WA: The shooting went smoothly. All the crepe-hanging prognostications were—as usual in show business—incorrect.

EL: What were some of the crepe-hanging prognostications?

WA: It would take me six times as long to shoot anything in Venice because you pile into the boat all the time, but it was six times as fast *because* you piled into the boat. There was no traffic and you got to the next location in sixty seconds, whereas in New York City you got there in sixty minutes. Going to a few different countries is going to be expensive.

EL: Did you have much trouble with reshoots?

WA: I think I did a few, but as the years have gone on I've done less and less reshoots. One, I haven't had the money. But it was more than that. I reshoot as I go along. If I don't like the dailies on Thursday, I reshoot it on Friday. I don't wait to the end of shooting like I used to. When I was acting with Keaton, or with Mia, I knew I could always get the two protagonists on a moment's notice. Now, I don't know. These people can be in Africa doing a film and I can't get them back. So I try to look out for that. I try to anticipate the problems in advance, *and* I've gotten a little more savvy so I can obviate some of the pitfalls that caused me to reshoot in the past.

July 2006

In London, I accompany Woody to see dailies for Scoop. *His English producer meets him at the door and warns him that he might find a scene in a staid London club to be too deeply red and yellow, too saturated with color. I am surprised by her concern; Woody has talked to me in great detail about his love of rich color and it is evident in some of his movies, such as* Radio Days *and* Sweet and Lowdown. *We talk after the screening.*

EL: You're not going to tone it down, are you?

WA: No, of course not. I love the way it looks. I always err on the side of warmth, of red and yellow. The problem is, we're making parallel movies here. They think they're making Alfred Hitchcock. I think I'm making Bob Hope.

November 2006

Woody has finished Cassandra's Dream. *His cinematographer was Vilmos Zsigmond, with whom he worked on* Melinda and Melinda. *A turning point in the film is when the two brothers (Colin Farrell and Ewan McGregor) go to their wealthy uncle (Tom Wilkinson) to ask for money and find that in return he wants them to kill a business associate who is going to reveal his financial misdeeds. The scene takes place beneath a sheltering tree. Much of it is in one shot and during it the camera shows not only the various conversations but Farrell's increasing nervousness and discomfort as he listens to his uncle and brother talk about murder.*

EL: How was it working with Zsigmond again? It seems you have different preferences in how you like to shoot.

WA: Vilmos is one of the top cameramen. He loves to do elaborate, challenging stuff. If you look at *The Black Dahlia,* that's right up his alley; he flexed his cinematic muscles there. I'm simpler than that and I didn't want anything elaborate in this case. But for me the test of a cameraman invariably is the lighting. To figure out the shots, compose the photo, they can do that, I can do that, we can do that together. But what separates the men from the boys is the lighting and he's wonderful at lighting.

EL: Is he on the Sven Nykvist side of that, doing it with very little, or the Zhao Fei side, using a lot?

WA: He's kind of in the middle. He doesn't need a ton of stuff [*pauses and chuckles*] but he wouldn't *mind* having it. He's used to doing big pictures and used to having cranes and effects and saying, "We'll do that later digitally." Working with him is easy.

EL: How did that shot under the tree come about?

WA: I had a very long talk scene. Colin's tale of woe, and then Tom listens to Ewan's pitch for money, then *he* makes a big pitch. There's a lot of dialogue there, and I was trying to figure a way to break it up. In real life I figured the uncle would take them back to his hotel, but that didn't lend itself to anything interesting. So then I thought to break up the scene and have them in the park because it would be private, and then if it suddenly started to rain, it would add a little oomph to the scene and it would go someplace.

Once they were doing the scene under the tree with the rain coming down, I thought we could dolly around the whole tree and see them. We had to cut out a

Tom Wilkinson explaining to Ewan McGregor and Colin Farrell in *Cassandra's Dream* that the price for his helping them with their financial problems is for them to kill one of his business associates.

number of leaves as we practiced the shot. We laid dolly track. We had to get the right amount of rain so they got wet but they had shelter under the tree. I just did two takes. To me the real problem was to have the camera operator and grip stop at the exact moment an actor said something. The first time they got there a little early but the second time they got it right on the nose and so did the actors.

EL: The apple tree in the Garden of Eden came to mind while I watched the scene.

WA: I had no intention of that, but I did think that some people would see that tree as the birth of an evil idea.

5

DIRECTING

May 1973

*Woody is shooting part of Sleeper in and around Denver. All is being readied for a
bedroom scene between Woody and actress Chris Forbes. It is a parody of cinematic romance: the man making sure he looks just right and assuming as debonair
an aura as possible; the woman, soft, silky, and desirable, spread languorously on
the bed.*

*Woody rehearses the scene a couple of times. Looking into a mirror, he puts on
an aviator's cap, affixes a moustache, and puts around his neck a white silk scarf
that will be blown by an off-camera fan. Then he turns to the crew.*

*"Here's what I'm going to do. I'm going to fix myself up, scent the room twice.
Then the fan blows the scarf and she's sitting on the bed eating yogurt, or strawberries and cream, or whatever it is they eat. Then I go over and start working on
her a bit, biting her, and the fan blows harder and harder. . . . We do have a fan,
don't we?"*

*He looks over at the property man, who says he has a fan but from what Woody
describes it won't blow nearly hard enough.*

*"I want something like a tornado," Woody tells him. The prop man rushes off to
rent two huge fans. Woody turns back to the crew.*

*"We need a gallon of Jell-O, or a huge sundae with a couple of gallons of ice
cream," he continues. "She should be in bed eating with a huge spoon."*

*A check with the caterer turns up four gallons of cottage cheese and some
orange slices. The clear plastic bowl that held enough salad for fifty people at lunch
is filled up and brought in, along with an appropriate spoon. Woody approves, still
thinking.*

*"You know," he muses, "it would be funny to me if I could open up a little cube
when I get over to her and have a little man come out and run all over her body."*

The fans arrive and do fine in a trial run but Woody is still thinking.

*"You're in for a big surprise, Chris," he says with a slight smile. Then he adds to
no one in particular: "It would be funny if I had a snorkel and wet suit instead of the
aviator's costume." The crew laughs. Woody smiles. "You think I'm kidding, but I'm
not."*

*The wardrobe man and the policeman assigned to the film for traffic and crowd
assistance get into the police car and roar off toward downtown, the lights flashing
and the siren blaring, to get the equipment.*

*"This is what I'm notorious for," Woody says as the crew moves off to wait.
"That's why it's not fun for my crew. But then, only so much can be done in
advance. Things occur to me on the set and it's a shame not to do them if we can."*

The wet suit arrives. Woody puts it on and flops around in the fins, then stops for a second, peering through the mask. "If people don't laugh at this, then I'm giving up," he says. The scene is shot. The crew laughs uproariously after "Cut!" is called.

But for some reason, the hilarity of the moment does not translate to film. The laugh isn't there when he screens the scene during editing and it doesn't make the finished version. He is not particularly surprised that what was funny in person is not funny on film—it happens often—even though the action is exactly the same. A few days after shooting the bedroom scene, he makes this observation on the difference between performing before an audience and performing before a camera.

WA: Monologue material is different from film scripts in that you have to do it yourself. You go up on a stage and find you write a portion of your monologue there—you start editing fast. You go up with ten jokes and when you're on joke four you know joke five isn't going to get a laugh; you're no longer in a closed room titillating yourself. It's totally an instinctive thing. You just know that if you grimace a little more they'll keep on laughing, and if you grimace another quarter inch it'll be overdone.

Your body dictates what to do. When I was in Sicily promoting *Bananas* and the whole audience spoke Italian and I went onstage, I just knew that I could get laughs from them. The instinct is different from writing in a room. Of course, that doesn't mean I'm always going to make it funny, but what I'm doing is different than when I conceived it.

But that has nothing to do with films. Something happens in film that gives it another dimension, good or bad. I know that when I fell yesterday that I was doing the proper thing that these people around here would think was funny. [*The fall, unlike the bedroom scene, translated to film and got a big laugh.*] I know that if there were a thousand people in the audience and I was in the middle of a play and I fell like that, I would get a big laugh. But I can't guarantee that it would look like that on film. That's what makes you crazy. We're all at the mercy of the dailies. I'll watch them and I'll think, None of those walks looks funny and I'll reshoot them and when I go to edit the film and I cut in those walks, the two worst ones in dailies will get the biggest laughs. That's why film comedies are so hard.

A week or two after the bedroom scene, he is in the Rocky Mountains above Denver, setting up the shot of Diane Keaton and himself trekking through the woods. It is a sunny morning. It also is 20 degrees Fahrenheit. Most of the ground is covered in snow. Woody, bundled in a thick down parka, is not happy.

"I hate it here," he says, but he is hardly being site-specific. "If I were in L.A. I would be hating it, being unable to wait to get back to New York, where probably nothing is happening anyway."

He and cinematographer David Walsh each look through the camera. The shot is almost good. They try a 250 mm lens, then a 100 mm lens. Woody mutters to himself. They try another lens.

"The trouble is, I want to make it funny and pretty and the two are opposite," he says with frustration. "It's a real pain in the ass."

(I am reminded of what his producer Jack Grossberg said a few months before, when Woody was shooting the very stylized Italian sequence in Everything You Always Wanted to Know About Sex: *"The butterfly has come out—and he has red hair.")*

Woody and Walsh try another angle: "Too arty." Then another. Woody looks through the camera again, followed by Walsh, then Roger Sherman, the camera operator.

"Does this shot bother you the way it bothers me?" Woody asks Walsh. "No? Then argue with me. I think it needs more of a sense of trees. There aren't enough in the frame."

Walsh does not argue for the shot. Instead, he and Woody and assistant director Fred Gallo take off in a station wagon to scout other possibilities. After they return, we talk.

EL: Getting this to look good is one of your problems, but what are your other concerns?

WA: There is a great skill in blending together good performances and a good story. Enormous finesse. But there is no mystery to it from a technical point of view. Millions of people who have gone to the movies all their lives could make a movie. Technically, they're wonderful, they could direct circles around me. They get everything going beautifully; their photography is great and their movies are beautiful. But where they fall short, like many TV commercial directors who make movies, is that they don't have a dramatic sense or a sense of comedy. That's why Buñuel's films can look terrible and still be masterpieces, because overwhelmingly what's important is the content. Every piece of junk that comes out looks good, because a director can just go out and hire a first-rate cameraman and a first-rate editor, and they all know what to do.

He hopes that Sleeper *will tap into a larger audience than his first films did. One day shortly before it is released in December 1973, I visit him in his apartment. The film was shown to Los Angeles critics the night before, and a little earlier in the day he has heard that Charles Champlin of the* Los Angeles Times *likes the film a great deal; he is pleased because with* Sleeper, *he is trying to move on to new ground, and he is more openly ambitious than I have ever heard him. (After* Annie Hall, *he will stop reading reviews.)*

WA: *Sleeper* is a picture every kid in America could see and find funny. It's exactly the kind of picture that I used to see as a kid and love. I don't want to be confined to intellectual humor, especially since I have zero intellectual credentials.

Chaplin had some very hip jokes in his stuff. I'm tired of being thought of as special for that Third Avenue crowd.

I don't think I'm a special comedian. I think I've had the same problem with my movies that I had with my cabaret act in the beginning: I believe once the audience is in the theater, they'll like the act or the picture. I like to feel that I have a broad commercial base like Chaplin, for instance. I'd like to do a series of commercially acceptable films. Instead of opening at small New York theaters and knowing we're going to break even, I'd like to be able to open a show the way you do a James Bond picture and get millions of people in to see it. I'd like the film to make $30 million [*his films to date have made only a few million*]; not for me—it could all go to the cancer foundation. There's no reason for this to be like an art object. They're not art. [*But there will be no Bond-like openings of his films in two thousand or more theaters, although there will be many financially successful pictures, among them* Sleeper, Annie Hall, Hannah and Her Sisters, Manhattan, *and most notably* Match Point, *which earned over $80 million worldwide.*]

And I think I've turned the corner with *Sleeper.* I heard *Scholastic* magazine liked it. I heard *Parents'* magazine liked it. I'm glad about that. I heard *Seventeen* magazine loved it and that [New York Times *critic*] Vincent Canby did, too.

(*Woody's wish for the film largely came true. It earned more than $18 million in U.S. domestic release alone—about $60 million in 2007 dollars—plus a considerable amount more around the world and in television and DVD sales.*)

November 1987

Woody is blocking the steps for Philip Bosco and Gena Rowlands for a flashback/ dream scene in Another Woman *that is being shot in a theater on lower Broadway. It is a plain room. The brick walls are unfinished, the stage is black, the seats red.*

After stepping through the actors' moves, Woody rides the camera to be sure it will film properly. In rehearsing the choreography, Rowlands starts the line, "Stop it. I can't live like this anymore," then asks Woody, "You want me to cross here?" She says another line, then, "Where would you like me to wind up?" He is graceful in his movement as he quickly walks around the stage, showing the actors their steps.

There are sixty-five crew and others sitting in the theater seats, out of the camera's scope. Woody points at them and says, "There are more people in here than will see the movie."

In the first takes he allows Bosco and Rowlands to do the scene the way they each envision it, then he moves them the way he wants as they work into it. He squats or stands as he watches the takes, occasionally whispering into camera operator Dick Mingalone's ear as the camera rolls.

This scene will be reshot three times before Woody is satisfied that he has the best angles for the pan between the two actors: here again in December, then in January at the Union Theological Seminary in uptown Manhattan, near Columbia University, and once more in mid-February. During one of the reshoots, I ask him how much he rewrites on film.

WA: Basically, I shoot the script. I like to get a first draft on film and then see where I am. I discover radical things I never would know otherwise. A script is only a guide for the work to come.

EL: Do you think you have distinctive writing and directing styles?

WA: It's hard to know one's own style. If I made a picture and didn't put my name on it, would you know it's mine? Now of course if I'm in it, that's a big clue [*he laughs*]. But if I wasn't in it, would you know it's mine? If you saw *Purple Rose*? I can't tell. I always try to fit the style of the movie to the content.

I think I have my own clichés. For one thing, I think I very clearly have an urban orientation. In all my movies you'll see people walking and talking in streets and sitting in restaurants and living in apartments. I feel that there are certain issues and questions that repeat themselves in the movies over and over again, though maybe not in every movie. And I think in the last ten or twelve years or so I've developed a photographic style that with the exception of a picture like *Zelig*, is marked by very long takes and never shooting any coverage of anything. I know I've mentioned this to you before.

EL: You're shooting this film with a superb cinematographer, Sven Nykvist, who epitomizes the European style of filmmaking that you admire so much. You both like to rely on long master shots in which you can see both or all characters talking, rather than cutting back and forth between them like in most American films.

WA: Sven was asking me the other day why American directors always do both a master shot as well as coverage of each of the characters—it's why he doesn't like to make movies here. The only reasons I could give him were that, one, American films have always been largely narrative, with lots of plot, and that's the simplest way to tell the story. And two, there were always factory-made studio films, so there was always a grinding-out formula that ensured nothing could go wrong. Everybody hit their mark, everybody had the right amount of makeup on, there was the master shot, the coverage. It was always very important to the producers that there were enough close-ups of the stars. To this day you'll hear producers complaining that the stars don't have enough close-ups, they want their money's worth from those people.

Whereas European films never did that. When I first started, I did that kind of shooting because I didn't know any different. When I did *Take the Money and Run,* I made sure that I had coverage because later in the cutting room I found I could save myself from a lot of grief if I had choices to cut to. Then, as I got more confident and more relaxed in filmmaking, I started to abandon that and I would say that by the time we did *Manhattan* that was the end of it. I remember just stringing masters together in *Manhattan.* The same thing in *Hannah.* And in this picture, too. We're in our third, fourth week of shooting and there hasn't been a scene in the picture where there have been back-and-forth cuts between people.

You'll never miss it if I do my job well. It gets tricky sometimes, like in *Another Woman.* In the dream sequence [*a two-minute scene between Marion and Larry, the man she most loves but drove away*] you see Hackman, and then Gena comes into the shot and it's a two-shot and she goes away and it's a single of her and she crosses back and we lose her and it becomes Hackman. And in a certain way you're doing star close-ups but you're not doing it in that crude way. You're giving the people their opportunities on screen. A lot of that was in *September.*

EL: What else about European-style filmmaking appeals to you?

WA: European films, Bergman's included, are more roughly hewn. American crews are sticklers. One of the things I like about European films is their lack of perfection. Actors do go out of focus now and then. European filmmakers never had the money, so they don't have the time to get that slick, decorated feeling. The camera moves are not always perfect, the zoom may jump. I like that, generally. [*In* Husbands and Wives, *made twelve years later, the handheld camera moves are deliberately jumpy.*]

February 1989

A few weeks later, in Woody's apartment.

EL: You've just finished a dramatic picture [Another Woman] shot with a lot of subtlety, and now you're doing a broad comedy [Oedipus Wrecks]. When we were looking at dailies today, you lamented that part of your unhappiness with the color in the film is simply because comedy has to be shot in brighter light than drama.

WA: In serious films you can do some very pretty things, some very poetic things. Like the sequence in *Another Woman* with Gene Hackman in the theater or Gena [*Rowlands*] in the empty apartment. You can move the camera a certain way and the compositions are poetic and the cutting is poetic and the clocks tick and you get a certain hypnotic rhythm going. But in this kind of comedy you can't do that. You gotta be [*snaps fingers twice quickly*]. If people on Columbus Avenue are looking up at my mother [*who has materialized in the sky*] you don't want the camera falling from face to face. You want [*snaps fingers again*] somebody yelling something. And when you go over to my house or to Mia's house you don't want a stunning kind of apartment with shafts of light coming in through the window. Everything has to play against mundane circumstances or else it's not funny, so everything in the picture is subjugated to the comic premise. Nothing can be allowed to get in the way of that. You have to simplify a lot with comedy because although schmaltzy stuff is fun to do, it always spoils the laughs. Everything becomes a vehicle to getting the good comic line across.

EL: How about the dialogue in drama?

WA: Well, it has to be just right, of course, especially these days. In early films it was, say, cowboys out on the plains and there was very little dialogue. It's beautiful. But modern times demand dialogue. People express themselves verbally. It's true of Ingmar's movies as well. When he can get less verbal, he goes into period. So *Cries and Whispers* is very, very nonverbal. It's wonderful—these people in this house. But in New York or any city, people talk, so I have a lot of it in my movies. In my films, nobody chases anybody else or wrestles on the side of buildings, and there are no moments of exacting tension between people like there is between the sisters in the house in *Cries and Whispers.*

EL: You write, direct, and edit all your films and act in so many of them and score virtually all as well, which seems to me to pretty well cover the definition of an auteur filmmaker.

WA: I read an interview with Steven Soderbergh, who made *Sex, Lies, and Videotape* [*which had been recently released, to great fanfare*], a film I like very much. He said he didn't believe in the auteur theory because you can have too much power. I don't know what that means. There obviously are people you would call auteur filmmakers, only meaning that it is clearly their own product, 100 percent. It expresses them. I don't know why as a director he'd object to power. He won't feel that way if some studio guy tries to tamper with his work.

EL: But you do know what it's like not to have enough power. For instance, when you told David Merrick, who was there in his business suit telling you what would work in *Don't Drink the Water,* that "I've made over a million dollars in my life not listening to men in blue suits," or when your material was being butchered by Charlie Feldman and others on *What's New Pussycat?*

WA: Usually I have civil relations with everybody. It's been very rare that I've ever gotten mad in a professional situation. I wasn't even mad at Merrick when I chewed him out. It wasn't an ugly situation. It wasn't that kind of mad. There was the one time making *What's New Pussycat?* when I told somebody to fuck off. It was either [*Producer Charles*] Feldman or one of his minions.

I had a less charitable view of Feldman than I did of Merrick, by far. Feldman was supposed to be one of those charming, wonderful guys who was tough to deal with but was a prince compared to other producers. But I didn't see that so much. In retrospect he may have been worse.

I was not experienced at seeing dailies and I did not realize that dailies look terrible all the time, because you don't get the sound effects and the mix effects and it's just bald, terrible stuff. These guys were mutilating my script and they were telling me what was funny and what wasn't funny. So I got frustrated and mouthed off.

EL: But now there is no one ordering you to do something. Is there a drawback to total freedom?

WA: I find the most difficult part of it is diagnosis. When I have a slightly unsatisfied feeling, I'm not completely clear on what it is that's bothering me. I think that the film I'm screening tonight [*a newly edited version of* Another Woman; *a screening several days before made him realize he did not yet have the characters in the film in proper balance*] would be much more to the liking of those who saw it the other night, who objected to too much narration.

EL: Is *Another Woman* close to being the film you envisioned? [*See page 13.*]

WA: No, it's not. When you work on something like this that takes six months or a year and requires so many people and such coordination of artistry of costumes and actors and writing and directing and lighting and all that, to a certain degree, unless you're lucky or a happy accident occurs or you're such an overpowering genius—but it's hard to imagine that this happens to anybody—a project starts to assume a life of its own. There are things you didn't anticipate. Sometimes it assumes a bad life of its own and you kill it and go on to something else, or you change it. But other times it assumes an interesting life that's fuller than you thought of at the inception and you go with that.

For instance, originally I thought Marion would be a cold person surrounded by nicer people. But that wasn't the impression that was formed as we filmed. And I wasn't sure. At first it occurred to me that this was even more interesting than I had planned because she's not as one-dimensional. So I started to add scenes to show her depth. I added the one with Kathryn Grody where she says Marion's a wonderful teacher, because I wanted to make Marion very nice. Maybe I tipped the balance too much. But the film keeps growing organically. Now I'm starting to develop a relationship between Martha Plimpton [*who plays Marion's stepdaughter*] and her. Originally there was no sense of Martha ever saying to her boyfriend, "She's so judgmental." [*Though later she finds that's not the case.*] Then I saw that that would be a fertile thing to mine. Now I'm going to do some more scenes with her so that by the end of the movie you'll have her calling on the phone at the party, which I never had. And then you'll have her going up to the old family home with Marion. I took out the philosophy discussion in the drive up, which I didn't like and was going nowhere. There also will be a scene at the end where she and Marion walk together with a better understanding of each other, so that will have grown into a relationship. And it's not what I sat down to write exactly. [*Smiles.*] It's called floundering.

EL: In film it seems you have more leeway with what you write, that you can change it on the spot.

WA: In Kazan's book or Bergman's, I'm not sure which, the author talks about how a play script is literature, language, but a film script is architecture—it's really a plan—and that's right. I write the script fast, as you know. And then I adjust, like when I was filming in the art gallery, where I knew I needed a moment between Gena and Mia—not when they first meet, but seeing the Klimt and Schiele. So first I shot this elaborate scene where you pan the whole art gallery and they're talking about Gena's first husband. But that was dreadful. It didn't even make the first cut of the movie. I knew they would have to be at the art gallery because that was where they were headed. So I told them, "We have to go back to the art gallery." But I had no idea for a scene, none whatsoever.

So I went to the art gallery with the two actresses and I thought, Well, they should be sort of getting to know one another, just talking about art. But that was tedious. We were all lit and they were standing in front of the pictures. And it occurred to me at that moment, this may be a place for Gena to say, "I may want to get back to my art." And that suddenly gave the moment more meaning. Both actresses responded to that idea immediately. So we ad-libbed it. I wrote it down for them on the back of an envelope like the Gettysburg Address and they quickly did it. And now it's a nice little scene in the picture. [*Marion, looking to buy an anniversary gift, enters a shop and finds Hope crying by a large print of Gustav Klimt's painting of a naked and pregnant red-haired young woman. Hope (herself pregnant) says the painting makes her sad. Marion tells her that the painting is meant to convey the opposite feeling—it is entitled* Hope. *The two women talk some about their own artistic efforts and Hope, echoing a theme of the film, says, "I guess we all imagine what might have been."*]

At the time, though, I was thinking to myself, Well, maybe I should get them both back at the art gallery and make even more of that. That has often happened to me, that I shoot more and then throw it away because I realize that it was fine the first way, that the very brevity of the new scene is contributing to its success; just because it's a good idea does not mean you can elaborate on it. Sometimes you can and sometimes you can't.

EL: What have you learned from this film?

WA: I think that it will definitely help for the next one. This is a hard film to make successfully; the demands are so rigorous. If you do a comedy, you can clock the laughs at a screening and know where the problems are. It's looser and it's more flexible. Something like this, you're aiming at a fairly sophisticated audience. It's an original piece of writing; it's not like you're dealing with a play, where you've been able to sort out what works. A dramatic story has to be without flaws—if you see little faults in this kind of thing, it's fatal, whereas in a comedy it's not such a terrible thing. The broader the comedy the more flexibility you have. I could get away with murder in *Bananas,* less in *Hannah,* and even less in this. It's the most demanding because it's fairly intense drama between people, and deals with adult problems. It's so easy to fail in the writing, so easy, because it's hard to write good dramas. It's certainly hard for me.

Then once you've written a good drama, you've got to get the actors to seamlessly execute it; they can't be unbelievable in any way. And their qualities are very, very important. You have to be more specific than in comedy. Any little characteristic that the actor has becomes very meaningful in the piece. If an actor has a slightly mean streak in him or a slightly loveable streak, that becomes very, very meaningful in his character on the screen.

EL: Do characters ever change during shooting, or even though you've written them, do they confuse you?

WA: I know when there's a false step. I can see it in the dailies when something's wrong. But I don't know exactly what I'm doing; I just know when it's not right. So I tell the actor, "Just do what you're doing." Hannah was a character neither Mia nor I understood at the start, and at the finish. We could never figure out whether Hannah was indeed a lovely, nice person who was the bulwark of the family and the spine who held everyone together, or whether Hannah was not so nice. In the first scene, the father [*Lloyd Nolan*] says, "We owe so much to Hannah, this lovely Thanksgiving dinner." And she turns and says to her sister, "Are you going to go for a singing audition?" Mia looked to me for guidance and I could never give it to her. I could just say, "Well, play this scene and let me see as you play it instinctively and maybe I can change something." But I'm in the dark a lot of times that way.

EL: How easy or hard is it to direct yourself?

WA: There's nothing to it. If you're in a scene with one or three other people, or sitting around a room, or running away from them—whatever it is—you're pretending to do this thing authentically. And you can feel as you're doing it whether it's authentic or not, if someone is off. You can just see the scene. An actress comes in and slams a book down and she either looks phony doing it or it looks completely real.

You can feel it at the time. It's like being onstage with an audience. You know when you're being funny and you know when you're missing. You can't miss feeling that. This is not to say that you should always be able to act perfectly. It doesn't work exactly that way because you act the scene and you're always locked into the limits of what you can do. Let's say I'm doing fear or panic—it's not going to be as good fear or panic [*laughs*] as Marlon Brando can do. But I know when I'm doing my own best or worst.

EL: You tend to use actors again and again in both major and supporting roles, like Diane Keaton or Mia [*this was five years before their breakup*] and, say, Wallace Shawn. Do you think there's something that comes across on the screen when people know each other well in life?

WA: Yes. When you know the people I do feel that for me, it relaxes me more and I feel more confident. I also think there's a chemistry between Diane and me, just as there is with Mia, and Tony Roberts. If I'm doing a film with them or with Diane Wiest or Judy Davis, I feel loose as a goose as an actor because I feel they've played with me and were willing to do another movie with me, so they couldn't have hated it that much.

Spring 2005

The Manhattan Film Center. We are in the screening room, which has not changed over the years. The walls and plush chairs are still avocado velour; his loveseat beneath the projection window is still covered with beige fabric with a little black in it, though it has been reupholstered. The eclectic and thorough collection of records with music of the 1920s, 1930s, and 1940s is in open drawers along one wall. Detritus of his latest film fills boxes in a corner. We sit, as ever, facing each other in chairs by the record collection. Nor has he changed perceptibly. His clothes are the same— corduroys, heavy sensible shoes, a well-worn cashmere sweater. He is in his seventieth year.

He is preparing to go to England to shoot Scoop. Match Point, *filmed there in the summer of 2004, will be shown at Cannes in a couple of weeks. Woody, uncom-*

monly pleased with the picture, will make himself available for a barrage of inter-views. A phrase he repeats often in talking about the movie is "We just lucked out."

EL: Was it really just good luck?

WA: Yes, just good luck. Actors would fall in, people I never heard of just turned out to be great. If we needed a sunny day, we got a sunny day. If we needed a gray day, we got a gray day. Whatever we needed for our shooting just worked. If we needed a location, we got it. We had no anxiety on the picture.

EL: Are you going to use the same group on the coming film?

WA: I'll have a lot of the same people. There are a couple I couldn't get because they're on jobs in other countries.

EL: Every decision about a film—location, casting, editing, and so on—falls to you.

WA: Yes, it should. But it's not that difficult. You write a script and you know what story you want to tell because you wrote it. So you just go out and pick the locations that seem best for telling that story, get the actors who do the job best. It's just following some common sense. It's obvious that this location won't work and this will, and that this actress is too saccharine for a part.

EL: Hitchcock famously did a storyboard for his films. Scorsese does. I've never seen you with one. Do you?

WA: No. I'm not conscientious. People think I'm facetious when I say this, but it's true. I'm a very lazy filmmaker. When I worked for Paul Mazursky, acting in *Scenes from a Mall* [1990], he was so meticulous, so rehearsed, he knew every shot before we started production. Hitchcock storyboarded, Jerry Lewis storyboards, maybe Marty, I don't know.

I come in to the set of, say, *Husbands and Wives*—and of course Carlo Di Palma was exactly the bad kind of companion because he was as lax as I am. So maybe I see that we're going to do the scene where Sydney Pollack tells Judy Davis he's going to divorce her. So we look around and we see that the sun's over here at this hour, so we say, "Let's shoot in this direction." And then I'd say, "Gee, if only there was a big urn over there" [*laughs*] and Santo [*Loquasto, his set designer*] would say, "Why didn't you *tell* me this?" And I'd say, "I didn't *know,* I just thought of it *now.*" And he says, "Let me see what I can do."

But I never plan anything. I don't rehearse anybody, I don't post-sync anybody [*rerecord their dialogue and match it to their lip movement on the screen*]. I don't do a lot of coverage, as I said. People think this is part of my style, but actually it's the lazy man's style. A conscientious filmmaker will go in and, as you know, shoot the conversation, the two, the singles, the over-the-shoulder shots. I won't do that. I'll shoot the two-shot and move on. Once in a great while I will say, just before we leave, something like, "Just give me one quick shot of that ashtray, just in case I need to go from take to take." But I almost never do that.

Doug McGrath [*his collaborator on* Bullets over Broadway] asked me when I made *Husbands and Wives* why I shot it like that. He was a younger guy trying to profit from my experience, trying to get what alleged wisdom I might have gleaned from years of directing. And I think I disappointed him—certainly startled him— by saying, "I'm lazy." I wanted to do a film where we didn't have to wait. We had a handheld camera and we just used it. I cut when I wanted to cut and stuck anything on I wanted. I didn't care about the niceties of it. I did it with no sense of having to make a film properly. I did it fast and effortlessly and unconscientiously. I wanted to get home early to practice my horn, watch the Knicks, eat.

That's why when I've said over the years that the only thing standing between me and greatness is me, I've been completely right about that. I've been given more opportunities than anybody. I've been given the money and freedom for thirty-five years now to make whatever I wanted: A musical? Okay. A detective story? Fine. A drama? Absolutely. Another drama, even though the first one failed? Go ahead. Whatever you want.

So there's been no reason for me not to make great films. Nobody was coming in and saying I have to do this subject or that, or that they want to see my script, or that I can't cast a particular actor, or they want to watch my dailies or my editing. Nothing. I've had carte blanche for thirty-five years and I've never made a great film. It's just not in me to make a great film; I don't have the depth of vision to do it. I don't say to myself, I'm going to make a great film and I'm going to be uncompromising. If necessary I'll work nights and go to the far ends of the earth. That's just not me. I'd like to make a great film provided it doesn't conflict with my dinner reservation.

I don't want to travel. I don't want to work long days. I want to get home in time to eat, to play my clarinet, to watch the ball game, to see my kids now. So I make the best movie I can under those circumstances. Sometimes I get lucky and the film comes out good. Sometimes I'm not lucky and it doesn't come out good. But I certainly have been, not irresponsible, but lazy.

EL: You once told me that you hear the voices of the characters all through the writing and then the first word uttered on the set makes it completely different because the voice is not the one you heard.

WA: Yes. In most cases it gets farther and farther along from the original as the film progresses. One of the nice things about being in England [*laughs*] is that the English voices sound a lot better. As I've said many times, when I don't have to meet the test of reality, when I'm at home writing, I can imagine an argument going on at the edge of a pier between George C. Scott and Paul Newman. Then I do the film and I get good people but the voices don't sound like Newman and Scott and the pier doesn't look the way I envisioned—he can't jump off the pier because [*laughs*] he'd break his neck. So now he has to run to the end of the pier and do something else.

Everything keeps evolving and evolving, or more frequently, devolving, and that's the problem. Ninety percent of the stuff is worse than you conceived it. You may once in a while get a laugh on something you did not expect to get a laugh on, but much more often you don't get a laugh where you were sure there was one. You're always gambling against the house.

EL: Does this happen on every film?

WA: Almost all of them. One of the few that didn't is *Match Point.* It seemed I was actually enhancing it as I mounted it. Tennessee Williams writes *A Streetcar Named Desire* and he gives it to Kazan and he mounts it with Marlon Brando and he enhances it, he makes it beautiful [*laughs*]. I don't do that. I've got a different approach. I write the thing and imagine [*laughs*] it's going to be good when it's not that great.

I start to do it and all my laziness and each of my mistakes ruin ten things that could conceivably work. You know, they're paying you for it to work. It's like the hitter in the ball game who strikes out with men on base. It's very upsetting.

EL: And the same is true with artists?

WA: Yes. The artist is always under the gun. At first you can't understand. You say, "Hey, all I tried to do was make a film. Maybe I struck out, maybe it's not so good, but why do you hate me so much?" But then, the truth of the matter is that you deserve that opprobrium. When I watch someone else's movie, I do the same thing. In reality you have to understand that if you do a movie or a play or a book or whatever and it doesn't succeed or please a person, you will be loathed and you have no right to expect not to be. He has every right to loathe you and you have no right to expect to be anything except an object of contempt. They're paying you to hit home runs, not try to hit them.

People sometimes refer to "an honorable failure." But that's a lot of bull. It's like a team that loses a game by one point—it's an honorable failure, but it still goes in the loss column. [*He grimaces, then grins.*] Am I suffocating myself in sports analogies here?

EL: Let me give you something fresh. In hindsight, do you think some projects are doomed, no matter how much you rewrite and reshoot?

WA: There are certain projects that are doomed from the beginning, yes. They're dead in print. Certain times you get an idea for a movie and you don't know it as you're going along but you're dead in the water right away because you've miscalculated or guessed wrong and the audience is never, ever going to buy into it. They just don't feel the same way you do.

Parenthetically, the biggest personal shock to me of all the movies that I've done is that *Hollywood Ending* was not thought of as a first-rate, extraordinary comedy. [*A film director, played by Woody, suddenly becomes blind from the anxiety of salvaging his career.*] I was stunned that it met with any resistance at all. I thought it was a very, very funny idea, and I thought that I executed it absolutely fine, and that I was funny and that Téa [*Leoni, as his ex-wife and current executive at the studio financing the film*] was great. I thought it was a simple, funny idea that worked, and could have been done by Charlie Chaplin or Buster Keaton, Jack Lemmon, Walter Matthau. I didn't think I blew it anywhere along the line—in performance, in shooting it, in the jokes, situations.

When I showed it to the first couple of people, film writers, they said, "This is just great. This is one of the funniest movies you've done." But that's not what the subsequent reactions were. And I was so shocked. Again, it didn't matter to me from any financial point of view; it was an inexpensive picture and worldwide it did its business and maybe made a little money. It was the biggest surprise for me of all the films I've done, because I generally don't love my own finished product but this one I did. I don't think many people would, but I would put it toward the top of my comedies.

EL: Have you ever been surprised by people latching on to a film you didn't think much of?

WA: Yeah. People really latched on to *Manhattan* in a way that I thought was [*laughs*] irrational. And *Annie Hall* was a much-adored picture. I mean, it's fine, but I've done better pictures than that, though it may have had a warmth, an emotion, that people responded to.

EL: You've been making films a long time now. How has the landscape changed?

WA: Well, I grew up going to films and adoring films. And now it's not a film culture I live in, really. It's not a culture of people who wait for the next Truffaut or Bergman film. That's a phenomenon that doesn't exist anymore. There are no new Fellini films. The guys who run the industry, most of them are pretty sad. Some very good directors emerge, but they have to fight and struggle. But there isn't that sense of everybody going to the art house theater and buzzing the next day about the film. And all the heroes of my young adulthood are pretty much gone. Truffaut is gone. Bergman is still here but he's elderly. Buñuel's gone and Kurosawa's gone and Fellini's gone and De Sica's gone. There was a time when you wanted to work and get their approbation and become one of them. That was the fantasy.

The same in the theater. Arthur Miller is gone, Tennessee Williams is gone, that whole theater phenomenon's gone. There was a time I wanted to work in the theater and be one of those playwrights, but there is no landscape to be part of anymore. If you are a good playwright you don't function in the same arena. The structure of their presentation is different. They're in some Off-Broadway house and if they're lucky and the play is a success they bring it to Broadway. And it isn't that the whole town is buzzing about it the next day and it's a must-see and it's interesting and that it affects people. The same thing in movies.

The younger generations are not that film savvy, they're not that film literate and familiar with the great films, and their idea of what good films are has changed. I'm not making any value judgment; it's just different from mine. The movies they like don't interest me. I'm not saying there aren't a couple of good films every year, there are—but, you know, there are hundreds of films made and a couple of good American films sneak through, usually by independent people, but more often than not it's the European films or foreign—they could be Iranian or Chinese or Mexican now—that are interesting. And you're the only one who sees it. I'll call Keaton in L.A. and say, "Did you see this?" And she'll say it hasn't been released there or she doesn't know where it's showing.

EL: You have your own screening room, but do you go to theaters just to be part of the crowd and experience it with them?

WA: I don't go out to movies much. That used to be part of the joy I had, to go to the theater. The whole ritual was fun for me. I liked looking at the pretty girls and I liked looking at the guys and hearing the talk and the building of forepleasure, and then the film. And afterward, if you were knocked out by it, you couldn't wait to get home and tell your friends about it. But that phenomenon no longer exists; there's a different social dynamic now. People rent the videos; they experience the material a different way. It doesn't interest me as much.

EL: You once mentioned that many people tell you *Broadway Danny Rose* is their favorite of your pictures. What are *your* favorites of your own films?

WA: I like *Match Point,* and I like *Purple Rose.* [Pauses.] *Husbands and Wives.* [*He turns cautionary.*] It's possible, if I reviewed all my films—if I actually *saw* them—I would think, Oh, what was I so delighted about? I don't think so, but maybe I'd get a good feeling about one I didn't like. It's hard to imagine that. I don't say that in a self-deprecating way. It's just hard to imagine that if I didn't like a film I would see it twenty-five years later and think, Hey, that wasn't as bad as I thought.

It's conceivable, but I can see it happening the other way around more easily, which is why I'd just as soon not see them.

I still like *Stardust Memories*—this has now dropped down a notch—and *Zelig* [*long pause*].

EL: What about *Take the Money and Run,* because it was your first one?

WA: I haven't seen *Take the Money and Run* in a long time, so I don't know, but I can't imagine it would be among my favorites. *Manhattan Murder Mystery* is a picture I like very much. I'm not a good judge but when I think off the top of my head I think *Match Point* came off, I think *Husbands and Wives* came off, I think *Purple Rose* came off. *Bullets* too. There's no correlation between my taste and public taste. That's true on my films and on other people's films, even on classic films. I can't really tell you how idiosyncratic my personal taste is because [*he laughs*] it would confirm people's worst feelings about me.

EL: Try it.

WA: I don't want to hurt anybody's feelings but [*pauses*] I'll just give you a taste, just a taste, but don't press me to go beyond it.

EL: Okay.

WA: When Aljean Harmetz was writing her book on *Casablanca* she called me because of *Play It Again, Sam.* And I said to her, "I'm the wrong guy to interview because I've never been able to sit through it. I've never seen it, really. It's never held my interest enough to sit through."

Now, people reading this are going to think, Who does this jerk think he is? You know, he does all these shitty films and he can't sit through a film that is so superior to anything he's done.

I'm not saying that they wouldn't be completely correct in saying that. I'm just expressing my opinion. I have many opinions that would surprise you and make me look even more stupid.

EL: Let's take your taste in the things you can talk about, about the things you really do gravitate to. I know you love *Streetcar Named Desire.* Can you give me some examples of the positive side of your idiosyncratic taste?

WA: Well, if I made a list of the ten best films ever made, with the exception of *Citizen Kane,* there would not be any American ones on it.

EL: What *would* be on it?

WA: *Grand Illusion* and *The Bicycle Thief* and *Rashomon* and *The Seventh Seal* and *Wild Strawberries* and *The 400 Blows* and *Rules of the Game*—I'll have to write them down. You know, an idiosyncratic choice of mine, one of the best American films for me, was *The Hill.*

EL: With Sean Connery and Ossie Davis [*1965, Sidney Lumet*].

WA: Nobody has seen it. Many, many lesser films are more revered. Now, someday, I will tell you of all the iconic films and movie stars that have never meant anything to me. And I've never denied that all of the directors and writers and actors [*laughs*] do better work than me. It's not a question of my feeling superior to the person. Not at all. I'm talking about if I'm home of an evening and I want to watch something, there are certain things considered iconic that I would nod off at.

[*A brief digression: A month or two later, Woody sends me what he calls his "insomnia list" of favorite films, with this note:*

When I awake during the night, to quell my existential panic I make lists in my mind. This sometimes helps me fall back asleep. Almost always the lists are of movies—adding and subtracting titles, substituting. My tastes seem to me unremarkable except in the area of talking plot comedies where I seem to have little tolerance for anything and certainly not my own films.

Fifteen of My Favorite American Films in No Particular Order:

The Treasure of the Sierra Madre	*The Informer*
Double Indemnity	*The Hill*
Shane	*The Third Man* (English)
Paths of Glory	*Notorious*
The Godfather: Part II	*Shadow of a Doubt*
Goodfellas	*A Streetcar Named Desire*
Citizen Kane	*The Maltese Falcon*
White Heat	

**Twelve of My Favorite European Films
and Three Favorite Japanese Films:**

The Seventh Seal	*Throne of Blood*
Rashomon	*Cries and Whispers*
The Bicycle Thief	*La Strada*
Grand Illusion	*The 400 Blows*
Rules of the Game	*Breathless*
Wild Strawberries	*The Seven Samurai*
8½	*Shoeshine*
Amarcord	

(Note: If we take *Citizen Kane* from the top list and put it in the second list, this would be my list of the best films ever made.)

Silent comedies are all taken up by Buster Keaton and Charlie Chaplin.

Stringing together a list of musicals there are many that I enjoy but the very best ones seem to me as I lay in the dark, pitiless night:

Singin' in the Rain
Meet Me in St. Louis
Gigi

They're in a class by themselves as American movie musicals. Close behind are:

My Fair Lady
The Band Wagon
On the Town
Oliver!

I put comedies in two categories—comedian's films which can be awful save for the comedian's work and comedy movies that have plots. Of the comedian's films or broader sillier films that I always laugh at are:

Duck Soup   *You Can't Cheat an Honest Man*
Monkey Business   *Never Give a Sucker an Even*
Horse Feathers   *Break*
A Night at the Opera   *Casanova's Big Night*
A Day at the Races   *Airplane!*
Monsieur Beaucaire

Of talking plot comedies, I'm hesitant to say my list because my taste is eccentric and there are any number of comedies I love that would make me seem foolish or should I say, more foolish in the eyes of the world. Plus there are any number of iconic comedies that never have and never will give me a laugh and I don't like to hurt the feelings of anyone who turns such a tough dollar making screen comedies or even their descendants. I will admit my list is always topped by *The White Sheik*, and when I think of American comedies my conviction is that no finer ones exist than *Born Yesterday* and *Trouble in Paradise*. Also *The Shop Around the Corner* is pretty damned good (I get a lot of fishy looks when I tell people I think *Born Yesterday* is the best all-time American stage comedy but it's the way I feel. A close second is *The Front Page,* the play). After the above four, my insomnia list gets dicey for public consumption with a few predictable choices but many very personal ones. Incidentally, my list never includes my own comedies, not because I hold myself out of the competition but because I've yet to make the list.

End of brief digression.]

EL: I remember thirty years ago when you were in Los Angeles, making either *Everything You Always Wanted to Know About Sex* or a portion of *Sleeper,* I suppose, and you rented the projection room at the Beverly Hills Hotel and screened *Monsieur Beaucaire* and *My Favorite Brunette* and I think *Casanova's Big Night.* You were showing them to Diane Keaton, among a few others, and I remember the complete and sheer delight you had in sharing these Bob Hope films with the four or five of us, who in some cases were seeing them for the first time.

WA: *Monsieur Beaucaire* is a funny movie. When you turn on the TV and see an old Bob Hope movie, in any of them there are some bad moments, some out-of-date moments. But you gotta look beyond that. You have to look at the good moments in the better films. Someone will say to me, "What *is* it that you see in Bob Hope? What's funny about the guys on an island and the gorilla comes along and picks them up and carries them off?" Well, yes, that's a stupid moment, not a funny moment. But there are phrases, long moments, long scenes in *Casanova's Big Night,* in *Monsieur Beaucaire,* in any number of Hope's films that are wonderful and his skill is on display brilliantly, just brilliantly. Maybe the movie will take a silly turn, but *he* rarely does. People always think of the road pictures [The Road to Singapore, The Road to Morocco, The Road to Rio, *and others with Bing Crosby between 1940 and 1952*] but the road pictures were not the great pictures, though they had some nice moments in them.

But when Hope became a star as big as or bigger than Crosby, there were moments in *The Princess and the Pirate,* moments in these others I've named, moments in *Road to Bali* and *The Great Lover.* Sometimes it will just be a minute. Sometimes it'll be five minutes. Sometimes it will be big scenes in a picture, long scenes.

EL: One of my favorite scenes is the very beginning, when they're on the camel singing, "We're off on the road to Morocco."

WA: Well, the music in all those pictures was great. You know, those guys were wonderful musical talents. If you see Bob Hope or Jerry Lewis dance, they are great. I saw Jerry Lewis once do an imitation of Fred Astaire. It was *astounding.* When he wanted to, he was a wonderful dancer. They were vaudevillians. And Groucho too.

EL: You say when you're acting, you're transported into the scene. Is the director part of you aware during that? Or does the director part of you know after the scene if it has worked or not?

WA: You've got the story and you're shooting a piece of it out of sequence and your commitment is to be sure that the pages you shoot that day are done well. All you think about is doing that little small thing well and putting it in the bank, and coming back to it later when you put the whole film together.

I don't need to be outside looking at it because I've planned the shot; I know where everything is going to be, so I know the mechanics of the shot work. I know that's not going to be a problem. It's just a question of if the acting in the scene will work.

I don't do a lot of takes, as I said, because [*laughs*] I get bored quickly. But if I did twenty takes of something, I know before I get into the editing room that the sixth and eighteenth were really good. It's very rare that I'm wrong about that.

EL: And you're pretty aware of your performance as well?

WA: Completely.

EL: When an actor is struggling with a line or with a scene and you've made five or six takes and he's just not getting it, will you ever say, "Let's print this one," even knowing you wouldn't use it so he'll have the relief of knowing you have at least one take?

WA: What I say is, "Okay, that was great. That was a good one." Then after I get the scene I tell the script girl, "Don't print that one." I have the annoying habit—to actors—of stopping in the middle of a scene. When they go wrong, I don't have the patience to go to the end of the scene. I figure, why should we? We're dead in the water now. But sometimes after I do that two, three, or four times, I figure I better stop and let them go start to finish no matter how awful it is.

EL: I remember once when an actress simply couldn't get the scene; you had to reshoot it another day. There seemed to be no way to help her that day.

WA: [*Wryly*] Yeah, not by me. I've often heard stories about how a director gets brilliant performances out of these people who have never before shown brilliance, or out of kids. I can't do that. I'm not one of those people who can get a brilliant performance out of someone that doesn't have it in them to start with. I just can't figure out how to do it. To this day it baffles me. I work with the actor and try all kinds of subterfuge, even to the point of saying the lines myself out loud so he or she can hear how I'd like it.

EL: Do you ever have times when you take an actor away from the set to try to help him through?

WA: Yes, there have been times when I've asked the assistant director to get rid of everybody from the set and let me just stay there with the actor and play around with it. But I prefer preventive medicine—the best way to cure cancer is not to get it, you know? And the best way to get a good performance is hire an actor who can give you one.

EL: Do actors ever say, "I wish we could rehearse, that we could spend a couple of weeks sitting around the table and reading lines and become an ensemble"?

WA: They don't. You have to remember that actors in general are so insecure and they're so happy to get a job that they're afraid to assert any desires—whereas I'd be sympathetic to it if they did. [*Pauses and smiles.*] But not to rehearse. Still, they needn't be afraid, but a lot of them are timorous. But most of them have no problem with not rehearsing whatsoever. Over the years I've worked my way and I've gotten wonderful performances from the actors—I don't get them *out* of the actors. The actors come in, they don't rehearse, they only have their sides [*their scenes rather than the whole script*] sometimes, they come to the set [*snaps fingers*], and go just like that and they're just wonderful. And when they see the picture, they couldn't be more delighted with their performance. So no one has ever complained to me about it before, during, or after. No one has ever said, "If only we could have rehearsed this more."
Nor has anyone ever complained to me about not getting a full script. I tell them the way I work, and even stars who don't have to worry about being fired find it fine. So much of the business is garbage, starting with the many, many meetings and the endless time in getting the project on, and the money wasted and the pretensions. You know, it's just common sense, getting together and doing it. It's proven all the time by people who don't have any money and don't have any time and get together and do perfectly fine work.

EL: Why don't you rehearse?

WA: For a number of reasons. One is I get bored. Another is basically I'm a comic performer; I don't like to do it until you have to do it.
When I was on Broadway in *Play It Again, Sam,* I hated rehearsal. Joe Hardy [*the director*] would make us do it again and again and I hated it, but when the

audience was out there, the dynamic changed. The electricity changed. You do it for them. You're on the line with them. A different chemistry sets in.

EL: *Husbands and Wives* has the look of a film in which none of the camera moves or even much of what the actors did was either rehearsed or even spelled out beforehand.

Sydney Pollack was in it. How was it using a director who occasionally acts, as a central character?

WA: It was such a dicey thing for me because I couldn't hire him for that big a part without him reading. But I'm thinking to myself, God, I'm going to read Sydney Pollack. What if he doesn't read well? I'm going to say, Sydney, you don't have the job? I didn't know what to do. Of course, he couldn't have been more gracious and understanding about it. He said, "Tell me if it's no good. No problem." He made it easy as could be. And, of course, as soon as he started reading, he was terrific.

EL: You have a narrator for this story, as you do in many of your films. Was it there from the start?

WA: The narrator was always there. I wanted a kind of documentary style for the relationship and with the documentary style comes interviews. [*Jeffrey Kurland is not only the interviewer, he was the costume designer for this and several other films.*]

EL: But you also use a narrator for non-documentary-style films. Why?

WA: It comes from one of two things: either my days as a stand-up comic or my wanting to be a writer of novels. But I'm very attuned to the voice of the person telling the story. I know Billy Wilder said that of himself. He used it in *Double Indemnity* and *Sunset Boulevard*. And I feel the same way. I feel addressing the audience or talking to them in the voice of the author or the main character as a way of gathering them up and putting them through the experience along with him—him usually being me, but not always.

EL: Is there anything else about *Scoop* that's fresh today, in terms of what you were aiming for or wish you had gotten?

WA: No, the only thing I have against *Scoop* is a self-indulgent lack of ambition. I don't think that I screwed the movie up. I think that the movie's cute—that the jokes are funny, that everyone performs well, that an audience will have some laughs and not want to tar and feather me when they come out of the theater. But it's not ambitious enough. I wanted to do a comedy and enjoy myself and make Scarlett funny and tell some jokes myself, and I indulged myself and what I wound up with at the end is, uh, you know, a light comedy, a dessert. Not worth more than that.

February 2006

EL: You've told me that when you showed Doug McGrath several ideas to choose from to collaborate on, you were surprised he chose *Bullets over Broadway*. [*See page 95.*]

WA: Yes, because it was not the one I would have chosen.

EL: The one you liked was a political story, right?

WA: It was a political story, a satire he didn't think much of. But he really liked *Bullets*, so I went ahead with it and it came out very successfully. The idea that the thug—who is the real artist—kills the girl because her acting is ruining the play made the story.

It was very successful because of a few things. One, Carlo's photography was very beautiful. And it was period [*1920s*]. He could always make period stuff beautiful. And I had a *great* cast. Everybody in the cast, like in *Match Point*, contributed to the success of the movie. Dianne Wiest was her usual brilliant self.

EL: From the way you've described it, you gave her more direction than perhaps any actor.

WA: Because she couldn't figure out how to start. She started [*pauses*] tentatively. Sometimes actors do that. I remember the three young girls [*Natalie Portman, Gaby Hoffmann, and Natasha Lyonne*] in the musical I did [Everyone Says I Love You], when they were in the store and the handsome guy walks in. I had to *kill* myself to say, "No, you guys have to do it like *this*" [*mimics near hysteria*]. Sometimes the acting is tentative because the actor is insecure or he can't believe I mean him to be that broad. My instinct in broadness is very strong. So I'll put my hand on my face [*makes very broad gestures*] and I want them to go all the way, I mean really all the way. So I expected the kids to act that way and they didn't. They were much milder, much more inhibited. I finally got them to do it and it looks funny on the screen.

The same thing with Dianne Wiest in *Bullets*. I didn't have to give her any direction at all except for those first sixty seconds. I kept saying to her, "You have to really make it like Norma Desmond, really extreme." And the first couple of times I guess she didn't believe I meant to be as stupid as I was demonstrating, but I did, because in her hands it comes out great.

EL: I understood when you first talked about this that there was more to it.

WA: Everything important that happened [*laughs a bit*] was on the set, but she did talk about it a couple of times before we shot. She said, "I'm not sure about this. What do you want here? Do you really think I should play this character?"

But again, she's one of those actresses who's like all those girls I went to school with. They'd tell you [*playing a teenage girl*], "Oh, I did so terrible on that test." I'd always come out, "Oh, I knocked that thing off," and then they would get 100 and I'd get 55. Well, that's how Keaton was, that's how Mia was, and Dianne Wiest was like that: they can't, they can't, they can't, but in the end, they're brilliant. [*Dianne Wiest won the Best Supporting Actress Oscar for her role as Helen Sinclair, the Broadway diva.*]

EL: Does Judy Davis fit into that category?

WA: Judy Davis is a special case. She and I never had any communication at all because there was no need for it. I would think we haven't exchanged a hundred words in our lifetime, and we've done three or four pictures [Alice, Husbands and Wives, Deconstructing Harry, Celebrity]. Now, if we were thrown together on a location, sitting around a house or something, we may have exchanged a few awkward words for sixty seconds. But I've never had to give her any direction at all. She comes to the set a truly great actress—intimidatingly great for me.

Judy Davis, Joe Mantegna, and Kenneth Branagh in *Celebrity.* Davis appeared in four of Woody's films in the 1990s.

EL: How so?

WA: I'm afraid to say anything to her because I don't want to tamper with her work, I don't want to misdirect her, I don't want to get her angry at me, I don't want to bother her [*starts to laugh*], I don't want to make noise. She comes to the set *great*. She does her thing *great*. She's always ten times greater than how I wrote the part. She goes back to her camper and I don't see her again or speak to her until she comes to the set the next time.

EL: Is this by mutual consent?

WA: We can't consent because we don't talk. [*He laughs.*] I think she's happy not to be bothered by a director and I'm [*laughs*] scared to death of her. She's intense. [*Pauses.*] There's one picture she did with me when she was nursing her baby. There were a number of actresses nursing their babies on my pictures. I think during *Sweet and Lowdown,* Uma Thurman was nursing her baby.

I was just reading Richard Schickel's book on Kazan, which is the best show business biography I've ever read, and Kazan directed very differently. He put in a lot of time with the actresses. He wanted to and they wanted it from him. I have just the opposite feeling.

Of course, I think there's no right or wrong way. I get very good performances out of my people by rarely or never speaking to them. And he gets great performances from his people spending *lots* of time. My guess is that if I had worked with someone like Marlon Brando, who would have been totally intimidating to me, I would never have spoken to him. I mean, Kazan spent a ton of time dealing with him. Now, I would have spoken to him if he was playing the character with an English accent and I didn't want him to, or made some *egregious* mistake—like if Judy Davis or Dianne Wiest came in and was suddenly playing with a Hungarian accent or a stutter. But if an actor comes in and plays with the common sense that the part dictates, then I never speak to him.

EL: There's a complicated shot in *Small Time Crooks* of you and Tracey Ullman on the rooftop, timed against the sunset, that obviously you had only one or two chances to get.

WA: It was tough because we had to make an establishing shot first, wide. And we did the wide shot and everybody was screaming as they always do, panic-stricken, like the *Titanic* is sinking. "Hurry, the sun is sinking!" [*Starts to laugh.*] "Hurry, get the camera here!" And literally you're vibrating like a tuning fork and you've got three minutes so you do it, then you do it again and the sun is now considerably lower, and then you look at the dailies and hope you got one that has enough sun. I think we put a cut in there someplace and when you put a cut in there

Woody and Tracey Ullman in a long master shot in *Small Time Crooks* that was timed against the sunset

they've got to hurry to set up the camera and shoot in the middle of the scene right away and you haven't lost the light continuity—so the sun hasn't noticeably moved.

EL: Were you caught up in the nervousness of setting up for the shot?

WA: Yeah, yeah. Me especially. I'm frantic because I'm the guy who suffers the most. If we don't get it, we have to come back there and someone yells at me because I'm spending too much money and I've got to sacrifice on some other aspect of the picture.

EL: Was it more nervous-making as an actor or as a director?

WA: Not as an actor; as a director, as the one who's in charge of the project. I never worry about my acting. If I'm in trouble, I make dialogue up. I never worry about what I'm going to say. That's never a problem.

EL: Let's spend a minute on your love of New York City, particularly Manhattan. I remember—I'm pretty sure it was during the filming of *Crimes and Misde-meanors*—you looking for footage of old New York so, you said, you could "demon-strate in a completely biased way that the city was a nicer place then." There is always homage to New York in your pictures, at least those shot here, which until very recently is virtually all of them. For instance, there is the piece in *Hannah* where Sam Waterston gives the architectural tour to Carrie Fisher and Dianne Wiest and in *Husbands and Wives* when Liam Neeson does it with Judy Davis and Mia Farrow. New York City amounts to a character in your films.

WA: Well, I love the city and have always loved it, and whenever I have a chance to show it in a flattering way, I do. You know, I was able to show architecture for its

Ike (Woody) and Tracy (Mariel Hemingway) in a horse-drawn carriage in Central Park in *Manhattan*

sake in that scene with Carrie Fisher and Dianne Wiest and I was able to show the city in the four seasons in the musical [Everyone Says I Love You]. People have said to me, "We don't know New York as you show it to us. We know the New York of Scorsese; the New York of Spike Lee we understand."

I selectively show my New York through my heart. I'm always known as a New York filmmaker who eschews Hollywood and in fact denigrates it. No one sees that the New York I show is the New York I know only from Hollywood films that I grew up on—penthouses, white telephones, beautiful streets, waterfronts, going through Central Park on carriage rides. Locals say to me, "Where is this New York?" Well, *this* New York exists in Hollywood movies of the 1930s and 1940s. The New York that Hollywood showed the world, which never really existed, is the New York that I show the world because that's the New York I fell in love with. A friend said to me after seeing me walk out of my house in *Hannah and Her Sisters*—showing beautiful black-and-white doors over on East Seventy-second Street—"Where *are* these places? I saw New York in your movies with foreigners and fans in Belgium and France and Italy. When I came to New York I wanted to see the New York I grew up loving in your films. It's more beautiful in them than it is in reality."

The fact is, when I first chose to portray New York as a character in a movie in a significant way, in *Manhattan,* I made the film in black and white because most of those movies I grew up on were in black and white. In those films you would see nightclubs and the kind of streets we've been talking about; actors would be walking on Riverside Drive or on Park Avenue, or coming out of their houses with furs on and getting into cabs. And, you know, where Jimmy Stewart goes through the park in that movie [Born to Dance, *1936*] singing "Easy to Love"—the Cole Porter song—is exactly where I placed the scene with Mariel Hemingway and myself in the horse-drawn cab in *Manhattan,* because that's where I got it from. I feel I owe nothing to reality in my movies in that sense. That's my vision of the city and I'm creating a work of fiction, and that's what I want to create.

6

EDITING

June 1972

Woody is in the small makeshift editing room on the top floor of the duplex offices of his managers Jack Rollins and Charles Joffe on West Fifty-seventh Street in Manhattan, near Carnegie Hall. Surrounded by shelves holding more than three hundred boxes of film, he is sitting with his post-luncheon chocolate bar (a "cocoa bean steak," he calls it), an unmerciful eye, and his film editor, Jim Heckert. They are hunched over a Moviola, a pre-digital-era film-editing machine with a small screen attached to it, trying to make a rough cut of twenty-five minutes for a sequence in Everything You Always Wanted to Know About Sex, *which in the final version will last no more than fifteen minutes. There are thousands of feet to choose from. Since much of the dialogue is improvised, each take has slightly different lines. They spend an hour to put together about a minute of film. If one doesn't like whatever is on the screen, the other usually goes along. I ask if this is the norm.*

"In the eight months we edited Take the Money and Run *and now this, we've never had a serious disagreement, have we?" Heckert asks.*

"That's because neither of us knows where the laughs are," Woody answers, staring at the images on the screen, looking for the laughs.

Then he adds with a sigh, "Well, if nothing else, we can make this into a series of six dazzling radio spots."

EL: This is a new kind of film for you. *Take the Money and Run* and *Bananas*, like the films of the Marx Brothers, Buster Keaton, and Charlie Chaplin's two-reelers, the comedian and the laugh are all that count. Photography, plot, lighting, slickness, and sets are secondary. The camera is simply placed facing the comedian and he is turned loose.

WA: The safe way to do my kind of picture is to subordinate everything to the laugh. Basically, you have to do that or you won't survive, because no one will care if the sequence looks good, only if it works. I used brightly lit sets and uncomplicated shots in my first pictures and deliberately never moved the camera in *Bananas*. This is the first time I've set out to make a picture look good without sacrificing the laugh. Not pretty, like *My Fair Lady*, but something with a little style to it.

Summer 1973

"Digging a grave at a cemetery would be funnier to watch than two guys cutting a comedy," Ralph Rosenblum says as he and Woody edit Sleeper *in New York. Rosen-*

blum, the editor of twenty-five films including The Pawnbroker, A Thousand Clowns, Long Day's Journey into Night, *and* The Producers, *did the final edit of* Take the Money and Run *and then* Bananas. *A deft editor as well as a realist, he says that no matter how well he and Woody edit the film, in the end how the audience sees the finished product "finally funnels down to an Italian or Jewish projectionist reading the* Daily News *while the manager buzzes up and says, 'Hey, Eddie, focus it.'"*

Rosenblum and Woody joined forces after Woody was not satisfied with the original cut of Take the Money. *Rosenblum suggested that Woody score with sprightlier music; use pieces of a long interview with the parents of two-bit crook Virgil Starkwell (Woody), most of which had been cut out, as a funny bridge between segments that did not naturally flow into one another; and add more of narrator Jackson Beck's interviews with Virgil to link the mélange together. (Narration will become a favorite tool of Woody's. In* Zelig, Radio Days, *and* Husbands and Wives, *among others, it is the thread that binds the story.) Still, it took a bit of serendipity for them to continue to work together.*

"*I ran into Ralph on the street while I was doing* Bananas," *Woody tells me later,* "and he said, 'You never talked to me after* Take the Money and Run.' *I said, 'Well, I just assumed you came in to help at the end but you were unavailable.' He said, 'No, not at all.'"*

While Woody works on one sequence, Rosenblum, a burly man with thick black-rimmed glasses and a trimmed salt-and-pepper beard, works on the one that follows; then they show each other their cut and collaborate on any changes.

["Woody is the opposite of most writer/directors, who have trouble throwing something out," Rosenblum tells me fifteen years later. "His sense of ownership as a writer is nonexistent. He was ruthless in what he would throw out. In Bananas, *I was fighting to keep material in. He wasn't prepared to deal with all the film he photographed. He didn't know any of the nuances of cutting, what to leave in, what to leave out, what to shorten, what to transpose. It was the hardest technically to edit. He had less control over what he was doing as a moviemaker. He was shooting skits. And he was less sure of himself. It wasn't a case of following the story, which was nonsense. It was a case of trying to preserve all of the various elements of some very funny skits. I hated it when I couldn't make some of them work. But he learned. Now he doesn't need anybody like me."]*

There is a tremendous amount of exposed film—about 240 reels, or forty hours. This has to be reduced to about ninety minutes.

"*The most important thing for me to get from Woody is what he considers his best reading of a joke or his best performance," Rosenblum continues. "I can't think of one thing he reshot that he doesn't appear in."*

Yet in many cases the first shot is the best, at least as long as the scene remains unchanged. Sometimes, as in the ending for Sleeper, *much of the scene is rewritten, then shot again, and it plays better than the original.*

Woody with editor Ralph Rosenblum at a Steenbeck editing machine, ca. 1977, in the days before computerized digital assembly. Snippets of film from scenes they're working on hang behind them.

"But when it comes to the physical stuff," Woody says one day after reshooting a scene, "I always feel that the first take will be the best, like lifting weights—the first snatch is the one that's going to be the strongest. When I was fighting at the future farm [Woody gets in a fight with the caretaker and they repeatedly slip and fall on an eight-foot banana peel] *the first couple of takes went really well. And when I saw them I thought, Hey, I didn't think I could do it that well. I'm going to go back and really perfect it. But none of the reshoots was as good, even though I had the benefit of seeing the early stuff and knowing it looked funny. I never improved on any of those things."*

Woody screens versions of the film to friends or friends of friends and notes where the audience consistently fails to respond. Then, no matter how much they like the scene or the joke individually, out it goes. One cut scene, a dream sequence shot on a salt flat in the Mojave Desert, may have been visually the best in the picture.

November 1987

We are in the Manhattan Film Center. Woody and Susan Morse, known as Sandy, his editor since Manhattan *(1979), are working on scenes 42 and 43 of* Another

Woman, *which come about a third of the way into the film. They work in soft conversation, in an orderly way. Three assistant editors make certain that any needed footage is available on a moment's notice. Woody is relaxed but thorough. He looks closely at every frame, doggedly tries variation after variation of a scene until he feels it is as good as it can be. As earlier in his career, he is completely unsentimental about lines or shots no matter how much he likes them; if they don't work, they're cut.*

Along the wall above the editing machine are eleven-by-two-inch posterboard slides with the number of every scene in the film along with a succinct description. The assistant editors do odd jobs at workbenches in the twenty-five-by-twenty-foot room. There are fourteen takes and trims hooked by open paper clips through a sprocket hole and onto a horizontal pole that drops into a canvas basket similar to a small hotel laundry hamper. Eight other reels of shots are on a counter; three are on one of the two Steenbeck editing machines, latter-day Moviolas. (Woody says that the addition of the second Steenbeck was a great idea because "we can do more — and because I came in here one day raring to go and the machine we had broke.") There is order at all times. An assistant editor can find a suddenly wanted take in seconds.

The scene is one of Gena Rowlands following after Mia Farrow, but it is hard to show them at a proper distance. As Woody watches the various combinations, he almost never says something is good. Rather, about the best judgment he can muster is, "That's not so terrible."

WA: My inclination is to drop the 100 mm shot forever. It makes it look as though Gena is closer than she is.

SM: Let's just look at it. [*It is a shot of feet. Mia's go into shadow, the frame turns all black, then the feet come out.*]

WA: Let's try beginning with her coming out of the black. [*It doesn't look right.*] There's no sense of movement. Leave her going into and coming out of shadow. We're not creating sufficient distance between them. It looks like Mia should be in the shot with Gena [*in front of a lighted window they both pass*].

SM: Want to use the second dolly shot? [*The camera moves to follow the action.*]

WA: [*They try it and he nods in acceptance.*] We're going to be fine because all these work together to one degree or another. The question is, Is there one combination that's more fun than another? The first two cuts, you can get away with. On the third, we need to do something. You want to see the distance between them. The only shot we haven't looked at is the wide shot from last week. Shall we look at it and see if it's magical?

[*It works okay, but the next cut doesn't do anything to advance the scene. He shakes his head, still looking at the screen.*]

It's not sweet. [*He pauses for a minute of thought.*] Let's wait and think about this. [*No solution presents itself and he speaks with resignation.*] The combined wisdom of the script girl, myself, and [*cinematographer*] Sven [*Nykvist*] and we still don't have a piece of cake on this thing.

SM: [*Not ready to admit defeat*] It's not as bad as you think.

WA: [*Slightly perked up by her optimism*] Let's talk this down. We could use Mia's feet, then the last half of Gena's shot.

SM: The choices are the 50 [*mm lens shot*], the tied-off [*no camera movement*], and the 100 [*mm lens shot*]. There's also the shadow [*Mia Farrow's along the wall*].

WA: The 100, the boat's sailed on at this point. [*A favorite phrase of his, meaning it's too late to do something. Still, he agrees to see it. Afterward he continues.*] We could try Mia to Mia—the 100 to the corner. [*Two shots from different perspectives and with different lenses. He speaks while Sandy is setting it up.*] If this works we could be in much better shape. We could go to the 50 and move the shadow to where you wanted to try it, or switch it with the feet [*the shot of her feet walking*] because the feet are less of a risk. If we can get the fluidity of that cut, it will help us. [*But after seeing it he is still unhappy.*] Philosophically speaking here, you're not bothered that she goes off in this direction and then fishhooks in the other? [*She is going one way in the first shot, then moving at a different angle in the next.*]

SM: It would be a problem for me if there were an acute angle there.

WA: That's what indeed is happening. [*There is a pause as he watches.*] This is going to work. I can just feel it. [*The edit now has Mia crossing the street, cuts just before she reaches the corner, then picks her up in the crosswalk. It makes for a more seamless scene.*] That's better. The eye fluidizes. [*He pauses, then smiles.*] I'll buy that. [*But in the second viewing the smile disappears.*] It doesn't work. I'm going to have to shoot it again. We've tried every conceivable way and it's graceless.

SM: [*Still not ready to give up*] What about the wide shot [*which shows much more to Mia's left and right*] and then the 100 [*mm, which is tighter*]?

WA: [*Hopeful once more*] Uh-huh. Let's take a look at that. What might also work, although I don't like to cut that way, is double-cutting the wide shot [*using parts of the wide shot twice in the scene. They decide to give it a try anyway. As*

Sandy and the assistants piece together this version, he continues.] If the cutting works properly here, then the logic is okay and Gena doesn't look like a fool coming to the corner. [*But after they've watched it he is not enthusiastic.*] It's just not a nicely cut shot. I don't think it works. You could try the shadow here to see if it works here and get a sense of it. [*The shadow is cut in. He suddenly brightens.*] I think this is going to work. We got lucky with that wall—the texture and geometry. [*There's a pause as he brightens even more.*] I'm starting to feel better now. [*He pushes back from the editing machine.*] So the much fussed-over 100 mm shot finds itself in the trim bin, relegated to the outtake reel forever.

[*Two hours and twenty minutes have passed. He gets up to go to the outer office while Sandy and the assistants get ready for the next scene. As an aside he says with a touch of amazement, "When Sven and Ingmar were shooting* Scenes from a Marriage, *they were obliged to shoot twenty minutes of usable film a day because they had no money to linger. They'd come in in the morning, rehearse, shoot ten minutes, go to lunch, rehearse, shoot another ten minutes."*]

Later that week, Woody and Sandy are working on the shot where Marion hears her brother Paul in a shed. It is an early fall day, the leaves bright red and orange. We first see him as a boy, then the camera pans out the door and adult Marion comes into the frame through a screen door. Woody had wanted to have the camera come over a silhouette of Paul, but the shed was small and cluttered and it was too hard to get the right angle. Seeing what he has instead, Woody bangs his fist on the table, then puts his face in his hands. "Shit, I just want to kill myself. This is so prosaic compared to the shot I wanted to make. I thought of it at the time and now it's too late. The actor is in a play in Philadelphia and it's a big deal to bring him up and besides, there are no leaves now."

They continue and edit what is there.

SM: Still want the music on the tail of this?

WA: [*Calm now*] Now we don't need it so much. The shot works.

He takes a break and the two of us head for the screening room, where we can sit and talk. In the office area between the editing and screening rooms, Jane Martin, his assistant and good friend, is photocopying Mary Tyler Moore Show *scripts.*

WA: [*Rather amazed*] Why?

JM: To see how a sitcom is written.

WA: I would think you'd want to know the reverse.

Some of the vexing shots in *Another Woman*
that took Woody and editor Susan Morse
hours and hours to make a satisfactory scene

We settle into two of the stuffed chairs.

EL: Most of the people you work with on your films have been with you a long time.

WA: I see no reason to change people if they do a good job. I much prefer long-term relationships.

EL: That's certainly been the case with Sandy Morse. Jim Heckert worked on a couple at the beginning, Ralph Rosenblum did six, and this is Sandy's twelfth. [*She will do twenty-two before leaving in 1999.*]

WA: Jim Heckert did *Everything You Always Wanted to Know About Sex* because I shot that in California, where he lives. But I felt a deeper relationship with Ralph because I had gotten close with him—professionally close, anyhow—on *Take the Money and Run* and then on *Bananas*. Also, he lived in New York and in many ways we spoke the same language. Ralph and I parted company after *Interiors*. He had other interests, so I thought I'd go with a different editor and that was fine with him, too. I looked around at major editors and then I got a call from Sandy saying she'd like to work with me. I thought, It wouldn't have occurred to me to use her. She was quite young.

EL: Even though she was constantly in the room with you and Ralph as one of his assistants, it seems you barely knew her. What made you decide to hire her?

WA: She's naturally a soft-spoken person. She was working just as an assistant or maybe even a second assistant, for all I know. I don't even remember. I know she was hanging up trims [*frames trimmed from a shot to make it shorter*] and putting away bits of film no longer needed. And, you know, I really like to sit there and edit. Then I got a phone call one night from Sandy. I had hardly said two words to her before then. She said, "If you don't have an editor, I'd love to work with you." And I thought to myself, Why not? I'm in on all the editing, I don't turn it over to anyone. This may be exactly right because this is a young woman and I'm not going to have to work with another eccentric in a certain sense. Ralph had his little crazies. I said to Sandy, "This is fine with me, but I want you to know that I want to be able to work Sundays and all hours, and I don't want to go out for lunch—you know, that stuff with Ralph: 'It's twelve o'clock, let's take our lunch hour.' " He always used to look at me and say, "So, we'll finish the picture an hour later. You'll deliver it March 14 at two o'clock instead of one o'clock." [*He laughs.*] That used to drive me crazy. She was in no position to say no because she wanted to go from assistant to editor and was looking for an opportunity. Sandy has grown in confidence. She really runs the editing room and is enormously responsible. We've had a very good relationship. It was very lucky for me that she called that day, because it would never have occurred to me to call her when she was so young.

EL: How are you feeling about *Another Woman* so far?

WA: So far, it's been the smoothest things have gone in years—under budget and grooved for our reshoot. And I'm at this point sanguine about the picture in this sense: the individual scenes have come out fine. Stringing them together is another thing completely, and when I look at the final result, my feeling can range anywhere from crushing disappointment, which *can* happen, to surprising excitement, which has *never* happened. More likely it ranges from crushing disappointment to the middle range where you think, Well, some of it works nicely but clearly it doesn't build to a big enough climax, or it starts too slowly, or there are too many scenes in a row of a similar type, or we don't know enough about this character to make it work. Generally my experience has been that it's individual things rather than a big problem and you just want to die. The first time I saw *September* I knew I had to do it over. I felt that way about *Zelig* when I first saw it. *Manhattan*, two weeks before it came out I wanted to buy it back. I remember saying to [*his manager*] Jack Rollins, "I just can't believe with my experience in the game that I could come up with this picture."

EL: You cut back and forth in time a lot in this film and many others.

WA: Time in movies is easy to play with. It's not like on the stage, where you're lumbered by being there at that moment. It's like a novel, where you can just snap your fingers and be a thousand years earlier or later. It's much tougher onstage. It was done to a degree in *Death of a Salesman* and quite successfully, but it's hard and requires great skill.

EL: How do you usually feel after you edit a film and screen the rough cut as a whole for the first time?

WA: I've pretty much always had a disappointed feeling after seeing films for the first time. That's why I'm sure I'll be disappointed when I see this picture. Sure, individual scenes cut very nicely, but it's of course how they add up. A lot of my work is done in the reworking and rewriting and reediting, like in *Hannah*, where the entire second Thanksgiving party was something that I did after the initial filming.

A week later we are watching the dailies of scene 74, Marion's [Gena Rowlands] dream where she walks into a psychiatrist's office and sees Hope [Mia Farrow], then her father [John Houseman]. It was originally shot with Marion talking to the psy-

chiatrist, then him moving out of the frame, and then seen later. It was reshot so that the psychiatrist is in the background, slightly out of focus. There is a continuous shot of Marion coming into the hall, pushing the door open, seeing Hope and the doctor and listening to them, watching Hope leave and then her father enter.

It is more effective and dreamy this way, but there has been a rare miscommunication with the camera operator about where Marion should look after her father enters. It appears she is looking where he isn't; the camera crew thought that was the way Woody wanted it. Moreover, her look is catatonic, not curious, as Woody thinks it should be. He normally says nothing until dailies end, but now he blurts out, "God, where is she looking?"

Several attempts with Sandy to cut around the odd stare don't work because Woody doesn't want the father walking into the empty frame. Since a reshoot is in order, Woody and Sven talk in the cutting room on how to make the shot tighter—there is more ceiling and wall than necessary—and also to show the father's face as he enters as well as Marion's so everyone knows it is her father and not a random elderly male patient. Two assistant editors break out the several takes to see if one has an angle that can be cut in. Woody and Sandy run them again and again. During the fifteen minutes this takes, Sven stands nearby watching while producer Bobby Greenhut and production manager Joe Hartwick stand farther off, afraid of the cost of another day's shoot but sensing there is no way to avoid it. After deciding there is no alternative but to reshoot, Woody gets up and says, "Well, onward and sideways."

The need to reshoot means that John Houseman, who is set to leave the next day because until a moment ago his work was finished, will now delay his departure. Everyone takes these changes calmly and in stride.

"After years and years of this you get used to it and it's not so depressing," Greenhut says later. *"On nine out of ten movies you'd go with the half cut* [finessing the problem by having the father walk into the empty frame] *Woody and Sandy found. But he wants it to be seamless. Orion* [the financier and distributor for the film] *knows we do this but probably not to the extent we do. But as long as we work pretty much within our budget, it's okay. And no one from the company sees the dailies, so they don't know."*

January 1988

Woody has hoped to have a first cut of the movie to show by now, but he tells me there is still a way to go. "It's a little choppy still. I saw the first reel [a reel is ten minutes long] *and I'm not pleased with lots of it. I'd be discouraged if I screened the whole film now. There are so many cuts* [individual shots within a scene] *and scenes missing. I think I can fix things with ten days of reshoots. They're more technical problems than anything, especially in the beginning. There's such disparity between what Marion* [the lead character and narrator] *says and most of the footage we shot. If we used it as is, the movie would be endless. I have to make the beginning more succinct to fit with the narration."*

I ask if he can explain the basic problem. "The movie starts slow because there's a lot of exposition. I made lots of cuts and used a device I haven't used in many, many years, a pre-title sequence [showing part of the film before the titles appear]*, and I hope that will speed along the beginning." By the time he is done, he will reduce the voiceover in the first reel by half.*

After considerable additional work he looks at the whole first reel again. He perks up as it plays. "I like this a hundred times better already," he says after a couple of minutes. "She has lots of energy and it moves much faster with these cuts." But after all ten reels have played and the picture is finished, he says, "A great idea for a comedy sacrificed on the altar of art."

At Sandy Morse's suggestion, he has used the third movement of Erik Satie's Trois Gymnopédies *as the opening music. He tries Schubert's* Death and the Maiden *quartet in its place but immediately dislikes it: "It's too lively, much too lively. Go back to the Satie."*

Woody rests his head on his right arm on the Steenbeck, listening to takes of Hope's [Mia Farrow's] *emotional voice-over. After hearing them all he says, "Get Mia back. She's too weepy. We're going to have to do it again. I want to try her slower with a quieter reading. She should get up to tears eventually, but it's too hysterical now and not interesting." After a few seconds he adds, "It's hard to judge what one wants clarified and solidified for the audience. I don't want to miss something that would give them a bit of knowledge that would make this viewing more interesting."*

The next day Woody is back in the editing room with Mia's rerecorded voiceover. Something still is not right. "Maddening," he says. He tries a shot that stays on Marion much longer before going into Mia's voice. The effect is to slow it up, which is what he wants. He continues: "Ideally we want a middle ground between yesterday's weepy anguish and today's flatter reading. The reason I'm so obsessed with this is because if the audience doesn't buy this, if this moment doesn't come off, we've got nothing." He tries another variation. "It's like writing, when you obsess over a few words, but it's much more cumbersome on film."

After more than two hours of laying in the voice-over and fiddling with the scene, he says without affect, "This isn't going to work." Then "Something's wrong with this." Then "What's going wrong here? I'm almost certain that it's Mia's reading. It's half again as slow as what I want."

After a few minutes, he tries again.

He spends another afternoon moving scenes around or proposing new ideas. One suggestion involves moving or changing the order of thirteen scenes. Finally he pushes away from the Steenbeck, still unsure of precisely the problem.

He gets up to leave for the day. "Thank God," he says as we go out the door, "the public only sees the finished product."

In early February he finally has a cut he's ready to screen for a few friends. As they take their seats in the screening room he says as we walk in to take ours, "If I had done this right, I would have made two movies—this one and a comic one where I overhear Keaton or Mia and run out and do whatever they want. That would be the one that could make money and be successful and this is the one they would cut up for guitar picks."

July 1988

A sound mixing room at Forty-seventh Street and Broadway. It is the first day of the process that will balance all sounds in Another Woman *as well as lay in the secondary sounds, such as footsteps, doors closing, and so forth. Woody wants to see how the work, supervised by Sandy Morse, is going. Two technicians sit at a computer-run console with hundreds of buttons. The technicians play the first seven minutes of the film. Woody says that one line is a little cramped on the next and asks them to change the sound balance on a couple of others but otherwise everything is fine. He tells Sandy and the technicians to keep going as they are, with a caveat. "Don't surprise me. No crickets or people flushing toilets or birdcalls."*

We talk in the car as we're driven back to his home about the weeks of editing and reshooting of some scenes that he has done.

WA: You want to make changes off the movie, not off the printed page. You change as much as you can off the printed page, but in the end, you've got to shoot the picture, edit it together, and put in your music—then you look. And suddenly everything becomes clear to you. You realize you need only one tiny scene and the audience knows you love the girl. You don't need four scenes. My films are really made after I get that first draft mounted. Then there's that dreadful moment when you screen the rough cut and you think, This is boring. It's not so bad at that stage because you feel you can fix things. It's later on that it gets brutal, when you can't fix it anymore.

EL: Do you figure this into your budgets or is working this way a bit of a luxury?

WA: It's not a luxury because I have to stay within my budget to do it. A film breathes, it's organic, and you go with it wherever it takes you. When we're budgeting, Bobby [*Greenhut*] will say, "It's a $10 million film." I'll figure I need $8 million plus $2 million for reshoots. So the reshoots are figured in from the start.

February 1989

Woody and Sandy are seated in front of the Steenbeck editing Crimes and Misdemeanors. *It is the third film in quick succession; work has often overlapped on* Another Woman *and* Oedipus Wrecks.

Sandy proposes a change in how a scene plays. Woody gets up to look at the scene-by-scene breakdown on the wall beam above them that lists a bit of action or dialogue and is color-coded for the main actor in it. For example: 37. Babs to Cliff: "I can't say it"; 39. Jack and Judah: "A hit man?"; 65. Judah sees Del's eyes; 73. Guilt: Judah w/Jack.

"This isn't our movie," Woody says, puzzled, looking to the far left side. "Where's our movie?" Sandy laughs and says, "There are three movies up there and they're all ours."

There are fifteen columns of listings. The first one has bits from Oedipus Wrecks. *The fifteenth has material from* Another Woman. *Two through fourteen are* Crimes and Misdemeanors.

Woody filmed most of the scenes as master shots, which both limits his choices and makes editing easier. He is concerned that some of the film is too wordy. "You can disguise it some with camera work and pacing, but it's far different from films with no words, like Cries and Whispers," *he says. "But that is a period piece, not dealing with a high-tech contemporary society. People walk and sit and talk. It's words, not deeds."*

He turns to a scene at the start of the film where Cliff, his character, comes home after seeing a movie with his niece, Jenny, and his wife, Wendy (Joanna Gleason), asks where he was. She's best in the first take, Woody in the second.

WA: You probably like the second better.

SM: Actually, the first.

WA: She's angrier in the first. I'm better in the second.

SM: [*Smiling*] Did you think I'd like the second because you were better?

WA: [*Shrugs and smiles in return*] There's nothing at stake here. It's not one of my great one-liners I'm killing.

March 1989

"Well," Woody says after seeing the first assembled version of Crimes and Misdemeanors, "the good news is it's better than I thought, apart from some obvious necessary cuts and trims. The bad news is, Mia's and my story doesn't work." (They meet; they work together on a documentary film; he falls for her.) But he is not distressed. "This may be the best I've ever felt at this stage. At least I don't want to blow up the place."

The finished film is the most rewritten and reshot of his movies to date. Over the next few weeks he throws out fully one-third of the story and revamps the story line and plot; in the end he will reshoot 80 of the film's 139 scenes at least once. In the original version, Hally (Mia Farrow) works as a geriatric social worker instead of the television producer she is in the finished film; she is married to a magazine editor whom the audience meets, and is also having an affair with a married man the audience briefly sees as Cliff (Woody), who also is married, and his niece Jenny (Jenny Nichols) secretly trail her through Central Park (she is not married in the final version nor is she having an affair); the documentary film Cliff makes so he can spend more time with Hally, with whom he has fallen in love, is of ex-vaudevillian patients in the nursing home where she works, not the funny and damning filmwithin-the-film he makes of his brother-in-law, Lester (Alan Alda); and the ending has Cliff passing himself off as a TV producer at the climactic wedding scene in order to foster a liaison with an aspiring actress, played by Sean Young, with whom he is caught in an indelicate position when a curtain in the ballroom is accidentally opened—her character does not appear in the finished film. The last shot in the original version is of him with Jenny, his only real friend; in the final version it is the sequence with Cliff and Judah (Martin Landau), the ophthalmologist who has gotten away with the murder of his mistress, Del (Anjelica Huston); the audience sees he has come to peace with his crime—and that leads into the rabbi Ben (Sam Waterston) dancing with his daughter at her wedding. In addition, the story line with Cliff and Jenny is much stronger in the first than in the final version, as is the story of his romance-seeking sister, Babs (Caroline Aaron).

The refashioning of the film starts, in what has become standard practice, with Woody and Sandy Morse in his screening room. Over the next several hours, they discuss how to reshape the movie.

Of Judah's story he asks, "Did we go too fast?"

"You don't want lots of expositional material to slow things down," says Sandy.

"Right. There's a question of whether we're strong enough with the religious aspect at the beginning. Put another way, do we want a clearer statement of the argument of the movie: no higher power is going to punish us for our misdeeds if we get away with them? And that knowing that, you have to choose a just life or there *will be chaos, and so many people don't do that that there is chaos. Then we go on to prove or disprove that."*

Both are pacing around the room. Woody goes on, thinking aloud, unhappy that in the first two scenes between Judah and Del, who threatens to expose Judah's mis-appropriation of a charitable foundation's funds if he ends their affair, Del is hysterical in both. Then he considers a scene between Judah and his brother Jack (Jerry Orbach, who arranges for Del to be murdered). He is displeased with a guilt-stricken Judah saying, "How did we become what we are?" and wants to redo it.

"Judah is secular but there is a spark of religion from when they drive it into you as a kid," he says. "I feel we're getting two blocks of information at the beginning: Judah and his secret [the affair with Del] *and also the religious stuff. I want to make it all one at the start. Do I have her flash through his mind while he's making his speech?" (The film opens with Judah being honored for his charitable work.)*

After an hour and a half of this they order out for lunch and move on to Hally (Mia Farrow). Woody still paces as he talks.

"What you want with Mia is the essential line: we meet, I fall in love. Finding out she is married is a stall but still viable." He stops to think and concludes, "It's an artificially introduced obstacle—her husband that I don't know about. I meet a girl, someone you'd think too mature and sober for Lester, and she winds up with him. Then I conveniently don't notice her wedding ring for at least a week. There's no other meat in the story with Mia. It's all the slow playing of arbitrary information."

"All that it needs to me is some sense that she could come to you," Sandy tells him. "I wish you had more reason to hope than there is. I wish for more intimacy in the champagne scene [after Hally tells Cliff in his editing room that public television is interested in the film on a professor that he has been shooting for years] *and at the jazz club"* [where Cliff and his wife and Hally and her husband go one evening. In the final version, the scene is with Cliff, his wife, Hally, and Lester].

Woody shakes his head. "There's no special plot with Mia here. It's all dredging up and trying to find stuff." He tries, unsuccessfully, several paths to find a way around. "The original notion was that she's married and having an affair. Why? And what does it give us?" He works through the ramifications of different dialogue and concludes that he has to lose the amusing and beautifully filmed scene where Cliff and Jenny follow Hally through Central Park. "It breaks my heart that I can't follow her."

Woody now redoes scenes aloud in different voices. "The surprise has to be that she picks him. In comparison to Judah's story, I'm not getting big enough things happening." After a long silence he tries out a couple of possible scenes with Lester and the professor but comes up empty, then moves on to the scenes with Cliff's sister. For the next hour he talks through possible dialogue for several scenes and then returns to the problem with Cliff and Hally.

"Is there anything to this?" he asks, trying yet another tack. "I'm married and I fall in love with Hally because my marriage is not a very happy one. And she's sin-

gle and I'm falling for her and Lester is pitching her in a superficial way and finally she says to me, 'You're married,' and I think that's the thing standing in her way when she's really being polite. Then she goes to London to do a show on foreign people. . . ." He throws up his hands. "It's no good. It's too masochistic, like a German movie of the twenties."

By midafternoon, after talking through many variations of plot and character changes, he has a pretty clear idea of what he needs to do. "This may be neurotic speculation," he says, "but I like to squeeze and squeeze until I've gone as far as I can. It would be self-destructive not to." He shrugs. "The worst that will happen is that people will get upset with me and it will cost me money."

There are ten scenes to rewrite and reshoot, the availability of actors and locations to check on and arrange. "We just need a few little finesses," Woody says. A little grin appears. "A million dollars' worth of finesses."

September 2005

EL: You're involved with the details of every step of a film, and I've noticed that you do not delegate any part of its creation, even assembling a first cut from takes you've already selected.

WA: To me the movie is a handmade product. I was watching a documentary on editing on television the other day and many wonderful filmmakers were on and wonderful editors and everyone was talking briefly about how they edit. Years ago, they would turn it over to an editor. Or there are people I know who finish shooting and go away for a vacation and let the editor do a draft; then they come back and they check it out and do their changes.

I can't do that. It would be unthinkable for me not to be in on every inch of the movie—and this is not out of any sort of ego or sense of having to control; I just can't imagine it any other way. How could I not be in on the editing, on the scoring, because I feel that the whole project is one big writing project? You may not be writing with a typewriter once you get past the script phase, but when you're picking locations and casting and on the set, you're really writing. You're writing with film, and you're writing with film when you edit it together and you put some music in. This is all part of the writing process for me.

EL: That makes all the sense in the world to me. I can't imagine not making every change on the page.

WA: But there are guys who make wonderful films who will go over dailies with the editor and point out the takes they like and then they go to Little Dix Bay for three weeks and have fun and they come back and the editor presents them with the takes they chose in a strung-out order and with some common sense. Then they say, "No, no, no. This was great but this shot goes on too long." I just can't do that.

I always go for a fine cut my first time. It doesn't do me any good to make a rough cut. I don't learn anything. My idea is to cut the film like it was going to come out, the best I can possibly cut it, the first time and then see what I did wrong. Of course, I've always done a million things wrong; I just don't know it. Then I start cutting away at it.

EL: How is it, having written a script, acted it, and shot it over several months, and seeing the dailies all that time, then going into the cutting room where you're going to have to see yourself, having to judge yourself as an actor?

WA: Very easy. You watch yourself and say, "I'm dreadful there," "I stink there," "I'm completely fake in this one," "There, I think I'm quite good, it's completely believable to me, and I think I'm being amusing and not overacting or mugging too much." It's not hard to pick out the good stuff. Of course, I'm sitting here with an editor and maybe somebody else, and sometimes someone will say, "I know you love take two but I gotta tell you . . . ," and then I'll look at them again and sometimes they'll be right, and I'll say, "Well, okay, if you prefer number eight, to me they're both good but we'll use eight."

It's not hard. What's hard is when your inspiration fails you, when my vision of the whole piece was faulty.

EL: I watched *Play It Again, Sam* the other night and noticed that there are built-in pauses for laughs.

WA: It was probably [*director*] Herb Ross's editor [*Marion Rothman*] who timed it that way. I don't do that because I don't have the confidence that the laughs will be there. And to me, pace is very important, so I would never do that. But the Marx Brothers did it.

EL: Yeah, they worked many of their films out on the road and knew just where the laughs were before shooting.

WA: I can't do that.

EL: *Take the Money and Run* is completely devoted to the jokes. Clearly you knew how to deliver the joke verbally. I guess your challenge was to find the best way to deliver the joke visually.

WA: Yes. It was easy to edit for the most part. The problem was how I used—or didn't use—the music. I took the picture with no music in it and I showed it to audiences under the worst kind of circumstances. You know, people you'd flush in off the street.

EL: You once said you got twelve soldiers from the USO and took them up to a screening room on Broadway.

WA: Yeah. They didn't know me, there was no music in the picture, they'd see this rough cut with crayon marks from the editing—and I'd panic and started to take things out of the movie because I thought from the reaction that they weren't funny. And then finally I was in trouble with the movie and the company said, "Why don't you bring in Ralph Rosenblum? He's a brilliant guy, and he'll help you with it."

Ralph had a wonderful sense of humor. He just loved the jokes and the comedy. It was like opening the doors and letting in a burst of fresh air. He said, "You're crazy for taking these things out, this is all hilarious stuff," and he put it all back in. And he said, "You need a piece of music behind it. Take some records and put some temporary music behind it," and he showed me how to do that. All of a sudden stuff started coming to life. He said, "Of *course* you're going to die if you show a rough cut with no music to twelve servicemen from Montana."

EL: How great was his contribution to the finished film?

WA: Quantitatively, 80 percent of the picture is what I gave him. But the 20 percent that he did completely saved the picture and turned it from a failure into a success. Most of what he did was show me that I didn't have to do things literally; I could do things very quick, very fast. For instance, I had a block of material that was very funny but it made the beginning of the picture get off very slowly. [*The first eight and a half minutes, narrated by Jackson Beck, introduce us to Virgil, a small, bespectacled boy whose glasses are stomped on by bullying children and adults alike; who takes up the cello (but, his teacher points out, "had no conception of the instrument. He was* blowing *into it") and plays it in a marching band; who steals a gun from a pawnshop to rob an armored car, only to find in a shootout with the guards that his weapon is really a cigarette lighter. The sequence ends with him entering San Quentin and then the titles come up.*] He left the beginning exactly as is, but he took the titles and he put them later. So you come in and the picture starts and you're seeing scenes being played and [*snaps fingers*] then the titles come, so all the material prior to the titles isn't really an expenditure of time for the audience. And so you've seen several minutes of funny film, storytelling without any cost to the pace of the picture. Now, it would never have occurred to me in a million years to do that.

Apart from my instinct in editing, which was really my instinct as a storyteller in writing, I learned everything from him. I couldn't have gone to school with a better guy. I've often said the two guys I went to school with—Gordon Willis and Ralph Rosenblum—taught me a huge amount about movies. Now when I reject something of theirs, a precept of theirs, I at least know what I'm doing. I can only do it because they explained so well to me the correct way to do it.

EL: In working on your twenty-two films from 1979 to 1998, did Sandy bring anything new to you? Did you change much in how you edit?

WA: Sandy and I both, I think, learned many things together. We struggled through tons of problems on films. She was always in there with me, helping me solve the problems, shooting down my ideas or encouraging them and pitching her own. Very frequently we asked her husband [*the writer*] Jack [*Richardson*] to come and look at the film and he would give quite cogent criticisms. She was a fine editor.

EL: Did she have the same sense of timing and sense of humor as Ralph?

WA: She had her own sensibility. She was helpful, too, in terms of relationship problems. She frequently had good insights into what was romantic and what was not.

EL: I remember watching the two of you edit *Crimes and Misdemeanors.* Characters were being taken out and new stories put in. As the film went along, stacked on one side of the screening room were increasingly more boxes of film with scenes of characters who were no longer in the picture. As I watched different cuts of the film I realized I had become attached to some of those people, even though their stories no longer worked.

WA: Right. We cut people out of films all the time, almost never having to do with their performance but strictly because of what makes the story work best. Of course the actor, being by nature insecure, always thinks it's the performance. He always thinks he was cut out because he was no good, or that he didn't get the part because he didn't read well or was no good. But it's really rarely that. It's overwhelmingly some other reason, usually traceable to me. Either I pick the wrong person at the audition or when I see the film and get a little more into it, that person seems wrong then. Or most of all, I've written it badly and don't realize it until it's up on its feet being shot.

Over the years I've cut out many people. I cut Vanessa Redgrave out of *Celebrity,* and she's as fine an actress as there is in the world. Obviously it had nothing to do with her acting.

EL: *Manhattan* was Sandy's first film. Was that a tough one or pretty straightforward?

WA: Not overly tough but normally tough. Some are simple, some are *very* tough. I had to do some reshoots on that. I had to reshoot the ending to get it right.

EL: Do you remember what the first ending was?

WA: Well, the very last shots were always the same. [*Tracy is about to leave for six months of theater work in London. Isaac suddenly realizes what he is losing and asks her not to go; he doesn't "want that thing about you that I like to change." She says she has to catch her plane and then, "Why couldn't you have brought this up last week? Look, six months isn't so long. Not everybody gets corrupted. Look, you have to have a little faith in people." Ike stares at Tracy with a quizzical look, then smiles. The "Rhapsody in Blue" orchestration swells and the film cuts to a series of shots of magnificent skylines of Manhattan.*] But there was a missing climax where I went to Yale's classroom and confronted him. That was never there. [*Yale is played by Michael Murphy. Both men are romantically involved with the Diane Keaton character. There are full human and ape skeletons that Woody makes some funny references to in what is largely a dramatic scene—see page 34.*]

EL: Were the skeletons in the script or did they just happen to be in the classroom?

WA: I think they were just there. I would not have thought to write them in. As I was saying the other day, people who have to sell scripts have to write in a lot of details. And they'll write, *Shot of him walking up the stairs. His face is grim. Cut to skeleton in classroom that matches his face.* They have to really project the picture to people who are giving the money. I never did that, so my guess is that's just how the classroom was. You know, you see something and you use it.

EL: I would guess *Crimes and Misdemeanors* counts as a tough one to edit.

WA: Yes. In *Crimes and Misdemeanors,* I thought the crime part [*laughs*] was riveting. I think people became involved with it. At one point I thought, Hey, who cares that I have another story going [*a more comedic one about Cliff*]? I should have made only this picture. Sometimes I still think that. As I've said, the original idea was that Mia and I were doing a documentary on old-age homes; we visited at least one that I recall and shot in it. But the whole story just didn't come off *at all* and I had to reshoot the entire "misdemeanors" part.

EL: The editing as you describe it is storytelling—it's a secondary part of the writing, something that has to be done to correct the story. For instance, as we've discussed, after you screened the first cut of the film, you completely rewrote the Alan Alda part and you came up with the devastatingly mocking film-within-the-film about him shot by your character.

WA: Yeah. He was my annoying brother-in-law. In the first version, Channel 13 [*the New York City Public Broadcasting Service station*] was making a film on him and I resented that all these legitimate sources fell prey to his charm. And so I had the idea of, Why don't *I* make the film and integrate the story more? And then it came to life.

EL: What was another tough one?

WA: Oh, *Zelig* was very, very hard.

EL: Because of the technical aspects?

WA: No, the technical part of *Zelig* was not hard, yet it is what amazed so many people. I believe Gordon Willis finally got his first Oscar cinematography nomination for that picture—which is a *laugh* because it was relatively effortless for him. [*A second came in 1991 for* The Godfather: Part III.] He's revolutionized the industry on twenty other pictures and went unrecognized, whereas his work on *Zelig* was great as always, but it was not *nearly* as complex as many of my films. You know, we'd turn on the kind of lights the newsreel would have and shoot. So the technical part of it and making it look old was not hard.

The problem with *Zelig* was, because of the limitations of that kind of story, we didn't have access to the private lives of the real people Zelig is shown with; you can only show them walking up steps or going into cars or at a banquet.

The white-room films, therefore [*in which psychiatrist Eudora Fletcher records her interviews with Leonard Zelig*], were a stroke of great good fortune. When I finally put it all together, the movie was [*laughs*] forty-five minutes. I couldn't stretch out the newsreel and documentary shots because I was unable to do scenes between people. So I had to figure out digressions and story and other things to do. And even now, it's one of my shortest films.

EL: Eighty minutes.

WA: Plus, I had to keep the funny things going. It was one of my more successful films. Successful meaning that I had a vision of something and I brought it off. The truth of the matter is, though, that I was going to do the film without using documentary technique. I was going to do a realistic story about someone who becomes whomever he's around. I liked the idea that you want to be liked so you give up your personality to whomever you're with. So if you're with people who liked the show at the Mark Hellinger last night, you'd say, "Oh, yeah, I really did enjoy that." But if you were with people who hated it, you'd say, "Oh, I didn't like it." It gets bigger and bigger and ultimately leads to fascism, because you give up your personality completely to be part of the group, to mix in with the group.

The content of the picture didn't resonate as deeply as the technique did at first because at that point that was a sort of startling technique—to do a black-and-white period documentary. And as the years have gone by and the picture's been shown a lot on television and people have seen it, the point of the picture started to dawn on people. There was something behind it.

And how many people forgot that I had used that technique in *Take the Money and Run*? It wasn't new at all. I started my movie career doing a documentary.

EL: What other difficult editing jobs come to mind?

WA: There have been individual problems in lots of them. *Annie Hall* was extremely difficult because it started out to be a stream-of-consciousness picture from Alvy. But as I said, when Marshall Brickman saw the first cut—he was co-writer on it—he couldn't follow it.

EL: Is this the cut you threw into the reservoir in Los Angeles?

WA: No. That was on *Sleeper*. When I was doing *Sleeper* in California there were scenes I hated so much that I didn't want anybody ever to see them. Of course, moronic as I was, I never threw the negative in the reservoir. The negative resided in a vault somewhere. But I did throw a print in the reservoir.

EL: You've told me that your instinct from *Take the Money* on has been not to edit a picture while you're shooting. Why?

WA: To me they are two completely different phases. At the end of the day, I'm tired and I'm cranky and I want to go home and live my life. I don't want to go to the editing room and start obsessing over film. I like to get all of the material shot and then come in fresh and cut the picture. That just works for me.

If I cut while I was going along, there are two schools of thought. One is that it might save me some money because I'd be seeing my mistakes while I was there and I could fix them. But the other is that I become obsessive and I might never stop shooting. In the same way, I don't work with a video monitor, although many, many people do. It works well for them but it wouldn't for me. I have this fantasy of going and looking at it on the video monitor and then going back and shooting it again, and then shooting it again, and again.

EL: But as you said about people who saw the early version of *Annie Hall* and always wanted to know more about the story between Alvy and Annie, it's the relationships between those characters that drive the picture.

WA: Yes, there is a relentless drive, like a Pac-Man that's eating you all the time, of what happens next. That's what people really want to see in movies and on the stage. No matter how abstract you make the picture, no matter how you disguise it and modernize it, it's like jazz. In jazz there's a melody and you want to come back to it. Even people who did modern jazz, like Charlie Parker, had a great respect for melody. They'd go wild, but they got the melody in there. And when eventually players abstracted so much that they didn't get the melody, people lost interest in jazz to a huge degree.

The same is true in movies or the theater. It's fine to be very fresh and original in structure, but you've got to always come back to what happens next because that's what the viewers want to know. And that was true of *Annie Hall.* It was full of what I thought at the time were very clever connections and turns. I thought, Oh, this is brilliant and this cuts onto that quite logically from a stream-of-consciousness point of view. But when you lose the thread of what happens next, it's very irksome to the audience.

You can't confuse the temporal arts with painting. Painting, you can look at Jackson Pollock and get a great, great buzz out of it and that buzz can be over in two seconds—or two hours if you care to stand there that long. But in the theater or the movies, where music is going along with time, the audience has to get involved in something and move forward with it.

EL: You told me a long time ago that when you're editing, you have to end the movie like a house afire because as you get to its end, time collapses.

WA: In comedy, yes. When you're doing a comedy the audience gives you a lot of goodwill the first twenty minutes or so and then you've got to really put out to earn the rest. It gets tougher and tougher. They've been sitting there now for an hour, and then an hour and fifteen minutes, and they don't want to make any more investment.

EL: As you constantly recut *Annie Hall* did you lose any scenes you particularly liked?

WA: We had a scene at dinner with Colleen Dewhurst [*died 1991*] that just ran too long. But then there was a scene where I'm sitting around with Annie's parents and Annie is watching television and clearly I've influenced her in a way antithetical to her parents' upbringing. We're talking about something and suddenly Annie snaps at them, "Well, quantity affects quality." And they say, "Who said *that*?" And she says, "Karl Marx." And then Mrs. Hall says in this naive way, "Oh, I just had the funniest dream the other night. It was just so funny. I was in the dream and Dad was in it and he was trying to fix a TV and I came down and he was angry and I just took the TV antenna and broke it off." It was a very funny scene revolving around the naiveté of people who had no sense of Freudian interpretation. I had it in the picture for a time but it didn't make the final cut.

EL: *Take the Money and Run* was a difficult one for you. Was *Bananas* easier?

WA: *Bananas* was a lot easier because as I was going along I kept thinking [*snaps fingers*], Don't worry about a thing here. They're going to laugh at this. We'll put a piece of music here and they'll love it. Yes, it was a lot easier.

EL: How about *Interiors*?

WA: *Interiors* had plenty of problems. I was inexperienced in doing that kind of film. I wish I could do *Interiors* today. I could really make it an indisputably good picture, I feel. I had bitten off a lot because I wanted to do a drama and I didn't want to do what passed for drama in, you know, popular American films. I didn't want to do melodrama. I wanted to do drama in the heaviest, most European sense. [*He pauses and shakes his head.*] I had a great idea and I got a percentage of the potential out of it, but now I could really do it. . . .

EL: What would you do now?

WA: The main thing is I would have made it much less poetic and much more realistic. I also would have brought in Maureen [*Stapleton*] much, much earlier in the movie and made the conflicts big and nasty right from the start so it would have crackled with conflict throughout. Here, I was working with different tones. So Ralph and I worked very, very hard. In fact, the first dialogue in that picture [*E. G. Marshall as Arthur, the husband of the troubled Eve, played by Geraldine Page, looks out a picture window at a panoramic view of the New York skyline, his back to the camera. In narration he says, "I had dropped out of law school when I met Eve. She was very beautiful. Very pale and cool in her black dress . . . with never anything more than a single strand of pearls. And distant. Always poised and distant"*] came from seventy pages later in the script. Now, in a poetic picture you can have more freedom to do that.

A few days later, he has just finished the rough cut of Scoop *and he is not in a good mood. The picture clearly isn't what he hoped it would be.*

WA: I'm almost always disappointed after the first screening. [*Small laugh*] It's a cold-shower moment. It's never as wonderful as you'd hoped it would be. And this certainly wasn't.

EL. Can it be saved?

WA: [*Long pause*] My own honest feeling is that it cannot. This doesn't mean that it will not be a commercial success. [*It will be.*] Why certain films are remains a mystery to me.

EL: When you're looking at it just in small bits, formerly on the Moviola and now on the computer screen, do you get an inkling of what it's going to be like or is it hard to see until you've strung it all together and looked at it whole?

WA: As I'm cutting it [*sighs*] you don't get an inkling of what the whole effect is going to be. No. You're putting it together, it's all very self-congratulatory and confident and buoyant and optimistic, and then you see what you wrought. [*He laughs ironically.*] And your heart sinks. It's always too long, it's always too slow. Invariably, stuff you thought was funny is not very funny and stuff you thought was so wonderful is not wonderful and relationships you thought would go a certain way don't. You know, everything that can go wrong goes wrong and nothing is as good as you hoped it would be.

EL: Is this an instance where you feel the directing was not up to par?

WA: No. I didn't feel that I directed it badly. I felt I mounted it fine. No director in the world would have done better with the material I had written. I mean, yes, some scenes they would have done better and some scenes I did as well as could be done. But it's the writing, it's almost always the writing. It's hard to write something between an hour and a half and two hours' duration that's interesting and fresh and original and believable and moving. That's where everybody strikes out, and me certainly.

EL: Any scenes you can tell me in particular that you looked at and said, "Oh, gosh, this just isn't going to work"?

WA: Well, I can say this: the first cut was two hours and fourteen minutes and now it's an hour and forty minutes.

EL: So what have you taken out?

WA: A lot of junk. There were many scenes I thought were funny in the picture—you know, chasing and following and romantic scenes with Hugh Jackman and Scarlett, and many jokes of mine that I thought fell flat.

EL: Did you find yourself wishing that you could reshoot it now that you're back in New York?

WA: [*Pensive for a moment*] Yes, it's a shame. [*Pause.*] I don't know if they would make a big enough difference, but there are scenes I wish I could reshoot. As you move along in editing, you just *feel* at the editing machine that you want to move to the next thing, you don't want to stop and wait for this and I look at the editor and she looks at me and we both know the same thing: who wants to stop for *that* now?

November 2005

I have seen Scoop. *We meet at the Manhattan Film Center to discuss it.*

EL: *Scoop* came in at about ninety-one minutes—standard for your comedies—after ruthless cutting. Is there anything in terms of the editing you could make note of?

WA: The most prevalent problem was keeping it moving along. It's a comedy, and a *light* comedy, and you don't have a lot going for you except a light story that has to bounce along amusingly. Once you bog down, it's death.

EL: So much exposition between Scarlet and her roommate disappeared, and you cut a lot about relationships and the setup with Hugh Jackman.

WA: Yes. You know, I learned this—I never learned it, I observed it and failed to learn it—on my first play, *Don't Drink the Water*, where I wrote a ton of extra material. You tend to write too much to make things clear and developed. I wrote about five pages between Tony Roberts, who was playing the ambassador's son, and the daughter of Lou Jacobi and Kay Medford, and the second the family walks in with the young daughter and she looks at him and he looks at her [*snaps fingers*], you didn't need any of it. It was all superfluous. You could see they were attracted to each other and five pages of soporific dialogue bit the dust.

This kind of thing holds true in the movies. I've learned it [*laughs*] a thousand times and I always screw it up, and that's what I did with this movie.

EL: Everything you need to know is in the viewing.

WA: Right. You think the audience is not going to get it, so you explain it, clarify it, but the truth of the matter is, they're *always* far ahead of you. [*He smiles.*]

EL: Which I guess is a help in ending a comedy like a house afire.

WA: [*Smiles again*] When I think about ending one of my movies like a house afire, sometimes I feel I should put the negative in a house and burn the place down.

7

SCORING

October 1973

A hallmark of a Woody Allen film is his almost exclusive use of American jazz and popular standards from 1900 to 1950 and a reliance on classical music for much of the remainder of the film's score. Woody's passion for New Orleans jazz began in his early teens. At fifteen he took up the clarinet, playing at home in accompaniment to George Lewis records for the first few years. Lewis, one of the great New Orleans–style clarinetists, died in 1968, but his sound—big, expressive, not clean-cut like Benny Goodman's, but rather blue and sweet with a plaintive tinge and a pronounced vibrato at times—can be heard often in Woody's playing; there is a picture of Lewis on a bookshelf in his home. (His film production company is named Perdido in honor of the New Orleans street synonymous with jazz.)

Now and then the music of New Orleans finds its way into his films. The style has a 4/4 beat that sets toes to tapping and a melody that all the players stick to rather than improvise on (the case with Kansas City and Chicago style). Harmony is not as important as the melody and the beat, and so while each player has his own part, and each has solos, they all play together for the benefit of the band. Because so few musicians work at playing New Orleans jazz, it is a vanishing art form. It developed into soulful, happy music at the turn of the twentieth century out of the traditional marches and hymns the city's bands played in funeral processions and jam sessions.

Woody practices his clarinet long tones [playing a note and holding it, again and again] every day, whether filming or not, and when he plays he appears to be lost in the music. Often when standing around he whistles one jazz tune or another. His absorption in the music is complete. One day during a lunch break while editing Sleeper *in the summer of 1973, I browse with him in a record shop on Eighth Avenue in Manhattan and pick out a couple of Lewis's records. I ask if they will serve as a good introduction. He studies the list of songs on the album cover, then nods and says wistfully, "I'd give anything to be you and hear these for the first time."*

Even though Sleeper *takes place two hundred years in the future, Woody plans to use New Orleans jazz for the background music because, he says, "I don't want to use the stereotyped Moog synthesizer music usually used for futuristic things. I want the music to play against the story"—a mélange of science fiction, romance, slapstick, and chases. That fall, after the film is edited, I accompany him to New Orleans, where he plays four sessions with the Preservation Hall Jazz Band to record the score with its longtime players. Trombonist "Big Jim" Robinson, eighty-three years old, gets a wonderful sound by playing almost out of the right side of his mouth alone, his left cheek flat and his right out like a balloon. Chester Zardis on bass, seventy-four, is about five-six and sits on a stool while playing. When he solos, his right leg shoots out in time to the music. Emmanuel Sayles, the banjo player, and*

Woody with the Preservation Hall Jazz Band while recording the soundtrack for *Sleeper* in 1973

Sing Miller, on piano, flash their teeth when they sing solos. Sayles has several gold teeth in the back right-hand side of his mouth, which he contorts to display them; Miller has only one large lower-front tooth. Percy Humphrey, the trumpet player and leader of the band, has a dour look but magisterial movements. Josiah "Cie" Frazier, on drums, smiles and smiles. All are at least sixty years old.

Preservation Hall is unlike any normal recording studio. In fact, it is unlike almost any music hall. The room is perhaps forty-five feet long and half as wide. The wood floor is worn; the walls are partly covered in pegboard (it was once an art gallery), with the rest bare wood or peeled plaster. It looks pretty seedy, but the acoustics are great. There are two rows of benches that begin three feet from the band that accommodate a couple of dozen people; the remainder of the two hundred or so fans who cram in stand.

Woody comes into the hall in pressed army fatigue trousers, a flannel shirt with a tie, a maroon corduroy jacket, and a khaki rain hat, hangs his coat behind the piano, and sits beside Humphrey, who without saying anything plays a couple of soft notes and on the beat they all join in on "Little Liza Jane." He does the same for each number.

"He has a wonderful ear," Humphrey says of Woody after the set. "He did what you should do when you play with another man's band: he played along with what we played. He didn't try to be a celebrity."

Between sets people buy recordings by the band and ask the musicians for autographs, including Woody, who of course does not play on the albums. He would rather duck out and catch a few minutes of the World Series. Instead, he finds himself in the path of a young man about five feet five inches tall; Woody is five-six. "If I'm shorter than you, I'm committing suicide," the young man announces, then walks away.

Woody stares blankly after him for a second. "[Dick] Cavett always has a witty riposte for these people," he says to me. (At lunch earlier that day, a not unattractive woman handed him a note. If you're who I think you are, *it read,* I've always wanted to fuck you to death. *He looked up at her. "Who do you think I am?" he asked.)*

Between recording sessions, Woody listens to the tapes in the sound truck parked on the sidewalk outside the hall. He especially likes the rendition of "Savoy Blues" and "Climax Rag."

Before one session Woody tells Allan Jaffe, a tuba player who founded and runs Preservation Hall, that for chase scenes he needs something a little faster-paced than he is getting, but he knows he can't ask the band to play faster. "Asking a band to play faster is worse than asking them to play 'When the Saints Go Marching In,'" Jaffe says later. So during a lull Jaffe casually asks Humphrey, "What would you play if it was 12:27 and you wanted to get to the clubhouse at 12:30?" The trumpeter thinks for a second and then they play "Bye and Bye" at a pretty fast pace.

Woody knows he will not get everything he needs and already has set up a recording session in New York with his band, the New Orleans Funeral and Ragtime Orchestra.

"For some scenes," he says during a break, "I need to choose music to fit where I'm running, for instance, and with my band I can tell them to play faster or slower, or when I need a break, or a tuba solo, or where I can play a couple of riffs. I can't do that in another man's band. It will be interesting to have a contrast with both bands."

At 12:30 A.M. on the second day the last session ends. Albert Burbank, probably the premier New Orleans–style clarinetist now, comes over to congratulate him. Then Jim Robinson walks up.

"Did anyone ever tell you you sound like my old friend George Lewis?" he asks. There is no finer compliment he could give Woody. "What's your name again?"

"Woody," he mumbles.

"Willard? You're real good, Willard."

November 1989

It's a Saturday, and therefore no filming on Another Woman *today. We meet in the living room of his apartment overlooking Central Park. As part of a conversation about his evolution as a filmmaker, we talk about how he found New Orleans jazz as a kid, then spend a few minutes on his earliest pictures and how he learned to use music to his advantage.*

EL: From things you've said over the years, it seems that jazz was one of the strongest bonds between you and your friends.

WA: Yes, we were very knitted together by traditional jazz. There was a DJ who eventually went blind named Ted Huesing, who played it. My friend Jerry Epstein was one of the first to own a tape recorder, a big, cumbersome machine. He taped what I later found out was a Sidney Bechet concert in Paris. [*Bechet's fervent arpeggios and broad vibrato distinguish his confident, strikingly personal style.*] I heard that and I thought it was wonderful, and this small enclave of friends became more and more interested in traditional jazz to the point we became in a certain way—I don't mean this in a pompous way—we all became experts in it. Like kids do, we knew every player on every record and every bit of jazz lore and history. I was thirteen or fourteen. I took up the clarinet soon after that.

EL: You said in a 1965 interview with Ralph Gleason of the *San Francisco Chronicle* that "the second night I saw Sidney Bechet—at a concert in New York; I'd seen him before but under bad circumstances, in the place above Birdland—was the most fulfilling artistic experience of my life." What brought such an overwhelming response?

Woody and a few of his friends fell in love with New Orleans jazz early in their teens and he took up the clarinet soon after.

WA: I went there with stupendous anticipation and he fulfilled it. Bechet was a startling musician; his ferociousness was incredible. I was struck by the total majesty of his playing.

EL: I know you played sports a lot. Did you put as much time into music?

WA: We spent many, many, many hours doing nothing but listening to that music. We'd come home from school and congregate at a friend's house. My friend Elliott Mills was one of the first people to have hi-fi equipment. I had a twelve-and-a-half-dollar phonograph that was a little suitcase kind, you put the top up. We just never stopped listening to jazz. I mean obsessively to note after note. So very often after school when everyone would hang out at Cookie's, the neighborhood joint over by the El, and have sodas and sandwiches and socialize and pair off for the movies or the poolroom, I was always home hovered over the record player in my bedroom.

EL: There is a lot of jazz in *Take the Money and Run,* but you didn't originally score it that way. What happened?

WA: I had never done a picture before and I had no perspective on it whatsoever. I was making all kinds of terrible mistakes; I hated everything; I didn't put music into many of the scenes, so they just played coldly and dryly. When Ralph Rosenblum came aboard he said, "Look, you've thrown out a ton of funny material, and you've got to put a piece of music behind that," or "You can't put a dreary, dirge-like piece behind a scene."
There was a scene where I go out on a date with Janet Margolin. [*His clothes hang in an old refrigerator, his shoes are in the freezer.*] I'm turning on the bathtub and getting into the shower, looking in the mirror and various things—and I had on the gloomiest piece of music, the saddest piece of music. Then Ralph took a piece of Eubie Blake ragtime and said, "Look. Look what happens when you put a piece of lively music behind it." And the whole thing just came to life. I was suddenly just bouncing along. It made all the difference in the world. And there are a million little things I just didn't know. I feel Ralph saved me on that picture. [*The sequence, an above-the-waist shot, ends with Woody going out the door dressed in a coat and tie to the end of the music. The camera lingers on the closed door—then after a few beats, Woody comes back in and we see he has forgotten to put on his pants and is wearing only a towel around his waist.*]

EL: Do you have an idea of the music you want for the film as you're writing it?

WA: I usually know at least some of the music I'm going to use, if not all of it. I don't necessarily mean the specific songs, but I know that this movie [Another Woman] is going to have, say, a classical motif and another movie is going to have

Virgil getting ready for a date in *Take the Money and Run.* Editor Ralph Rosenblum's suggestion of a sprightly tune by Eubie Blake for this scene and other suggestions changed the whole tone of the picture.

Rodgers and Hart. In *Manhattan* I had the music first and was sometimes doing the scenes to fit the music—the opening montage, for instance. [*Rhapsody in Blue plays as the film opens with a series of quick shots of the New York City skyline: dawn, the Empire State Building in silhouette, other skyscrapers, parking lots, streets teeming with pedestrians, the Brooklyn Bridge, neon-lit giant advertisements on Broadway, a Coca-Cola sign, several hotels, snow-covered and lamplit Park Avenue and Central Park, the garment district, a street demonstration. Then as the music swells over the scenery, Ike's voice (Woody's) comes in, as if reading what's he's written.*] Chasing over to Tracy's [*Mariel Hemingway*] house at the end [*to "Strike Up the Band" as he runs down a Manhattan avenue*] I wrote specifically to accommodate music. I knew I wanted a block of musical indulgence, and a number of times I would stretch things out so I could leave myself a lot of room to do a big dose of Gershwin. I rarely do that, but because I knew what music I was using, I very consciously extended scenes to create space on the screen to play it.

But in this one there will be a Mozart clarinet concerto or a Bach piano piece for source music to accompany a dinner scene, say, but the score will use dissonant music.

March 1989

Woody and Sandy Morse are seated in the screening room of the Manhattan Film Center trying to solve two scoring problems in Crimes and Misdemeanors, *one small, one big. The small one is finding the proper place to use "Sweet Georgia Brown." Woody first tried it over a shot of Alan Alda (Lester) walking down a street.*

"It's too much music for that short a cut," he says after seeing the scene. "It should be at the beginning of a longer montage. Do we have anything more we can

Ike running to see Tracy (Mariel Hemingway) at the end of *Manhattan* to the accompaniment of "Strike Up the Band." The scene is purposely long, Woody says, "so I could leave myself a lot of room to do a big dose of Gershwin."

cut in?" *A cut of Lester and a college professor walking while Cliff (Woody) films a documentary is put in.*

The big problem is at the finale when Ben, the blind rabbi played by Sam Waterston, dances with his daughter at her wedding as the music continues into the end credits. Woody has planned to use Irving Berlin's "Always," but when he hears Steven Spielberg is making a film with that title, "like a schmuck I had the office call Spielberg's and ask if the song is a big part of his movie because if so, I wouldn't use it at the end of mine. They are, so I'm dropping it." In the end Berlin's estate withheld permission to use the song; Woody regrets asking Spielberg because he can't find anything as appropriate. An added problem is that with Ben's blindness, a title with "eyes" in it, such as "I Only Have Eyes for You" or "Jeepers Creepers (Where'd You Get Those Peepers?)," makes an unintended joke. Woody and Sandy suggest titles to each other, occasionally getting up to check the backs of albums on the shelves in a large case against a side wall or look through the ASCAP title book (listing all songs registered with the American Society of Composers, Authors and Publishers). He knows virtually every decent song written between 1900 and 1950.

"We've used 'Make Believe' before, in September," Woody says. " 'We'll Meet Again,' but Kubrick used it in . . . in . . . Dr. Strangelove. It has the right sort of schmaltzy sound. 'Speak to Me of Love' . . . 'If I Loved You' . . . 'I Only Have Eyes for You.' [He laughs.] I always do that by accident. It's too bad. It's such a pretty, schmaltzy song. 'As Time Goes By' can't be used. 'I Dream Too Much' we first used up on the roof with [Bob] Balaban. I wouldn't want to use Gershwin because of Manhattan. Cole Porter is the wrong person for end music. 'Falling in Love Is Wonderful,' but a Berlin song can't go beyond the picture. [Meaning Berlin's estate requires that the music must accompany the story.] How about 'I'm Confessin'?"

"That's in September also," Sandy says.

"Okay. [Pause.] I want something with the feel of 'Lara's Theme,' that's a waltz. [Another pause.] 'I'll Be Seeing You' is in Oedipus Wrecks. 'You're Too Beautiful,' we've used. 'Bewitched' we used. 'Isn't It Romantic?' . . ."

"*You don't think that would have gotten away.*" (*It's in* Hannah and Her Sisters.)

"*Nothing by Vernon Duke? Certainly nothing by Duke Ellington. Too jazzy. Porter's too sexy, more of a Latin beat. That's not right. Anything of Leonard Bernstein's? On the Town . . . My Sister Eileen. [Pauses again.] It's all fun in retrospect. It's being faced with the power of decision. There are so many to choose from.*"

(*Weeks later he ends up using "I'll Be Seeing You" because he can find nothing better.*)

.

Not long thereafter, there's a similar problem while scoring Oedipus Wrecks. *Before tackling it, there is a music cue he's still unhappy with and wants to fix. It is for "I Want a Girl" and it comes as his character, talking about his mother to a psychiatrist, says, "I love her but I wish she would disappear." Woody listens a couple of times and then says, "I want to make sure that the hit is a nice rim shot from the last punch line."*

That resolved, Woody stands by the turntable in the editing room, trying to find a piece of piano music to replace Frankie Carle's rendition of "If You Were the Only Girl (in the World)"; the rights are not available. Beside him is a stack of perhaps twenty records he has culled from his shelves. He repeatedly picks up and drops the Victrola arm into the groove of a candidate from Erroll Garner, Earl "Fatha" Hines, and George Shearing, among others, but to no avail. He finds one "too baroque," another "too sweet," a third "like a cocktail bar." His frustration begins to show. "I want a piece of the right age, not too old, no Fats Waller. I want a straightforward melody," he says as he puts on yet another record.

April 2006

EL: What should the music in a film do?

WA: For me, the music enhances the film and sometimes is a lifesaver to a scene—without the music, the scene doesn't work; with the music, it does. If you have a good picture and you put in good music, it's like pushing a winning hand in poker. It's a good feeling. If you have a mediocre picture or a bad picture and you put in good music, you can help yourself a little bit, but you can't save a bad film just with music.

EL: Like the scene in *Take the Money and Run* where you had heavy music behind a comic moment and it didn't work, and then Ralph Rosenblum suggested the Eubie Blake tune.

WA: Yeah, that's a very good example. And it can also be true of a lot of movies when there is no music on the sound track. In a big science fiction picture or an adventure picture you'll see these dazzling scenes and what you're responding to is the sound track. If you look at the cuts without the sound track, you will see a cut of a guy jumping back and a cut of something falling and a cut of a train moving, and the cuts are fine but the cumulative effect is nothing special. But then there's an explosion and you can hear things smashing and screeching—it's alive.

In comedy, I find music is really a help. You can do a dramatic movie and not have any music in it and it can still be very effective. It's not that easy to do in a comedy. I did it once, in *Annie Hall,* but it's better to use music. And sometimes I've used tons of music. It's part of the pleasure of a certain kind of movie that you deliver to the audience. They're getting not only the comedy scenes and the romantic scenes, but those are underscored with the music. As Noël Coward said, "It's extraordinary how potent cheap music is."

EL: We talked before about the scene in *Oedipus Wrecks* where you come home from dinner with Julie Kavner with a boiled chicken leg in tinfoil she's sent with you and you unwrap it with its dripping chicken jelly as you think of her and "All the Things You Are" starts to play. [*"It seems to swell a hair late," he says during editing one day in 1989 while adjusting the timing of the song to the action on the screen. Just a few frames of film either way can make a huge difference.*]

WA: Yeah, the Jerome Kern song.

EL: So anyone who knows the title of the song gets a second emotional cue.

WA: In that picture, too, when those two little old women come to visit me and "Sing Sing Sing" is playing, the music enhances their entrance. [*As mentioned earlier, Woody's character, Sheldon Mills, watches in horror as his mother and aunt make an unannounced visit to his law office. Gene Krupa's beat on the tom-tom signals trouble when his secretary interrupts a meeting with the head of the firm to tell him of the visit, then Benny Goodman's clarinet swings up as the scene cuts to a long hallway where the two little old ladies wearing* Cats *buttons march inexorably toward him. "Ominous," Woody said, red-faced with laughter as he watched the scene with music for the first time.*] I used "Sing Sing Sing" again in *Manhattan Murder Mystery* when we're chasing after the killer and he disposes of the body— it enhances the excitement of that scene.

I remember once sitting in the cutting room with Dick Hyman while I was scoring *Broadway Danny Rose.* I asked him, "Which do you think is more effective?" I had him look at a fast song at the end and he said, "I love that." Then I had him look at a slow song, and he said, "Hey, wait a minute, I love *that,* too." Because each one gave a completely different feeling at the end. And I must tell you [*he starts to laugh*], I haven't seen the picture in a long time and I don't really know which one we wound up using. [*It is a slow Italian piece.*] It's funny, they all melt together.

EL: Most of the time you use existing songs, almost always from the 1920s through the 1940s. Why?

WA: When I started, I worked with Marvin Hamlisch [*who wrote the music for* Take the Money and Run *and* Bananas], which was great. I had a couple of pictures scored after that. But it's always a hassle. First of all, it's an expense—not that clearing permissions for existing songs isn't—and you're dependent on the composer coming up with the right score. He goes home and he writes his heart out and then he comes in and he plays the songs—and you think they're not right. And the guy is heartbroken and tries to sell me on it and I don't really want to be sold on it; I just don't think it's right. Even though the music may be beautiful, I just don't feel it for that spot. Then he has to write something else and then maybe something else and he becomes surly because he's on the third version and you keep turning down what he does. Then I feel, Gee, I can't keep doing this to the guy. It's not right. Or he writes it to fill the scene and then at the last minute I decide I want to cut down the scene by six feet, so then his music cue doesn't fit anymore.

Choosing the music myself, I'm sitting in the cutting room and I have a gigantic library of the world's music and I go in the other room and pick out a recording. If it doesn't work, I take it off. If it's expensive, I don't use it. If at a later date I decide that the scene is going to be half as long and it doesn't work, I take it right out and find another song. And the audience always has the pleasure of the extra evocation of the song. If the audience is hearing an original score and if the composer happens to write a dazzling score and you're going to be humming it like the *Gone with the Wind* score fifty years later, that's one thing. But short of that, when you hear

In *Oedipus Wrecks* Sheldon (Woody) ponders a chicken leg sent home with him after a meal cooked by Treva (Julie Kavner), the nice Jewish girl his mother vastly prefers to the WASP Lisa (Mia Farrow) to whom he is engaged.

my scores, you can be hearing Django Reinhardt or Erroll Garner or Coleman Hawkins playing a beautiful tune by a great composer, playing it with a lot of feeling and a lot of rhythm and it gives you a good feeling just to hear the music. Frequently the music I have in is better than my movie—a great artist is playing Cole Porter or George Gershwin. It's what Marshall Brickman calls "borrowed grandeur."

I use popular songs of the 1920s, 1930s, 1940s—the golden era of song: Gershwin, Kern, Porter, Berlin—because it's my kind of music. I can't think of doing it any other way. The best time I have is scoring. What I'd like to do, which I haven't done in years and years, is score something with my band, myself playing. But you've got to have the right movie and I haven't had the right movie since *Sleeper.*

EL: You have all that music literally at your fingertips, both physically on the records but also in your head. Could you do it as well if you didn't have the music in your memory?

WA: I have a casual but pretty good knowledge of music because over the decades, when I get in the shower in the morning and when I shave and get dressed, I'm always listening to something—it can be jazz, classical, opera, pop—so I've heard a ton of music and I can always dig out something from my memory. But there are plenty of times when we will call up the Colony record shop on Broadway and say, "We need something like 'Sing Sing Sing,' something in a kind of minor key. What have you got there?" We call them "the fishmongers" [*laughs*]. What's fresh today?

EL: What is it about jazz that makes you want to draw on it so much?

WA: I put in the music that I like to listen to because it's my movie [*laughs*]. A certain kind of jazz is great music for comedy because it's up and lively. I really

don't go beyond the swing era because it's important that the beat be simple and the music melodic. It would be hard to do a score with Charlie Parker and Dizzy Gillespie—in a *comedy*. You could use their music for a serious film. And once in a while I can sneak some Thelonious Monk in there.

Also, I can't score easily with my idols. I'd never use Jelly Roll Morton or George Lewis. I've only used two pieces by Sidney Bechet. Once in *Sweet and Lowdown*, and I only used it because the lyrics [*of "Viper Mad"*] were great for the party Sean [*Penn*] goes to in the movie; I also used a very, very atypical Sidney Bechet record, where he plays "Tropical Mood Meringue," which he did do not that well and not that successfully and is not considered part of his serious work in any way. I've never been able to use Louis Armstrong for scoring. I've featured him, as I did in *Stardust Memories,* but like Lewis and Bechet, I can't use him innocuously in the background; it would bother me too much, their music is too meaningful for me.

Now, I also love many of the people who I do use for background music. I've had a lot of success with Ben Webster, Coleman Hawkins, Django Reinhardt, Erroll Garner, because their music is highly melodic and it swings. I've used Benny Goodman a lot, who's not really an idol of mine, though I love his background sound.

EL: When you don't use jazz you often use classical music. For instance, you were going to use Stravinsky to score *Love and Death* but you changed to Prokofiev, which gave the film a very sprightly sound. Because the movie takes place in Russia I understand why you'd want Russian music as a counterpoint, but why did you change composers? And what of Stravinsky's would you have used?

WA: I've since used a little Stravinsky. I used the Concerto in D in *Melinda and Melinda.* We would have taken some of the ballets, some of *The Rite of Spring,* some of *Dumbarton Oaks* and integrated them, but they were all too dissonant— and expensive. Ralph Rosenblum said we should try Prokofiev's *Lieutenant Kijé Suite* for a spot and it worked very well. So we tried another and another and made it all Prokofiev. [*Among the other pieces are the* Alexander Nevsky *cantata and* The Love for Three Oranges.]

EL: Why did you make the choice to have so little music in *Annie Hall,* including over the titles and end credits?

WA: At that time I was very much interested in Bergman's work and Bergman never used music; I felt he must know something. [*Bergman once said that the combination of music and film is "barbarous."*] I figured, he's so good, if he doesn't think music is right, I probably have a blind spot. I used source music [*music already recorded*]. And I didn't use music in *Interiors.* But as I started to get a little more confident I thought, Well, that's really not the way *I* feel movies. I feel them with music. To me, music has a special importance, a special meaning.

EL: Will you define that a little more?

WA: It's really a very consistent part of self-expression, and my movies have been very self-expressive; that's mistaken for autobiography. They're expressive of observations of mine or feelings of mine, but what you're seeing on the screen much more often than not are total fabrications, but those fabrications are in the service of my feelings. So in its most reduced, silly form, I'm, for example, not going to make a film that extols Nazism, whereas I will make a film that has a politically Democratic point of view. I'm always going to make films that express my personal feelings about the meaninglessness of life and the horror of existence.

EL: We talked about *Everyone Says I Love You* about five years ago but I want to check up on it now. I know you wanted people to sing songs you like, in regular voices.

WA: There are people who adore and revere voices like Frank Sinatra and Barbra Streisand. These are miraculous voices of our time. But there are other people like myself who get a kick out of Jimmy Durante's voice and Jerry Lewis singing. And then there are people who walk down the street singing or who sing in the shower, and it's perfectly fine listening to them—for me. Someone else can hate it but I don't, so I made a film of that. It fulfilled the desire that keeps me working.

EL: Do you sing in the shower? Do you break into song from time to time like the characters in the film?

WA: I have. I used to do it more. Then I found the shower was an extremely good place to think, as I mentioned earlier. It's a change of environment and a relaxing one and a total refresher.

EL: You say the music of the 1920s, 1930s, and 1940s gives the picture a certain style, but you're also able by picking a song with a title to give a subliminal message to the audience. An obvious example is in *Manhattan,* when you play "Someone to Watch over Me" as Mary and Ike [*Diane Keaton and Woody*] sit on a bench in Sutton Place after talking all night, silhouetted against the East River and the Queensborough Bridge by the breaking dawn. The music tells us that two people who didn't get along are now quickly falling for each other.

WA: Right. I very often try to pick something that has some kind of irony or some kind of relation to the movie. This is particularly true in the title music of pictures. So I'll use, say, "What Is This Thing Called Love?" [Husbands and Wives] or "With Plenty of Money and You" [Small Time Crooks], because there's no action on the screen. If I'm scoring in the picture itself I might have a piece of music that fits the action of the scene perfectly even if the title of the song or the lyrics don't, because it's so appropriate. I can do anything I want and that's always fun for me.

EL: Apart from the musical and *Radio Days*, was the scoring of one film particularly pleasurable?

WA: There are a few; for me the music in *Stardust Memories* is sensational—which had nothing to do with me. I just put the records in. [*"Stardust," played by Louis Armstrong and His Orchestra; "If Dreams Come True," performed by Chick Webb and His Orchestra; Django Reinhardt's renditions of "I'll See You in My Dreams" and "Body and Soul"; Lester Young with Count Basie and His Orchestra playing "Tickletoe"; Dick Hyman's "Hebrew School Rag," Cole Porter's "Easy to Love" and "Just One of Those Things"; Mussorgsky's* Night on Bald Mountain; *Marie Lane singing "Brazil"; Burt Kalmer and Harry Rubin's "Three Little Words"; the Original Dixieland Jazz Band (the first band to make a jazz recording, in 1917) playing "Palesteena"; Sidney Bechet playing "Tropical Mood Meringue"; Count Basie's "One O'clock Jump," "Sugar," and "Sweet Georgia Brown"; and Glenn Miller's "Moonlight Serenade."*]

EL: We've talked about this in another context, but are there times when you're writing a scene when you think, Say, Coleman Hawkins would be great here?

WA: I have done it at times, though I can't recall them at the moment. But I do recall when I was doing *Manhattan*, thinking, Shoot this scene much longer, because I wanted to have material up on the screen to accommodate the Michael Tilson Thomas overtures. Now, we did the Gershwin music with Zubin Mehta and the New York Philharmonic because it was a Manhattan picture. But I was writing and shooting to accommodate music, things that didn't make any sense unless you knew the music. When we were filming, some of the crew were wondering, Why is this taking so long to do? But I was thinking to myself, When you see this with the music, you'll see what I mean. And in most cases I was right because the music was so pretty. But as usual, not in every case, and I had to throw that stuff away.

EL: Any other times where you were writing the script that you knew the music?

WA: Yes, when I was writing the murder part of *Crimes and Misdemeanors* I knew that I was going to be using the Schubert piece [*the first movement of his String Quartet in G*], which is ominous and dramatic. I knew when I was writing it that the Martin Landau character was going to be getting out of his car and going to find the body.

EL: I like the opera music in *Match Point.* It is perfect accompaniment for some very operatic action. When did you get the idea for Caruso?

WA: We had no money for a score and I said to [*associate producer*] Helen Robin, "Maybe I'll do it like I did years ago, with no music whatsoever." *Interiors* had no music and even *Annie Hall* had only source music, as I said. I needed some opera because the people in the film go to the opera and it occurred to me that we could get some of these vintage opera arias off foreign labels very inexpensively. And then it just so happens—luck again, like so much with that film—that a company was putting out a package of all of Caruso's work. And when we told them we were interested in using some, they gave us a fantastically good price on it. The package was coming out simultaneously with the movie, so it was mutual advantage.

EL: You chose the music after the film was done? You had no thought of this beforehand?

WA: Right. And I wanted the recordings to sound old on the tracks, to have the audience hear the crackles and to know that it was old recordings, not score. They lent a warm and interesting feeling. Without it seeming like old recordings, the music seemed too slick for me. I always hate what they do on old jazz CDs to sanitize them. They always sound terrible but "clean" for people who are buying clean and have no connection to the music. So I always buy LPs. Here I was able to get the real old sound.

EL: Are there other instances where you've thought of the music in advance?

WA: I always knew that I was going to be using [*Albert W. Ketèlbey's*] "In a Persian Market" in both the mother in the sky [*in* Oedipus Wrecks *the mother of*

David Ogden Stiers as the malevolent Voltan hypnotizes insurance detective C. W. Briggs (Woody) and his coworker and nemesis Betty Ann Fitzgerald (Helen Hunt) in *The Curse of the Jade Scorpion.* Woody feels that "it may be the worst film I've made."

Woody's character appears in the sky over Manhattan and kibitzes with pedestrians] and the hypnotist scene in *Jade Scorpion* [*in which David Ogden Stiers maliciously hypnotizes Woody and Helen Hunt*]. I only wish I could have used it again. It would have been great for some places in *Scoop*.

EL: Do you have the same feeling of relief—or is it pleasure—when you get to the point where you can score the movie that you have when you've thought through the screenplay and are finally able to begin writing?

WA: Yes, it's very pleasurable. When you get to the scoring, you've cut the picture together and every addition you make is going to be a plus. There's no downside. You can't do anything but enhance your picture. If one piece of music doesn't work, you try another one, and another one. And if nothing works, then nothing works.

EL: Do songs come to mind when you're watching dailies and editing? Do you make notes?

WA: I make them all the time—sometimes when I start to shoot on the set I think to myself, This will be a great scene if I score it with classical music and not jazz. Or sometimes when we're editing, we edit with the music as we go along. That is, we don't go to the next scene until we have this one scored. When you don't, you often have to make a lot of trims subsequently. Because when you are editing a chase scene or a walking scene or a driving scene without scoring it, you make it to a length that's appropriate when it's silent. And then suddenly you put this piece of Django Reinhardt or Benny Goodman behind it and you think, Oh, it should be triple this length. It's very disappointing that it runs out here. Or vice versa.
Then again, sometimes we're hot on the editing and if I don't have a particular song in my head I don't want to say, "Let's take a half hour off and figure the perfect piece of music for this scene."

EL: Did you do that with *Match Point*? Some of the scenes, like when he shoots the women, seem so perfectly matched.

WA: No, all that was silent for a long time. Then when we stuck *Othello* behind it it just seemed right.

EL: Did you have to tweak much?

WA: I had to tweak the music a bit to make a musical cut. We had a lot of fortuitous matches between sections, but we didn't have one when Scarlett was coming up in the elevator and I had to get to a different part of the music. [*Nola is returning to her apartment to meet Chris, who has led her to believe he is ready to leave his wife for her but actually is lying in wait to kill her. The music plays as the action cuts back and forth between Nola traveling home and Chris loading his shotgun; the musical cut is made in the last sequence, in which she rides in the elevator and is shot after getting out.*] So if you know *Othello* or speak Italian, you'd notice it, but I don't think you'd notice that much because you're engrossed in the movie. I've spoken to opera people who have seen the movie and none of them have said to me, "Hey, what did you do there, you put a cut in *Othello*?" [*He laughs.*] That will come later, after it's hung around for a while.

EL: When ideas come to you about which music to use, do they stay in your mind like plotlines do when you're thinking through the story, or do you have to write them down?

WA: Months later it's still there. It's no effort. Once you think "Sing Sing Sing" would be great in a given spot, when you're editing it three months later, it's the first thing that comes to mind.

EL: Music from the 1920s through the 1940s is a signature of your films.

WA: Yeah—if I was satirizing my movies [*pauses and smiles*] I would do the black-and-white titles and some sort of jazz music, Duke Ellington, say, and then probably have somebody talking to the audience and do broad stuff about the meaning of life.

EL: Apart from playing with your band to do a score and doing an original musical, is there anything special with music you'd like to do on-screen?

WA: I've always wanted to do something about New Orleans jazz, but I could never get the budget for it. But if someone would give me $80 million, $100 million—which they'd be insane to do—I could do a great American jazz movie. I don't mean a story about a guy who plays the trumpet and his girlfriend leaves him [Sweet and Lowdown *is, among other things, the story of a jazz guitarist whose girlfriend leaves him*]. I mean a story about the beginning of jazz and how jazz evolved in New Orleans and came to Chicago and New York and spread all over the world.

I've always wanted to trace the lives of Sidney Bechet and Louis Armstrong because these were two young kids who met in New Orleans and grew up in there—two emerging geniuses and two absolutely dazzling soloists. I've always felt Bechet was superior to Armstrong, although at that level it's like saying Velázquez was better than Goya. Louis was an internationally beloved icon, worshiped beyond all measure, and nobody worships him more than me, yet I get embarrassed when people say, "This is the greatest musical talent of the twentieth century." I don't necessarily feel that way even though I do feel he was magnificent beyond compare. Sidney was magnificent, too, yet he is almost totally unknown and has had no real commercial life and certainly no iconic status except some in France for the past years. And as Louis's life led him to dining at Buckingham Palace, Sidney was serving jail time for shooting somebody. I could make a great film about it.

EL: For years I saw you doodle "American Blues" on scraps of paper while you edited. Now I know why.

WA: Yeah, I would love to make that movie. I feel I could re-create New Orleans and the birth of jazz better than anybody else because I think I'm the only film director around who has that particular passion and knowledge. But I'd need a carload of money.

EL: What makes it so expensive?

WA: You have to re-create New Orleans at that time, then you have to go to Chicago, to some of the clubs, then New York. Sidney went over to Europe. This little thing that started with slaves chanting to each other and singing spiritual songs in church grew to be America's major contribution as an art form and after a period of time it's revered all over the world, from Africa to England to Japan.

The big guys squander $90 million, $100 million, $120 million left and right on films they lose their shirts on. So they can lose their shirts with me. [*He laughs heartily.*] I could *guarantee* it.

EL: Is there another musical film you'd like to do?

WA: Yes, I'd like to do an original musical in the United States. That would interest me. I would have somebody write the score and lyrics and I would do a book musical. I would have fun doing that.

You know, the musical has developed and progressed, but it hasn't always progressed in a direction that interests me. The kind of musicals I like are old musicals. I don't know if there is an audience for them. If tomorrow some of the musicals I like opened on Broadway for the first time, I wonder if they'd be successful at all or as successful as they were.

It wouldn't be like *Everyone Says I Love You*. For this I would need real singers because it's a different concept entirely. But again, I don't think anybody's going to wake me up in the middle of the night to give me the money for it.

EL: Have you seen *The Pajama Game*? [*A revival has recently opened on Broadway.*]

WA: No.

EL: Is that beyond the period you like? [*It debuted in 1957.*]

WA: It's just about the transitional period. It's okay but wasn't one of my emotional favorites.

EL: Which are?

WA: I like the ones that everybody liked—*Guys and Dolls, My Fair Lady, The Music Man.* Of the movies I liked *Singin' in the Rain,* of course, and *Meet Me in St. Louis,* and *Gigi.* And I also liked the film version of *My Fair Lady. The Band Wagon* was fun. From an earlier era, *On the Town.* That antiquated style is more fun to me. Same thing for me when I see a play in a theater. I can appreciate other things, but I really like when the curtain goes up and regular human beings are in a predicament of sorts, emotional or external, some kind of predicament I can get with. I've never seen a production of *Waiting for Godot* that I can sit through. I would not dare to presume to be critical of Samuel Beckett, but no matter how you cut it, I don't enjoy the play. It just doesn't mean anything to me. When the curtain opens I like it to be about people like those in *Death of a Salesman, A Streetcar Named Desire,* or *Who's Afraid of Virginia Woolf,* plays in which I get sucked into the lives of the people.

EL: What are your budgets for music these days?

WA: Currently, other than *Match Point,* I'm working on very tiny musical budgets, so I've really got to use ingenuity. One of the areas in which the budget for the Paris film escalated so much was music; because of the nature of the film it could not be done on a minuscule music budget. [*The film, to be shot in the summer of 2006, was cancelled two months before work was to begin because it had become too expensive.*] My normal music budget is about $750,000—a lot, considering the last couple of films I've only had between $150,000 and $200,000 to work with. So fortunately opera worked for me on *Match Point* and I was able to be parsimonious with *Scoop.*

EL: You've often said that you don't like any music after about 1950. In fact, you once told me, "I don't know anything about music after about 1950. Listening to it is a punishment. I only like classical and jazz."

WA: I got lost in the shuffle of contemporary music. When I see someone like Billie Holiday or Frank Sinatra singing a Cole Porter tune or a Jerome Kern tune or Gershwin quietly, you can hear the lyric and hear the melody. Then you see four guys with guitars and ten thousand people lifting their friends up over their shoulders and the guys are all bare-chested and the audience is bare-chested and the guys all have streaks painted on their faces and they're smashing their guitars and the music is amplified beyond belief—it just doesn't mean anything to me. It's clear that I've been left behind, but that's okay with me.

I'm sure it's my loss because all the people I know and respect—Diane Keaton is a prime example—love contemporary music. Music that came with groups post–Elvis Presley, they have a tinge of ruralness to me, which I don't like. They are mostly all guitars and drums—that's the instrumentation—and a singer will be talking to you sounding like Winston Churchill, then he will start to sing and he sounds like Grand Ole Opry. They go into their bluesy or down-home voice or whatever it is. I like cosmopolitan instrumentation—a singer in a piano bar, someone playing trumpet quietly. I don't want to hear him singing like a country singer, or a white guy singing like a black singer. It's like when I go to a movie: If on the first shot they throw a flag on a taxi meter, I stay. If they throw a flag on a mailbox, I don't. There's something that puts me off. Maybe what I'm really saying is that I want what I grew up on, and younger people are saying, "I want what *I* grew up on." But I've been able to put the music I want in my movies, the music that's meaningful to me.

EL: I'm reminded of a number of times you've turned to first Sandy and now [*film editor*] Alisa [*Lepselter*] to help you find a contemporary song. There is the scene in the comic part of *Melinda and Melinda* where Will Ferrell sneaks downstairs and listens at Radha Mitchell's apartment door, where she's with a guy. You wanted to hear a seductive song coming from inside. After a couple of minutes someone suggested Barry White. All the editing assistants, in their twenties and thirties, jumped on it and one went out to get a CD and suggested using "Come On," which you did. But of course, you had never heard of him.

WA: Whenever I want source music that's contemporary I always have to say to them, "Who would you be playing at this party?" And they always put their heads together and come up with a singer.

I remember when I was doing the promotion for *Melinda* some girl was saying to me, "Your choice of the music was so brilliant," and she mentioned Barry White and I said [*starts to laugh*], "Well, *of course*. Who else am I going to get for something like that?"

Fall 2006

Editing and scoring for Cassandra's Dream *is about done.*

EL: Before you left to shoot *Cassandra's Dream,* I asked you if you had given any thought to the music for it. You said you hadn't and added: "I know the picture is dramatic enough that if it doesn't have any music it will still work. So at least I don't feel panicked that if we need a certain kind of music I won't be able to afford it. I do know that because it's dramatic it probably won't be lilting jazz. It will probably be something special. I don't think standards are indicated in the script. I may between now and when we start shooting in July write something into the script so I can get the music I want. For instance, just as we're talking now, there's a line where a character is looking for a house and he says, 'I need someplace where I can practice my trumpet and I'm not going to be disturbed.' Now, this doesn't figure into the story in any way other than that line. But it's conceivable—I'm making this up right now—that if I have him enjoy the music of Miles Davis, that would give me an organic sound for the whole movie."

But you abandoned using Davis and instead asked Philip Glass to write a score. What happened with Davis? And what made you think of Glass?

WA: I couldn't come up with a way to use him. The closest I could do was the guy's trumpet. But then when I found out what Miles Davis cost . . . [*He rolls his eyes.*] The trumpet line is still in the movie. In retrospect I don't think Miles would have worked and there was no way we could have afforded him.

The idea for Philip Glass came after a lot of small talk with my assistant Sarah [*Allentuch*] and with my friends about what would be good for this picture. Nobody had any really great ideas because there were no really great ideas to be had. I was always aware that hiring someone to score the picture is affordable. A composer is less because with all those jazz records you're not only getting the rights to Miles Davis, you're paying the musicians or their estates and paying the record companies. In the past I've had extremely high music budgets, I've had *ridiculous* music budgets on pictures where I use twenty songs and those songs cost $5,000 or $10,000 each and more. We've paid in the twenties and thirties of thousands for songs. We've spent around a half million dollars just to score a picture.

The idea of Philip Glass felt very good for the movie. As soon as I mentioned it, everybody said, "*I* was going to say that," and they were because he's the logical choice for the movie. The movie is kind of tragic in feeling and he seemed like someone whose work was full of, you know [*smiles*], suffering and angst. It seemed like it wouldn't be a Hollywood score, it would be a score full of feeling that was appropriate to the story.

So we called Philip Glass and showed him the script and he was very interested. I didn't know him at all, but of course I know his work and I was trepidatious about not only working with a composer but a very strong composer where I might have had problems, which has happened before. But it's worked out very well. He's given me very good music and I found him very pleasant and easy to work with. You know what you're buying, to begin with, so there wasn't going to be a big discrepancy between what I wanted and what he provided. There were times when I would say, "No, that's a little too heavy" or "That's a little too light" or "A little too much music there." The usual finessing of cues. But I found him to be no problem whatsoever. I guess he's so good that he's confident and so there's never a sense of threat or ego.

EL: How different was it to work with him?

WA: It was interesting. Scoring before was tedious and took months but with Philip it's nothing like that. He came in and saw the picture and four days later we had a ton of music. We didn't know in the beginning where we wanted spots so we erred on the side of having him write too much. But if you have a ton of music it starts to get overwhelming, and I said to him, "I don't want this to be *Frankenstein* or *Dracula*."

Then whenever I needed a different cue I'd call him and say, "Your cue didn't work here," and he was never defensive. The next morning you'd get a new cue. It was like having the record collection—give me this one.

The funny thing is, his music is so riddled with apprehension. I'd say, "This is a casual scene. The music seems too apprehensive." And he'd say, "Oh, no, that's the *romantic* stuff. The apprehensive stuff I'm saving for the murder."

I was thinking, My God, what is going to happen? But he's wonderful. He was always enthused over our ideas and very compliant. It's still easier for me to use recordings, but then you don't get to work with a genius.

8

THE CAREER

January 2000

Woody has written and directed thirty films in the past thirty years and grown from a comedian who has taken up filming his own work into one of the world's most respected filmmakers. His influence (though he will deny it) is visible in a new generation of moviemakers. Just as Take the Money and Run *and* Bananas *were successors to the anarchic comedy of the Marx Brothers, the faux documentary style of* Take the Money *paved the way for what has become known as mockumentaries, among them* This Is Spinal Tap *(directed by Rob Reiner), the films of Christopher Guest* (Waiting for Guffman, Best in Show, A Mighty Wind, *etc.), and, of course,* Zelig. Annie Hall, *considered a romantic comedy, might more appropriately be thought of as funny but much more as a story about the psychological underpinnings of romantic relationships. Without* Annie Hall, *it is hard to imagine, say,* When Harry Met Sally, Sleepless in Seattle, *and a wave of independent romantic films that followed.*

Woody and I talk over several days about his life and work. He is sixty-four at the time and—there is no better word—content, a feeling I seldom have seen in him. He and Soon-Yi Previn married in Venice in 1997 (they have been together since 1992) and are recent parents of a daughter, Bechet, named, of course, in honor of Sidney Bechet. (In 2001 a second daughter, Manzie, after jazz drummer Manzie Johnson, came along.) He and his family and his jazz band had just returned from a string of concert performances in Europe; Woody says he "was shocked by how much I loved Barcelona and Madrid. I thought they would be nice cities and that would be that, but they're incredible. Spain is a strong market for my films. In Europe I generally do pretty well. In the United States, as you know, even when I get critical support, it often doesn't translate into box office."

EL: To what do you attribute your longevity as a filmmaker?

WA: [*Pauses a moment*] I was thinking in the not too distant future of writing a piece entitled "How Have I Lasted?" I toyed with it but I thought it was too self-centered. I was turning sixty-four and I'd been working since I was sixteen and I wondered how I lasted. For example, who's my audience? My audience was never college kids when it should have been. It's certainly not college kids now. It's not red-staters, not Bible Belters, not most of America. It's not intellectuals, either—I could point to a whole slew of them who have never supported my work. I've never been a big money earner, always demanded total artistic control of my movies even in the face of a string of unprofitable pictures—and I've gotten total control always. I mean, talk about irrationality.

Richard Schickel [*author and longtime film writer for* Time] wrote a very nice essay about me once, saying that my audience left me at a certain point. And I thought that was the one thing he had wrong. It was that *I* left *them; they* didn't leave *me.* They were very nice and if I had continued to live up to my end of the contract, they showed no signs of wanting to leave me and be anything other than a nice affectionate audience. *I* was the one that moved in a different direction, and a good-sized portion of them felt annoyed and betrayed. They didn't like it when I did *Interiors* and *Stardust Memories.* One critic said that *Interiors* was an act of bad faith. I thought that was an overreaction. I tried to make a particular film and if it didn't work, it didn't work. That's fine. I completely respect the opinions of those people for whom it didn't. But it wasn't made in bad faith.

Then *Stardust Memories* put people off and over the years the audience got more and more uncomfortable with me, unsure of what my next movie might be and less assured they'd enjoy it. A lot of people still think my best films were around the era of *Annie Hall* and *Manhattan,* but while those movies might hold a warm place in their hearts—for which I'm delighted—they're wrong. Movies like *Husbands and Wives, Purple Rose of Cairo, Bullets over Broadway, Zelig,* even *Manhattan Murder Mystery* and *Sweet and Lowdown,* are far superior. Of course, these things are matters of opinion, but I go by my own just as others go by theirs.

Now, it's true after the first few films I gave up caring about popularity or audiences or what's written about my movies, but this was not out of arrogance or any feeling of superiority. It was just that that part of the process—the so-called reward—wasn't making me happy or satisfied. People often misread my shyness for aloofness, but it's not. I needed a spiritual center and being an atheist, they're hard to come by. So I experienced a kind of apathy toward success or failure and, sadly, even life in general. Both success and failure have proven not to mean much to me in ways I thought they would when I was starting out. Neither does much to rectify the real problems of life.

The flip side of being what my friends call "immune to criticism" is being unable to enjoy the pleasure a resounding success brings. This is not to say I hate the money but, put succinctly, despite all the adulation in the world one remains annoyingly finite. [*Shrugs, then laughs.*] So as I was saying, my shyness and my inability to shake off a dark cloud that comes with coming to grips with reality causes people to think I'm distant or not approachable, but I'm not at all aloof or even reclusive—which is another description of me that's not accurate. Incidentally, this doesn't mean I wouldn't share many of the severest criticisms of my work if I hear about them. I have a very critical eye for my work and for other people's. I used to read about myself but I completely stopped, because talk about unhelpful distractions—the absurdity of reading you're a comic genius or in bad faith. Who needs to ponder such outlandish nonsense?

I will say Soon-Yi has opened me up more. I wish I had met her when I was younger. I always bounced in and out of relationships, none of them really working for me—or for the other person—then, in the most absurd, accidental, preposterous way I stumble awkwardly into a relationship with a young Korean who I've got very little in common with and it works like a charm. My theory has always been, when it comes to relationships, you can try and try but you have to luck out, and I lucked out. I mean, what am I doing with a woman who's got her master's in special education with an interest in teaching learning-disabled children and who never has seen *Annie Hall* nor three-quarters of my movies and [*laughs*] whose idea of lunch is a tuna melt?

Anyway, you ask how have I lasted—particularly given all my flaws, my limitations both artistically and as a person, my phobias, my idiosyncrasies, and my artistic pretensions and absolute creative demands in a venal, cutthroat industry—operating with only a minor gift? Here's the answer: As a kid I loved magic and might have become a magician if I hadn't been sidetracked. And so, using all my sleight-of-hand skill, my misdirection, my subtle subterfuges and showmanship—that is, everything I've learned from poring over my magic books as a kid—I've been able to pull off a brilliant illusion that has lasted now over fifty years and includes scores of movies. Houdini, Blackstone, Thurston, all the prestidigitators of my youth would have been proud. [*He shrugs.*] I wish I was kidding.

November 2005–November 2006

This is an unsettled period for Woody. First he is set to film a drama in London in the summer of 2006 but at the last moment he pulls out because the deal is not quite right. Within two or three days, there is an opportunity to make a romantic comedy in Paris, a favorite place. He quickly puts the script into shape—the story is different from the one for London—and starts to cast it but then finds to his great sadness that there simply is not a large enough budget to make the film he envisions and give it the right score, as mentioned earlier. Yet all is not lost, as soon after that, the London deal comes together satisfactorily.

"I love the Paris picture," he says in June, days before going to London, "and I had already cast a couple of people that I love. Michelle Williams, who's so gifted, was just perfect for the girl. As the guy, I cast David Krumholtz. I've always wanted to use him and he was just right for the role. But the budget escalated so precipitously that even with the complete contribution of my salary, which I was more than willing to do, it still was millions over. [He laughs ruefully and shakes his head.] *But I was so looking forward to working in Paris and living in Paris for an extended period of time and shooting there. It just broke my heart, but there just was no way to do it. So I switched over and went from doing an extremely romantic fanciful movie to doing a very serious movie, like* Match Point.*"*

EL: Will you make the Paris film another time if someone has the money?

WA: Oh, in a second. I'm hoping that somebody will step up at some point. Maybe if I have a couple of commercial successes someone will ask, "How much do you need for that Paris film?" I'd need an additional $5 million, and then some I'd contribute part of my salary.

EL: This will be your third summer in a row in London. Does it feel like going home?

WA: Well, it's a very comfortable feeling because the people are wonderful and it's wonderful to make a movie there. And I'm going to the best weather that I could hope to shoot in, the summer—gray and cool.

EL: Have you given more thought to writing that piece called "How Have I Lasted?"

WA: No, not serious thought. But it is still a mystery to me. I've been around for years and I've done so many pictures that have not made very much money and I've been able to maintain myself in the business with a lot of freedom—total freedom. It's a combination of good luck, deception [*starts to laugh*], and overestimation.

EL: I'd like to go through your work, starting with the kind of oddball ones that are unrelated to your writing and directing. [*I hold up a piece of paper on which I've written every film he's been in. Those he has written and directed to this point total thirty-seven, but there are a dozen others as well.*]

WA: Those are mine? [*He looks at the list a moment.*] Uh-huh. [*Not impressed or surprised*] Well, sure, I keep working. I keep adding to it.

EL: We've talked a lot over the years about *What's New Pussycat?*

WA: Yeah. Not a nice experience.

EL: Has anything changed to make it any better?

WA: No, no. The big lesson from that was if a picture is successful but you're not happy with it, it's an unhappy experience not worth anything. At that age [*he was in his late twenties when he began work on the film*] I had, or fancied myself having, an artistic temperament, and I was plunged into Hollywood at its most venal.

EL: Is there anything mitigating in that it allowed you to get started on your own?

WA: At the time it came out, Charlie Joffe said to me, "Well, it's successful but the studio people are saying, 'It's all Peter Sellers and Peter O'Toole.'" And I remember thinking to myself, Someday the importance of that picture will be that it was my first foray into movies. That was the kind of moronic confidence I had when I was younger [*laughs*].

Then I was at the video store a year ago, looking for something to rent, and I saw a copy of *What's New Pussycat?* And on the box it headlined, "Woody Allen's debut film," so I got a sort of ironic pleasure out of that, a guilty pleasure of being unjustifiably self-confident [*laughs*].

EL: Do you think you needed that kind of high confidence to get started?

WA: I had great confidence when I started. Not just when I started in films but in show business.

EL: You've told me you knew you could make your friends laugh.

WA: More than that. When I wrote my first television show [*Stanley, starring Buddy Hackett as the operator of a cigarette shop in a posh hotel lobby; the show aired live during the 1956–57 season*], one review said that "Buddy Hackett could

Woody in his first scene (it's with Peter Sellers) in *What's New Pussycat?*, shot on his twenty-ninth birthday

ad-lib a funnier show than this." I cut that out and put it at the head of a scrapbook I was keeping at the time and I got great pleasure out of it because I thought, Oh, this is going to be just perfect in its irony later. That kind of confidence can only come from being very young—I was nineteen, twenty years old—or just a kind of stupidity that I also had [*laughs*].

EL: There's that scene in *Pussycat* you did with Peter Sellers on the quay. I've always thought if they could have showcased both of you it would have been funnier.

WA: Yeah, but he was a monster star and a monster talent. One of the few deserving talents, I felt.

EL: I've never asked you how it was to perform with him.

WA: It was just fine. Peter's problems [*drug and alcohol abuse, a compulsion to do impersonations—"It was like being married to the United Nations," his first wife said*], which I was never privy to but they were sort of legendary, were always off-screen. It was absolutely fine to act with him.

EL: Did he ad-lib a lot?

WA: He did ad-lib a lot, yes, but I liked that. He was someone whose ad-libs were valuable, and I ad-libbed a lot, too. So that was just fine.

EL: How were you feeling when you did that? I know you were confident of your talent, but people were messing terribly with your script.

WA: I'd never written a movie before, but I felt if everyone would get out of my way, I could make a funny movie here. But the studio, represented by Charles Feldman, was too powerful and too hands-on. The director [*Clive Donner*] was a very sweet guy. Peter O'Toole was a wonderful guy. Peter Sellers. The women in the cast—Paula Prentiss and Capucine and all of them—were very nice people. But Charlie Feldman ran that thing with an iron hand. And I kept thinking, Just get out of my way and let me show you how to do this.

EL: The interesting thing about Feldman was that twenty years before then and for a long time leading up to this film, he had a sharp sense for the right idea, but it seems that this was really the end of his run.

WA: Yeah, I remember people said to me, "If you think *Charlie's* trouble or a monster, he's like Mr. Charm compared to the other studio heads and producers. He's one of the best ones in terms of going out to dinner with and hanging out with." And from that point of view he was fine. He just had a block, some kind of psychological block, which prevented him from telling the truth. So it was hard to work with him.

I guess the redeeming thing about the film was that I got to spend eight months in Paris and I developed a love for the city. I have a regret, or a kind of semi-regret, that I didn't stay there. Two of the girls who did the costumes [*Mia Fonssagrives and Vicky Tiel*] liked Paris so much they stayed and lived and worked there. I didn't have their independence of spirit or originality.

EL: Can you imagine what might have happened if you had stayed there?

WA: It took a more adventurous soul than me to do it, and it's a shame. There are many people I know at my age who say, "I have no regrets." [*Big laugh.*] I have nothing but a million regrets. [*Smiles.*] I don't really have a million regrets but that is one. [*Then a bit wistfully*] It would have been nice.

Now it would be very difficult to do that, pulling the kids out of school. They both speak French, but pulling them out of school . . . And Soon-Yi's friends are all here, she's made a *lot* of friends. And I know this sounds funny, but all our doctors are here—the fabric of our life: my cutting room is here; my jazz band's here. But there are times when I've said to her, "Why don't we broaden our perspective and think about living in London or Paris?" And if she said, "That would be very exciting; I'd love to do that, we'll put the kids in a French school," I could be had. But she's not like that—she knows it sounds great but it's really not practical. "You could shoot a picture there, but our whole life and friends are here."

EL: Tell me about *Casino Royale.*

WA: *Casino Royale* was a totally nothing experience for me. I went over to England and stayed as a guest of the production. I made a lot of money and was given a lot of per diem. I never started a day's work until I was already on overtime. I wrote a certain amount—I wrote *Don't Drink the Water,* my play. And I played marathon poker games from nine o'clock at night to eight the next morning, night after night after night after night. I eventually quit because it was too time-consuming. Time passes very rapidly when you're gambling.

EL: Where did you play?

WA: Sometimes in a room at the Hilton Hotel. At the time *The Dirty Dozen* was being made there, so I often played with Lee Marvin and Charlie Bronson and John Cassavetes and Telly Savalas, who were in the cast, but everybody that was in town played. Howard Cosell passed through town and played. Producers who were producing films played. Everybody. William Saroyan played.

EL: What about acting in the movie?

WA: Acting in the movie was *nothing*.

EL: Did you write your part? [*He played Jimmy Bond, the neurotic nephew of the retired Sir James Bond (David Niven). Also in the cast were Peter Sellers, Ursula Andress, Orson Welles, Deborah Kerr, William Holden, Charles Boyer, John Huston, and Jean-Paul Belmondo. All that star power produced a very dim film with an impossibly confusing plot. It did, however, have a very 1960s sensibility. Burt Bacharach and Hal David won an Oscar for their song "The Look of Love."*]

WA: I have no idea who wrote the script. [*Wolf Mankowitz, John Law, and Michael Sayers are the credited writers. Those uncredited are Val Guest, Ben Hecht, Joseph Heller, Terry Southern, Billy Wilder, and Peter Sellers.*] I did not write my part [*though he, too, is listed as an uncredited contributor*]. I ad-libbed a joke here and there. I didn't write anything in the movie, never saw the movie, never cared anything about the movie. I knew it was a moronic enterprise as it was unfolding. It took no great observer to see that it was all dumb chaos. I did have the thought, My God, I'm in a movie with Deborah Kerr, I'm in a movie with Charles Boyer, with David Niven. But I only met Niven.

EL: What did you think of him?

WA: Very, very nice. Exactly what you see on the screen. I remember having lunch with him one day and his life sounded so great. He said, "We're doing a movie in London and we wrap the week at five o'clock or six o'clock on Friday afternoon. I go right out to the airport and I'm in my swimming pool in the south of France by seven-thirty." He liked that.

EL: But you never saw the finished product.

WA: No. Just from seeing what I was in, I don't know how anyone could sit through that. Every once in a great while when I was with Charlie Feldman he would say, "Oh, you've got to see these dailies," and he'd show me with great pride ten minutes of dailies that John Huston had shot or someone else had shot. [*There were five directors—Val Guest, Kenneth Hughes, Huston, Joseph McGrath, and Robert Parrish; each did a portion.*] And I thought, God, this stuff is just awful. These guys have no chance with this at all.

And Charlie Joffe said, correctly, "Just shut up and be in the movie. You're trying to get into the film business. It's going to be a big picture and you'll be in it with a lot of stars, so it will help to get you launched in the movie business. And you're having a nice time in London and getting a chance to do work on your play. You're enjoying yourself playing cards and visiting all the museums and doing all the tourist stuff, so just shut up and . . . [*pauses*]

EL: Deal. But you did write a draft of *Don't Drink the Water* there. What was the genesis of the play?

WA: I wanted to be a playwright like George S. Kaufman. I was searching for a Kaufmanesque idea and that *was* a Kaufmanesque idea, one that he would have liked. Max Gordon, who had produced a number of his plays, loved the idea and wanted to produce it. But I wrote it with insufficient skill, so that when Max Gordon saw it he said, "I don't think you've brought this off." He, correctly, bowed out and said, "This is not for me. I don't think this is going to make it."

EL: Did he offer any ideas for improving it?

WA: He sent me to his friend Howard Lindsay—no, no, Russel Crouse. We sat down and he gave me some pointers—I don't remember what the pointers were, but they made sense at the time and I was very thankful. And I was writing away and everyone was telling me how funny the play was as they read it but they didn't have Max's Broadway acumen. Finally I brought it to David Merrick and he said, "Oh, I want to produce this, it's funny." And then when I got it on its feet and we did it, all the flaws that Max had seen in it came out. It was an immense struggle to bring life into it.

EL: What were some of those flaws?

WA: Oh, tons of stuff didn't work. I had the wrong director for it [*Robert Sinclair, whose credits included the Broadway versions of* Pride and Prejudice, The Women, *and* Dodsworth *but who had not directed a Broadway play for perhaps thirty years*], but I can't blame him. It wouldn't have worked if I had Mike Nichols. It just wasn't there in the writing. And I found myself, as Merrick had said, up to my ass in show business. I was in hotel rooms in Philadelphia and Boston writing until two o'clock in the morning, making changes, the cast playing half of the old show and half of the new show. Then changes in the cast and a new director [*Stanley Prager*] coming in. Then in Boston I got terribly sick and had to remain in bed for seven or eight days. It was just a dreadful experience.

And yet, interestingly, there were other plays in Philadelphia and Boston at the time that were much heralded and playing to packed houses and great reviews and those plays came into town and died and closed. And my play got just enough life in the reviews to let it run. And it ran and ran and ran and ran, for two years or so. It was not a good play, but its heart was in the right place. The idea was a good idea, but I didn't have enough experience or skill to write it properly.

EL: How was your relationship with Merrick?

WA: I did argue with Merrick, but I liked him. He was good and he was right with me as often as he was wrong. In my desperation I would suggest things and he would say, "Forget about it, it's terrible." And he was right. And he would suggest things that were not very good and I would argue with him and I was right.

But I liked him. He was a good producer, he had good instincts. I always used to watch football with him on Sunday afternoons in Philadelphia. He'd say, "Look, I went into the business because that's where you meet pretty girls. You meet none of them in a law firm." And his attitude was, "I'm [*the theater critic*] Walter Kerr. He's going to say what I say. If I think a scene is boring or a play is boring, *he's* going to think it's boring. If I think it's really wonderful, nine times out of ten he'll think it's wonderful."

It was a very sensible, correct appraisal. That stuff is really obvious. You give yourself a million rationales and lie to yourself and denials, but you can see. When I finish a movie, I can almost always see, This is boring. People are going to be bored by this. Or, I've done a good movie and people are going to like this.

And Merrick was like that. It was Merrick who put me on to Tony Roberts. And he insisted that Tony play the part in *Play It Again, Sam* years later because we were going to cast another actor, and he said, "I think Tony Roberts is available and if he's available, I think we should use him." The "I think" meant [*laughs*], "We're going to use him."

EL: Did you become friends with Tony in *Don't Drink the Water*?

WA: We liked each other but I think I went out with him once during the whole run. We didn't become friendly until he, Keaton, and I were thrown into proximity

Woody and Diane Keaton between shots during the filming of *Play It Again, Sam* RIGHT: Woody, Diane Keaton, and Tony Roberts (in a scene from *Annie Hall*) have been friends since *Play It Again, Sam* was on Broadway in the 1960s.

in the Broadway run of [*the play*] *Play It Again, Sam* and then the three of us became very friendly. We all spoke the same language.

EL: What do you think of the film version of *Don't Drink the Water* [1969, directed by Howard Morris]?

WA: The one with Jackie Gleason? Oh, it's abysmal. It's a textbook of how you buy a play and ruin it. I'm not saying they were buying *Born Yesterday* and ruining it, but I did it a hundred times better when I put it on with Julie Kavner on television. As I say, it's not a great play to begin with by any means. Not even a good play. But it's [*pauses*] an easy laugh vehicle. If you're ready to suspend your critical judgment, it's an evening of laughs, even if the PTA is doing it.

Both the movie and the first casting in New York eschewed Jews, and that proved to be a very big mistake. Gleason was an absolutely brilliant comedian and no one is a bigger fan than me, but he was just wrong for the part. I had written it for Lou Jacobi and a Jewish actress at the time, Betty Walker, who's a riot. And Merrick was so sensitive about that that he wanted Paul Ford to play it, who was wrong for it and was unavailable, or didn't want to play it, I don't know which, so Jacobi stayed. He got the woman from the *I Love Lucy* show, Vivian Vance, and Vivian was just wrong for it. Kay Medford, who is not a Jew but is Jew-*ish,* came in one day, did it, and the part came to life suddenly. Jacobi always was alive because it was written in that Jewish idiom.

There was a time when I was writing it that I thought it could be made into a movie which I'd direct with Jimmy Stewart playing the lead. It's true Stewart was an arch-gentile, but I could have slanted it for him. It would have had a different feel to it and I would have written it much differently.

But anyhow, although it was not a great play, the stagehands in the Morosco Theater told me they had never heard laughs like that in any play there, wire to wire,

they just roared and roared. That sounds better than it is. But as a laugh machine, it got huge laughs.

I always wanted to play the part of the father and got the chance years later with the great Julie Kavner playing the mother and Michael J. Fox playing Tony Roberts's part. And Dom DeLuise was in it. He was *so* funny that I used to have trouble doing scenes because I would be laughing at him in the scene. He made me laugh so much that sometimes I couldn't keep a straight face.

EL: The idea is one's worst nightmare about travel, that you inadvertently get swept into trouble and have to seek refuge in an embassy.

WA: It was an idea that George S. Kaufman and Moss Hart would have made great capital out of, but I didn't have the savvy.

EL: You said the other day that you now know how to improve *Interiors.* Do you know what you would do with *Don't Drink the Water*?

WA: I can't be specific, but I wouldn't let myself get away with stuff that I let myself get away with because it worked but is not really that believable. I would have been more ingenious than I was, because it was a very good idea. At the time I was writing it there were people who were stuck in embassies and couldn't get out, and I thought, What if my *parents* were stuck in the Hungarian embassy or the Czechoslovakian embassy? My *God,* my father and my mother and their complaining; it was such a funny idea. But it was too big a comic idea for me to handle.

EL: Character or structure?

Woody with
Julie Kavner
in *Don't Drink
the Water*

WA: Structure and writing. It should have been less of a jokey cartoon. I should have taken a little speed off the fastball and, you know, been a little better, a little more realistic, with plot and characters. It was so unrealistic; it was such a flimsy cartoon that I had nothing going for me but the laughs, so I had to keep it up with the laughs, imagining that I had seen that same kind of thing with Kaufman and Hart years earlier. But I misperceived. Those guys made characters and made a story and you were involved in the story. If you look at *You Can't Take It with You*, for example, it isn't just a billion crazy people and laughs. There's a story about the lovers that you're interested in, and although the laughs stop for those scenes, nevertheless that's what makes the story go. Whereas I never stopped. It was just one burlesque after another. I could keep the laughs going, but at a fearful price.

EL: Even though you wanted to do a Kaufman and Hart type of play, didn't you once tell me that you went to another play, *Teahouse of the August Moon,* for a guide to structure?

WA: Yes. That's something that Danny Simon showed me years ago; very often when writing something he would use an already existing structure. Of course, his material would be completely different. One would be about Martians and the other would be about cowboys. He had seen that structure already play onstage or someplace and knew by using that structure what problems he was going to have and how fast he was going to have to move and what he had to do. So if you structured it like that, you knew that if your idea was good and your jokes were fresh, it was going to work because good jokes with that structure had worked before. I'm explaining this badly, but that's what it was.

EL: So after a play that was quite successful and two films that were awful but also successful, you were able to get someone to finance a movie for you.

WA: Eventually. When I wrote *Take the Money and Run* with Mickey Rose, Jack Rollins didn't want me to appear in and direct a film because he felt like there might be some kind of backlash, like, "Who is this wunderkind? Who does he think he is?" And I didn't care about directing it. I just didn't want somebody to ruin it. So it was hard to get anybody interested in *Take the Money and Run*.

For a while I had Jerry Lewis interested in directing it, but the studio didn't want to go along with that—it was United Artists who made *What's New Pussycat?* and *Casino Royale.* Palomar Pictures was a new company and they couldn't deal from strength. They liked the script and it was a million bucks and they figured, Yes, we like him, we've seen his act, we think he's funny, we've seen that he has written for the stage, he's written for the movies a little bit. He seems like a rational guy at meetings. We've got to take a chance on someone. And they took a chance with me, and that's how I got it on.

The first person at United Artists who took a chance on me in a big way was David Picker, after *Take the Money and Run*. He pushed for me there. They made a three-picture deal with me to write and direct, and the first thing I brought them was a version of *Sweet and Lowdown*. They were so taken aback and disappointed. They thought they were going to have to tap dance and do all kinds of things because I had a contract that said they had to do what I wanted to do. But the second I saw that they were unhappy, I said, "Don't give it a moment's thought. If you guys don't want to do this, I won't do it. I'll write you another one. I mean, it's not a big deal. I'm not going to make you do a picture you don't like."

EL: They must have been bowled over.

WA: Yes, they were surprised because they were used to people holding them to the contract. But we liked each other and we were not barbarians and I was never going to make a film company put money into a picture they didn't want to. They behaved very well with me and I certainly felt obligated to behave well with them. A month or so later, I came back with *Bananas* and David was high on it and I made it. I worked there for a long time and gradually [*company head*] Arthur [*Krim*] came to value me.

EL: Was that first film called *The Jazz Baby*?

WA: Yeah. And in that period Marshall Brickman and I wrote something called *The Filmmaker*, which would have been a good film but which for some reason [*long pause*] I think it never got past Jack Rollins and Charlie Joffe. I asked them to read it. They were not high on it and their opinion meant a lot to me.

EL: Have you ever gone back to it?

WA: No, now I wouldn't. It would have been very sophisticated for its time. It was about a guy having a relationship with a girl who had serious mental problems.

EL: You said you came back a month later with *Bananas*. Was *Bananas* already written?

WA: There had been a book. I can't remember the name, it was like a nonbook, that Sam Katzman, a producer of low-grade films [Earth vs. the Flying Saucers; Riot on Sunset Strip; Hot Rods to Hell], had asked me and Mickey Rose to adapt for Robert Morse. And we started to write it and the book was so uninteresting and so bad that we just dumped it and went into our own style of joke, joke, joke, joke, crazy joke, crazy joke. The book had been about South American dictatorships—

nothing like what *Bananas* was at all; *Bananas* had *no* plot. We brought it to Bobby Morse and he was not high on the script. He thought, What is this? I expected the book and I get *this*.

So the whole project got scuttled. Later when United Artists didn't want to do *The Jazz Baby*, I said to Mickey, "We've got to write something. These guys definitely want a film from me." And we thought, What about the South American dictator thing? It wasn't in great shape but in a couple of weeks we could finish it. David loved what we did and we went ahead with it.

EL: You improvised the chamber quartet with no instruments because the instruments failed to arrive in time. [*Fielding Mellish (Woody) visits the palace of the dictator. Four musicians are in the balcony, miming playing various strings. Of course, they make no sound, but the joke is very clear.*]

WA: People have talked about that. Yes, I did, but so what? It's no stroke of genius and not even a very good sight gag. In those days, I did what I had to. I never knew the director could say, "I'm sorry, I'm not going to shoot. When I ask for a string quartet I expect them to have instruments." In those days I didn't care, as long as I could keep going and make the day's work.

EL: But when you came to shoot the scene and there were no instruments, you thought, Wait a minute, it would be funny if the players just mimed playing the instruments.

WA: Yes. I didn't think it would be riotously funny, but I thought, What are my choices? I can't wait around for instruments. If it looks okay on film, I'll leave it in. So I had them mime it. I just kept moving along on the stuff so I could finish.

There was supposed to be a string quartet playing when Fielding Mellish (Woody) visited the dictator's palace in *Bananas*. The instruments hadn't arrived by the time he was ready to shoot, so he filmed them pantomiming.

EL: How much changed as you shot? I know you and Louise [*Lasser*] ad-libbed a lot. What about Howard Cosell [*who does a play-by-play commentary of their two characters consummating their marriage*]?

WA: He had the structure of what to do but he was ad-libbing some.

EL: I love the scene with the one thousand green generic New York deli take-out bags. [*A few of the rebels are sent from their jungle hideout to a hole-in-the-wall café in the city to get lunch for the whole group. They place the huge order and when they return to pick it up, the thousand sandwiches are lined up in individual bags.*]

WA: Charlie brought them. He went home [*from Puerto Rico, where the film was being made*] to New York for the weekend for some other thing and I said, "I need the kind of take-out bag you get"—there used to be a drugstore on the corner of Fifty-seventh and Seventh with a fountain—"I need those kind of take-out bags." [*Laughs.*] And he brought them all back.

EL: Do you look on that film with pleasure?

WA: I never think of it. It was boring being in Puerto Rico. There wasn't anything to do. The food wasn't good. The weather was hot and humid. The moviehouse leaked and I found a dead mouse in my room. I don't like to dwell on the past.

EL: We skipped over *Take the Money and Run.* Did you go into it saying, "I have a lot to learn"?

An army marches on its stomach, so the rebels in *Bananas* send emissaries from their jungle hideout to a small village to get lunch—1,000 grilled cheese (one on a roll), 300 tuna, 200 BLT (with mayo on the side for all), and coleslaw.

WA: I never had a moment's doubt about anything because I wrote the script and I knew what the jokes should look like. It was a simple matter of that. I knew how they should sound. Mickey and I acted the jokes out.

One of the producers said to me, "Tell me [*very sincerely*], do you ever stop and think, 'I am responsible for a *million dollars*'?" And the answer to myself was, No. Not for a *second*. I didn't see the million dollars, it was an abstract thing. It never occurred to me. And I never had any doubts [*laughs*]—until I saw the first cut. Then I asked for my cyanide capsule.

To me, the biggest thrill was going into San Quentin, the first day of shooting. The excitement was not "I'm doing my first day on my first film," but "I'm going into *San Quentin* today and I'm going to see these guys in the *cells* and the kitchen and the jute mill." I was more excited about that than making the movie.

EL: Is that when they told you—"If you get taken hostage, we're not coming after you"?

WA: That's what they told us. They said, "We'll do anything to get you out but we will not let anybody out. So stick with the group." And the inmates seemed happy that we were there. It broke up the monotony of the day for them. And they were happy to be in the film as extras. We gave them cartons of cigarettes, which is what they wanted. We weren't allowed to pay them.

Now I'd be scared out of my mind. But at that time it didn't bother me for a second. We came back two weeks later to reshoot a scene and I recognized a guy from the first shoot and I said, "Hey, hi, you still here?" He laughed.

EL: [*Assistant director*] Freddy Gallo told me years ago that you drove yourself to the set on that film and your driving was an adventure. You had, I think, a red convertible and they'd be all set up and you'd go zooming past—I think he embellished this story—but watching you drive was . . .

WA: [*Smiles.*] Better than the movie.

EL: Didn't you often call your analyst from a phone booth?

WA: Yes, sometimes. I was in a deep Freudian analysis at the time and I was continuing my sessions on the phone. Sometimes it would be easy but there were times in the middle of the day I'd be shooting on the street and we'd take our lunch break and I'd go over to a phone booth, and it would be a hot, sunny day, stifling in the phone booth and I'd be free-associating [*laughs*] in a standing position. But I did it.

And I had a perfectly nice time. Everybody on the film had a nice time; they were all sorry when the film wrapped. The film came out okay.

EL: I'd argue more than okay. It is what it is, a series of laughs.

WA: Yes, it is what it is. No one had done that documentary approach. We didn't think twice about that. I had originally wanted to shoot it in black and white because it was a documentary and all the documentaries were black and white at the time. I remember telling that to Jerry Lewis and he said, "They won't even *play* the picture in certain countries if it's not in color." Then he suggested I shoot it in color and it could be changed to black and white here but in Thailand and places like that it will be in color. But in the end I couldn't shoot it in black and white. The studio wouldn't let me.

EL: Were you spending a lot of time with Jerry Lewis then?

WA: Not a lot of time with him, but I did spend a little time with him. I spent a whole evening at his house in Bel Air. He couldn't have been nicer. He got into his car and drove me back to my hotel in Beverly Hills himself. And then Keaton and I went up to see him when he played the Concord or Grossinger's, somewhere up in the Jewish mountains [*the Catskills, in upstate New York*], and, of course, he was brilliant onstage. We spent a little time with him up there. I think he's a tre*men*dous talent who if he had been used more selectively would have made a stupendous contribution, because all the talent is there. It's just immense.

EL: You were performing in Chicago and you had the idea for *Play It Again, Sam.* Is that right?

WA: Yes. I was at [*the nightclub*] Mr. Kelly's. I wrote it in Chicago while I stayed at the Astor Tower.
Again, not a good play, but, you know, it got what it deserved. It was a modest hit. Not a bad play, but it's nothing special. It's worse than nothing special. It's not a good play, either. It's a lightweight commercial kind of comedy. There are funny things in it. And it was a fun experience.

EL: How much of the play changed on the road?

WA: There were things that changed in rehearsal all along. They changed at [*director*] Joe Hardy's suggestion, they changed as we rehearsed and cut things out. We opened in Washington. We were kind of successful right away, though not immensely. And then we opened in Boston and were stronger, I think.

EL: Was this another case of rewriting all night and people learning lines the next day?

WA: No, because we were not in deep trouble with this.

EL: It was David Merrick who suggested—who *commanded*—that you use Tony Roberts. Where did Diane Keaton come from?

WA: Strictly an audition. We were auditioning women and we were told that Sandy Meisner of the Neighborhood Playhouse said this next girl was the most talented girl in his class. She came out, I read with her onstage, and she was clearly wonderful. Then Joe and I put her down as a very strong prospect for the job and we debated. She was about my height but with shoes on she was taller, and we didn't want that to be the joke and distracting. We auditioned a number of other women, but a few days later we had to agree that she was clearly the best one we saw.

EL: Were you immediately attracted to her?

WA: I wasn't attracted to her, but I wasn't *unattracted* to her. We were just friendly. I remember that we were in rehearsal before we left town and I had a date with a girl the next night and Keaton and I went to have dinner together the night before during a rehearsal break. I had such a great time with her when we were at dinner I thought to myself, Why am I going out with this other girl tomorrow night? What am I doing? This girl is great. She's wonderful. I did go out with the other girl the next night, but I never called her again.

When we opened in Washington, Keaton and I got serious with each other. We went together, on and off, never sure, just on and off until it was time to go away and make *Bananas.* At that time we had to make decisions and we decided in favor of each other. [*He smiles.*] She came with me to Puerto Rico and then we lived together in Delmonico's Hotel for about five months while they finished the renovation of my penthouse. And then we lived there for a couple of years.

EL: Did the three of you—you and Tony and Diane—have great chemistry from the start of rehearsal?

WA: We all played well, but the chemistry between Diane and me developed over time. It was something that happened offstage as well as on. In fact, our relationship offstage became the chemistry that translated for us accurately into movies. She's *so* funny and I laugh at her all the time and she knows just how to react to me.

EL: *Manhattan Murder Mystery* was done ten years after your last film together and your chemistry is really evident. Did the three of you start out awkwardly in the play or find a rhythm right away?

Woody and Diane Keaton did not begin to appear in movies together until after their personal relationship had ended in the early 1970s. This scene is at the end of *Manhattan Murder Mystery*.

WA: It was never awkward. It was always graceful, easy, but it wasn't special. It only became special with Keaton as I got to know her and we developed a relationship.

You know, I didn't work with Keaton in film until we weren't living together anymore and we had broken up for a while. We were never in a film while we were going together. When we worked together, she was living with someone else.

EL: She told me that long into the run you would do things to break each other up, and some nights you would just speed through it. Is that right?

WA: Yeah, a year into the run. Sometimes we would do things to keep us interested. Keaton would sometimes do the whole play as Marlon Brando. [*Laughs.*] The audience never noticed anything. They enjoyed it completely. There was a time Keaton and I broke up onstage, we just couldn't go on, we were so broken up with laughter. The audience never had any idea that it wasn't part of the play.

EL: Do you remember what it was?

WA: I was giving that big speech to her: "Someday we'll look back on this and the problems of two little people won't amount to a hill of beans. . . ." And [*laughing*] there was a time that I sneezed onstage—there is a theory that actors never sneeze onstage, but I did [*laughing still*]. Once Tony Roberts didn't come on. He was downstairs pitching one of the pretty girls [*laughing harder*], and I was like Gleason [*he makes a big face*] when he goes "homina-homina-homina"—it had never happened to me—and one of the other girls in the show jumped right into the breach and kept the show moving brilliantly. She just picked up the cues and kept going and finally Tony came on.

I'd be onstage and Tony would say to me [*whispering*], "Max [*his nickname for Woody*], the guy in the second row." And there would be some guy, you know [*laughing*], with a propeller beanie or something, and I couldn't stop laughing for the whole show. Or there'd be some beautiful girl in the first or second row and both of us couldn't take our eyes off her for the whole show.

But it is true in a show that you can do your laundry list waiting for a cue. I'd be sitting onstage and Tony and Diane would be talking and I could be thinking, Let's see, should I go to Elaine's for dinner? Should I take them there? Where should we go? We went to Elaine's last night, why don't we try the Chinese restaurant?

Then I would hear, "So what do you think, Allan?" And [*snaps fingers*] I'd come right back into the thing.

It was so much easier than anything I had ever done—so much easier than being a stand-up comic and talking directly to the audience. That was so terrifying and so nerve-racking. This was—I've given this example before—I'd be eating my sandwich, the curtain would be down [*mimes eating a sandwich fastidiously*], and then, "Places!" "House to half!" [*Mimes putting down sandwich.*] "House off!" And I'd be calmly on.

When I was in a nightclub I couldn't eat breakfast, knowing I was going to perform at ten o'clock at night. And here, because you're on with other people, you're not alone—the simple difference between being alone or not is all the difference in the world. It's like when I play with my band. We do our thing. If the audience likes it, great. If they don't like it, too bad. The same thing with the play. You play the play. That was always the direction from Joe Hardy, too. He always used to say, "Don't play the audience. Just play the play and they'll like it or they won't like it." Very good advice.

EL: So when it came time to make a movie of it you obviously made changes to open it up, but for the three of you it was just like putting on a comfortable shoe, I presume?

WA: Yes, it was very easy. Interestingly, Herb Ross, who was hired to direct it, asked me to do the adaptation and when I gave it to him he was very disappointed. *Very* disappointed. He said, "It's like you wrote the play again. It's all indoors."

He flew to New York, came to my house, sat down, and said, "Here are my notes. On page one . . ." And he proceeded to give me five notes per page. "Do this, if you could bring this outside . . ." After a while he said, "Aren't you going to take any notes?" I took no notes but I listened to him and remembered what he said about each thing. He must have given me a hundred notes. Three days later, I sent him back the script. He couldn't believe it. He said, "Bravo, all the changes I wanted." So a lot of the adaptation, he should have credit for. And when we got out to do it, it was easy to do because we'd done it.

Herb told me that whenever he tried to make changes, he came to realize how tightly the play was structured—and it was. He had a lot of trouble making changes and couldn't in spots because it was so tightly written. But having said all this, it's not a very good play. It's a serviceable commercial romantic comedy. Trivial and amusing and it plays. It works if you play it in dinner theater. Dudley Moore played it very successfully in England.

EL: It's still produced all the time, isn't it?

WA: Yes. So is *Don't Drink the Water,* which proves it's a myth that the good things endure. For the same reason you can still turn on television and watch the Three Stooges. They've endured along with Shakespeare. You know, a play is an annuity. If you write a good potboiler comedy, it just gets played. A week doesn't go by that we don't get a request for someone to do *Don't Drink the Water* or *Play It Again, Sam* in some form, somewhere. *Writer's Block* [*his two one-act plays "Riverside Drive" and "Old Saybrook," produced in 2003*] was done quite successfully this past year in Italy.

EL: Did you ever want to direct the film version?

WA: No, I didn't want to direct it and I never had any interest in directing on the stage; I just wanted to sell the movie.

EL: Was it yours to sell or Merrick's?

WA: Merrick, but I think they would have had to have my approval. Originally they wanted to do it with Dick Benjamin and Paula Prentiss because Dick was a star. And Dick told me that he didn't want to do it because he felt that it wouldn't be good for his image to play such a loser. And I disagreed with him. I felt it wouldn't hurt him at all because everyone knew he wasn't a loser. And he regretted that mistake, he told me after. I think it was not a good decision because he would have been wonderful; Dick and Paula would have been at least every bit as good as me and Keaton, maybe better.

EL: By the time these three films were out—*Take the Money, Bananas,* and *Sam*—you were pretty firmly established.

WA: Yes, from that point on I was feeling my oats. I was up and coming and the next film I did after that was the sex film, right?

EL: Yes. You left San Francisco and went to L.A. to start it.

WA: Right, my feeling at that point was that I could have an idea like that and I could go to United Artists and they would be simpatico right away. I felt that I was not so much a plaintiff anymore. I had a very positive relationship with them. They thought highly of me and they treated me respectfully.

EL: Had Arthur Krim become your great supporter by then?

WA: He was a fan but we had only been introduced a few times before in a political context. He clearly was seeing, without spending a lot of time with me, that I was a good thing for the company. The sex film opened and it was successful. Then I did the Russian film, *Love and Death,* and he liked the fact that that was also a successful film. I was a winner for their company. Then I did *Annie Hall* and it won the Academy Awards [*1977 Best Picture, Best Actress, Best Director, and Best Original Screenplay*] and by that time he felt very proud. He was very generous about *Interiors.* He said, "Look, you've earned the right to do what you want. Whatever you want to do, go ahead."

EL: When I interviewed him, in the late 1980s—by then he had been completely on your side for fifteen years—he said: "I came into the film business with Charlie Chaplin and I'm going out with Woody Allen."

WA: Yeah. [*Laughs.*] Depends on his inflection when he said it. . . . Arthur gradually became my champion and I did many films with him. I've said to you and I've said publicly, the three big factors in my professional life are Arthur Krim, Jack Rollins, and Vincent Canby. Those three guys made my professional life.

EL: Let's stay with *Sex* for a while. There is a rerun of the Carson show on in the background and you hear yourself answering the question "Is sex dirty?" with "It is if you're doing it right." I remember when you were making the film, Dale Hennesy [*who won an Oscar for* Fantastic Voyage (*1966*)] was doing the sets—

WA: Yes, a wonderful art director.

EL: —and there were times that what you wanted built and the constant changes you were asking for were driving him nuts, but it was the most good-natured nuts I've ever seen. He was pulling out his hair trying to get it right and still laughing.

WA: He was in a tough position because [*associate producer*] Jack Grossberg had to keep the lid down on the money and Jack was brutal with him; Jack was

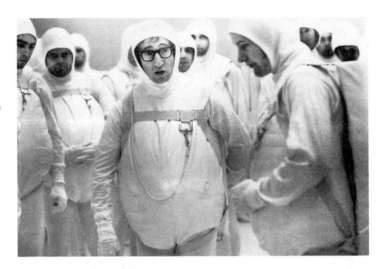

Woody as one of the sperm in the sequence titled "What Happens During Ejaculation?" in *Everything You Always Wanted to Know About Sex*

great, ingenious, with no money and coming up with things. And Dale was Jack's guy. Jack wanted him and pushed for him.

I have one significant regret on that picture. From the beginning, the opening sequence of the picture was meant to be the sperm sequence and the closing sequence of the picture was the giant breast. When I showed the picture, and I showed it a number of times, nothing could top the sperm sequence [*in which many sperm—Woody is one—prepare for action in a parody of periscope reconnaissance and parachutists making ready in World War II movies*].

I was talking to Pauline Kael about it and she said, "It's so funny. You know, the problem with the picture is it's so hard to follow the first sequence. You led with your best one." The people at UA said, "We can still switch." And I, contrary to my instincts, switched and opened with the court jester and put the sperm sequence at the end, but that picture was not meant to be seen that way. It was meant to open with the sperm sequence and close with the breast sequence. And I've regretted that cowardly mistake ever since. I betrayed my muse and I deserve whatever opprobrium is directed to me. [*Pauses, then his voice brightens a bit.*] But I was young, and a lot of people were prevailing upon me to do that and I wasn't confident enough to say, "I'm sorry, but I want to do it this way."

EL: If that's the worst treachery you've performed against yourself . . .

WA: [*Quickly*] No, no, it's not the worst, but it's one of the ones that if I wake up in the middle of the night that will keep me up.

EL: Has your muse demanded retribution since? [*He laughs.*] You've said that you satirize the things you love.

WA: Yes, that's what I wanted to do, not what I was doing. And you may ask, "Well, why didn't you do it?"

EL: Well, why didn't you do it?

WA: I lacked the smarts or the character. I couldn't find my way out of the box at the time. I was a comic talent. It was very hard to get into the movie business. I had no credentials. I didn't know about cameras or editing. I knew comedy. I knew if I got into the movie business I could make my comedy work for me. And once I had, I was getting plaudits on my comedy. It had always served me well. But I didn't have the nerve to just say, Wait a minute. Despite the fact that I've led the audience and made a tacit contract with them, I'm backing out, I'm going to go in a different direction. No more comedy.

Now, by doing that it might have been that no one would have been willing to give me a nickel to make a serious film. Certainly after *Interiors* nobody was interested. So I kept going with comedy, but what I really wanted to do was what I was satirizing in the Italian sequence.

EL: I don't want to sound like a cheerleader here, but you followed with a pretty good string of pictures: *Sleeper, Love and Death, Annie Hall, Interiors, Manhattan, Stardust Memories.*

WA: Yeah, *Sleeper* and *Love and Death* are fine for what they are. It's just that I quarrel with what they are.

EL: *Interiors.*

WA: I hoped when I did *Interiors* that if it had been more commercially successful that I might have been able to stay on the dramatic track. But it was not remotely commercially successful, though it was kind of critically successful. I always tend to think of it as not critically successful, but one day I was throwing junk out of my house and I came across an ad in which there were a lot of quite good quotes. But despite that, people were not entertained enough by it to come, or tell their friends to come.

EL: Actually, I know a lot of people who, seeing it after twenty years, have said, "Hey, this is pretty good."

WA: But you know, something happens in the passage of time. Your defenses let down and so a lot of stuff that was not very interesting when it came out appears better when you see it years later on television. I don't know if it's that it was always good and people didn't realize it, or that when a picture comes out you have expectations for it and it doesn't meet those expectations. Then years later you're sitting at home and it's raining out and you turn on the television and it's free and you watch it and you say, "It's not so bad, really."

EL: People have so identified you as the guy that you play, from your stand-up days and appearances on television and early movies, that to do something that different that quickly was like suddenly turning off the hot water in the shower, a complete change of temperature, and one's first reaction was to jump from it and say, "I didn't see this coming." A problem throughout your career is that people think that you're the person on the screen and everything conflates. So when you gave them something so different for the first time, it was off the scale; no one knew where to put it, it didn't fit anywhere they knew.

WA: Right. I never like to take the easy way out in any project that I do, so I always accept the worst said about anything of mine. I always feel you can always make a case for yourself, but it's so deceptive, it's so easy not to be true to yourself, so easy to be self-deceptive, that if you just believe the worst that's said about you, you're safer. I could argue about any of my movies and make up some case to you about why this is wonderful and that is wonderful. But it's too easy to fool yourself, to come up with rationalizations. If I come out with a movie and people think it's no good, I accept that. And while I don't read about myself or solicit anyone's opinion, now and then someone offers a pat on the back or a critique and even though I may dismiss opinions, the negative critique always rings true.

EL: Let's go to *Sleeper*. There's a series of three California movies—*Sam, Sex, and Sleeper*—shot one right after the other.

WA: *Sleeper* was a step forward for me, as I said earlier, because it was not *Take the Money and Run*. It had a real plot. At the start I had the insane idea to make it a four-hour movie with an intermission. The first two hours were to be me in New York living my life. It would hopefully have been funny. And at the end of it I was to fall into a vat of liquid nitrogen and freeze. Then there would be an intermission and after it the entire New York landscape would have changed—it would be two hundred years in the future and everything would be white and strange.
But [*laughs*] I found it so hard to write such a big thing; it was really two movies. Finally I said to myself, "Hey, do I really want to write a film just so I can [*laughs*] fall in a vat of freezing juice?"

EL: How far did you get?

WA: I don't know. Twenty pages, forty pages.

EL: But the problem of the four-hour movie didn't throw you off, it was writing two movies for one picture. You got lazy?

WA: Yeah. There were things like the Kubrick film, *2001*, *Gone with the Wind*, intermission movies . . . *The Godfather*. It was a very bold idea. But I just didn't have the stick-to-it-iveness or the energy.

EL: You solved the problem by collapsing a two-hour film into a couple of nice lines about the Happy Carrot health food store that you ran two hundred years earlier.

WA: Yeah, I figured, Let's just do the second half, let's just do the future, when the guy wakes up. I mentioned it to Marshall Brickman and he liked the idea and we worked on it together. I had the idea while I was making *Everything You Always Wanted to Know About Sex*. As soon as it was over I knew that's what I wanted to do.
Somewhere in that time I acted in *The Front*.

EL: You did *The Front* after *Love and Death*.

WA: After *Love and Death*, right, and before *Annie Hall*. I have no outstanding memory of *Sleeper*. I don't think of it very much. Again, it's one of those films. It seems to have worked fine.

EL: Just after you made *Sleeper* you told me how much you liked the exchange between yourself and Keaton, where you're fleeing the police and you want to be sure she knows the name of the secret project in case you're captured so she can continue to help the underground. You say to her with intensity because you're in danger, "It's the Aries Project. The *Aries* Project. You got that?" And she answers earnestly, "*Yes, the Jupiter* Project."

WA: You know, I was portraying her as a Buster Keaton heroine. Peter Bog-danovich noticed that and he was right. Chaplin's heroines were just idolized. Keaton's heroines were dummies who he was stuck on the train with and she's throwing little pieces of wood on the fire and he's looking at her. I wanted to have more of a Keatonesque Diane Keaton.

EL: Which came first after *Sex*, the notion that your next movie had to have a plot, or you had an idea and it had a plot?

WA: I had the idea for *Sleeper*. I knew it was not going to be a joke-by-joke movie. It was a tale that had to be told. And we had very little money to do it. I was running very long on my picture and this was still in the getting-to-know-how-to-work-with-me period for United Artists. They sent some people out to Colorado and I showed them some dailies and, as usual, they were nice as can be. They said, "Leave him alone, he's doing fine."

EL: Talking about Keaton and Chaplin, in *Sleeper* you were able to use some silent comedy. Tell me the difference between doing silent comedy and verbal comedy.

WA: Well, I find silent comedy easier than using words for comedy. It's like chess and checkers. You have just two dimensions. You look at the screen and there's no dialogue, so you're doing the gags. And some people can do them skillfully and some can't. Chaplin could do them, Keaton could do them. When they had to talk, they were lost. They just weren't good when they spoke. It's harder.

EL: These guys started off doing the silent but couldn't do the verbal. You stared out doing the verbal, then demonstrated you can do silent very well.

WA: The physical is easy. I can make an audience laugh with just physical comedy. But it's not easy to be a physical genius the way Chaplin was. For those guys, it wasn't just a question of executing a sight gag. Keaton and Chaplin had a particular beautiful grace—physical genius.

EL: They were balletic.

WA: Yeah, they were balletic. They were amazingly good at that. If there was a festival of silent movies and I had to write a script, it would just become a question of working out the silent jokes. I could execute them, I feel, decently. Keaton and Chaplin could make them into art.

EL: You said the idea for *Sleeper* came while you were doing *Sex*. Did the notion for *Love and Death* come up during *Sleeper*?

WA: [*Pauses to think*] No. What came up was the murder mystery that started out to be *Annie Hall* and years later turned into *Manhattan Murder Mystery*. I wrote it with *Annie Hall* characters, with Annie and Alvy, but it was the story about the guy down the hall having killed his wife.

I told everybody that I was working on a New York murder mystery. And I don't know what it was, but it didn't come out to my liking. I wrote the whole thing, including the memory montage that was eventually used at the end of *Annie Hall*. Tony Roberts was an actor who she gets romantically involved with, to my chagrin—and I didn't like it. But something was wrong with the script. I don't know what it was. And I had no idea what project to do.

I was pondering around in the living room in my penthouse and I saw a book on

Russian history and I thought, Hey, why not do *Love and Death*? I've always said those are two subjects I'm interested in and it would be like *War and Peace.* And I wrote that in no time at all and showed it to Jack Rollins and he thought it was hilarious and I went off to do it.

I shot most of it in Paris, but United Artists, in the interests of saving money, had me shoot some in Hungary. I scouted in Yugoslavia, I scouted in Hungary. I was freezing when we made it in Hungary. I was so cold I can't tell you. I have memories of myself trying to practice my clarinet out on a field where I couldn't move my fingers to play the horn, it was so cold. Every single night I'd go back to the hotel and stand under a hot shower for twenty minutes. I hated my experience in Budapest.

EL: But the Paris part seemed fun for you, at least during the time I was there.

WA: The Paris part was fine. But cold. I had to move some of those scenes into interior. I didn't want to, but I had to. The crew was wonderful.

EL: You do a number of great Bob Hope impersonations in the film. The scene where Boris is arranging to meet the countess could have been in *Monsieur Beaucaire.*

[**COUNTESS** My bedroom at midnight?
BORIS Perfect. Will you be there too?
COUNTESS Naturally.
BORIS Until midnight then.
COUNTESS (*Pressing his hand to her bosom*) Midnight.
BORIS Make it quarter to twelve.
COUNTESS Midnight.
BORIS But of course.]

Boris (Woody) with the countess (Olga Georges-Picot) arranging a rendezvous in *Love and Death*

WA: Yeah, I was doing him all over the place. I remember when it came out, I was having a pizza downtown with Marshall Brickman and he said, "Come on, I'll go with you to get the reviews"—that was when I still read the reviews. We went uptown and bought the *Times* and [*Vincent*] Canby loved the picture. Actually, the picture was loved all over America, and I suggested to United Artists—they wanted an idea for an ad—that they just do wall-to-wall quotes so that there's no border on the page and it's just quotes from every newspaper in every state. It was a very impressive ad because it was a much-liked picture.

EL: With *Sleeper* you began to give your comedies a really good look, but *Love and Death* was particularly rich in its colors.

WA: Yeah, I picked a very good cameraman [*Ghislain Cloquet*] and, of course, it was period, and when you do period you can get more beauty in it. And I got good weather, great Parisian weather—

EL: Yeah, apart from seeing your breath it was fine.

WA: [*Smiles.*] —and winter light. I was starting to get more interested in what the pictures looked like. And *Sleeper,* too. I started to get more interested in my profession.

EL: Was it a case of being more interested or just suddenly seeing what you could do?

WA: I was thinking to myself, Now I've established myself a little bit and I don't want to do just joke comedies my whole life. I wanted to start to make more interesting pictures and start to make better-looking films and cut the films better; not just make the joke reign supreme but take advantage of the cinema more.

EL: You shot *Zelig* and *A Midsummer Night's Sex Comedy* almost simultaneously.

WA: Yes, but we edited *Midsummer Night's Sex Comedy* first because we had to put that out. *Zelig* took a little time because we had to research all that stock footage and order it. It was a pain in the neck. But the shooting was a cinch.
The writing was very demanding because you have to sustain interest in that story without benefit of personal scenes, as I touched on earlier. It was very tricky, doing the white-room tapes [*interviews by psychiatrist Eudora Fletcher of Leonard Zelig*] and seeking out ways to get footage that would be completely valid—the camera would naturally have had to be there. So much of the time it's me walking out of a car and into a building.

That put me under a lot of strain. I never gave in to the temptation to do anything that couldn't happen in a documentary. I didn't want something for the sake of the story that could not have been in a newsreel or real documentary.

EL: You talked to me years ago about your former school principal Eudora Fletcher, someone who is such an awful person in your memory, and yet you gave the heroine of the picture her name.

WA: There's my compartmentalization. If someone has done me wrong and they're right for the part [*snaps fingers, starts to smile*], that doesn't matter. If someone's name's great and they have not been very nice to me or they're not a nice person, it doesn't matter. I can separate those things easily.

EL: In the writing of *Zelig* were you ever stuck or were you able to move it along pretty well?

WA: I was pretty able to move it along, but I learned a lot in the shooting of it. I couldn't use actors because actors were not realistic. If you got a guy off the street, he sounded like a real person.

EL: Why isn't that a problem in a movie? Is it because the audience views a documentary as being real life?

WA: Yeah. If I had a woman talking to you as Mia's mother, no matter how great an actress she was—if she was Geraldine Page or Maggie Smith—they're not real in a documentary style. Whereas if I just get my housekeeper and sit her down and tell her, "Just say she was nice to work for and she paid you a lot of money and it was a great job," and I cue her: "Was she terrific to work for?"
And she'd say, "Yeah."
And I'd say, "Well, how was she? Did she stand over you?"
And she'd answer, "Oh, no, she never stood over me. She let me work freely." All of a sudden the whole thing is as real . . . it *is* real.

EL: The untrained voice is the natural voice?

WA: Yeah, the lack of technique, lack of theatrical presence.

EL: Did you have a lot of actors to start?

WA: Yeah, I had some actors, but I never used them. I used *Teamsters,* they'd drive the cast in.

EL: The line you wrote in the finishing sequence: "In the end, it was, after all, not the approbation of many but the love of one woman that changed his life." I imagine many people thought, Well, maybe this happened in his life and he's written about it.

WA: But that isn't so. When I made *Zelig* it had no relation to what was happening in my real life. When a psychoanalyst and I talked about the film in a public program, a lot of people asked me questions and I tried to explain that I had no point of view to a lot of this stuff that they think. My dedication is to artistic effectiveness. Telling a good tale.

If I ever have an analyst, for example, who is a character in a movie, if the story is that the analyst is the hero, that's great. If the analyst is a murderer and that's what's good for the story, the analyst becomes a murderer. But I don't have any doctrinaire point of view in making up fiction about analysts or Jews, women or Americans—it's whatever serves the story. So that line served the story at the end of *Zelig*. But if Zelig suddenly went crazy and stabbed Dr. Fletcher, or if Dr. Fletcher suddenly flipped out and went away and broke his heart, and that was the most effective ending for the movie, then that would have been the ending.

EL: As we've talked about, it's so easy for viewers to confuse the person I'm talking with now with the identically dressed person who's on the screen, who sounds precisely like you.

WA: Right, they confuse it. That, of course, may be that's why they come to my movies and I'm lucky they confuse it. I don't know. But it's been something that I've denied my entire life and they look at me and smile and say, "I know, I know, you're *right,* you're *right.*" But they don't really believe it and there's nothing I can do or say. They think it's me.

EL: *Another Woman is* an interesting story of someone taking stock of her life.

WA: I know I've talked some about this before, but the great idea for me was hearing conversations through the wall, which could be played for comedy, which I later did in the musical [Everyone Says I Love You, *1996*] or for this. The metaphor for me at the time seemed that she was a cold woman who didn't want to face up to anything bad in her life, or didn't want to hear anything bad and avoided everything and finally she came to a point where she couldn't avoid it anymore and she was starting to hear it coming through the wall.

It was the kind of drama that interested me, that kind of odd, poetic, metaphoric drama. It was hard to handle. I did the best I could with it. I had such a great actress in Gena Rowlands, and Ian Holm was tremendous.

EL: I remember having a good time watching the film come together. It had been about ten years since I spent more than a few hours on one of your sets, and what struck me was how easy it seemed for you.

WA: Yeah, from a professional point of view. At that point I had made many movies. There is a certain level of professionalism that even the most [*laughs*] phlegmatic types learn. So I can get out on the set and I know what I'm doing technically. But at the end it doesn't mean anything. Well, it's better than the first-time director who's not sure and makes certain silly mistakes. You can learn 1 percent and the other 99 percent is what you're born with. Like being a nightclub comic.

Jack Rollins used to say, "You have to learn the technique and do it over and over." And yes, you learn 1 percent. There is the guy who goes out the first night and the guy who's been doing it for two years. The guy who's been doing it for two years has got a 1 percent edge in technique. But the guy who's doing it the first time, if he's better than the other guy, the other guy can have been doing it for twenty years, fifty years, it doesn't matter.

EL: This is the film that had Gene Hackman in it.

WA: [*Enthused*] Yeah, yeah. I'm always intimidated by people like Gene Hackman or Gena Rowlands or Geraldine Page or Maureen Stapleton. You want not to make a fool of yourself in front of them.

EL: Were you happy with how *Another Woman* came out? You were optimistic about it when you were making it, but when we talk it never comes up as a favorite.

WA: No. I could make that better now.

EL: What would you do?

WA: I have sometimes gotten myself in this bag—I did it on *Interiors*, too—that because I'm working with some cold characters, I don't heat up the movie a lot. So there's a kind of coldness that the lead character in *Another Woman* has that permeates the film. It's a little colder than I wanted it to be. And I made some clumsy mistakes.

EL: Such as?

WA: I didn't deal well with her husband. It was in the writing. I had Ian Holm and he got me off the hook a number of times the way he performed because he was very sensitive, very good. But I didn't write that character well enough. I should have made him more passionate and explosive early on. I would have been better off being less cerebral in my choice of atmosphere and characters.

EL: The line about the cardiologist who "looked into my heart and liked what he saw" comes to mind.

WA: I got some decent writing in it, just like I got some decent writing in *September,* too. They are very ambitious dramas. They are not melodramas, so I didn't give myself any of the support of the cinema. I didn't exploit my medium. They could have been plays in the theater. They were cerebral. And they were aiming high—not achieving, but aiming high. And I didn't have sufficient mastery.

You do a comedy and you don't have sufficient mastery. The result is *Take the Money and Run* and there are a million things wrong with it and you flounder but the basic product when it's finished entertains people. And you try to learn from your experience if you can and apply it the next time to the degree that one can do that. But what you're left with is an entertainingly viable thing.

When you're ambitious and you're going for poetic drama like *Another Woman,* where a woman is hearing herself through the walls and following people and they lead her back to her past and things like that, well, when you don't make it, you're not left with *Take the Money and Run,* an entertaining little thing that pleases a crowd. There's not enough for the audience to enjoy.

And those three dramas—*Interiors, September,* and *Another Woman*—were very ambitious. So when I struck out, it was apparent and egregious and not entertaining.

The impulse was honorable, the attempt was honorable, I did the best I could. I was not settling for playing into my strength and doing another crowd-pleasing comedy, and not doing the drama that passes for drama in American movies. I was doing what passes for drama in European movies. So to the degree that I was swinging and missing, you can become irate and I take the blame.

EL: What would be some of the tricks of the cinema you could have used?

WA: One is creating action. You can't do a cowboy movie on the stage. Just like *Waiting for Godot* doesn't translate to the movies; it's for the stage. In *Match Point,* I took advantage of the medium. The guy's a tennis player and there's killing in it and there are passionate scenes.

EL: Right. And here you're following people through hallways and it's static and they're hearing things through the walls.

WA: Yeah. So the idea is good, but I didn't maximize the potential of it.

EL: We've talked a lot about the genesis of your ideas but not about how you decide among the many ideas which to do. Can you give me a couple of examples of how you came to do the film you did at a particular time?

WA: I had the ideas for *Small Time Crooks, Curse of the Jade Scorpion,* and [*pauses*] *Hollywood Ending,* all three on the desk. And I said, "Hey, I'd like to knock off these three comedies and get them off my desk." And I did them one after the other. There were people who said, "Gee, he's doing trivial movies. He's doing these lightweight comedies." But I don't think that way. I just think, I want to do this one because it's on my desk. That's the idea I wanted to do at the time.

When that was over, I had the impulse to do *Anything Else* because the idea had been floating around in my mind for years, about an older guy who's really crazy and has a crazy view of the world and is advising a younger kid about his life, and the kid idolizes the older guy and is taking lots of advice from him. But the older guy turns out to be, you know, practically a psychopath. I make what I feel in the mood for at the time and I hope people enjoy it. If not, I still do what I want the next time out and hope again. I suppose if no one ever enjoyed my films I'd have been out of work long ago, but I luck out often enough.

EL: This is an oversimplification, but there is a theme you can find. Not long ago in talking about *Zelig* you pointed out the danger that conformity can lead to fascism. Here's a kid listening to a guy who figuratively turns out to have tinfoil on his head so he can hear the extraterrestrials. There's an underlying sensibility that it's really dangerous if you're not willing to be yourself.

WA: It's a lose-lose situation because you get into plenty of trouble when you're yourself [*laughs*]. It's just that you *feel* better. It's like an athlete, a prizefighter or something. You don't want to fight the other guy's fight and lose. If you fight your own fight and you lose, you lose. But if you fight the other guy's fight and you lose, then you feel crappy.

That's often what happens when you make films. If you try to make the film to accommodate something outside yourself, or please an audience or please the critical community or for commercial reasons or even artistic goals—if you're doing it for some calculated reason that you're not comfortable with and you strike out with it, you really feel bad. Whereas if you're doing something that you really care about and feel and are doing it for pure pleasure and it turns out to be a disaster, you feel better there finally than with *What's New Pussycat?,* where you hate the thing although everybody else loves it. But if you're getting no pleasure out of it yourself, what's the point? If I do a picture that I like and other people don't like it, at least I'm getting some pleasure out of it. Whereas if I don't like it and they like it, you know, yes, they're selling tickets at the box office, but I'm not getting any pleasure out of it.

EL: Who has had the most influence on you?

WA: I adored Bergman so much when I started making films—I still think he's the best filmmaker I ever saw—and when you think of me then, what was I really? I was a nightclub comic, a Broadway gag writer. I was not an intellectual; I was not a brooding, somber person. I was out at the ball games and eating at Elaine's. I hadn't seen the inside of a camera, I didn't know what I was doing, and my biggest influence is Bergman. It's so incongruous and silly, the disparity between the people who were influencing me—Bob Hope and Ingmar Bergman [*starts to laugh*]. So of course you're going to get a strange hybrid picture that's full of George S. Kaufman or Bob Hope kind of wisecracks and a certain stylized dramatics that characterizes the heaviest of Swedish films from a nonintellectual nightclub comic treating subject matter that's quite serious and quite profound. So you get this strange mishmash [*laughs*]. Yet for better or worse, the films apparently were amusing to people, and different—I *wasn't* doing the conventional thing. But I was, as anyone starting out, a product of my influences. And my influences were so antithetical.

I've always said that I am not artist enough and not commercial enough. To the average person, my films might seem, for want of a better word, arty. And to people who know art, they don't. So it's a strange limbo I've lived in with my movies. They've been—I don't know what to say. Not commercial and not art [*pauses and then laughs*] and yet some accidentally are enjoyable and even profitable.

EL: Are there pictures of yours that are personally satisfying, that came out of a personal feeling or personal notion that you wanted to address? I'm leading to something here.

WA: *Interiors* expressed my feelings about life, that it's a cold, empty void we live in and art won't save you—only a little human warmth helps. That was something that I was writing didactically. A number of my ideas, if you add them all up, would sound pessimistic. *Crimes and Misdemeanors*, you can commit a crime and get away with it because the universe is godless. If you don't police yourself, then no one is going to police you. In *Purple Rose of Cairo*, my feeling was, as I've said before, you have to choose between reality and fantasy and, of course, you're forced to choose reality and it always kills you. In *Interiors* there was a lot about how cold and incommunicative we are with each other and life is a terrifying thing and death is terrifying and nothing can help you. Add them all up [*chuckles*] and it sounds grim.

EL: Or realistic. When you were at Cannes with *Match Point*, someone asked you if the film was cynical. You answered that "cynical" is just an alternative spelling of "realistic."

WA: I do feel that way. [*Sighs.*] But it's not the stuff of popular entertainment. It doesn't wear well in popular entertainment. People may agree with you completely but they don't want to dwell on it.

EL: But *Match Point* is the exception here. It's proved very popular. Has its wide acceptance given you a lift?

WA: It helped my confidence in this sense: I've always wanted to be [*a small laugh*] a *serious* filmmaker. Any time I've done a serious film, I've never had a large audience for it at all. *Match Point* was a breakthrough for me in that the film could be serious, without jokes in it, without comedy in it, and it had a real audience—an audience like *Manhattan,* an audience like *Annie Hall,* that had a *big* audience. Big for me, that is. So it's given me the confidence to do the one I'm doing now because I feel people may actually even enjoy it. It won't read to them like homework. It will be entertaining as well as with some measure of substance, to the degree that I can do that.

My theory with movies is that at my stage of life, people have made up their minds in advance. People who like my work go and see it and overlook my faults. People who don't like it only see where I screw up because I always screw up [*laughs*] a certain amount in everything. That's why I'm so knocked out by *Match Point,* because despite the fact that I'm such a screwup all the time, in *Match Point* I feel I didn't screw up. *Hannah and Her Sisters* is a film I feel I screwed up very badly, but people who like me chose to like my work. Famously, I felt I screwed up *Manhattan* and people overlooked it.

EL: How do you feel you screwed up *Hannah,* apart from the happy ending?

WA: Yeah, that was the part that killed me. Almost every film I've done, even the ones I've loved, like *Purple Rose,* there were things I felt I should have done differently. I remember them although I haven't seen the films in years, thinking, If only I had made it move a little faster here, or a little more full of feeling in this moment. But *Match Point,* everything just fell in. [*There is a tone of wonder in his voice.*] Maybe I won't feel *Match Point* is good if I look at it ten years from now, maybe I'd think to myself, Oh, God, I thought it was so perfect and look at this and look at this [*laughs*]. But of course I won't be looking at it for precisely that reason.

This morning on the treadmill I was watching an old film and I was thinking, I haven't seen this film since the sixties. And I remember when the star in this film emerged publicly—she was so gorgeous and I couldn't wait to see her. And when I saw her now in the old film she didn't seem as beautiful as I remembered her. And I was thinking, What happened? She was a famous beauty and now I'm looking at her and I'm thinking, Have standards changed? Have my tastes? Was she never really that beautiful? [*He smiles ruefully.*] Never look at your old movies. It's too scary.

EL: How far ahead are you thinking?

WA: A year or two. We're negotiating with people for the next summer or summers. There are some situations where foreign people want me to do films wherever I want and others where they want me to do them in their country. There even has been a modicum—a *modicum*—of American interest. But I'm wary of that because domestic money often comes with artistic strings.

There was recently an article in the *Times* that said the average cost of a picture is now $96 million. I make mine for $15 million. I would think they'd be breaking down my door: here's a guy who makes them for $15 million, $14 [*million*], never above $17 [*million*]. They're almost a sure thing to break even with ancillary rights and worldwide box office and the downside risk is small. I'll never bankrupt anyone. Plus I always get good people in my movies. And you would think someone spending $96 million would say, "Have him make a half dozen movies for us and I'm sure one of them will make some money and each of them will probably either break even or make a couple of million dollars and our money's relatively safe. And when it's all over, if we make $2 million on each picture we'll make $12 million."

I know it's not $250 million, but there'd be a lot of product and maybe they'll luck out and one will be *Match Point* or *Manhattan* and they won't make $2 million, they'll make $100 million. But I'm sure there's something I'm not seeing because that's not the case.

Some guy wanted to back a film of mine and wrote that he understands all my freedoms and would give me *x* amount of dollars, which was a little on the short side, and all he requires is a five-page synopsis. And we e-mailed him back that I don't do a five-page synopsis even for *me*. I don't do a *one-page* synopsis for me. I've never given anybody who's done my film more than three or four lines so that the basic survival fears are mollified: that it's in color, that it's contemporary [*laughs*]— because they don't want period black and white, nothing that takes place in the fourteenth century deals with the silence of God. So I try to give them a vague idea of what I'm doing, but I don't like to pin myself down because sometimes while I'm writing, the very thing I'm writing inspires me to a different idea, and I want to be able to switch over to it.

The funny part of it is, for years people have kvetched to me about period films, and every time you see a period film—whether it's *Titanic* or Mel Gibson's film or *Gone with the Wind* or *The Godfather*—they all go through the roof in profits.

EL: You've told me about the New Orleans jazz film you'd like to do. Is there another film you'd like to make?

WA: I guess I'm starting to feel—because I'll be seventy-one this year—that I'm never going to do that Bob Hope movie where I glide through it in every direction. I always wanted to do a road picture with someone, maybe Keaton or another comedian, like the Hope-Crosby road pictures, not [*laughs*] a road picture like *Easy Rider*.

If a studio came to me and said they'd like to do a picture in the Hope and Crosby tradition, I could really make it great. The fatal error people always make when they update pictures is overproduce them, overelaborate them. But I wouldn't do that. I'd make one that was *in the tradition.* It would be a funny movie, but no one's going to be interested [*laughs*], either making it or coming to see it.

EL: I know that you're the most satisfied with *Match Point,* but on a couple of occasions you've told me that *Purple Rose, Husbands and Wives,* and *Match Point* are the three you like best. Does that still hold?

WA: [*Answering quickly, although he seems a bit reluctant to like even this many*] Yes, if I had to pick three. [*He turns cautionary.*] All these appraisals could change if I actually saw the films again. *Bullets* gives me a fond memory—*Zelig.* [*He pauses, frowning.*] I'm reaching.

EL: I want to ask you a couple of summing-up queries. Years ago you wrote a funny spoof of commencement addresses for *The New Yorker* called "My Speech to the Graduates." But do you have serious advice to pass along to would-be filmmakers?

WA: When I talk to groups they always ask me for advice and I can never really give it, because there is no set way a person gets into the business or becomes a director. Everyone does it differently. They do it by hook and crook and manipulation. Marty Scorsese goes to film school and becomes great, and Leni Riefenstahl [*laughs*] courts Hitler and becomes great. So the only advice I can think of is that it's only the work that counts. Don't read about yourself, don't have big discussions about your work, just keep your nose to the grindstone. And don't think about any of the perks. Don't think about the money or laudatory things. The less you can think about yourself, the better. It's like being a baseball pitcher; the less you're conscious of your motion the better you pitch. Just do good work, don't waste time thinking about anything else, don't join the show business circus, don't pay attention to the distractions that people send your way, and everything else will fall into place.

If people don't like your work, keep doing your own thing and either they'll wise up or you'll find yourself out of work and deserving to be. If people hate your work, let them—they may be right. Or not. And if people even call you a genius, it's very important to run because you have to ask, If you're a genius, then what is Shakespeare or Mozart or Einstein? With me it's always modified downward—"a comedy genius." I'd say a comedy genius is to a real genius what the president of the Moose Lodge is to the President of the United States.

As I get older, the word "legacy" always comes up and I personally have no interest whatsoever in legacy because I'm a firm believer that when you're dead, naming a street after you doesn't help your metabolism—I saw what happened to Rembrandt and Plato and all those other nice people. They just lie there. There may be some small financial legacy to my children, not a great one, but when I'm dead, it wouldn't matter to me for a second if they took all my films and the negatives of my films—apart from this small financial sum for my children—and just dumped them down the sewer. The great Shakespeare's no better off than some no-talent bum who wrote plays in Elizabethan England and couldn't get them produced and when he did you fled the theater. Not that I think I'm totally untalented, but I don't have enough to get my blood circulating once rigor mortis sets in. So legacy doesn't really matter at all. I said it best in my quip: "Rather than live on in the hearts and minds of my fellow man, I'd prefer to live on in my apartment."

EL: What about the audience that comes along after you're gone and enjoys the work?

WA: That's fine for them and if for any reason any of my films give pleasure to people after I'm gone, great; I'm not against that. But I couldn't care less what happens to my work when I'm dead. When you're younger you think in terms of glory, adulation, immortality, but when you look up and see where your paths of glory are headed—that's why when they talk about the legacy of presidents I wonder, What are those politicians so worried about with their libraries and their tapes, with their faces on stamps and coins? It's hard to look presidential when you're in an urn.

EL: You often talk about how work has to be fun.

WA: It has to be fun when you're doing it because that's the only pleasure you get from it. When you're younger you think fame and the financial rewards are going to transform your life but then you find that they don't really do the trick. Once the film comes out, if someone comes to me and says, "Hey, your film was very well received," I'm delighted. Then what? If they say it was not very well received, I say I wish it had been. But it doesn't make much actual difference either way because the real fun was in doing it—the planning and the execution and the busywork. After, I don't want to see it again. I don't have any DVDs of my films. I couldn't care less about them. I did them. It's like poking around half-eaten slices of pizza. It was last night's take out—fun last night, but I ate it.

EL: When did this change take place?

WA: After my first couple of films I saw I had a good time making them and once they came out, the fact that many people loved them didn't mean anything to me. I mean, I was happier than if a mob showed up at my door with a rope. But I was still sitting alone at home on Saturday night having to decide if I'm going to order from the Chinese restaurant or make myself eggs, and dumbfounded the girl with the long blond hair and the tanned legs at the gym didn't appreciate the value of a "bright new film comedian." It didn't change my life at all. And then when my first negative criticism came in, when for the first time people didn't like a film of mine, I had thought it would be so demoralizing to me and I found it didn't hurt that much at all. Incidentally [*laughs*], the blonde *still* wouldn't look at me. I don't know if it's a blessing or a curse. No high end, no low end, only the focus on doing it—like making a nice collage. Busywork at the sanitarium keeps the inmates occupied and tranquil.

EL: Is there a continuing small core of people you rely on?

WA: In the film business you're inundated by people with all the answers from every side but you have to keep your own head. You're in a constant state of trying to do a good piece of work in spite of all the pressure and advice from money mavens and film experts and finally you're up against the biggest obstacle, your own limited talent. It's so hard for anyone to make a good film. You have to rely on your family or your closest friends who share many of your values—that's what probably draws us together—and make your own little world of values and taste and criteria and then be true to that world. If you can do that, it helps you rather than limits you. If everyone in the world is celebrating this song or that play, you have to hang in with your own beliefs, adverse as they may be. You'll find it's not so hard to do. If I like something or someone I couldn't care for a second if no one else does, and if I don't, I don't. When I finish a film there are a couple of people whose opinions I care about and I'm anxious to reflect on their comments because I respect their taste, even when it's different from mine.

If you can't divorce yourself from hearing about yourself and your work, which is not all that hard to do, then I'd advise you not to believe the compliments and the good things said about you. A good portion of them are insincere, a good portion are wrong—which leaves a very small portion to get excited over. Most hype about your work is show business flattery. Always remember: Many of the people honoring you at one of those black-tie events on T.V. won't return your phone calls a week after the dinner.

EL: How much can criticism help or hinder your work?

WA: I wish the artist could—it would be a big help—but the artist can't adjust his work according to criticism. I can accept criticism as true but there's nothing I can do about it in the next film. I'm not going to change my style or my subject matter because someone criticizes it. I couldn't if I wanted to. I'm limited, or as Marshall Brickman so brilliantly put it: you're fucked by who you are. The work exists independent of all the talk about it. If the thing is good, it remains good despite the pro or con palaver about it. And if it's not good, it drifts away no matter how popular it may seem at the moment. Of course, it's nice to have that popular moment, no matter how fleeting, because by the time they realize the movie stinks, you have their money.

Most work by most people, my own included, is bad because it's hard to do good work. So you have to assume going in that most of the work by filmmakers, authors, playwrights, painters is not first rate. Once in a while you come across an authentic talent or even a genius but it's rare. We're all saved because the public is not very demanding and a thing needn't be very good to succeed. But I must be lucky.

When I started out I would cut out the bad things written about me and put them in a scrapbook because I was so certain that it would be ironic one day in light of how great I intended to become. Now the verdict is in and what I thought were carping notices don't seem so. So I have no illusions about my work. Recently I was given the Prince of Asturias Award [*a prestigious Spanish award "to acknowledge*

Woody as a writer in **Play It Again, Sam,** and **Deconstructing Harry**

scientific, technical, cultural, social and humanitarian work carried out interna-tionally"]. The night I got it, so did Arthur Miller and Daniel Barenboim. And when they notified me of my selection I honestly thought it was a clerical error, that some poor guy in Spain had made a terrible mistake. I thought it was a funny idea for a movie; this poor inkstained Spanish wretch had to explain to his superiors why this craven mediocrity from Brooklyn was coming to get an award more suited to the discoverer of, say, radium or at least Tupperware. Of course, I refused it but then I got calls from people in Spain saying I couldn't, that the king and queen would be there and it would be a terrible insult. So I went. Now I've got this shiny medal.

EL: Okay. Last question, at least for now. Give me an assessment of your career so far.

WA: My objective feeling is that I haven't achieved anything significant artisti-cally. I'm not saying this ruefully, just describing what I feel is true. I feel I've made no real contribution to cinema. Compared to contemporaries like Scorsese or Cop-pola or Spielberg, I've really influenced no one, not in any significant way. I mean, a number of my contemporaries have influenced young directors. Stanley Kubrick would be a prime example. I haven't been *any* kind of an influence. That's why it always struck me as strange that so much attention was paid to me over the years. I never had a big audience, was never a big moneymaker, never did controversial themes or paid any attention to current fashion. My films have not stimulated the talk of the country on social, political, or intellectual issues. They're modest pic-tures done for modest budgets making extremely modest returns and making no real ripple in the show business world. Young directors are not running out imitat-ing me and shooting films the way I shoot them. I never had enough technique or sufficient depth to my ideas to start anybody thinking. I'm a Brooklyn-Broadway wisecracker who's been very lucky.

I think I'm sort of—without the special genius that he had—like Thelonious Monk in jazz, who was just a separate thing apart; nobody really plays like Thelo-nious Monk or wants to, but as I say, he had genius and I have merely a talent to amuse. [*Woody's artistic philosophy is also like that of Monk, who said, "Don't play what the public wants. Play what you want and let the public catch up."*] And I'm not an overly modest person. When I'm good, I appreciate myself. I'm not sad or confessionally masochistic about this but I'm smart enough to know I've maximized my limited gifts, made good money compared to my father, and most importantly by far have had my health.

When I was a kid I used to run into the cinema to escape—twelve or fourteen pictures a week sometimes. And as an adult, I've been able to live my life in a cer-tain self-indulgent way. I get to make the films I want to make, and so for a year I get to live in that unreal world of beautiful women and witty men and dramatic situations and costumes and sets and manipulate reality. Not to mention all the wonderful music and places it's taken me. [*Laughs.*] Oh, and sometimes you get to date some of the actresses. What could be better? I've escaped into a life in the cinema on the *other* side of the camera rather than the audience side of it. [*He pauses.*] Ironic that I make escapist films, but it's not the audience that escapes it's me.

Acknowledgments

Woody Allen has made our conversations a pleasure for half his life and even more of my own. I look forward to those to come and thank him for all we've had. The accumulated transcripts run to well over a thousand narrowly spaced pages. I am grateful to Kate Wolf and Allison Joyce for their help in sorting them into the categories of this book.

My thanks and appreciation to Jerry Ament, Barry Dagistino, and Maggie Adams at MGM, and to Dorrit Ragosine and Callie Jernigan at MGM/Twentieth Century Fox Home Entertainment; to Larry McAllister and Christina Hahni at Paramount/ DreamWorks; and to Ann Limongello at the Disney/ABC Television group for their generous help with the scores of photos taken from Woody's films; and to still photographers John Clifford, Clive Coote, and Keith Hamshere. Many thanks as well to Irwin J. Tenenbaum for timely aid.

Besides being a pleasure to know, Woody's assistants, first Sarah Allentuch and then Sage Lehman, helped whenever I called. Thank you. My gratitude as well to Helen Robin, and to Juliet Taylor.

At Knopf, thanks to Sonny Mehta, to Chip Kidd for what I think is the perfect cover, to Iris Weinstein, to Kathleen Fridella, and to Kyle McCarthy. Jonathan Segal has edited books of mine for more than twenty years and there is no one more deft with a pencil or devoted to his writers. The idea for this one was Jon's and I'm glad he had it. I cherish his friendship as much as I value his skill in honing themes and ideas.

I'm lucky to have friends like David Wolf, whose constant availability for much-called-on advice, and Will Tyrer, whose constant worry over the page count, are testament to the care of pals.

No amount of thanks can fully convey my appreciation to my wife, Karen Sulzberger, and our sons, Simon and John, for the life we have, but I offer it to all three with my love.

Punch Sulzberger has showered me with affection and kindness over the past twenty-five years, and he tells funny jokes as well. This book is for him, in small return.

Index

Note: Page numbers in *italics* refer to photographs; WA stands for Woody Allen throughout the index.

Index

Index

Index

Index

Index

Index

Index

Index

Photographic Credits

Courtesy of Woody Allen: 271, 302, 327

Annie Hall © 1977 Metro-Goldwyn-Mayer Studios, Inc. All Rights Reserved: 27 (6), 29, 333

Another Woman © 1988 Orion Pictures Corporation. All Rights Reserved: 275 (5)

Anything Else. Courtesy of Dreamworks and Paramount Pictures (© 2007 Dreamworks LLC. All Rights Reserved: 170 (left)

Bananas © 1971 Rollins & Joffe Productions All Rights Reserved: 337, 338

Brian Hamill. Courtesy of Metro-Goldwyn-Mayer Studios and MGM Clip + Still Licensing. All Rights Reserved: 197

Broadway Danny Rose © 1984 Orion Pictures Corporation. All Rights Reserved: 169, 224

Celebrity. Courtesy of Miramax Film Corp. © 1998. All Rights Reserved: 263

Clive Coote. Courtesy of Woody Allen: 42 (2), 81, 127, 167, 168, 171 (right), 220 (2), 229

Curse of the Jade Scorpion. Courtesy of Dreamworks and Paramount Pictures (© 2007 Dreamworks LLC. All Rights Reserved): 158, 313

Don't Drink the Water. Courtesy American Broadcasting Companies, Inc.: 334.

Eric Lax: 88

Everyone Says I Love You. Courtesy of Miramax Film Corp. (© 1996. All Rights Reserved): 154, 155, 216, 217

Everything You Always Wanted to Know About Sex° But Were Afraid to Ask © 1972 Metro-Goldwyn-Mayer Studios, Inc. All Rights Reserved: 5, 193 (3), 346

Hannah and Her Sisters © 1986 Orion Pictures Corporation. All Rights Reserved: 141, 171 (left)

Hollywood Ending. Courtesy of Dreamworks and Paramount Pictures (© 2007 Dreamworks LLC. All Rights Reserved): 226

Interiors © 1978 Metro-Goldwyn-Mayer Studios, Inc. All Rights Reserved: 112, 113

John Clifford. Courtesy of Woody Allen: 51, 124, 125, 129, 206, 211, 216, 217, 265, 364 (right)

Keith Hamshere. Courtesy of Woody Allen: 187, 235

Christopher R. Harris: 300

Love and Death © 1975 Rollins & Joffe Productions. All Rights Reserved: 69, 351

Manhattan © 1979 Metro-Goldwyn-Mayer Studios, Inc. All Rights Reserved: 34, 80, 266, 305

Match Point. Courtesy of Dreamworks and Paramount Pictures (© 2007 Dreamworks LLC. All Rights Reserved): 127, 171 (right), 220

Melinda and Melinda Courtesy of Twentieth Century Fox. © 2005 Twentieth Century Fox. All Rights Reserved: 57

Mighty Aphrodite. Courtesy of Miramax Film Corp. (© 1995. All Rights Reserved): 48, 49, 153

New York Stories (Oedipus Wrecks). Courtesy of Touchstone Pictures, © Touchstone Pictures. All Rights Reserved: 46 (2), 308, 309.

Play It Again, Sam. Courtesy of Paramount Pictures. © Paramount Pictures. All Rights Reserved): 8, 9, 70, 332, 364 (left)

The Purple Rose of Cairo © 1985 Orion Pictures Corporation. All Rights Reserved: 20, 21, 22 (3)

September © 1987 Orion Pictures Corporation. All Rights Reserved: 143

Shadows and Fog © 1992 Metro-Goldwyn-Mayer Pictures, Inc. All Rights Reserved: 173

Sleeper © 1973 Metro-Goldwyn-Mayer Studios, Inc. All Rights Reserved: 64, 170 (right), 177

Small Time Crooks. Courtesy of Dreamworks and Paramount Pictures (© 2007 Dreamworks LLC. All Rights Reserved): 265

Stardust Memories © 1980 Metro-Goldwyn-Mayer Studios, Inc. All Rights Reserved: 230, 231

Take the Money and Run. Courtesy American Broadcasting Companies. © American Broadcasting Companies, Inc.: 4, 133, 304

Zelig © 1983 Metro-Goldwyn-Mayer Pictures, Inc. All Rights Reserved: 72, 73

A Note About the Author

Eric Lax's books include the international best-selling biography *Woody Allen* and *Life and Death on 10 West*, both of which were *New York Times* Notable Books. With A. M. Sperber, he is the coauthor of *Bogart*, which was a finalist for the Los Angeles Times Book Prize in Biography. *The Mold in Dr. Florey's Coat* was a *Los Angeles Times* Best Book of 2004 and a *Discover* magazine Best Science Book of 2004. His writing has appeared in the *New York Times*, the *Los Angeles Times*, the *Atlantic*, *Vanity Fair*, and *Esquire*. He is an executive of International P.E.N. and lives in Los Angeles.

A Note on the Type

This book was set in New Caledonia, a typeface designed by W. A. Dwiggins (1880–1956). It belongs to the family of printing types called "modern face" by printers—a term used to mark the change in style of the type letters that occurred around 1800. New Caledonia borders on the general design of Scotch Roman but it is more freely drawn than that letter. This version of Caledonia was adapted by David Berlow in 1979.

Composed by North Market Street Graphics, Lancaster, Pennsylvania

Printed and bound by R. R. Donnelley, Crawfordsville, Indiana

Designed by Iris Weinstein